D1253776

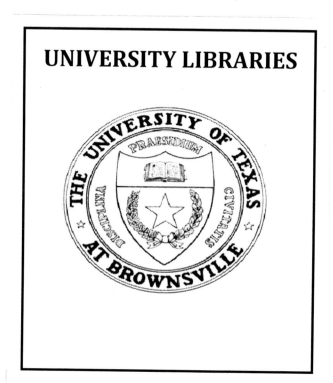

**UNIVERSITY LIBRARIES**

# The Firm

# The Firm

## The Inside Story of the Stasi

GARY BRUCE

OXFORD
UNIVERSITY PRESS
2010

**OXFORD**
UNIVERSITY PRESS

Oxford University Press, Inc., publishes works that further
Oxford University's objective of excellence
in research, scholarship, and education.

Oxford   New York
Auckland   Cape Town   Dar es Salaam   Hong Kong   Karachi
Kuala Lumpur   Madrid   Melbourne   Mexico City   Nairobi
New Delhi   Shanghai   Taipei   Toronto

With offices in
Argentina   Austria   Brazil   Chile   Czech Republic   France   Greece
Guatemala   Hungary   Italy   Japan   Poland   Portugal   Singapore
South Korea   Switzerland   Thailand   Turkey   Ukraine   Vietnam

Copyright © 2010 by Oxford University Press, Inc.

Published by Oxford University Press, Inc.
198 Madison Avenue, New York, NY 10016

www.oup.com

Oxford is a registered trademark of Oxford University Press

Library of Congress Cataloging-in-Publication Data
Bruce, Gary, 1969–
The firm : the inside story of the Stasi / Gary Bruce.
p. cm.
Includes bibliographical references and index.
ISBN 978-0-19-539205-0
1. Germany (East). Ministerium für Staatssicherheit—History.
2. Intelligence service—Germany (East)—History.
3. Secret service—Germany (East)—History.
4. Germany (East)—Politics and government.   I. Title.
DD287.4.B78 2010
363.28'30943109045—dc22
2010012023

9 8 7 6 5 4 3

Printed in the United States of America
on acid-free paper

*For Gabriel*

# Contents

# Acknowledgments

IT IS SAID that baseball is a team sport played individually. The practice of history is very similar.

The lead archivists on this project deserve my first thanks. Frau Hannelore Strehlow of the Stasi Archive's Potsdam branch (which at the end of 2008 was transferred to the central archive in Berlin), herself an excellent historian, worked tirelessly to prepare the material for my viewing. Her profound knowledge of the archival holdings and of Stasi history greatly enhanced this book. She even went so far as to delay her summer holidays to accommodate my research visits, something that took a toll on her leaky roof that required repair. Frau Kramer also made my stay in Potsdam a pleasurable experience, with her healthy supply of both cookies and stories of growing up in East Germany.

I am deeply indebted to Herr Detlef Niemann of the Schwerin branch of the Stasi Archive, who not only guided me to the most relevant material but championed the project. He put me in contact with a number of individuals, from volunteer curators at village museums to the president of associations for Stasi victims to the first federal commissioner for the Stasi files. His profound belief in the importance of the Stasi archive's work helped spur me on during the down times. I will also take away fond memories of our times at Brinkama's lamenting the fortunes of Hansa Rostock. Herr Haiko Hoffmann provided outstanding support and very pleasant conversation. Frau Marlies Lemcke and Frau Claudia Retemeyer helped locate materials in the labyrinthine archives. Although she was exceptionally busy, Frau Erika Schröder, the director of the Schwerin branch, made time to come by the reading room and check on my progress, a most welcome act of kindness. Given the distance to the nearest restaurant, I was grateful when I was invited to participate in the communal take-out order. Some of my best conversations about this project took place over "Hawaii-Kebabs" in the canteen.

Jörg Stoye, director of the Magdeburg branch of the Stasi archive, kindly guided me around Perleberg with individuals who had been involved in the revolution of 1989.

At the Brandenburgisches Landeshauptarchiv, Karin Braun went out of her way to accommodate my requests for information, as did Dr. Klaus Schwabe at the Landeshauptarchiv Schwerin. My last-minute plea for statistics on the districts was graciously answered by Annette Skorna of the Landesbibliothek Mecklenburg-Vorpommern and by Brigitte Thein at the Amt für Statistik Berlin-Brandenburg.

Stefan Wolle, one of the leading historians of East Germany, was kind enough to suggest three of his seminar students to assist me with arranging interviews in Germany. I could not have asked for more professional and enthusiastic colleagues. Jolanta Turowska not only helped plan interviews but assisted in developing interview strategies, offered insights on the project more broadly and served as an important contact in Berlin. Chapter 1 is based in large part on Antje Rickert's meticulous research on Districts Gransee and Perleberg during the Nazi period. Monika Starke also played an important organizational role at the outset of the project.

I owe a special thanks to the many people, both Stasi employees and "ordinary" Germans, who agreed to be interviewed for this book. They accepted me into their homes and talked with me as long as I wished. They were all gracious hosts. In keeping with their wishes, their names appear here as pseudonyms, except for two publicly known regime opponents, Dr. Ulrich Woronowicz and Dr. Jürgen Schmidt-Pohl.

Sven Lauk and Matthias Putzke, friends since our days playing basketball as students of Humboldt University in Berlin, make it difficult to leave Berlin when the time comes. Hartmut Mehlitz, Barbara Mehlitz, and their son, Joachim, all from Berlin, have been an important part of this project since the beginning. They have provided shelter, food, and companionship. Hartmut Mehlitz's book on the *Blindenvater* August von Zeune has been influential in my own approach to the writing of history. When I first conceived this project, I expected to write a scholarly history of the Stasi; I could not know of the people I would meet with whom I always want to stay a minute longer.

I have received tremendous feedback from my students, both undergraduate and graduate, as we discussed East German history and the pursuit of history in general. Although many more deserve mention here, I would be remiss if I did not acknowledge Mikkel Dack, Lindsay Dowling, Aaron Ducker, David Gall, Jonathan Kitay, Andrew Kloiber, Michael Murray, Amelia Howard, and Joshua Schultz. For his research assistance and for his help preparing the manuscript, I would like to thank my current PhD student Michael Pitblado, a fine historian in his own right.

Since my arrival in the department of History at the University of Waterloo, I have never felt anything but at home. I am grateful to my colleagues here who have provided me with the supportive intellectual environment in which to write this book. In particular Patrick Harrigan's keen eye for detail improved the book, and his sympathetic ear made it possible for me to focus on writing rather than on the demise of the Montreal Expos. Both Donna Lang and Nancy Birss provided much-needed administrative support, and Carl Bon Tempo's advice was instrumental at the prospectus stage.

To complete the research for this book, I undertook six trips to the archives over the course of six years, totaling some ten months in Germany. The substantial costs involved with this travel were offset by the generous funding of the Social Sciences and Humanities Research Council of Canada and the German Academic Exchange Service.

Nancy Toff at Oxford University Press is the consummate editor: gracious, fair-minded, critical, and available by email. Her emphasis on narrative vastly improved the book. Joellyn Ausanka and Sonia Tycko, who guided the manuscript through the final production stages, are masterful at their craft. I am also very grateful to the press's anonymous reviewers for their recommendations.

Chapter 6 draws in large part on my article "In our District, the State is Secure" in *Contemporary European History* 14.2 (May 2005). I thank Cambridge University Press for permission to use the material here.

Antoinette Duplessis has helped in countless ways, from sandwiches to sympathy. My parents have been supportive throughout my academic career, especially when I switched my major from chemistry to history those many years ago. My mum continues to be a great source of comfort. My dad was always greatly interested in my work, and, although he did not live past the early stages of this book, he is still very much a part of it.

Gabriel thinks that we already have enough books. For reminders like this, and so much more, I dedicate this book to him.

# Abbreviations

**AstA**   Antragsteller auf ständige Ausreise. Applicant to emigrate from East Germany

**FDJ**   Freie Deutsche Jugend. Free German Youth—the Communist youth organization

**GDR**   German Democratic Republic (East Germany)

**GHI**   Geheimer Hauptinformator. Secret lead informant

**GMS**   Gesellschaftlichter Mitarbeiter für Sicherheit. Societal co-worker for security—a low-level informant, generally not assigned to a monitoring operation

**HA**   Hauptabteilung. Main directorate within the Stasi

**HIM**   Hauptamtlicher Inoffizieller Mitarbeiter. Full-time unofficial co-worker—a designation used from 1979 for outstanding and long-serving informants

**JHS**   Juristische Hochschule des MfS. College of Law—a college for Stasi officers located in Potsdam-Eiche

**KgU**   Kampfgruppe gegen Unmenschlichkeit. Fighting Group Against Inhumanity—an anti-Communist resistance group based in West Berlin

**KP**   Kontaktperson. Contact person—informant not officially registered with the Stasi

**KPD**   Kommunistische Partei Deutschlands. Communist Party of Germany—fused with the Social Democratic Party in 1946 to become the Socialist Unity Party of Germany

**IM**   Inoffizieller Mitarbeiter. Unofficial Co-worker—a generic abbreviation for Stasi informant

**MfS**   Ministerium für Staatssicherheit. East Germany's Ministry for State Security, commonly known as the Stasi

**NVA**    Nationale Volksarmee. East German National People's Army

**OPK**    Operative Personenkontrolle. Personal surveillance operation—one of the two categories of operations the Stasi conducted to monitor individuals

**OTS**    Operative-technische Sektor. Section for operational technology—Stasi department responsible for providing crime labs for on-going investigations, and technology to secure Stasi installations

**OV**    Operativer Vorgang. Operational case—a more in-depth Personal Surveillance Operation

**POZW**    Partner des operativen Zusammenwirkens. Collaborative operational partner—a contact for the Stasi similar to a Contact Person (See above)

**SED**    Sozialistische Einheitspartei Deutschlands. Socialist Unity Party of Germany—East Germany's Communist Party

**Stasi**    See MfS

# The Firm

# INTRODUCTION

BORN IN SCHWERIN, the capital of the eastern German province of Mecklenburg-Vorpommern, in 1945, Jürgen Schmidt-Pohl apprenticed as a professional bookseller before obtaining employment at a bookstore on Friedrichstrasse in the town of his birth. At the age of twenty-three he was arrested for speaking out publicly against the new East German constitution, which had removed a catalogue of basic citizens' rights, and sentenced to twenty-four months in prison for what the regime deemed "rabble-rousing." Following his release, he returned to the bookstore for a short time before he was dismissed and forbidden to practice his trade anywhere in East Germany. For two years, he worked in a brewery as a manual laborer. Since he had come to the attention of the authorities, the Stasi (*Staatssicherheit*), East Germany's secret police, had hired thirty-four informants to monitor him, three of whom, he later found out, were his girlfriends. Schmidt-Pohl then foolishly, as he himself admitted, contacted an amateur group that smuggled people out of East Germany. He was arrested in June 1974 for "preparing to flee the Republic" and held for nine months in the Hohenschönhausen Stasi prison on the outskirts of East Berlin, before being sentenced to five years in prison and a further five years of removal of rights. He would have been banned from voting, the police could have searched his apartment at any point without a warrant, and his travel would have been restricted to a 12-mile (20-km) radius around the town where he lived.

As it turned out, Schmidt-Pohl served only one year in prison before Amnesty International brought attention to his case and West Germany bought his freedom. (Selling prisoners was an important source of hard currency for the GDR. In 1988 alone, the practice accounted for more than DM 230 million.)[1] His case was indeed a particularly grizzly one. During his time in prison in 1974, his retina detached and the Stasi arranged for an operation. Schmidt-Pohl recalls today that the surgeon insulted him before commencing the surgery. Following the operation, he was returned to prison in Cottbus and beaten by prison guards. His retina detached again, leaving him permanently blind in his right eye.[2]

In this story, the Stasi, like Odysseus, encounters the barbarian and destroys his sight, not in the grotesque fashion of tricking the Cyclops and then sending a smoking shaft into his eyeball, but through much more subtle methods—mishandling, neglect, abuse, and an operation that was conducted, to borrow a German phrase, *stiefmütterlich*, as a stepmother might do things. If Homer's hero presents us with the classic encounter between civilization and barbarism, and one with a nuanced question about how comfortable we are that barbarism was defeated in this ghastly fashion, then the conduct of the Stasi is even more difficult to judge. Although the Stasi did, on occasion, arrange for the murder of regime opponents,[3] this was far more the exception than the rule. Instead, the Stasi employed more refined methods of control—extensive behind-the-scenes monitoring by a vast army of informants, psychological methods to disrupt individual lives, prisoner neglect, blackmail, and coercion—methods, no matter how distasteful, that do not equate with a shaft to the eye or, in real terms, to the brutal torture methods of the Gestapo.

Because of the subtle nature of control in East Germany, the vast majority of those involved with the repression apparatus were never brought to justice after the fall of the Berlin Wall. Of the more than 91,000 full-time Stasi officers in 1989, thirty-three were sentenced by the year 2000. Twenty-eight of the sentences were suspended, four were settled financially. Only one of the full-time workers of the largest secret police per capita in world history went to jail—an unassuming watchman at a district office in the countryside, who, after having had too much vodka, drew his weapon and shot two people near the remote outpost. That watchman, Werner Funk, was sentenced in 1990 to ten years in prison.[4] It is frustration at what appears to be an appalling miscarriage of justice that has prompted Hubertus Knabe, the controversial director of the Stasi memorial site at Hohenschönhausen in Berlin, to write of "the perpetrators being among us," a provocative reworking of *The Murderers Are Among Us*, the title of Wolfgang Staudte's film about genocidaires walking free on the streets of postwar West Germany.

Questions about the nature of the Stasi are intimately tied to the nature of the German Democratic Republic. If the Stasi were merely an instrument of control, albeit a harsh one, in the service of a redemptive, utopian, fundamentally "civilized" regime that enjoyed a good measure of popular support, then its actions are more easily justified; its members were simply part of a "normal" secret service, typical of any modern industrial state. If the Stasi were a brutal instrument to forcibly push through a system to which East Germans did not subscribe, then the organization and its members must be judged more harshly. And, in the end, the question of responsibility for crimes—be it on the part of the population or the regime—remains the single most important question of twentieth-century German history.

I outline below the poisonous debates that swirl around the field of East German history, but it is worth mentioning at this stage that for all of the sophistication of ideas about the nature of the East German regime—whether it was a totalitarian state, welfare dictatorship, or hybrid bureaucratic-totalitarian welfare state, whether East Germans led perfectly normal lives or lived in a constant state of fear and paralysis, whether the stability of the regime is to be explained primarily by repression or by popular support and societal fragmentation—we still do not have an empirical study of the regime's most important tool for societal control at a grassroots level.[5]

What follows is a history of the Stasi in two ordinary districts of East Germany, District Gransee and District Perleberg, how they monitored the population, their daily operations, the people who worked for the Stasi, and, ultimately, their demise. Districts Gransee and Perleberg were but two fairly remote outposts of the 217 Stasi district offices (*Kreisdienststellen*) responsible for the lion's share of societal surveillance in East Germany. The distinctly unglamorous district offices of the Stasi employed only 13 percent of the overall staff of the Stasi (there were roughly 7,000 Stasi employees at the district level), yet ran just over 50 percent of all informants.[6] Erich Mielke, whose long tenure as minister responsible for the Stasi stretched from 1957 until its demise in 1989, was aware of the importance of these local offices in securing the country: "The district offices are the decisive instrument for the security of our workers' and farmers' state. The stability of our Republic...depends on the determined and self-sacrificing efforts of the members of the district offices."[7]

Apart from the bucolic natural beauty and the genuine friendliness of their people, there is nothing exceptional about Districts Gransee and Perleberg. This fact makes them all the more intriguing for a historian interested in the typical, day-to-day functioning of the Stasi rather than its atypical—albeit spectacular—foreign espionage successes like the placement of the spy Gunter Guillaume high up in Chancellor Willy Brandt's government or its involvement in the doping of East German athletes. Neither of the districts bordered on West Germany or West Berlin, although District Perleberg was on a transit road to West Germany. Neither had potential sites of unrest like universities or particularly sensitive industry. District Gransee did have a number of Soviet military installations that were a focus of Stasi work, but this was true of many districts in East Germany.

What led me to study these two districts was both their ordinariness and their advantageous archival situation. Given the attention in the press concerning access to East German secret police documents, the freest access to secret police files in human history, and to the mammoth holdings of the Stasi archives (more than 111 miles [180 km] of documents), it might come as a surprise that the amount of material collected by the Stasi in its nearly forty-year history was much greater than what now remains. Throughout November 1989, after the Wall had fallen but while East Germany was still in turmoil, Stasi officers methodically walked files from their offices to shredders, to the coal furnaces on site, to forests for burial, behind barns for burning, or to rivers where large sacks of documents were sunk. At the beginning of December, incited by smoke billowing from Stasi offices, local citizens stormed the offices and halted the destruction of documents. In some cases, however, it was too late. Almost nothing remains of Markus Wolf's famed foreign espionage branch, and many district offices saw vast destruction of documents.[8]

Such was not the case with District Perleberg, however, whose record group contains 450 feet (137 m) of documents, the most in the region of Schwerin and far eclipsing, for example, District Lübz where less than 23 feet (7 m) of documents survived the revolution. Although the holdings for District Gransee are less extensive, at only 39 feet (11.9 m), key record groups survived the revolution intact. In both cases, I examined the documents best suited to understand the manner in which the Stasi operated, namely the operational files when the Stasi launched a monitoring operation of an East German citizen (known as a Personal Surveillance Operation (OPK, *Operative Personenkontrolle*) or the more involved Operational Case (OV, *Operativer Vorgang*), the cadre files that outlined the life background of each employee with the Stasi, their recruitment and their career achievements, informant files that detailed the manner of recruitment and the informant's subsequent history with the Stasi, and *Sachakten*, the files that dealt with the day-to-day running of the branch, including directives from the center.

The files for Perleberg sit in a depository in a former barracks of the East German National People's Army in a farmer's field some 15 miles (25 km) away from Schwerin; those for Gransee in a former medical complex on the outskirts of Potsdam. Both are regional branches of the agency with the unwieldy name that administers this very sensitive collection: The Federal Commission for the Documents of the State Security Service of the former GDR. For as much as the commission has come under fire of late, it cannot be emphasized enough that the archivists and staff there offer superlative research assistance.[9] As has been well established in the literature, the Stasi was not a state within a state but rather served at the behest of the ruling Socialist Unity Party (*Sozialistische Einheitspartei Deutschlands—SED*).[10] Accordingly, I also examined the party files for Districts Gransee and Perleberg held in the *Länder* archives for Brandenburg and Mecklenburg. Although these contained valuable insights into the location of the Stasi in the information-gathering apparatus of the party, there was little to illuminate the often contentious relationship between the party and the Stasi at a district level.

The final pillar on which this book is based is oral history. I conducted interviews with fourteen former employees of the Stasi who worked in Districts Gransee and Perleberg (and one neighboring district)—some of them operational officers, some of them support staff—and twenty "ordinary" Germans who lived in the districts during the era of Communist rule.

## THE CONTENTIOUS HISTORY OF EAST GERMANY

For a small country that lasted briefly on the map of Europe, the attention accorded the German Democratic Republic is nothing short of astonishing. The history of East Germany, however, holds particular poignancy for current residents of eastern Germany, where those complicit with the regime are neighbors of those who suffered under it. This fact of the GDR being very recent history is indeed the rub, as Ulrich Plenzdorf observed: "That the GDR is dead is a myth. The people who were the GDR are still alive."[11]

In recent years, the debate about East German history has garnered worldwide attention through the enormously successful movies *Goodbye Lenin!* (and the less successful abroad but very popular in Germany as *Sonnenallee*) and the Oscar-winning *The Lives of Others*. Since the tragic elements of *Goodbye Lenin!* were more or less ignored (such as the painful scene in which the daughter discovers the letters from her father, who was separated from the rest of the family by the Berlin Wall) and the comedic moments around Spreewald pickles accentuated, the movie's reputation is that of a comedy, one that portrays life in the GDR as a light-hearted affair. Even the exclamation mark in the title suggests a note of frivolity. Like Jaroslav Hasek's famous *Good Soldier Švejk*, East Germans appear as a group that bumbled along the path of life, oblivious to the repression around them or pretending to be naïve so as not to get caught up in the system. The image of an East Germany where life was simply a connection of happy events was reinforced in the early 2000s with several major German TV stations running variety shows about the GDR. Katarina Witt, the East German ice skater and star of the Sarajevo Olympics, appeared on RTL's *Die DDR-Show* wearing a shirt from the Communist youth group *Young Pioneers*, reminding her viewers that "there were also some very nice times" in the GDR. When queried about the negative aspects of the regime, her co-host answered: "It makes no sense on an entertainment show to invite a border guard to the studio and ask him about his orders to shoot."[12] On SAT.1, the former boxer Axel Schulz co-hosted *Die ultimative Ost-Show*, the job description for which was apparently to exclaim *"Dat war der Hammer!"* (literally "That was the hammer!," or "That was awesome!") whenever the topics of Trabants (East German fiberglass cars), the East German rock groups City or Die Puhdys, or camping on the Baltic were raised.

*The Lives of Others*, on the other hand, deals far more squarely with the repressive features of the regime. In Florian Henckel von Donnersmarck's film, set in the mid to late 1980s, the Stasi captain Gerd Wiesler (played by Ulrich Mühe) is the case officer assigned to monitor the oppositional playwright Georg Dreyman. From his listening post in the attic, Wiesler comes to know the intimate life of his subject, is moved by the music and poetry he is exposed to in the course of surveillance, and ends up as a quasi-guardian angel for Dreyman and his companion, for whom he has developed more than just a passing fondness. Apart from a major historical inaccuracy that makes the entire premise fall apart (a Stasi officer of that rank would never have been the one donning the surveillance headphones), there was not one instance in the entire history of the Stasi when an officer went over to the opposition in the manner suggested by the film. The film is laced with ideas of redemption overcoming sin (an understandable central motif for any German movie about the German past), of the fundamental humanity of the central character, and the fact that he becomes the "good man" of the sonata that Dreyman plays while Wiesler secretly listens in. Overlooked in this interpretation of the film is Wiesler's career both before and after his association with Operation *Laszlo*.

When the movie opens, Wiesler is mercilessly interrogating a prisoner for assisting in the escape of his friend over the border. After several nights of interrupted sleep and Wiesler's threats to the well-being of his family, the prisoner suffers a breakdown and confesses to the "crime." At the Stasi college in Potsdam-Eiche, Wiesler uses this case to instruct the next generation of Stasi officers in how to extract confessions from prisoners. If it is indeed the sins of that life that Wiesler wishes to redeem by protecting the playwright and his companion, it is odd that following Operation *Laszlo*, Wiesler opens personal mail for *five years*. This action would not have been a benign, make-work project for a fallen secret police officer, but would have had very real consequences for those whose mail was opened. As a case in point, the 154 Stasi personnel who worked in Department M (mail monitoring) in Region Halle in the southern industrial area of East Germany inspected 15,779,715 pieces of mail in the first quarter of 1989 alone, and sent out 85,478 memos to appropriate Stasi departments regarding the content of the letters.[13] Does a "good man," following his redemption, open other people's mail for years on end? To see this film as a morality play in which goodness overcomes the dictates of ideology is to miss a much more complex picture about the institutional barriers that *denied* opportunities for good to triumph in the East German dictatorship.[14] For Ulrich Mühe, the actor who played Wiesler, the film itself must have been a cathartic exercise: unbeknownst to him until after the fall of the Wall, his wife was a Stasi informant throughout their entire marriage.[15]

To a certain extent, what has happened in the field of popular culture, where films and television shows about daily life in East Germany far away from the repression apparatus dominate, has been mirrored in the historiography of East Germany. Initial scholarship following the collapse of the Berlin Wall in 1989 tended to highlight the dictatorial, repressive, and controlling aspects of the SED (*Sozialistische Einheitspartei Deutschlands*) regime. Recent works, however, have moved away from a top-down model of the GDR toward one that emphasizes the plurality of relationships between rulers and ruled, the myriad ways in which East Germans participated in the dictatorship (albeit with varying degrees of willingness), and the degree of "normalcy" that characterized the lives of most East Germans. In many ways, 1993 represented a highpoint of a school of thought that can be broadly characterized as "totalitarian," with the publication of two major works, Armin Mitter and Stefan Wolle's hefty *Untergang auf Raten* (Decline in Stages) and a seminal article in the influential *Vierteljahreshefte für Zeitgeschichte* (Contemporary History Quarterly) by Klaus-Dietmar Henke titled "On the Use and Evaluation of Stasi Files."[16]

Mitter and Wolle's superbly written book, one of the first to mine the new archival material in any real depth, argues that the GDR was in a constant state of war with its own citizens and enjoyed virtually no popular buy-in. Accordingly, the regime developed sophisticated instruments, like the Stasi, to keep the population in check. Henke's vision of the GDR was not far off that of Mitter and Wolle, as he contends that the Stasi at least from the 1970s was an instrument of blanket surveillance (*flächendeckend*) and served a vital role as an organ that could help mold society toward the ideals of the party. The following year Clemens Vollnhals backed Henke's description, suggesting that the Stasi was an instrument of the exercise of totalitarian power.[17] Among totalitarian historians, descriptions of the regime vary from "gentle totalitarianism,"[18] to a "subtle" dictatorship,[19] to that which practiced a "soft" form of repression.[20]

The totalitarian model soon fell on hard times. Some historians claimed that East Germans did not see themselves in the stark hero-or-victim story of GDR history as portrayed in works like Mitter and Wolle and in the mammoth reports of the parliamentary commission tasked with writing the history of the GDR. Academics became increasingly uneasy applying a concept that did not seem to adequately capture the extent to which citizens themselves had agency in society and the regime, rather than their portrayal as hapless victims of a regime run by nebulous "others" who were somehow not part of society.[21] Furthermore, the concept seemed to be a strain of post–Cold War triumphalism akin to Francis Fukuyama's arrogant declaration that history had ended in favor of Western democracy.[22] Scholars were also concerned about applying the same term for East Germany that had been developed for Nazi Germany, a country that had, unlike East Germany, plunged the world into war and undertaken systematic extermination of Jews.

Klaus-Dietmar Henke, a supporter of the totalitarian concept for both the GDR and Nazi Germany if appropriate qualifiers are applied, rightly reminds us that the two regimes can be compared but must not be equated with one another.[23] In place of totalitarianism, a flood of alternative terms poured into the scholarship, including "welfare dictatorship" (*Fürsorgediktatur*), "post-totalitarian bureaucratic dictatorship," and a "thoroughly ruled society." In promoting his model of a "forced through society" (*vermachtete Gesellschaft*), Klaus Schroeder outlines obvious pitfalls with the alternatives: Since "thoroughly ruled society" can apply to democracies as well, the central question remains the degree of "thorough ruled-ness" in the different political systems. To suggest that the GDR was a "welfare dictatorship" is to suggest that individual well-being, rather than ideology or power, stood at the center of the GDR state, and is therefore, he believes, to thoroughly confuse matters.[24] Most recently, Mary Fulbrook has proposed the term "participatory dictatorship" to capture the seemingly large number of East Germans who were active participants in the system, rather than simply hapless victims. In championing this approach to GDR history, she writes: "A very small ruling elite, with a linked apparatus of repression and injustice, was supported and sustained by a very much larger number of people who played key roles in trying, under exceedingly difficult circumstances, to build a better society…through engaging in such communal activities as attempting to beautify their village, construct a new swimming pool, or organize a youth sports festival."[25]

Instead of focusing on the areas that the regime controlled, some historians turned their attention to the *inability* of total control, pointing instead to the boundaries of dictatorship, to those points at which society becomes impenetrable.[26] In many ways, this approach was a complete dismissal of Martin Malia's plea: "Totalitarianism does not mean that such regimes in fact exercise total control over the population; it means rather that such control is their aspiration."[27]

The latest works by historians of the GDR have analyzed the multiplicity of GDR society, the various ways that the regime met the wishes of the population, and the general, mundane day-to-day experience of most GDR citizens that suggests at least some level of co-existence.[28] As one historian has written, "Life in the GDR was ordinary for the majority of the population,"[29] or, in the words of Mary Fulbrook, most East Germans led "perfectly normal lives."[30] For these historians, the true experience of the vast majority of GDR citizens was away from the political sphere, in a private life of making do, and, at times, of a certain degree of loyalty.[31] Rather than seeing East German history through the lens of top-down "blanket surveillance," historians began to explore dominance (*Herrschaft*) as a social practice.[32] Sense of one's self (*Eigen-Sinn*) often collided with the regime, causing both sides to compromise.[33] To be sure, East Germans knew both where the physical, international boundary of the GDR ran, as well as the invisible domestic boundaries, a fact that has prompted Thomas Lindenberger to invert Bessel's "boundaries of dictatorship" description to "dictatorship of boundaries."[34] On occasion, the ruling SED, in the interest of stability, was required to reach out to the population, whether in the form of allowing rock concerts for youth, more freedom in the cultural sphere for writers and artists, or allowing renegade church leaders to continue initiatives that were not in line with state policy.[35]

For the workers, arguably the most important social group from the SED's point of view, this translated into a certain degree of power vis-à-vis the regime in terms of working conditions and wages.[36] This fact of accommodation by the regime helps to explain the relative stability of the GDR beyond the "repression" paradigm.[37] In short, many historians do not see in the SED a menacing, totalitarian party that aimed to control all aspects of society, but rather a flexible albeit dictatorial ruler that was prepared to accommodate where need be and that endeared a certain amount of loyalty.

By 2006, one of the leading historians of East Germany in the English-speaking world would go so far as to state explicitly that her goal was to kill, once and for all, the totalitarian model: "I want to use the diverse books gathered here for review in part to critique what is (or should be) by now a fairly dead horse, the totalitarianism model, which nevertheless appears remarkably resistant to terminal burial."[38] Nevertheless, the totalitarian concept lives on. Supporters of the concept, such as Peter Graf Kielmansegg, argue that there is no need to throw the baby out with the bath water; although the totalitarian concept has its limits, it is nonetheless a useful categorization for a regime that, after all, enjoyed a monopoly of power and controlled all of the armed services, including the Stasi.[39] Hannah Arendt's totalitarian concept, for example, centers on the use of terror to control a population. Since in this form the concept is ill-suited to capture the much less physically brutal Stasi, Kielmansegg suggests that the overall concept be maintained, with an emphasis instead on the Stasi's power to control life opportunities, rather than to control through terror.[40]

In many ways, whether East Germans led "perfectly normal lives" is a red herring, more reflective of what East Germans recollect now rather than relevant to a historical investigation of the system of government that existed in the GDR. It is deeply rooted in humans to remember personal aspects of their life rather than broader historical developments. Naturally, East Germans today remember their vacations on the Baltic, their first love, hikes in Thuringia, the view from the TV Tower in East Berlin, meeting under the World Clock at Alexanderplatz, school trips to the "green vault" of Dresden, birthdays, weddings, and funerals, rather than the order to shoot at the Berlin Wall. There is a self-defense mechanism at play against what appears to East Germans to be a suggestion that because the country in which they lived was the country of the Stasi and the Wall, their triumphs, achievements, personal relationships, even their lives were all for naught. Because one lived in a "bad" land, so the accusation seems to be, one lived a "bad" life.[41] That, however, is another story, one that begins rather than ends in 1989 and is closely tied to human memory and the nature of oral history.

Because East Germans recall living a "normal life" does not mean that the regime must therefore have been benign, ordinary, and normal,[42] but rather suggests that the passage of time alters our memories of what once was, especially in Germany where many unfulfilled postunification aspirations have certainly affected views of the GDR. Surveys of East Germans conducted after the revolution of 1989 suggest that there is indeed an increasingly positive view of the GDR. In evaluating the statement "One felt spied upon. You couldn't trust anyone," 43 percent of East Germans answered "True. That's exactly how it was" in 1992, but only 25 percent gave the same response by 2004. Similarly, 72.6 percent of East Germans claimed in 1990 that there was "complete surveillance" in the GDR whereas only 42 percent would agree with that claim in 1995. Although the term Ostalgie has been shunned of late, it is nonetheless plain that as time marches on East Germans increasingly believe East Germany to have been less of a surveillance state—and, by extension, the Stasi to have been less harmful— than they originally thought.[43]

As important as the descriptor of the regime historians choose for the GDR, is the *perception* of the regime by East German citizens. Even if East Germans led ordinary lives and accommodated themselves to the regime, there was overwhelming secret police pressure to do so, a fact of which East Germans were fully aware. East Germans *thought* that they were being monitored by the regime. The fact that millions of East Germans have applied to the Stasi Archives assuming that the Stasi had information on them cannot be written off as macabre fascination, but would better be seen as a broad belief in a pervasive secret police presence. This subjective belief clearly had implications for how East Germans would live their lives. Indeed, the fact that the Stasi was a "risk to be calculated with" may well have prompted many East Germans to live as unnoticeable life as possible.[44]

It is also clear from the course of the revolution of 1989, when regional Stasi offices were stormed in December (and the headquarters in January 1990), that East Germans thought that the Stasi had files worth protecting. Citizens did not storm the archives of the Communist Party. East Germans wanted Stasi files protected because they believed that there were personal files on themselves and other East Germans, not because they worried about destruction of bureaucratic directives or guidelines or (alas) to secure the records for future historians.

A word must also be said about the sheer size of the Stasi. Here, historians should be grateful for our level of access to East German secret police documents in contrast with other countries of Eastern Europe: the number of informants and full-time workers in the Soviet Union, for example, remains a best guess, whereas we know that in 1989 there were precisely 91,015 full-time Stasi employees and 173,000 informants.[45] Helmut Müller-Enbergs estimates that in the course of GDR history, a quarter million East Germans were full-time Stasi workers and nearly 600,000 were informers.[46] Some will take issue with these staggering numbers and claim that Western democracies, too, have their security services, including the American FBI and CIA, the West German Office for Protection of the Constitution, and the Canadian Security and Intelligence Service. One example demonstrates the vast disparity between the two. On October 1, 1989, the Stasi Regional Administration Halle employed 1,829 Stasi personnel, with a further 1,539 in the district offices, while the Regional Administration Magdeburg employed 2,685 with a further 895 in the district offices. In total, then, there were 6,948 Stasi employed for domestic surveillance in these two regions, leaving aside the informants.

In contrast, the Department for the Protection of the Constitution (housed within the Ministry of the Interior) for the German province of Saxony-Anhalt today employs eighty people to monitor roughly the same territory.[47] Put differently, the Stasi was nearly 9,000 percent larger than its equivalent in the new united Germany. Canada's relevant security apparatus, at 2,449 full-time employees, was dwarfed by the Stasi's 91,000 officers, although the Canadian population was twice as large as that of East Germany's.[48] The result of this enormous apparatus was four million index cards on East Germans and two million on West Germans, along with countless photos, sound recordings, and scent rags (pieces of cloth containing the scents of suspects, which could be used by tracking dogs if they went underground). It is difficult for those who have not seen the mammoth holdings of the Stasi archive to imagine the extent of material collected by East Germany's secret police. If it takes roughly two minutes to read one typewritten page, it would take one historian close to seven thousand years to read all of the material—assuming that she read every minute of every day.

What is also noteworthy is that the Stasi established an informant infrastructure even in out-of-the-way places. In District Perleberg, there was one informant per roughly seventy-six pre-retirement adult East Germans in 1988, a period no more eventful than previous years. As a point of comparison, at the height of the Great Terror the Soviet security apparatus, the NKVD, had one informer for every five or six families in the capital city of Moscow, understandably a sensitive operational area. In one high school in the Donbass region in the latter half of the 1930s, thirteen out of twenty staff members were secret police informants.[49] But in the Ukrainian regional district capital of Kharkov, the Soviet secret police had one informer for every 16,800 people.[50] What is remarkable about the Stasi is its penetration of the most ordinary, ostensibly nonthreatening, areas of East Germany. Even within Eastern Europe, the pervasive surveillance in the GDR was exceptional. The secret services of the USSR (1:595), Czechoslovakia (1:867), or Poland (1:1,574) did not even come close to the ratio in East Germany of one full-time secret police officer for every 180 East German citizens.

The clear scholarly emphasis of late on daily life in East Germany and on the aspects of the regime that were "not so evil"[51] has meant that works on the Stasi, repression, opposition, and resistance have been less in evidence. Even recent important works on the Stasi itself have tended away from a top-down history of the Stasi toward a model that investigates the mutual influence between society and the regime's instruments of control.[52] How do historians square this circle, then, of East Germans leading "perfectly normal lives" in a country with the Berlin Wall and the largest secret police per capita in world history? Respected, thoroughly trained historians come to polar conclusions on this question, frequently eschewing the nuanced answers to which the profession has become accustomed. Thomas Lindenberger argues that East Germany was a society where individuals were able to assert control of niches, their own free space away from the state, whereas Stefan Wolle insists that there were *no* niches, *no* refuges, *no* free spaces.[53] The debates have gotten to the point where one historian publicly cancelled his subscription to a journal for a negative review of a work on the "everyday life" approach to East German history.[54]

If we cast our view to other regimes as a point of reference, Sheila Fitzpatrick's analysis of everyday life in the Soviet Union under Stalin suggests a similar conundrum with Soviet citizens attempting to live ordinary lives while continually running up against the state "in one of its multifarious aspects."[55] Although comparisons with Nazi Germany must be made with the greatest of caution, there is some aspect of Yehuda Bauer's description of day-to-day life in the Third Reich as "colored by the criminal regime" that has echoes for the German Democratic Republic.[56]

It is difficult to imagine that a dictatorship with the range of instruments that the GDR had could not color, in very real terms, the ordinary lives of East Germans. Of course, daily life in East Germany cannot be reduced to the Stasi, but daily life in East Germany cannot be understood without taking it into account. In Hubertus Knabe's view, the Stasi's effect on daily life was palpable: "Precisely the hidden, but for every citizen tangible omni-presence of the Stasi, damaged the very basic conditions for individual and societal creativity and development: Sense of one's self, Trust, Spontaneity."[57] Given the very real manner in which East Germans were conscious of the Stasi's existence as they went about their lives, concepts such as "boundaries" of dictatorship seem inadequate to capture the diffusion of the Stasi in society. One can no more place a boundary around the Stasi than one can encircle a scent in a room. To go even further and suggest that the "impact of the Stasi on East German society should not be overstated" and that the "Stasi hardly touched the lives of most East Germans directly" is preposterous.[58]

I do not wish to suggest, as Hubertus Knabe has done, that histories of daily life are leading to a whitewashing of the regime.[59] There is no question that societal systems can be understood only within the context of state-society interactions and that histories of daily life are vital in this equation. Given the level to which society was politicized, however, and the fact that the state-society relationship was not one between equals, histories of dominance and power structures must form an integral part of the discourse.[60] The lessons of the historians' debate of the late 1980s in this regard are crucial. Apart from the nonsensical comparison of the suffering of the Wehrmacht with the suffering of Jews, the assertion that the Holocaust did not really alter the day-to-day existence of most Germans missed the manner by which German society was infused with Nazi racial ideas.[61] It is my hope to offer a sense of the integration of state into society, of the tendrils of the regime's repression apparatus even in small-town East Germany, the power that the Stasi was granted within governmental structures to carry out its mission, and the manner by which Germans internalized the Stasi presence.[62]

## DENUNCIATION AS PARTICIPATION?

For many scholars, the barometer for participation in a regime is the willingness of citizens to denounce fellow citizens. As is to be expected, historians differ as to what constitutes denunciation. Whereas Katrin Dördelmann defines it as the "voluntary passing-on, anonymously or not, of information about politically unwelcome talk and actions of other people,"[63] Sheila Fitzpatrick and Robert Gellately define it as "spontaneous communications from individual citizens to the state (or to another authority such as the church) containing accusations of wrongdoing by other citizens or officials and implicitly or explicitly calling for punishment."[64] Moreover, "denunciation" has an inherently negative connotation but may also be conceived of in purely neutral terms such as reporting a crime to the police, a phenomenon that is by no means restricted to dictatorships and has, to a large degree, a positive connotation. Denunciation need not always have a formal element to it; gossip and reporting to friends can serve as a "horizontal" form of control within society.[65]

Karl-Heinz Reuband's caution on the issue of denunciation as a demonstration of regime support is worth noting, though. Denunciation in Nazi Germany was never a mass phenomenon (or, phrased another way, the vast majority of people in Nazi Germany did not denounce anyone), so the extent to which we can conclude that denunciation indicates regime support is questionable. Nevertheless, in the sweeping change that has occurred in the literature on Nazi Germany, historians have turned their attention from the model of a totalitarian state that forces its agenda on an unwilling population, to that of the active participation of ordinary citizens in sustaining a dictatorship.[66] It has become commonplace to compare the Nazi regime with East Germany to demonstrate that there was greater frequency of spontaneous denunciation—and therefore support—in Nazi Germany than in East Germany.

Whereas the Stasi had 91,000 full-time officers at its collapse, the Gestapo employed a mere 7,000 in the prewar period even though the population of Nazi Germany (60 million) was over triple that of East Germany (17 million).[67] With the help of its informal network of denouncers, the smaller Gestapo was able to keep tabs on a much larger population. Robert Gellately was the first to explode the myth of a Gestapo agent that lurked at every corner[68] and to turn much of the responsibility for the Nazi terror system over to ordinary Germans who assisted the secret police, a form of collaboration for which women and men were equally guilty.[69] Although Eric Johnson believes that the Gestapo was not as dependent on unpaid informants as Gellately suggests, particularly in the repression of opponents among Roman Catholics and Jehovah's Witnesses, and that too much of the blame for Nazi crimes has shifted away from leading bureaucrats, the premise that ordinary Germans voluntarily partook to a large extent in the repression apparatus now seems entrenched in the literature.[70]

The Stasi at first glance seems fundamentally different from the Gestapo. Whereas the Gestapo appears as an arms-length participant in an essentially self-policing society,[71] the Stasi established and constantly refined a network of amateur informants and almost never responded to tips from the few East Germans who came to the Stasi. It would be a mistake, however, to think that the Stasi did not rely at all on assistance from the population, a point that underlies this book. On a regular basis, the Stasi requested cooperation from

East Germans on certain operations, dropped in on factory bosses to monitor employees, and heard from school principals about potentially oppositional students. To be sure, many of these individuals were approached by the Stasi, which was generally a much more proactive secret police than the Gestapo, but just as recent research has shown the Gestapo to have been more proactive than originally thought, so too was the Stasi more reactive than many accounts suggest. It frequently followed up on tips not from its well-groomed informants but from its casual contacts who were not signed-up informants, including school principals, landlords, police officers, even neighborhood acquaintances of Stasi officers themselves. If there was little institutional pressure in Nazi Germany to become a "self-policing" society, that was not the case in East Germany, where the Stasi was a sprawling institution that frequently coerced participation from its informants.

As research on Nazi Germany has demonstrated, motivation to denounce was often—if not primarily—personal, relating to landlord-tenant struggles or other instances whereby the "weaker" in the party denounced the "stronger" in order that the state take over the personal vendetta. In Essen, for example, wives often denounced abusive husbands ostensibly for listening to foreign radio.[72] Although there is considerable research on the motivations of East Germans who became Stasi informants, there is still much to be done on this other category of individual who worked for the Stasi on a casual basis, who, often in their role as contacts who had been cultivated by the Stasi, did in fact spontaneously denounce. For the most part, these were individuals who had privileged positions in society and some ongoing contact with the Stasi, not ordinary individuals off the street.

Although denouncing was a form of involving oneself with the state, it is an awkward fit with the concept of "participatory dictatorship." Some informants worked for the Stasi out of conviction, some for personal or material gain, some used the Stasi for personal vendettas, and many were coerced (a more appropriate descriptor than "persuaded").[73] It is difficult to judge the degree of *willingness* to become an informant, especially given the genuine concerns that many East Germans would have had about refusing a recruiting officer. As the first overseer of the Stasi files has said, to refuse the Stasi required a strong "I."[74] Moreover, the regime built broad popular involvement into its own extensive surveillance goals; it was the state infrastructure that permitted this negative form of participation. In fact, the apparatus for denunciation in East Germany calls to mind Gerhard Paul's description of the Gestapo in Schleswig-Hollstein as a "democratization of terror," or the establishment of structures that allowed for the active participation of ordinary segments of society in the repression process.[75] With reference to the surveillance apparatus in particular, with its myriad ways to involve ordinary individuals in repression, whether occasionally or regularly, and which, when necessary, crossed any "boundary" to carry out its surveillance duties, East Germany was not so much a participatory dictatorship as it was a regime that could dictate participation.

## THE SETTING: DISTRICTS PERLEBERG AND GRANSEE

Districts Perleberg and Gransee are both situated in the north German plain, a flat, windswept landscape north of Berlin that is today dominated by power-generating windmills. These quiet areas of Germany contrast with Berlin, the nearest big city, with its construction-crane-filled skyline, ubiquitous graffiti, and clamor of buses and trams. Unlike in major cities of the former German Democratic Republic like Leipzig and Dresden, it would be an oddity to see a North American backpacker walking the streets of Wittenberge, the largest town in either district.

District Perleberg was located northwest of Berlin, on the important train line between Hamburg and Berlin that accounted in large part for what industry there was in the area. During the Cold War, of course, there was considerably less traffic on this route, but direct rail access to East Berlin was nevertheless an advantage. District Perleberg is located in an area of Germany known as the Prignitz, a tranquil region of reeds and lakes, of thousands of storks with their large nests teetering on hydro poles, and an area punctuated by the historic Elbe River, which widens here as it begins its graceful descent to its estuary in Hamburg harbor. Cyclists today bike along the tops of dikes laid down to keep the Elbe floodwaters at bay; they enjoy the striking views of the river that looks as if it has no depth, as if it has been gently unrolled along the plain. The flat terrain, quiet roads, quaint villages, and well-developed trail system have made this region a mecca for cyclists and hikers from around Europe. Wittenberge in particular is banking on cyclists in its economic development platform. In many ways, this region, with its thin population, agricultural economy, and flat landscape contrasts sharply with the "other" end of East Germany, the industrial heartland far to the south and the craggy "Ore Mountains" along the border with Czechoslovakia. If that area is the Rockies, then Districts Gransee and Perleberg are the prairies.

Although the population of District Perleberg declined from a high of 90,761 after World War II to 73,229 in 1989 (most of the population loss occurred in the mass exodus of East Germans prior to the construction of the Berlin Wall in 1961), it was still the second most populous district in Region Schwerin at the time of the regime's collapse.[76] The employed population in District Perleberg was primarily working class. Of the 36,990 employed in the district in 1989, the largest groups by far were factory workers (nearly 30 percent) and agricultural workers (22 percent). District Perleberg represented the epitome of the "workers' and farmers' state."[77]

Most people in District Perleberg lived in one of the three cities: Perleberg, the administrative center of the district with a population today of 14,000; Wittenberge, at 22,000 inhabitants the largest city and main industrial area; and Bad Wilsnack, an elegant city dominated by the Late Gothic St. Nicholas Church. Perleberg and Wittenberge are archrivals, their hostility often spilling over in the soccer games, which are epic battles between the two cities. Today, residents of both cities will immediately inform you that the other city is receiving preferential treatment when it comes to the government's placement of offices or other services. Perlebergers were furious when a high school was moved to Wittenberge in the 1980s and a public swimming pool opened there instead of in Perleberg; Wittenbergers are today irate that the hospital in town has been downsized and a new one opened in Perleberg. For the most part, the rivalry stems from the social makeup of the two cities.

Wittenberge, with its three major factories and repair center for German rail lines, has traditionally been a blue-collar town, voting heavily for the Social Democrats and, during the 1920s and 1930s, proving a difficult town for the Nazis to penetrate. Even today, Wittenberge has streets named after socialists like Clara Zetkin and Salvador Allende, which survived the flurry of postunification name changes. (The small, rundown tavern boasting live soccer that occupies the corner of Marx and Engels Streets somehow does not live up to the billing that such an intersection would suggest.) Perleberg, on the other hand, is an administrative center and white-collar town, the houses a little better cared for, the air more pleasant than the stench from the rayon factory that sat over Wittenberge for years.

Because of Wittenberge's location on the banks of the Elbe River and the Hamburg-Berlin rail line, several industries settled in the town: The märkische Ölwerk (oilseed processing plant of the Mark Brandenburg), which produced margarine and similar synthetic-fat products; the gargantuan Zellstoff- und Zellwollewerk Wittenberge (ZZWW), which produced rayon and cellulose; the railway outfitting works; and the calling card of the city, the Nähmaschinenwerk Wittenberge, a sewing machine factory established by Singer in 1903 but taken over by the Communists after the war and continued to produce high-quality sewing machines. As the airship *Graf Zeppelin* flew over Wittenberge in 1928 on its maiden voyage across Germany, the passengers on board would have seen at the Singer plant below the second-tallest clock tower in Europe, still a symbol of the city. On any given day, in a scene reminiscent of contemporary China, the entrance to the plant was crowded with thousands of bicycles, many of them rusting from the salty spray of the rayon factory just up the road. No matter where one lived in East Germany, a sewing machine from Wittenberge (produced under the name Veritas) in one's home elicited looks of admiration (with perhaps a splash of suspicion) since their high quality meant that the vast majority were exported to the Soviet Union or to the West. One factory worker recalled the odd image of large Mercedes trucks backing up to the loading bay to take East German sewing machines over to West Germany.

Following German unification in 1990, the sewing machine factory, which had been producing 1,250 sewing machines a day, lurched along in the new economy but quickly fell behind, shutting its doors on New Year's Eve 1991 after eighty-eight years in business. The people of Wittenberge are deeply saddened by the loss of the factory, not only because of the economic benefit it brought but because it was a source of pride. All that remains of the once bustling factory is the clock tower and the word "VERITAS" in very large capital letters on a building at the factory's old site. The other major industries in Wittenberge soon followed suit. The Ölwerk closed in 1991 after 168 years in business, and in 1995 the last of the chimneys of the rayon factory demolished. On the site of the industrial park where the three industries resided now sits a restaurant and a man-made beach along the Elbe River that hosts a bar called the Elbe Beach Club that invites youth in the area, in somewhat awkward English, to "drink, lunch, music and chill."

The center of Perleberg, the second largest city in the district, is located on a small island in the Perleberg stream. Unlike modern cities such as Seattle or Calgary, Perleberg's layout resembles nothing of a chessboard but is characterized by streets with bends, public squares accessible only from one direction, and other twists and turns, a result of both its long history and the confines of the oval island on which it sits. The middle of the city is dominated by an open square tightly packed in by merchants' houses from the seventeenth and eighteenth centuries. The imposing St. Jacob's church and town hall sit back to back on the square, under the ever-watchful eye of the sword-wielding statue of Roland, a warrior of Charlemagne's court, at the other end of the square. Roland statues were erected throughout primarily northern and central Europe as symbols of the free status of the city. Perleberg's wonderful example dates back to 1498 and is one of only twenty-five original Roland statues remaining in Germany today. Throughout Perleberg, like most cities in eastern Germany, the Cyrillic alphabet and red stars remind that Russians fought and died here. A red star adorns an obelisk at the main war cemetery in Perleberg and just off the main street is a plaque to a Red Army tank driver who was killed well after the end of the war. Although the plaque in Russian suggests that the soldier was a martyr, the truth, known to most inhabitants in town, was that the soldier was killed by locals practicing vigilante justice because of the soldier's aggressions against German women.

Bad Wilsnack, the third and smallest city in District Perleberg with just over seven thousand inhabitants, has long been a pilgrimage site. In 1383, after the knight Heinrich von Bülow burned the town and church to the ground, a local priest sifting through the ashes of the church noticed something out of the ordinary. On the altar were three hosts that appeared to have drops of blood on them. The "bleeding hosts" received sanction from the local bishop as a miracle, launching several centuries of pilgrimages that finally petered out after Martin Luther declared the Wilsnack hosts to be a false miracle and had them destroyed. The massive, stark, cold church interior still has signs of those pilgrimages in the form of odd, wondrous objects like large mammal bones that pilgrims brought with them. The people of the Middle Ages who traveled to Bad Wilsnack looked for those things typically sought after by pilgrims: solace, cures for their ailments, guidance for a heavy heart. Today's visitors are little different, as they descend from the train and walk the short distance to the spa to take the thermal waters that permit the town to use "Bad" (bath, spa) in its name and to find respite from their travails on the many walking paths that wind through the forests surrounding the resort.

Some 56 miles (90 km) to the east of District Perleberg is District Gransee, a region of fields, lakes, and blowing grasses in the Neu Ruppiner plain that has been immortalized in Theodore Fontane's classic novel *Effi Briest*. For Effi, the region represented her refuge, her calm in a life of turmoil, literally her Eden; when she receives news from her parents that because of her conduct she is no longer allowed to return to her home in Hohen-Cremmen, she—as well as the reader—is heartbroken. Effi faces the same fate as her biblical namesake and is banished from paradise.

With only five thousand inhabitants, Gransee was one of the smallest administrative centers in East Germany. Today the almost completely intact medieval city wall circles the city, allowing passage in and out through the Ruppiner Gate. Beside the brick St. Mary's Church in the center of town sits the pride of Gransee, a monument designed by the eminent Karl Friedrich Schinkel to commemorate an overnight stop in Gransee made by the funeral procession of Queen Luise of Prussia in 1810 from her place of death in Hohenzieritz to the royal burial grounds in Berlin.

Gransee was roughly the same size as nearby Fürstenberg (5,241 inhabitants), but both were considerably smaller than Zehdenick (11,635), the other city in the district and the only industrial center.[78] Zehdenick, the gateway to the Mecklenburg lake district, was home to a large brick factory that was central to the construction industry of the GDR as well as a microelectronics factory that supplied the East German cargo fleet. Until 1938, the area around Fürstenberg was a destination for well-to-do Berliners who docked their yachts on the nearby lakes and enjoyed the coffee shops along with patrons who arrived in town on one of the Nazi-owned *Strength Through Joy* steamers.[79]

During the GDR, the military dominated District Gransee. In this relatively small district were located eighteen Soviet military bases (including that of the general staff for Army Group North) and five bases of the East German military. In Fürstenberg in particular, with more than fifteen thousand Soviet troops and only five thousand residents, the Soviet presence would have been a part of daily life and, it must be said, not always a pleasant one. Complaints about the Soviets ranged from the unbearable clatter of their tanks as they accelerated to ascend the hill on the edge of town, to their fishing with hand grenades, to their preferential treatment on harder-to-access goods, and theft. The local police were frequently called to bars where brawls between Soviets and residents had exploded. The image of the Soviet forces did not necessarily improve after the fall of the Wall, when the retreating soldiers ransacked their residences and took with them appliances and plumbing fixtures, leaving the German authorities little choice but to tear down the residences and build anew.

Fürstenberg's main point of interest today is the Ravensbrück concentration camp, which the Nazis established primarily for female inmates and which employed female SS guards whose ruthless conduct was on a par with that of their male colleagues. Most Fürstenbergers would immediately recognize the name of Dorothea Binz, a young local woman who was sentenced to death after the war for her vicious conduct as a camp guard.[80]

District Gransee had roughly half the population of District Perleberg, but like its counterpart it was primarily a workers' and farmers' district. Just over half of all working people in the district were connected with industry or agriculture.[81]

If it were not for the village of Neuglobsow, located between Gransee and Fürstenberg, it is likely that Hitler would never have visited the district. In 1936, a year in which Hitler was enjoying unprecedented popular support at home, Karl Litzmann, a World War I hero and victor of the Battle of Lodz, died and was buried in his home town of Neuglobsow. As word spread throughout the region that Hitler and his top ministers Joseph Goebbels and Hermann Göring would be passing through Gransee on the way to the funeral, locals began to file out to the streets. Initially disappointed because Hitler did not stop on the outward journey, the crowd waited patiently, hopeful that the Führer would get out of the car on the return journey. Hitler's impromptu stop in Gransee following the funeral was for many in the area one of the highlights of the period. Today, Werner Krause remembers vividly that June day in 1936 when Hitler descended from his car into the throngs that lined the streets and into his element—shaking hands vigorously and chatting at ease with his people and they with him. At one point in his short visit, a young girl emerged from the crowd and offered Hitler a drink of Gransee's famous apple cider. Believing that it was an alcoholic beverage, he knelt down and kindly explained to her that he did not drink alcohol. When she said that there was no alcohol in it, he took the glass, raised it, and drank it. The crowd erupted, and Hitler made his way back to Berlin.

# 1

# DISTRICTS GRANSEE
# AND PERLEBERG
# UNDER THE NAZIS

WHAT WOULD BECOME the east German districts of Gransee and Perleberg after 1945 were in the province of Mark Brandenburg during the Nazi era. Gransee itself was located in Landkreis (administrative district) Ruppin, whereas Perleberg and Wittenberge were located in the Landkreis Westprignitz. Even today, people in this area refer to themselves as being from the Prignitz. Due to its geographic proximity to the capital of the Third Reich, Mark Brandenburg was closely entwined with the development of Nazi Germany—both in military and political terms.[1]

Recounting the history of Mark Brandenburg during the Nazi era presents its own set of challenges. The last days of World War II witnessed a frenzied destruction of documents by nervous Nazis as well as collateral losses of archival material during the Allied invasion of Germany. To make matters more difficult, much material was captured by Soviet troops and brought to Moscow, where it remained under lock and key until 1992. The small portion of material that was returned to East Germany in the 1950s remained inaccessible to historians until after German unification and now resides in both the federal and *Länder* (state) archives.[2] By way of illustration, the Nazi administration region of Mark Brandenburg in 1933 was comprised of 46 district offices and 903 *Ortsgruppen* or local groups. Of these, there exists today material on only 9 district offices and 27 local groups, and virtually none of the material relates to districts in the west of the province where District Perleberg was located.[3] As a result, compared to other German provinces, especially those in former West Germany, the study of Mark Brandenburg during the Nazi era has just begun.[4] Credit should nevertheless be given to the work of amateur historians, museum personnel, and enthusiasts in the area who have kept the stories of the past alive in local newspapers and publications like the *Wittenberger Chroniken*. The affable Werner Krause, a teacher in Gransee, has worked tirelessly to publish stories of Gransee's Nazi past in the local newspaper *Gransee Zeitung*, stories, it should be said, that do not always paint the area in the best light, making his dedication all the more impressive.

On June 1, 1933, there were roughly 2.7 million people living in the province of Brandenburg, divided almost evenly between the regions of Frankfurt (Oder) and Potsdam. As is to be expected from northern Germany, more than 90 percent of the population was Protestant, 5 percent Roman Catholic, and there was a smattering of Jews and atheists. Pockets of industry cropped up in this largely agricultural area, where nearly 40 percent of the working population was employed in agriculture, animal husbandry, fishing, and forestry. Industry and manual labor made up the next largest segment of the economy, followed by trade and the public sector. This was by no means an area dominated by white-collar public servants (*Beamtenregion*), although there was naturally a certain amount of this type of employment in local government cities like Perleberg and Gransee. Women made up 35.6 percent of all employed, a fairly high number explained by the fact that the textile industry, traditionally dominated by women, was one of the major industries in the region.[5] The Gransee area was generally on the cusp of the industrial development taking place in the ring around Berlin, which included aluminum production in Lauta, a burgeoning aviation industry near Oranienburg (an abandoned airstrip off of the B94 highway is still visible) and Brandenburg, truck plants in Brandenburg and Berlin, and a robust television and movie industry in Babelsberg, just outside Berlin, the "Hollywood" of Germany and a major tourist attraction today.[6] Although these industries had a ripple effect into the regions around Gransee and Perleberg, these areas were still just outside the reach of Berlin and ended up developing industries that would service the forestry and agricultural sector. By the end of the World War II, many of the industries in Gransee and surrounding area (including Berlin) had become vital to the war effort, including the Hennigsdorf steel production facility (during the 1953 uprising the workers from this plant marched an astonishing 15 miles (25 km) into Berlin to take part in demonstrations),[7] the Heinkel airplane and airplane engine factories in Oranienburg and I. G. Farben's poison gas facility located in Falkenhagen.[8]

One notable exception to the predominantly agricultural economy of the West Prignitz was the highly industrialized Wittenberge. In 1934 Wittenberge was a city of 26,000 inhabitants, 95 percent of whom were Protestant, 4.9 percent Catholic, and 0.1 percent Jewish. Nearly 1,500 Wittenbergers were employed at the outfitting works of the German national railway, the sprawling yards of which still dominate the eastern part of the city, while many others worked in one of the nearly eight hundred small businesses that catered to the surrounding agricultural industry.

In the early 1930s, as the Weimar Republic teetered toward the brink, many of the six million unemployed fanned out across the country looking for food, shelter, and work, more often than not meeting with a frosty reception at one town before being sent on to the next. In Gransee, more than 1,600 unemployed came to town in 1932, some of whom were put up temporarily in the youth hostel or offered shelter for the night in the cells in the basement of the city hall.[9] Whether Hitler was directly responsible for the turn of the tide, he could easily claim credit for the vastly improved unemployment rate a year after he had come to power. In Wittenberge, the number of unemployed dropped from 599 in 1933 to 360 the following year, and those dependent on social assistance fell dramatically.[10]

## NAZI SEIZURE OF POWER

Although the Nazis originally had difficulties penetrating working-class-heavy Wittenberge, they eventually succeeded in becoming the most popular party in the city.[11] At the communal elections of 1929, only one Nazi was elected while the Social Democrats (SPD) won 12 seats. In the 1930 electoral breakthrough, when Nazi seats in the Reichstag jumped from 12 to 107, the Nazi fortunes in Wittenberge also improved. Although the SPD was still the most popular party, with 5,845 votes, the Nazis were now second at 4,195.[12] Perhaps aided by Joseph Goebbels's appearance at an election rally at Wittenberge's main stadium in 1932, the Nazis were the most successful party at the election later that year, receiving 6,565 votes to the SPD's 4,927. Almost immediately after the frail President Hindenburg appointed Adolf Hitler as Reich Chancellor on January 30, 1933, Hitler began to solidify his position, for Hitler was fully aware that his hold on the chancellorship was tenuous. He proceeded swiftly against his political opponents, the Communists and the Social Democrats, and within weeks of seizing power had opened Dachau concentration camp to accept political inmates. Communists in Gransee were outraged by the conduct of the Nazis. In February 1933 the communists held a major rally in the Gransee 10,000-seat *sportpalast* that featured Wilhelm Pieck, future president of East Germany, as a speaker. As was typical of the general lawlessness settling over Germany, police columns moved in to break up the rally in brutal fashion.[13] On the other side of the province, Wittenberge also witnessed the wave of violence brought on by the Nazi seizure of power in the form of assaults on two SPD deputies, Snudat and Deutschendorf, and storm trooper (*Sturmabteiling*—SA) attacks on ordinary citizens.[14]

The dome on top of the Reichstag in Berlin, the most popular tourist attraction in the German capital, was erected in 1999 to replace the one that had burned on the night of February 27/28, 1933. To this day, the circumstances around the Reichstag fire have not been fully clarified. Martin van der Lubbe, a Dutch Communist, almost certainly set fire to the German parliament, but it is highly unlikely that his actions were part of a Communist plot, as Hitler claimed. Regardless of what happened, Hitler identified an opportunity and seized it. On February 28 the German president issued an emergency decree that set aside many of the rights guaranteed in the Weimar constitution. In Wittenberge, the Nazis established a one-hundred-man protection squad (*Schutzstaffel*—SS) unit in order to "assist" the police while SA ransacked the homes of suspected Communists and Social Democrats.[15]

In the elections of March 5, 1933, the Nazi party gained 44 percent of the German vote. Although this was the best result it had ever achieved, the results were nonetheless somewhat disappointing for the Nazis, who theoretically still needed their coalition partner, the Deutsche Nationale Volkspartei, to control the Reichstag even though the Nazis had done their level best through intimidation and wanton arrests to control the electoral outcome. In Gransee and Wittenberge, the Nazis performed considerably better than the national average, obtaining (with the coalition partner) 71.2 percent and 57 percent respectively. Not surprisingly in this Protestant area, the Catholic Center party performed poorly. Two days after the election, a member of the SA ran the swastika flag up the flagpole at the Wittenberge high school (*Gymnasium*) against the wishes of the principal.[16] Werner Krause, a retired history teacher in Gransee who was seven years old in 1933, recalls the windows in his school decorated with swastikas and the SA marching through the streets to celebrate the Nazi electoral victory.[17]

The Brandenburg provincial election followed quickly on the national election and produced a clear majority for the Nazis and their coalition partner, the DNVP. A few weeks later, the new session of the Reichstag was opened at the Garrison church in Potsdam (rather than at the Reichstag, which was still badly damaged from the fire). There, by the grave of Frederick the Great, the eighty-six-year-old Hindenburg handed power to the forty-four-year-old Hitler, the generational change not lost on most observers. The town of Wittenberge marked the occasion with a massive torch-lit parade.[18]

Through draconian laws, intimidation, and outright violence, the Nazis had eliminated the democratic remnants of the Weimar Republic in a matter of weeks, so much so that by the November 12 elections to the Reichstag there was only one party left—the National Socialist German Workers' Party. In Wittenberge, 93 percent of the electorate turned up for the mock election, 16,542 voting for the Nazi party and 1,256 abstaining.[19]

## REPRESSION AND TERROR

The more than 37,000 members of the SPD in Brandenburg region had good reason to fear the Nazi takeover. Almost immediately, the Gestapo terrorized SPD members into emigration, into underground activity, and ultimately into prison, including in the city of Wittenberge, where the Gestapo confiscated party property and arrested twenty-two people (most of them SPD members) in May 1933.[20] Wiethold Schubert from Wittenberge, for example, campaigned against the Nazis, was arrested in February 1933, and eventually murdered in a gas chamber at one of the Nazi euthanasia centers.[21] Once the SPD was officially declared illegal in June 1933, SA troops swept through Gransee arresting members of both the SPD and KPD (Communist Party of Germany) and throwing them in the basement of the brewery in Neuruppin. Although many were released a few days later, August Fischer, a member of the KPD, died as a result of the interrogations.[22] By mid-1933, nearly 5,000 people had been arrested in the province of Brandenburg.[23]

The first concentration camps in the region originated in the era of the "wild camps," a time when zealous SA and SS hastily transformed various local buildings into makeshift holding pens. By 1934 the former brewery in Oranienburg, just north of Berlin, had become a camp for more than 5,000 prisoners, primarily Communists and Socialists.[24] This early violence toward Communists was not, however, a radical departure from the previous era. Police in the Weimar Republic tended to sympathize with the Nazis and to come down hard on the Communists. The middle classes in Germany, too, genuinely feared the Communists and their revolutionary fervor.[25] In 1936 a much larger, much better organized camp was established in Oranienburg, which would go on to become one of the most notorious of the camps. Sachsenhausen opened its doors on June 12, 1936, with a capacity for 8,000 prisoners. A second camp in Brandenburg, and for many historians one of the most intriguing, given that it had both female inmates and female SS guards, accepted its first transport (860 German women and 7 Austrian women) in May 1939.[26] By the end of the war Ravensbrück camp, which had been built for 3,000 female prisoners, held 70,000.[27]

As was the case with all of the concentration camps, Ravensbrück and Sachsenhausen built up a sprawling network of subcamps that fed into Germany's wartime demands. Near Gransee, more than 1,000 prisoners from Sachsenhausen worked in Dynamit AG in late 1944 while another subcamp of Sachsenhausen was established in Wittenberge, with nearly 1,200 female prisoners to support the Arado aircraft factory.[28] Wittenberge was also the site of a subcamp of the concentration camp at Neuengamme that held almost 500 prisoners. The emaciated prisoners of Wittenberge died at a rate of roughly one every second day due to the harsh conditions. One of the prisoners recalled:

> On January 8th, 1943, I was transferred from the concentration camp Neuengamme to Wittenberge....We worked on a construction site, under the most difficult conditions. We had to work from 6 a.m. to 6 p.m. with a one-hour lunch break, when we got one liter of turnip soup. Each morning we got 240 grams [8.5 oz] of bread for the whole day.... The barracks were unheated. After the signal to go to bed, the *Kapos* (prisoner-supervisors) would get violent....They woke us up at night, forced us into the washrooms and hosed us down with cold water....In 1944, a new head of the camp came, and the camp regulations were loosened a bit. We also got a new block chief. I often worked with civilian engineers. They were nice and sympathetic toward us. Sometimes they even brought us bread.[29]

Students of German history are often astounded to learn that there were hardly any Jews living in Germany when Hitler came to power. In 1933 there were 499,682 Jews in Germany, not even 1 percent of the population, and the vast majority of these (80 percent) were German citizens. The province of Mark Brandenburg had only 7,616 Jews, or about 0.28 percent of the population, a low number that is not entirely surprising: most Jews lived in cities and Brandenburg was primarily rural.[30] The very first anti-Semitic measure undertaken by the Nazis was a boycott of Jewish businesses, launched by Goebbels on April 1, 1933, in front of a large crowd in Berlin, where he claimed that it was a necessary measure to counter Jewish demands abroad for a boycott of German goods.[31] The images of SA men standing in front of Jewish shops with signs reading "Germans, protect yourselves. Don't buy from Jews" have become some of the most powerful of the Holocaust. This was, after all, the first anti-Semitic step on the long path to Auschwitz. Considering that the boycott was generally a failure since most Germans still desired the products that Jews sold, the events in the small town of Gransee around the boycott are that much more noteworthy.[32] During the night of April 1, almost all the windows of the seven Jewish-owned shops in Gransee were smashed by unidentified culprits, resulting in damages of nearly 13,000 RM.[33] The Nazis were careful not to encourage boycotts of larger department stores such as Karstadt because many non-Jewish Germans worked there, but once the boycott was underway it took on a life of its own. Several SA men assumed threatening poses outside the Karstadt store on Berliner Strasse in Gransee, prompting the company to complain: "Today, on this Saturday after-noon, six or seven SA men stood beside the sign [in front of the store promot-ing the boycott] causing us financial losses since many of our customers would not dare to enter the store."[34] Goebbels ended the boycott shortly after it began because of popular disapproval, claiming, however, that he had done so because Jews had stopped their anti-German propaganda abroad.[35] Other anti-Semitic measures took place throughout 1933 at a grassroots level. All teachers at the Wittenberge high school, for example, were required to prove that their par-ents were of Aryan descent while their students were made to learn ethnogeny (the study of race).[36] For years, a banner hung along one of Wittenberge's main streets, Adolf-Hitler-Strasse, stating matter-of-factly "Wittenberge does not want any Jews."

These were but the first of a range of measures against Jews. In the course of the next few years, laws would require Jews to register their property, pre-vent them from marrying non-Jews, require them to use the "typical" Jewish names of Sara and Israel along with their given names, and wear a yellow star on their sleeves. More than 1,970 laws and regulations would be passed against Jews from 1933 to 1945 that would confiscate their property, exclude them from professions and public places and, ultimately, murder them.[37] Anti-Semitism was plainly visible in Gransee in 1936 when the editor of the local newspaper proudly proclaimed: "I, too, have in the past accepted classified announcements and advertising from Jews. I would like to announce today, however, to citizens and businesses alike, that in future, no adverts or classified announcements will be accepted from Jews."[38]

For five years, Hitler kept his hatred of Jews somewhat in check. Although he harassed them through his laws and denigrated them to second-class citizens, he stopped short of physical violence against them. That changed on November 9, 1938, the Night of Broken Glass (*Kristallnacht*), when Nazis went on a rampage against Jewish shops and places of worship, in the process carting thousands of Jews to what were by then well-established concentration camps at Dachau and Sachsenhausen, and killing many dozens of others.[39] Making matters worse, the Nazis made Jews pay for the damaged cityscape. As they did elsewhere in Germany, the SA and SS in Gransee eagerly participated in *Kristallnacht*, attacking the textile salesman Raphael Michaelis, his wife, and his mother, smashing his store windows, and plundering his store. His possessions were thrown out of his second-story apartment and his valuable books and papers burned on Schinkel Square in the heart of town. In the words of a local historian and eyewitness: "After everything had been reduced to ashes in front of the eyes of the curious Granseers and the citizens had stood by helplessly and watched—including me, at the time twelve years old—we simply went silently back home."[40] The Michaelis family eked out a living as best they could until they were transported from Gransee in the spring of 1943 in a sweep of Brandenburg Jews. The family perished at the Theresienstadt concentration camp.[41] Other groups, such as the Jehovah's Witnesses, who refused to give the Hitler salute and enter military service, were deported. Some ten thousand of them were sent to concentration camps.[42]

The war fundamentally changed the ethnic makeup of this out-of-the-way area of Germany. For the vast majority of people from Gransee and Wittenberge, the war years were the first time that they had direct contact with people from eastern Europe. As the war dragged on, thousands of Poles, Russians, and other east Europeans were shipped into Germany as slave labor. Granseers soon became accustomed to seeing Poles—identifiable by the *P* on their clothing—undertake the backbreaking agricultural work in the fields around their town. Local residents recall the line of foreign workers, some of them in wooden shoes, being marched by SS men with dogs from their barracks to various factories in town.[43] Similarly, more than 14,000 foreign workers came to the small town of Wittenberge during the war, roughly 4,000 of whom were from the east.[44] For the most part, the foreign workers were put up in specially constructed barracks in the region, which soon became infamous for disease and malnutrition.[45]

By far the most important factory in the regions under study was the Phrix-Werk, established in 1938/39 in Wittenberge to produce rayon from straw with the help of cutting-edge technology. Wittenberge was chosen for its location on the Elbe River, which provided the vast quantity of water required to process straw, and its access to the Hamburg-Berlin train line. Production of rayon began in 1939 and by 1940 the plant employed 1,530 people, 400 of whom were foreigners including Czechs, Slovaks, Russians, Ukrainians, and French prisoners of war. The local employment office informed the plant that the Russians were to be kept behind barbed wire to guard against sabotage.[46] Of the 300 Polish Jews who worked at the factory in 1940, 160 had been sent back to Poland and certain death two years later. Although the fate of the remaining Jews is unclear, the historian Hermann Kaienburg believes that they were deported to Poland in the first months of 1943 as the Reich strove to become "free of Jews."[47] Foreign workers at the plant were responsible for the most difficult and dangerous tasks, including loading and unloading the heavy hay bales and, later in the war, for cleaning up bomb damage and detonating unexploded bombs.[48]

On March 6 and April 18, 1944, the Phrix-Werk was badly damaged by Allied bombing. In an unusual occurrence, the plant directors awarded money and a note of thanks to the prisoners who had helped put out fires and tend to the injured.[49] By October, however, because of war damage and the rapidly approaching Red Army, the plant ceased operations and sent the remaining prisoners back to the concentration camp at Neuengamme. After the war the plant was taken over by Communist authorities and renamed The People's Own Cellulose and Rayon Works.

The first bombs fell on Wittenberge in the early morning hours of October 26, 1940, when five bombs were dropped, likely unintentionally, causing minimal damage and no loss of life.[50] A few weeks later Wittenbergers encountered the horrors of twentieth-century air warfare for the first time. Beginning at 8.30 p.m. on November 13 and continuing for the next six hours, Wittenberge was pounded by sixty incendiary bombs.[51] From that point on the population lived in constant dread of the Anglo-American raids. Werner Krause recalls: "Beginning in November 1940 nights were continuously interrupted by air attacks. During the day, everything looked so romantic, with the long evaporated trails. When night fell, residents sought out air-raid shelters, basements of various buildings that had been determined to be the most secure. After a number of sleepless nights in the shelters, my father said to me one day: 'What is this nonsense anyway? If a bomb falls on this building, it's going to end up in the basement and we'll all be dead anyway.' Somehow I didn't find that very comforting."[52]

Following the release in January 1943 of the "Regulation regarding the wartime assistance of German youth with the Luftwaffe," all school children born in the years 1926 or 1927 were required to serve in the flak (anti-aircraft) defenses of the Reich. Wittenberge teens reported for flak duty the following month.[53] The flak defenses of Wittenberge scored a major victory in March 1945 when they brought down a U.S. bomber that crashed near Perleberg, its massive carcass an object of intense interest for young boys in the region.[54] In March and April 1944, deaths from air attacks were becoming commonplace throughout the area. In the course of those two months, 47 people in Wittenberge lost their lives, 360 in Oranienburg, 35 in Rathenow, and 28 in Brandenburg.[55] By 1944, the major industries in Wittenberge were being hit hard by Allied bombing. Local Nazis trying to bolster the morale of the population held a rally on Horst Wessel

Square in Wittenberge with banners reading: "In spite of the terror, we will fight to the end."[56]

As horrific as they were, the attacks on Brandenburg were much fewer than those on the capital of Berlin; since Brandenburg was nearby, many Berliners left the city for the less dangerous surrounding countryside. The Gransee chronicle reported: "The evacuated brought with them from Berlin furniture and furnishings, valuables and clothes. Even those who have to remain in Berlin bring their valuables out here to save them from certain destruction. Within no time in Gransee there was no barn, no attic, and no restaurant that did not have someone living there."[57]

## THE ENDGAME

As the Russians slowly and ruthlessly pressed on to Berlin, German refugees from the east began flooding into the province of Brandenburg. The most famous incident related to Germans fleeing from the advancing Russians involved the ill-fated ship *Wilhelm Gustloff*, which, in January 1945, was torpedoed by a Russian submarine on orders of the slightly intoxicated captain. More than 8,000 refugees perished in the frigid waters of the Baltic, the second worst maritime disaster in history and one that took five times as many lives as the *Titanic* tragedy. Günter Grass's novel *Crab Walk* masterfully recounts how the *Gustloff* has become the cause célèbre of the Far Right, since historians in their unwillingness to address German suffering have neglected the topic. Gransee was flooded with refugees, many of them in need of serious medical attention, having made the long trek from East Prussia. The first floor of the local school was converted into a children's hospital, staffed primarily with doctor and nurse refugees from the children's clinic in Posen.[58]

In February 1945, emaciated refugees from East Prussia dragging fragile wooden carts piled high with all of their belongings poured into Perleberg, where they found refuge in the girls' school in Wilsnacker Street. Teachers halted instruction and tended to the refugees, spreading straw for them to sleep on and occasionally assisting in delivering babies. The parking lot outside the school, overflowing with refugees' wagons and horses, resembled scenes from the old Wild West.[59] One observer commented on the number of wounded who struggled into town from the medical facility in nearby Kyritz: "Amputees, toiling on one leg and feverish, drag themselves down Berliner Street toward the city, collapse, and resign themselves to lying in the street."[60]

On January 26, 1945, the Second Soviet tank division of the First Belorussian Front finally crossed the former German-Polish border and brought the land war to Brandenburg. Simultaneously, the province around Berlin was hit by British bombers. On February 22, 1945, over the course of only eleven minutes, seventy-two B-17 bombers dropped nearly 865,000 pounds of bombs on Wittenberge's rail junctions and train-repair yards, killing eleven people in the process.[61] Almost every night from then until the end of the war, air raid alarms sounded in Wittenberge to announce incoming bombers.[62] The last bombing run against Wittenberge took place on April 10, when more than a hundred bombers dropped phosphorous bombs on the city center, destroying much of the once handsome city and leaving in its wake smoldering bodies. The following day, in direct contradiction to Hitler's orders to defend against the Russians to the last man, several leading Wittenberge citizens declared Wittenberge an "open city," one that the Russians or Americans could enter freely. This state lasted a matter of hours before Himmler and Bormann declared that any city freely handed over to the enemy would have its decision-makers executed.[63] Wittenberge reversed its decision, but this did little to alter the course of events. Once within range, the Red Army general Victor Kalyuzhny delivered an ultimatum to the mayor of Wittenberge, which demanded that "the mayor of Wittenberge present himself at Gross Breese where he will receive the conditions for the handing over of the city to Soviet troops." Failure to comply was to lead to the bombing of Wittenberge.[64] On May 3 Soviet troops entering the surrendered city were greeted with white flags hanging from the houses.[65]

This part of Germany found itself squeezed between the advancing Russian and American armies, so much so that on any given day it could be bombed by both U.S. aircraft and Russian artillery. Knowing full well that Germany had inflicted nowhere near the suffering on the Americans as it had on the Russians, many Perlebergers hoped for liberation by the American side. The anti-tank ditches that had been dug through the center of town and out into the asparagus fields by teenagers and older men of Hitler's *Volksturm* went for naught as the "Cossacks," as local residents referred to Soviet soldiers, entered the city on May 2, 1945.

In contrast to his counterpart in Wittenberge, the dentist-mayor of Perleberg walked along Pritzwalker Street and handed the city over to the advancing Russians without hesitation. The only shots to be heard were those of SS soldiers running through town firing at balconies where the white flag had been hung out, yelling: "You call yourselves Germans? You're traitors! Pigs!" As had been typical of the SS during the war, its members preferred to fire on defenseless civilians rather than on the far more dangerous Red Army. The peaceful surrender did not prevent the Russians from looting, drinking, and sadly, raping. Ever since the Red Army crossed into German territory, Russian soldiers had engaged in acts of rape that were so much part of the advance on Berlin that Norman Naimark has called it a "systematic expression of power and revenge over the enemy."[66] Albert Hoppe, a teacher from Perleberg who meticulously recorded the happenings in his area in his diary, attributes the hundreds of suicides by young women in the region after war's end to the conduct of the Red Army.[67] Locals claim that in 1945 the lake in the center of Fürstenberg was crowded with the bodies of young women who had drowned themselves.

In Gransee, a group of teens took a white flag stitched together by several women in town and hung it from the church tower, helping to ensure that the city would be handed over to the Russians without a fight. Remembering that event, a local historian has written that "children were the heroes of Gransee."[68]

The flat province surrounding Berlin that lay between the Oder and Neisse rivers was one of the hardest hit of the war. It was here that the endgame of the Third Reich played out. In the final eight months of the war, the number of deaths by bombing in the region was twice as much as in the previous six years of war.[69] Most of the damage occurred in Potsdam, Küstrin, Frankfurt/Oder, Schwedt, and Forst, while Gransee and some cities south of Berlin remained largely intact. The Berlin-Hamburg Chaussee, a vital artery that had been the target of numerous strafings and which passed close to both Wittenberge and Perleberg, was littered with burning cars and rotting horses. The official number of war dead in Gransee was 189, although a local historian puts the number at slightly above 200.[70] Wittenberge reported 776 deaths at the front, 216 bombing deaths, and 256 dead among the slave laborers.[71]

On May 18 the people of Perleberg gathered on the main square of their city, underneath the hulking statue of Roland with his gaze affixed on the city hall before him, and listened to mundane announcements by the local Soviet commander. They participated unenthusiastically in three cheers to Comrade Stalin and then cleared the square for a prearranged party. And so, for a brief time on that spring evening, Perlebergers forgot about the destruction around them and their uncertain future at the hands of the Russians, and danced under the wide Mecklenburg sky.

# 2

# IN THE SERVICE
# OF THE FIRM
## The Full-Time Stasi Employees

WHILE EAST GERMANY EXISTED, many East Germans had difficulty forming an impression of the individuals who worked full time for the Stasi. Germans did not even have a particularly vivid term for Stasi workers when referring to them privately among friends, employing mostly the generic "those ones" (*die da*). In smaller communities like Perleberg and Gransee, many townspeople would have known who was a full-time Stasi worker (though knowing the identity of an informant would have been considerably more difficult) and would have assiduously avoided coming into contact with them. As a point of comparison, the Stasi did not have a reputation of benign or ineffectual exercise of power like that of Italy's state police, the Carabineri, which is still the butt of popular scorn. In East Germany, citizens genuinely feared the Stasi, although it would be an exaggeration to say that they were terrorized by it.[1] After 1989, opinions on Stasi personnel ranged from the flattering—the "intelligentsia" of the Socialist world—to the disparaging—"ignorant," "uncultured," and even "possessing a distinct odor—like a mix of oil, floor polish, and sweat."[2] Part of the reason that the Stasi personnel remain mysterious is their general unwillingness to be interviewed. Of the plethora of works on the East German Stasi, very few authors interviewed Stasi officers,[3] a situation not altogether surprising given the fact that Stasi officers found themselves after German unification facing a public that at a minimum considered their line of work distasteful, and at the other end of the spectrum brought up questions of illegal conduct and possible prison sentences.

Apart from interviews, personnel files offer one of the richest sources of information on Stasi employees. Each Stasi official had such a file, which contained considerable detail on every aspect of their career with the Stasi—bonuses, notable successes, family relations, disciplinary measures, background, health, and so on. Section 5 of the personnel file, which contains the results of the thorough background check on the candidate, demonstrates how wide the Stasi cast its net in vetting a candidate. The investigation encompassed the candidate and his wife, the candidate's children and their wives, the parents and in-laws, siblings of the candidate, siblings of the candidate's wife and the spouses of those siblings, and close friends of the candidate. Because of the enormous task that this presented, the Stasi increasingly looked to the children of their own workers for the next generation of officers since the majority of the screening would have already taken place. Personnel files are entirely accessible to researchers except where the personal lives of the officers and their relatives is concerned. Ironically, historians are permitted to view the personnel file of Stasi officers, but the officers themselves are not.

In my talks with Stasi officers, I was frequently asked what their file contained, what the Stasi "really" thought of them, and if the Stasi was aware of their occasional breaches of security. Historians are permitted to know all work-related aspects of the employee's time with the Stasi, but the Stasi Files Law, which regulates access to the documents, protects the officers from prying into their personal lives. One important exception is that the researcher is permitted to know the names of the Stasi officers, whereas those who were spied upon (*Betroffene*—literally "the affected ones") by the Stasi are to remain anonymous to researchers.

Thus, historians interested in locating former Stasi employees can obtain their names from the files located at the Stasi archive. The Stasi archive has proved, however, to be one of two sources for names of Stasi officers. A Web site (www.cryptome.org) dedicated to exposing various murky government activities on a global scale, from Mexico's "dirty war" to dubious actions of the U.S. Department of Homeland Security, published a list of all Stasi workers at the time of dissolution of the Stasi, a list that was rapidly downloaded and printed throughout the country—including by Stasi officers themselves. The greatest shortcoming of this otherwise reliable list is of it being a "snapshot" of the roster in December 1989, and thus does not contain the names of individuals who retired even a few days prior. One Stasi officer mentioned how delighted he was that he had retired a few days before the list was published and therefore does not appear on it. Armed with the names of the Stasi officers, the task of tracking them down then presents itself—a task made much easier by the online German telephone directory. As is the case in many countries, Germans have to pay *not* to have their phone numbers listed and so, out of lethargy or cost, they let their names stand.

In the end, District Perleberg officers proved easier to locate than those of District Gransee. Ten District Perleberg employees (out of fifty-three) agreed to be interviewed (a secretary, a chauffeur, and a custodian; all the others were operational officers). Out of the entire complement of fifty-three workers, eleven were building security (and were not contacted for interview), two were cleaning staff, and three secretaries. Some could not be contacted for other reasons—one of the officers had moved to a new life in Sweden since 1989, and one, a new recruit at the end of the 1980s, got on the wrong side of drugs and the mafia and was murdered in Hamburg. In total, I interviewed six (out of twenty-four) operational officers in District Perleberg. Efforts to track down the last leader of the district office, Werner Ryll, in Hamburg and Berlin, locations that local residents suggested, proved futile. Werner Ryll's predecessor, Herbert Tilse, still lives in the area, and I was able to contact him by telephone. I spoke with him long enough for him to explain in between labored breaths that he had just had four teeth removed and that his health was rapidly fading. He was willing to talk to me but felt he was physically unable. Unlike some of the others I contacted, Herr Tilse was unfailingly courteous.

District Gransee's office was a much smaller office than District Perleberg's, employing only thirty-six full-time workers in 1989. Of the seventeen officers in operational duty in the last year of the regime, two had fled West after 1989 and settled near the border of Switzerland, and one had died. Three of the remaining fourteen operational officers agreed to be interviewed. Unfortunately, the last two directors of the District Gransee office, Siegmund Tamme and Hans-Jürgen Töpfer, proved impossible to locate.

The organization of former Stasi officers known as the Insider-Komitee, whose self-styled objective is to restore "balance" to the current literature on the Stasi by writing "objective" history of the Ministry for State Security, assisted me in locating an important Stasi officer for interview. Although the Insider-Komitee was not able to provide me with any additional names of those in the districts who were willing to be interviewed, they did find a leader of a neighboring district office who was willing to talk. Since that district was very similar to District Perleberg, I deemed it appropriate to include his interview.

## DISTRICT GRANSEE

The small Stasi office in District Gransee, with its responsibility to protect sensitive military installations in the area, was not a desirable posting. Stasi officers in District Gransee, constantly reprimanded for their sub-par performance, were the butt of jokes for other districts in the region. In 1954, the district office had only seven officers in operational duty, one leader, and one deputy leader. It was the second smallest of the fifteen districts in Region Potsdam and was dwarfed by districts like Brandenburg, which had twenty-five full-time employees. Even in the early 1950s when the Stasi was in its infancy, Gransee was about half the size of an average district office.[4] Following the restructuring of the East German states (*Länder*) into regions (*Bezirke*) in 1952, the Stasi itself was organized into 217 districts. This process of restructuring took some time, but by late 1953 the territorial organizational structure of the Stasi was in place.[5]

The overall structure of the Stasi was mirrored at the district level. Whereas the headquarters had main departments for key areas like counterespionage (Main Directorate (*Hauptabteilung–HA*) (HA II), the economy (HA XVIII), opposition (HA XX), and foreign intelligence (HVA), the next level down, the regions, had corresponding departments.[6] The district offices did not have departments as such, but assigned individuals to work along the departmental lines. Both districts Gransee and Perleberg had four sections, each employing roughly five to seven officers: (1) evaluation, the nerve center of the office, which analyzed the myriad reports from Stasi officers for a suitable course of action, (2) counterespionage, (3) opposition, and (4) the economy, these last three corresponding to departments II, XX, and XVIII. Although not a distinct section, the people around the district leader, including his secretary, his deputy, the radio and wireless operator, chauffeur, and head of building security, made up a sizable component of the overall complement.[7] In sum, the district offices can be safely considered representative of the broader Stasi, albeit in their territorially confined jurisdiction.

Although the files are far from complete, it has been possible for the most part to trace the leadership of the Stasi office in Gransee. The thirty-two-year-old Heinz Brosk started his career with the Stasi as leader of District Gransee, having spent time with the embryonic political police division (K-5) that was housed within the People's Police (*Volkspolizei*).[8] It was not at all unusual in those days for such a young man to take on a leadership position in the apparatus, given the fact that the entire Stasi apparatus (including its 217 district offices) had to be staffed very quickly by individuals who had no association with the repression instruments of the Nazi era.[9] Unlike the Nazis, who reached into the Weimar-era police for recruits to the repression apparatus, the Stasi was willing to sacrifice know-how for a clean break with the past.[10] Although the Communist "old guard" from the street battles of the Weimar era occupied the most senior leadership positions in the Stasi, youth were required in order to staff the apparatus. In 1952, about half of all Stasi employees were under the age of thirty.[11] Compared to what it would become, the Stasi was small in the early years, but it is worth remembering that by 1952, with 8,800 employees, it had already outgrown the prewar size of the Gestapo (7,700 in 1937).[12]

It is not clear who led the district between the time Heinz Brosk left in 1957 (to a lower position as an operational officer in District Rathenow) and the arrival of Dieter Melkers in 1966, but a document from 1963 lists a certain Verch as leader of the district in that year.[13] Melkers had been with the Stasi fifteen years by the time he was appointed district leader, and had arrived from District Oranienburg where he had been deputy leader. After Melkers moved on to the regional office in Potsdam as head of the assessment and evaluation group in 1971, Siegmund Tamme assumed the leadership of the Gransee Stasi office. The thirty-six-year-old Tamme had worked in counterespionage in the regional office in Potsdam, and this made him ideally suited for District Gransee and its many military sites. Clearly, one did not have to be a graduate of the euphemistically named Stasi University, the Potsdam College of Law, in order to be a district leader, as Tamme did not graduate from the JHS until after he became head of the district office. Tamme left the office in disgrace in 1985, severely reprimanded by his superiors for overseeing the weakest district office in Potsdam region.

Hans-Jürgen Töpfer, an electrician by training, took over from Tamme in 1985 and would go on to oversee the demise of the Stasi in Gransee four years later. Töpfer's father had served in the Wehrmacht and died on April 25, 1945, less than two weeks before the end of the war, when his son was one year old. Almost from the outset, Töpfer had shown himself to be a reliable Communist, heading up the Free German Youth group at his high school for two years. During the vetting of his relatives prior to his recruitment, the Stasi determined that Töpfer's fiancée had visited her grandparents in Munich twelve years previously, when she was nine. The fiancée agreed to end all postal contact with her grandparents in order to remove this obstacle to her future husband's work for the Stasi.[14]

Since Töpfer's recruitment by the Stasi in 1967, he had worked exclusively in the Rathenow district office in Region Potsdam, where he held progressively responsible positions: case officer (1969), working group leader (1972), operational group leader (1974), deputy district leader (1983), and finally leader of District Gransee in 1985. By 1976 he was already being groomed for a senior leadership position in the district, his superiors singing his praises. In an appraisal of his work, the leader of District Rathenow said that Töpfer had successfully concluded one Operational Case (*Operativer Vorgang*, OV) the highest level of operation the Stasi conducted, usually involving a number of secret informants and a complex array of other monitoring such as mail and telephone, and had already opened another OV. Furthermore, he had improved the reputation of the Stasi in the area: "Töpfer, in his role as operational group leader, has made a significant contribution to raising the profile of the MfS [Ministry for State Security] in the eyes of cadres in leading positions in industry and the party secretaries in the major factories. Due to his knowledge and comportment they acknowledge him as someone worth talking to and follow his advice."[15] A constant thorn in Töpfer's side had been the fact that his parents visited relatives in West Germany, an activity that was hurting his career. In 1980, Töpfer asked the Stasi to prevent further trips West by his parents, and it cannot be a coincidence that Töpfer was finally made district leader a few months after his wife's grandmother—a constant traveler to the West—died.[16]

In a sampling of twenty-three personnel files from District Gransee from the 1980s (in any given year there were about thirty-five people employed in the office), the varied backgrounds, human qualities, weaknesses, and workplace rivalries emerge, often in vivid color. The Stasi knew intimate details about its workers—what they were like as high school students, whether they engaged in marital infidelity, whether the individual was in financial difficulty, and how often they consumed alcohol. Often, the reports on the full-time employees sound like personal classifieds: "He likes to play soccer, paint landscapes, read history books, and go to the movies,"[17] "He spends his free time fixing up his house, and could do with losing a little weight,"[18] "She likes to dance," "She originally wanted to be a hairdresser, but her doctors advised against it because of a car accident that broke her leg,"[19] "He likes to hunt."[20]

The old Jesuit missive "Give me the boy until seven, and I will show you the man" rings true for how the Stasi approached its potential recruits. Family background, upbringing, and conduct in elementary school all factored into the decision to approach a potential recruit for Stasi duty. A report on Volker Ehmig, an officer who joined the Stasi in 1987 as a second lieutenant, stated approvingly: "He was brought up in his parents' house in a positive way, believing in our state."[21] In checking the background of a future secretary with the District Gransee office, the Stasi approached her eighth-grade teacher. Because of a car injury, the student never finished the grade, but the teacher judged that she would have been able to finish with a mark of "good."[22] Ideally, the Stasi desired a straight Communist trajectory from youth to adulthood—a working-class family with parents supportive of the regime, involvement and preferably leadership position in youth groups like the Free German Youth or the Society for Sport and Technology, the learning of a trade, and time spent as a worker. The oddity in this life-path is the number of individuals who were hired by the Stasi even though they were not members of the Communist, or Socialist Unity, Party (SED), *Sozialistische Einheitspartei Deutschlands*). In 17 percent of the files for District Gransee (and this number could be higher because the file did not always specify), the officer joined the Stasi without having been a member of the SED. Although the norm was to become an SED candidate fairly quickly, in one case the officer worked for the Stasi for three years before joining the SED.[23]

The Stasi looked favorably upon marriage, given the stability that this would provide to its officers in what was, ultimately, a very stressful line of work. A family man with a wife supportive of his work was the ideal Stasi officer. Most of the officers who joined the Stasi were already married upon recruitment, a reflection in part of the Stasi's concern about homosexuality. In its consideration of the recruitment of Carsten Hoeltke in May 1989, one of the very last recruitments in the District, the leader of the branch expressed thinly veiled concern that Hoeltke did not currently have a girlfriend: "His relations with the female sex are normal. The candidate had over a long period of time a loose relationship with a girlfriend."[24] In another case, the Stasi was very concerned about a bachelor recruit who was a pig breeder and seemed to be spending too much time on the farm.[25]

Of the thirty-six full-time employees at the District Gransee office in 1989, only three were women and none of these were in operational areas, occupying instead the positions of secretaries and cleaning staff. The district-level office was an even more male-dominated world than the rest of the Stasi, where about 15.7 percent of all Stasi employees throughout the 1980s were women, owing in large part to the fact that the district-level offices did not monitor mail, the staff for which was generally two-thirds female.[26] In the vast majority of cases (79 percent), the female Stasi worker was married to a male Stasi officer.[27]

In keeping with the larger trend in the Stasi, very few of the workers in District Gransee had graduated from high school. By 1988 only 20.9 percent of all full-time Stasi employees had the *Abitur*, university entrance qualification as distinct from the trade qualification, 61.6 percent had obtained grade 10, and 15.7 percent had passed grade 8. As a point of comparison, the proportion of the officer class in the National People's Army who had *Abitur* was at 72 percent during the same period.[28] Of the twenty-three workers examined here, only one had *Abitur* and two others had completed grade 12. The most common educational path to the Stasi in District Gransee was to complete grade 10 (48 percent of officers surveyed) and then to apprentice a trade. Qualifications to be a member of the building security or support staff, who were also full-time workers that made up the total complement, were often as low as grade 8 with some practical training.

Although most Stasi employees had had a career in a trade before joining the ranks of the secret police, the range of District Gransee employees' previous occupations ran the gamut—electrician, machinist, telegraphist, teacher, tractor repair, lathe operator, carpenter, metal worker, and, curiously, zoo keeper. Only three came from a white-collar job with the local city council to join the Stasi. East Germany's motto as the "workers' and peasants' state" captured the essence of the Stasi, a secret police of and for the working class, one that looked on previous intellectual achievements with disdain. What was important was whether a candidate for the Stasi had experienced a worker's life firsthand. To be sure, however, the Stasi in the later years tended to draw from the more highly trained workers, those with an expert qualification, rather than less-educated manual laborers as had been the case in the 1950s.[29] This is not to say that the Stasi disparaged all forms of education, but specifically only those that fell beyond its capacity to control.

The Stasi went to great lengths to use not only its own staff and training manuals to bring a new employee along but its own academies like the Stasi college in Gransee that offered courses in Marxism-Leninism.[30] (Apart from its main college in Potsdam and the smaller one in Gransee geared to new recruits, the Stasi maintained educational centers in Eberswalde, Teterow, Belzig (foreign intelligence center), Ahrensfelde, and a language school in Dammsmühle).[31] Several years later, if the employee were moving up through the ranks at an appropriate pace, they would be sent to the main training center for Stasi officers, the Potsdam College of Law (JHS), for four years. Here a typical slate of courses would include Marxism-Leninism, Political Economy, Scientific Communism, Problems of Imperialism, History of the German workers' movement, Psychology, Legal Theory, International Relations, Criminal Law, Criminality, the History of the Imperialist Secret Services, Imperialist Media, Border Controls, special training in operational methods, and Russian Language.[32] The terminal degree from the JHS was the *Diplomjurist*, or academically trained legal theorist, a degree that was also offered by distance education for officers who could not be resident in Potsdam for four years.

Stasi recruits were always sought out. They did not volunteer for service with the Ministry for State Security, and if an individual did approach the Stasi, he was likely to be rejected on suspicion of being a mole. There was a certain elitism to the Stasi in this regard, a snobbishness in particular toward the other armed organizations like the police and the army who accepted almost anybody. Secret police officers styled themselves as Chekists (members of the Russian secret police) with a historic mission to protect the advances of the Communist movement, not unlike the way the protectors of the Grail might have seen themselves. Given that Stasi recruits were sought out, the first and most obvious question for the organization was to determine whether an individual was at all inclined to, or suitable for, Stasi work.

The most common recruiting ground for the Stasi was the Feliks Dzerzhinski Guard regiment, by 1989 an 11,526-strong regiment that was primarily responsible for guarding Stasi installations in Berlin. In 1988 nearly 40 percent of Stasi personnel were recruited from the guard regiment, 21 percent from the National People's Army, and about 3 percent from the regular police.[33] District Gransee bucks a trend among Stasi recruits with only six full-time workers selected from the most obvious pool of potential candidates—the offspring of current officers—whereas in 1989 16 percent of all full-time employees had a parent with the Stasi.[34] Between 1968 and 1982, a full 47 percent of Stasi personnel had a relative in the secret police.[35] Especially beginning in the 1970s, the Stasi increasingly targeted the children of Stasi officers as a source for the next generation of secret police, but the guard regiment still made up the primary pool of applicants. When army recruits went to their sign-up locale, the recruit would be made aware of the possibility of carrying out their compulsory military service with the guard regiment instead of the regular army. Agreement by the candidate would be an indication of a favorable predisposition to the Stasi, given the nature of the guard regiment's duties. Candidates were not simply transferred to the Stasi at the end of their time in the guard regiment, however, owing to the Stasi's desire that their cadres experience life as a worker before entering into service for their defense. There was almost always a time lag of a few years between the end of guard duty and the formal entry into the Stasi. Once the Stasi had approved of a new recruit, and he had agreed, the Stasi simply informed the present employer of the fact that his employee would be leaving shortly, demonstrating some of the power that the Stasi wielded in its societal interactions. In one instance, a teacher was removed in order to join the Stasi shortly before the beginning of a new term: "Although the Candidate is in the education sector, it is still possible to remove him on short notice before the beginning of the school year."[36] Although the new recruit would sometimes be placed in an area of responsibility that would be familiar to them from their working career—a former teacher worked on the education line, a former member of an agricultural production collective was placed in the appropriate department, (economy)—a close match did not always occur.[37] Somewhat surprisingly, a close family relative living in the West was not a hindrance to becoming a Stasi officer—provided that there was no telephone or postal contact.

In District Gransee, 39 percent of employees in the personnel files examined had been in the guard regiment before joining the Stasi, 17 percent had served in the National People's Army border troops (one of whom distinguished himself by arresting three East Germans trying to cross the border to West Germany), 0.9 percent had been with the People's Police (*Volkspolizei*), and 26 percent had been informants prior to joining the Stasi as full-time officers. (Some of these categories overlapped; one could have been at the border and also an informant.) According to a former Stasi captain in District Gransee, the 1980s increasingly saw the Stasi recruit informants with an eye to eventually hiring them into full-time positions, a marked departure from previous practice where informants rarely made the transition from informant to full-time officer.[38] Fourteen out of the twenty-three Stasi personnel surveyed had their first posting with District Gransee and remained there their entire career. All others were either transferred from other districts, or had served briefly at the regional level in guard duty or in postal control. In sum, there was very little movement at the district level, with most officers spending their entire career in the small, thirty-odd-strong office, or, occasionally, moving from one district office to another.

As a rule, district level Stasi officers did not have experience at any other levels of the Stasi—whether at the regional level or at the sprawling headquarters in Berlin. Their entire experience of the Stasi was limited to the smallest territorial unit of the organization, the district. In District Gransee, there was one notable exception—an officer joined the organization, moved to Egypt where he was with the foreign espionage branch of the Stasi for four years, and then returned to District Gransee, despite his best efforts not to be transferred back to the small outpost.[39]

Movement through the ranks was generally contingent on operational activity, how well the officer was running informants, how often they met (seemingly regardless of the quality of those meetings), and what role the officer had played in operations to monitor citizens. In annual evaluations, the frequency of officer contact with informants played a major role in whether the officer received a positive review. Lothar Schrader, at the time with District Neuruppin, was praised for how often he met his informants: "In spite of his large network of informants, he consistently maintains a high average number of meetings per informant. Here he is the best in the district."[40] In general, officers could move quickly from their starting rank of *Feldwebel* (sergeant), through *Oberfeldwebel* (sergeant major), to *Unterleutnant* (second lieutenant ), often in the space of three years, by which time they would be making more than twice their already-generous starting salary. The next levels, *Leutnant* (lieutenant), *Oberleutnant* (first lieutenant), *Hauptmann* (captain), and major, were somewhat more difficult to obtain and could take much longer—as much as ten years for captain. The highest position at the district level followed major—that of lieutenant colonel

(*Oberstleutnant*). The military structure of the Stasi carried over to cleaning and clerical staff who also had military ranks, and whose annual evaluations were laced with Cold War overtones, such as that their orderly scrubbing of the floors helped sustain the Stasi's fight for world peace. Every member of the district office, including support staff and cleaning staff, were issued camouflage fatigues in case of an emergency situation.[41]

It would be an exaggeration to say that there were serious discipline problems among the District Gransee staff, but the personnel files do reveal a number of reprimands, ranging from one officer who drove a visiting Iraqi student to the train station and was informed that he had endangered national security,[42] to another who was sent to jail for ten days for losing his handgun while drunk and later losing his briefcase with keys to the internal filing cabinets.[43] Although the latter are quite serious breaches of security, they did not hinder his scheduled promotion to captain. It was also not unheard of for problem officers to be transferred, as was the case of Lothar Strempel, who consistently bickered with his colleagues. The following year he was demoted and transferred to Gransee, and earned a sharp rebuke from his superior: "Given his character flaws, Comrade Major Strempel is no longer able to undertake the duties of a deputy district leader."[44] In general, only under rare circumstances were Stasi personnel released for reasons other than age or health-related issues once they had passed their probationary month, a period which saw a number of Stasi personnel released because of "unsatisfactory standing." In 1989, more than 1,745 Stasi personnel were released, about 90 percent of these due to retirement, health, or unsatisfactory performance during the initial probationary month.[45]

The age breakdown of the District Gransee office matches almost exactly the broader trends in the Stasi, with an average age of 35.8 in 1989 compared to 35.7 for the Stasi overall.[46] The Stasi had aged over the years from its average age of twenty-eight in 1950. Still, the District Gransee office was a remarkably young organization, with only two officers in their fifties, and three under the age of twenty-two. Hans-Jürgen Töpfer, the leader of the District, was only forty-five years old when the regime collapsed—certainly young enough for another career.

## DISTRICT PERLEBERG

From its inception, the District Perleberg Stasi office was larger than the District Gransee office and would go on to sizably outdistance its sister office. From a modest complement of twelve full-time employees in 1953, the office tripled in size by 1972 and then grew slowly until it topped out at fifty-three employees at the time of the regime's collapse.

One of the most explosive eras of growth of the Stasi took place in the 1960s,[47] as it began to take on a range of duties atypical of a secret police and transformed into a bureaucracy of repression.[48] From 1957 to 1971 the Stasi ballooned from

17,400 full-time employees to 45,500 and then to a staggering 81,500 in 1983, with the most rapid expansion taking place between 1968 and 1982 during which time the Stasi doubled in size.[49] Unfortunately, statistics on District Perleberg for the 1960s are not available. Nevertheless, it is striking that the office tripled in size in the twenty years between 1953 and 1972 just as the overall Stasi did. In the following decade, however, District Perleberg ran counter to the increase in the overall Stasi complement.

This state of affairs had come about because of a relaxation of tensions between the two Germanies following the signing of the 1973 Basic Treaty that regularized German-German relations and increased human traffic between the Cold War adversaries. Ironically, the Stasi increased in size most rapidly during the period of détente and increased international recognition of the GDR.[50] District Perleberg's complement throughout the 1970s remained consistent, however, even decreasing slightly. The small dip in the number of employees between 1983 and 1985 corresponds to larger developments as the budgetary crunch emanating from the oil crisis of the early 1970s finally caught up with the Stasi. The days of ever-increasing Stasi personnel, regardless of costs, came to an end in 1983—if only temporarily—at a time when Stasi duties were increasing due to a burgeoning opposition movement and an exponential increase in the number of East Germans applying to emigrate. As a result, the Stasi came to integrate quasi-employees into their system of surveillance, including senior informants who were in charge of other informants. The division of labor paid substantial dividends for a typical Stasi officer who, in running two or three senior informants, ultimately oversaw fifteen to twenty informants without the taxing frequency of meetings. By 1989, District Perleberg, with its fifty-three employees, was the second largest Stasi office in the Region of Schwerin, second only to District Hagenow, which had one more full-time employee, and much larger than District Bützow. which had only twenty-three full-time employees.[51]

In 1985, the universally despised Werner Ryll took over for the retiring Tilse and led the office until dissolution in 1989.[52] Stasi officers resented the heavy-handed Werner Ryll, his high, billowy, thick hair reminiscent of Slobodan Milosevic, and his lack of compassion, a situation that did not improve with his excessive drinking. His chauffeur remembered that "anytime there was a function where alcohol was served, he was there."[53] Former employees did not mince words in their descriptions of him, denouncing him as a "pig,"[54] "a total shit," and "something less than a human being."[55] Frequently he would not say "Guten Tag" to his colleagues, something that was particularly grating in Germany where politeness and form of address are considered hallmarks of civilized society. Ryll cared little for the personal lives of his employees. Frau Paupst, one of the cleaning staff, asked to be relieved of her obligation to help cook at the Leipzig fair because her daughter was about to give birth. Ryll responded curtly: "What does your daughter's baby have to do with us?" and insisted that she cook at the fair.[56] Many Stasi officers longed for the days of Herbert Tilse, the former leader, who was firm but fair, even attending the wedding of his secretary and putting his chauffeur and car at her disposal—an act of generosity one can scarcely imagine of Werner Ryll.[57] On a lesser scale, Stasi personnel were also put off by the fact that Ryll wore the same suit to work every day. In 1988, several employees launched an official complaint about the manner in which he demeaned his colleagues, a complaint that Ryll brushed off by saying that the district needed more discipline.

Ryll's personality raises a larger question of the extent to which an individual was able to influence the nature of the secret police at a local level. There is no doubt that the last years of the District Perleberg office were the worst in terms of surveillance—an overburdened officer corps, low morale, increasing pressure to find informants, more meetings with them to launch operations, and the constant berating to be more aware of what was going on in the district. In District Perleberg, an unfortunate set of circumstances came together to intensify Stasi activities in the area—namely, a relatively large office with the necessary infrastructure for societal monitoring already well established, and a zealous, angry leader who was a dedicated Chekist willing to exploit to the full the apparatus at his disposal.

Werner Ryll came from a working-class family and dedicated himself to the regime and to Communism at an early age, voluntarily joining the German-Soviet Friendship Society and later the SED.[58] In the background checks on him, there is no indication that Ryll would later prove to be a problematic employee. One informant, who was assigned the task of monitoring Ryll, summed up his personality: "To end off, I'd like to say that Comrade Ryll is a young man with potential, one who believes strongly in our party and in our socialist system."[59] In this instance, the Stasi misjudged his home situation, claiming that his family life was harmonious—shortly before he divorced. In 1968 when Ryll was twenty-eight he joined the Stasi as an "Officer on Special Assignment." Seven years later he moved on to the Schwerin regional office where he worked in Department XVIII responsible for agriculture, which suited his trade training. After a two-year stint at the Potsdam College of Law, he became deputy leader of Department XVIII where he served for two years before becoming director of District Perleberg in 1985. Ten days later he was promoted to lieutenant colonel, the highest district-level position.

Similar to District Gransee, the Perleberg Stasi, in its search for the next generation of officers, closely inspected the upbringing of the candidates and their home environments, noting with approval when the candidate had been brought up in a working-class family. Also like District Gransee, the majority of officers had practiced a trade like machinist or lathe worker for some time before joining the Stasi. There are, however, some important differences between the two districts. First of all, the general educational level in District Perleberg was higher, with 18 percent of the twenty-two files sampled having completed *Abitur* (compared to 0.4 percent in Gransee). Second, the full-time employees of District Perleberg tended to have more relatives in the Stasi than those of Gransee. Whereas few Gransee officers had relatives in the Stasi, and then usually only one, the Perleberg Stasi was a real family affair. Sixty-one percent of employees surveyed had relatives in the Stasi, and of those 26 percent had more than one relative in the organization. One officer had a son with the Stasi in Schwerin, another son with the Stasi in a neighboring district office, a niece and her husband who worked for the Stasi in the Berlin HQ, and his mother and his father-in-law also worked for the Stasi.[60] A female secretary had three brothers with the Stasi in the Berlin headquarters, a sister with the Stasi's postal surveillance branch in Berlin, and her father worked for the secret police in the regional office in Schwerin.[61] Although it was not uncommon for husbands and wives to work in the same Stasi office, there are no cases in the files examined here where a son or daughter worked in the same unit as the parent. Third, in roughly 10 percent of the cases examined here, the Stasi was alerted to a potential recruit by an informant, an approach that did not occur in District Gransee. As was the case with Gransee, the Feliks Dzerzhinski guard regiment provided the largest single pool of Stasi recruits, but it is noteworthy that three of the twenty-three full-time employees had been informants prior to joining the Stasi.

In other respects, too, Districts Gransee and Perleberg were similar. It was the rare exception when a full-time employee was transferred from one district to another, or to other branches of the Stasi. For the most part, the district level Stasi offices knew very little turn-over.

The first few days on the job for a new Stasi officer were in many ways similar to typical American office jobs, namely reading and familiarizing oneself with general office procedures. Following a meeting with the leader of the district and the party secretary, the recruit would be introduced to his colleagues and then set to work on reading the mundane directives related to his position—vacation policies, disciplinary issues, and so on. The officer would then move on to read up on overarching principles of the Stasi ("On the importance of maintaining secrecy in the ministry for state security") and on specific operations that were instructive. Once these were completed, the recruit could attend the school in Gransee for further training in Marxism-Leninism.[62]

Women made up sizably more of the Stasi corps in District Perleberg (17 percent) than in District Gransee but still worked almost exclusively in a supporting role. The notable exception was Anne Lowe (later Anne Klenk), a secretary who started with the District Perleberg unit in 1960 when she was nineteen years old. By 1961 she had been elected to the party organization in the District Office and a few years later won the National People's Army service medal in bronze. Four years following her attendance of the Stasi school for Marxism-Leninism in 1971, Frau Klenk did something that was quite remarkable for a female Stasi employee—she left the secretarial ranks and began to work as an operational officer, eventually rising to the relatively high position of lieutenant. Although she did not engage in serious undercover work like some of her colleagues, her position in the evaluation branch of the district office was nonetheless an important one. She vetted all individuals in the district who had applied to visit West Germany, or whose work required them to travel there (based on countless informants' reports and on reports from official sources like the police and city council).

Her colleagues remember her scurrying along the hallways groaning under large stacks of files. She met regularly with the district leader to discuss individual cases, and more often than not her recommendation to grant or decline travel permission was accepted by the leader. Her diligence at work was rewarded in 1987 with the National People's Army service medal in gold.[63] Today, Frau Klenk lives with her husband, a former Stasi officer in the district, in a comfortable apartment in Wittenberge. She remembers fondly the good qualities that she took away from her time with the Stasi: discipline, order, and hard work.[64] As a whole, however, the Stasi did not seek to promote women into higher positions in the organization, with barely a handful in operational duty in the entire secret police. Antje Müller, the leader's secretary, worked at District Perleberg from 1973 to 1989, never rising above the position of secretary, although she had repeatedly requested more challenging duties, including learning foreign languages.[65]

In the late 1970s, the Stasi found itself dealing with a human resources issue that would soon become pressing—grooming the next generation of leadership candidates. Many of those who joined the Stasi in its early revolutionary days, and who now held leader, deputy leader, and section leader positions, would soon be lost to retirement and their positions filled from the massive influx of younger workers that had begun in earnest in the late 1960s. This fact was brought home in 1982 when Bruno Beater, a deputy director in the central Stasi office in Berlin, died, leaving only Erich Mielke left as the last of the founding fathers.[66] In order to ease the transition, the Stasi sought out candidates to be brought along for higher positions. Rudolf Schulze, who ended his career as a section head and major in 1989, was targeted for a leadership position in 1978, when the leader of District Perleberg outlined the rationale behind grooming the next generation: "In order to deal with the political-operational duties in District Perleberg in the next few years, we need to rejuvenate and improve the qualifications in those mid-level positions. Accordingly, we have to seek out and empower suitable Comrades for these duties."[67] Thus, Schulze was given the opportunity to work closely with the deputy section head.

The Department of Personnel and Training played an important role throughout the career of a full-time Stasi employee. Its power was visible in a number of ways, for example, its ability to secure housing for new employees in a country that had a chronic housing shortage, its role in finding work for spouses in the district, and how it arranged with employers so that the recruit could indeed join the Stasi. Moreover, the department closely monitored the private lives of its officers, mindful of wayward behavior or, equally troubling, marital difficulties. This was, after all, small-town East Germany where most citizens would know who was a member of the secret police, and the Stasi was well aware of the negative repercussions that "immoral" conduct would have on an organization that was already loathed. In one case, Werner Ryll, the leader of the district, berated one of his officers for having an affair and wanting to end his marriage. Amid threats that the result would be his dismissal from the Stasi and the loss of his apartment, Ryll also reduced the officer to tears by saying that he not only betrayed his wife but also his fellow members of the collective. In this case, the officer broke off the affair.

In many cases, however, the Stasi could not save the marriage as evidenced by the fact that the divorce rate among Stasi personnel was on a par with the rest of society.[68] Leading a "clean" life was considered part of being a professional Chekist, as the organization made clear in an order from 1964, which reminded Stasi employees of one of SED General Secretary Walter Ulbricht's commandments: "Thou shalt live a clean and decent life and respect your family."[69] Given that the previous year, the primary reason that Stasi personnel were dismissed was "immoral conduct with the opposite sex," the Stasi may well have been concerned about wayward behavior.[70]

District Perleberg Stasi employees were, with an average age of thirty-nine in 1989, slightly older than those of District Gransee. In District Perleberg the average age of operational officers was forty-two, matching a larger overall trend in the Stasi. The abrasive leader of the district was relatively young at forty-nine.

## THE INTERVIEWS

For all of the sound scholarly treatment of the Stasi, one disappointment in the accounts has been the absence of a human portrait of a Stasi employee.[71] Readers often come away without a clear mental image of who, exactly, worked for the Stasi, their names, dreams, weaknesses, hobbies, passions, and vices lost amid a sea of statistics. Apart from offering a flesh-and-blood portrait of Stasi personnel, including the important issue of motive, the following interviews also shed light on the vexing question of totalitarianism in the GDR. Historians continue to debate vigorously whether the regime aimed to control all aspects of life in East Germany, or whether there were indeed private "niches" to which one could retreat with more or less regime acquiescence; yet the most gaping hole in this discussion is what those involved in the repression apparatus thought about the nature of their work.

In the following pages, many of the individuals responsible for repression in the East German hinterland reflect on the issue of "totalitarian" control, a term that, because it derives from the academic world of political science, was never really in common parlance in the offices of the secret police. Rather, Stasi officials discuss the degree to which societal surveillance was *flächendeckend* or "blanket," but this term must be considered synonymous with totalitarianism.

Moreover, in the course of the interviews, the Stasi personnel provided key insights into the structures of the Stasi and crucial bureaucratic practices like running informants that, regardless of the case officer, lent totalitarian qualities to the work by virtue of the institutional culture that had developed in the Stasi.

One of the greatest challenges for any historian is to determine the veracity of the source on which their narrative is based, a challenge magnified when the source is a secret police officer who worked behind the scenes in a now defunct dictatorship. Even in Herodotus's *The Histories*, one of the earliest attempts at scientific history, written nearly twenty-four centuries ago, the author is aware that much of what he is being told could be fabricated. He distances himself from the source by using phrases such as "I say only that which the Libyans themselves recount" or "Anyone who finds such things credible can make of these Egyptian stories what he wishes. My job...is simply to record whatever I am told by each of my sources." Herodotus's confession of imperfect knowledge and his lack of accountability for his sources is a luxury of a bygone era. In one of the clearest recent examples of the explosive nature of handling historical testimony, Daniel Goldhagen opted to ignore all self-exculpatory testimony of Holocaust perpetrators in 1960s trials in West Germany. On the other hand, Christopher Browning believed that such evidence, when weighed against the rest of the testimony, could be considered truthful.[72] Some of what the Stasi personnel relate below is not worthy of belief and brings into question their entire testimony. Others, however, alternately divulged information that painted them in a poor light or expressed profound remorse; their testimony is far more believable.

I have respected the interviewees' request for anonymity. All names are pseudonyms.

## DISTRICT GRANSEE

### Florian Tenbrock—The Intellectual[73]

Florian Tenbrock lives in the quiet hamlet of Häsen about 50 miles (80 km) northwest of Berlin and a few minutes down the road from Gransee. The road heading toward Häsen is scenic, although in the late summer the sunflowers were just past bloom and looked like they had suddenly died of fright as they stood stiffly in the autumn breeze. As I approached the house for our first interview in 2003 on a hardpack dirt road, Tenbrock was standing outside chatting with a neighbor. He indicated where I should park my rented Alpha Romeo. (I have had the bad luck of getting upgraded from my economy-size car on almost every occasion that I have interviewed Stasi personnel. Arriving in an Alpha Romeo does little to dispel the image of an overly affluent West.)

Herr Tenbrock is a reasonable man. He is worldly, having spent five years with the East German embassy in Egypt, clearly concerned about his children (he wrote his memoirs to help explain to them why he worked for the Stasi), and intelligent. He was the only officer in District Gransee who possessed *Abitur*, the high school certificate. Although the interview lasted several hours, he broke into a smile on only two or three occasions. His earnest demeanor reflected his cold professionalism in the workplace. As he sat in a firm armchair in a pose like Lincoln in his monument, he answered questions calmly, often pausing for long periods before speaking. When referring to an incident in June 1987 when two teenage brothers were shot dead while running away from a Soviet military base, Tenbrock justified this atrocious act by saying that the teenagers were not exactly "pure as the driven snow." The living room where the interview took place was prim and proper, furnished with cheap but functional cabinets, sofas, and rugs. At one point, he took me upstairs to his bedroom, where he showed me, proudly displayed on his wall, a ceremonial dagger that the Stasi had awarded him.

At forty-eight, the youthful Herr Tenbrock is just starting to show signs of aging. Gray has crept into his full beard, and his physique is no longer that of the high school sports star whose athletic career was cut short by injury. His home today would be the envy of most North Americans—a large A-frame on an idyllic plot of land surrounded by leafy old-growth trees. Tenbrock always referred to the Stasi as *Die Firma*, the Firm. I interviewed Herr Tenbrock twice, three years apart, and on the second occasion he took me for a drive around the district in his Volvo, a Barbra Streisand CD somehow providing a comforting background. When I asked him if Gransee looked as it did during the GDR, he responded: "It looks the same. It's just more colorful now."

We had lunch at a villa just outside of the town of Menz where West German embassy representatives vacationed during the GDR era. "Of course, we had this whole place bugged," Tenbrock says while gesturing at the cluster of cottages hugging the lake. After a pleasant outdoor lunch of schnitzel and sundaes, I prepared to pay, but my gracious host would hear nothing of it. The main topic of conversation over lunch was travel, one of his favorite hobbies. Herr Tenbrock was enthusiastic about an upcoming cruise to Norway, a land that, like Canada, holds for him a Nordic mystique. He spends countless hours on the Internet tracking down bargains and seeking out exotic locales. Although he does not admit to it, perhaps Tenbrock realizes that nearly three decades of travel restrictions in the GDR has infused in him a desire to see the world on the other side of the Wall.

Driving back to his home, we pass a small lake, which reminds Tenbrock of an incident in the late 1980s. A Swiss historian/sleuth believed he had finally cracked the mystery of the Amber Room, the stunningly beautiful room that showcased the golden substance first in the city palace in Berlin until 1716, and then in St. Petersburg as the Prussian king presented it as a gift to Peter the Great in return for support in war against Sweden. The splendorous Amber Room remained in St. Petersburg for more than two hundred years until the Nazi invasion, at which point it was dismantled and shipped in dozens of crates back into Germany. Sometime in the spring of 1945 as the Soviets pushed toward Berlin and the Nazis evacuated their looted treasures to the interior of the country, the crates containing the Amber Room disappeared for good. The Swiss historian, believing that they had been deposited in a lake in District Gransee by the retreating Nazis, organized a dive mission to investigate. Stasi officers in the district monitored the expedition carefully and were no doubt relieved when no crates were found.

Tenbrock vividly recalls the day that he found out he would be working for the Stasi. The local district leader, Siegmund Tamme, had talked to Tenbrock several times at the District Council Office where he worked and eventually recruited him for the Stasi. One day while Tenbrock was sitting at his desk, a hulking man came through the door and said "Are you Tenbrock? You start with us at 8 a.m. on Monday morning. We've taken care of everything." Indeed, the Stasi had the tools at its disposal to take almost anyone it liked from a workplace and arrange for their transfer to the secret police. Tenbrock went to the regional headquarters in Potsdam with all the new recruits to swear his oath of allegiance in a hall awash in a sea of East German flags; several of the new recruits were selected to touch the flags on behalf of the entire incoming class while swearing the oath.

Like many junior officers, Tenbrock began his career with the Stasi as an investigator who performed background checks on candidates for jobs that might lead them into contact with the West, like sailors, truck drivers, and border guards. It was, in fact, this mundane background check on a would-be border guard that led the Stasi to the notorious war criminal Heinz Barth—the most spectacular success in District Gransee's history.[74] Tenbrock worked for the District Gransee office for ten years before joining Markus Wolf's foreign espionage branch in the East German embassy in Egypt; the details of his posting were kept hidden from even his closest co-workers. Five years later, and to his dismay, Tenbrock returned to rural, small District Gransee, which he thought he had left behind for good. Markus Wolf made a lasting impression on Tenbrock, who considers a book that Wolf signed for him one of his prized possessions and who, following Wolf's death on November 9, 2006, lamented the loss of a great man.

Tenbrock became lieutenant seven years after joining the Stasi; he would end his career as a captain. He attributes his swift rise through the Stasi ranks in part to a stellar informant whom he recruited, "Josef Nöcker," a doctor who was not averse to soliciting information from his patients on behalf of the Stasi. Nöcker's frequent trips to West Berlin for treatment of his lethal wasp allergy afforded Tenbrock rare insights into life on the other side of the Wall. The Stasi returned the favor by showering Nöcker and his family with special treatment, not the least of which was arranging for his daughter to be admitted to medical school.

A recurrent theme in interviews with Stasi officers is the utter disdain officers held for their party superiors.[75] Tenbrock was exasperated with local party officials who constantly badgered him about the reliability of his star recruit. In order to satisfy them, and unbeknownst to the informant, Tenbrock once recorded Nöcker by means of a highly sensitive microphone hidden in a wall and sent it off to a Berlin lab, which confirmed that the informant was indeed telling the truth. But, in his diatribe against the party, Tenbrock recounted an aspect of Stasi work that will no doubt surprise readers: the Stasi had office hours. Twice a week, citizens could enter the local Stasi office (a plaque on the building read "Ministry for State Security—Gransee District Office") and discuss with the officer on duty any issues of concern.

Many of the complaints centered around the lack of decent housing. In one instance, however, a trembling health inspector explained that the local abattoir was in violation of every major health code … and had been for years. The inspector could no longer, in good conscience, perform his duties if the state was not going to take action to ensure the safety of the public. Tenbrock, the officer on duty, reported the situation to his party superiors, but the abattoir continued to operate as it always had. Although this one incident revealed to Tenbrock the paralysis of the party, of far greater consequence for him was the party's constant urge to recruit more and more informants, equating a high number of informants with greater national security. It was this pressure from above that caused the Stasi to keep informants employed well past the initial reason for recruitment in order to report in a mundane capacity on the general "mood" of the population.

Some Stasi officers refused to regularly meet with these informants—what Tenbrock calls "card corpses" (Karteileichen)—and were severely reprimanded. Stasi officers became burdened with informants, upwards of thirty of them in the district and which was logistically unmanageable, according to Tenbrock, given the fact that officers had to meet their informants after 5:00 p.m. since informants held full-time jobs. Here, however, historians must be cautious of accepting this recollection at face value, considering the sheer volume of reports and meetings with informants. In the 1980s District Perleberg officers had a total of 2,500 meetings a year with informants, and those informants (or the controlling officer, as the case may be) authored roughly 5,000 reports in District Perleberg alone in that same time frame. There were certainly inefficiencies and differing levels of aptitude among informants, but given their high level of activity it would be an exaggeration to characterize the majority of informants as "card corpses."

Tenbrock has few regrets about his line of work. He likes citing his efforts to prevent medical professionals from "fleeing the republic" to demonstrate the importance of the Stasi. "Regardless of what you think of Socialism," he says, "if a dentist leaves our district for the West, then thousands of people go without dental care."[76] Tenbrock presents this evidence not as a man desperate to convince or to justify, but matter-of-factly, preferring those facts to speak for themselves. Tenbrock also points to the Nazi-hunting function of the Stasi. He is outraged that the new united Germany (which he refers to as a "banana republic," playing on the East German desire for bananas expressed during the 1989 revolution) allows swastikas painted on buildings to remain for weeks on end before being removed, and are often not investigated further. He recalled with thinly disguised pride a time during the GDR when the Stasi arranged for every student in the district (even the ones who were out sick) to write an essay in order to obtain a sample of their handwriting; this in an effort to apprehend the individual who had painted swastikas on a wall in Gransee. Although the Stasi never did find the culprit, Tenbrock nevertheless holds up this example as the bar that the new Federal Republic should meet.

On the issue of whether the GDR was totalitarian, whether the Stasi engaged in blanket surveillance, Tenbrock is blasé. Some things, he claims, were of no interest to the Stasi. A sixty-year-old parish priest in traditional robe preaching to twenty-five "omas" (grannies) did not concern him, whereas a twenty-five-year-old preaching in jeans did. Tenbrock was dismayed by developments within the Stasi in the 1980s, especially the make-work projects that the party continually foisted on the secret police. For years on end, Tenbrock provided summaries to his superiors on the general mood of the population; for this effort he received no feedback, never hearing what happened to his reports and having no indication that the party had responded to them in any meaningful way. On a regular basis, the district party chief stepped into his Volga car and drove to the Stasi Office in Gransee where he demanded the District Stasi director to look into a variety of issues that had suddenly taken his fancy.

As time passed, the Stasi increasingly took on duties that had been the responsibility of other jurisdictions. Investigation of those who left the GDR illegally, or who had applied to emigrate, were technically the purview of the police or the department of the interior in the district council, but over time these duties fell to the Stasi. The result of these extra duties was, according to Tenbrock, increased disciplinary measures against overwhelmed Stasi officers who had no choice but to neglect some of their duties.

Almost immediately following the unplanned and disorderly opening of the Berlin Wall in November 1989, Tenbrock and others in the office began the systematic destruction of documents held in the district office. Although an outside observer might think that East Germany, and the Stasi, could still continue to exist after the fall of the Wall—the government still oversaw the National People's Army, a well-armed police force, and a loyal secret police—it was by no means clear in the fall of 1989 that the end of the Berlin Wall would translate into the unification of Germany. Tenbrock recognized that the cause to which he had dedicated his life was on the brink of extinction. As he said: "Certain dreamers in intellectual circles thought that some sort of reformed GDR would continue. I was not one of those dreamers." Tenbrock helped pile the documents into trucks headed to a site outside of Potsdam where the documents were burned. This destruction of material, a terrible historical loss, which is often overlooked given the mammoth collection that has remained, continued into the first week of December when a citizens' committee occupied the local office. Unlike many other Stasi personnel, Tenbrock was not concerned about citizen retaliation against him or his family, stating with a cavalier disregard for the anger in the streets: "What was there to be afraid of? The Firm was a legitimate organ of the state. It's not like we were some wild underground enterprise."

As outlined in the Stasi Files Law of 1991, Tenbrock's membership in the Stasi prohibited him from the civil service, a very broad category in Germany encompassing railways, the teaching profession, the police, and other major employers. Almost immediately after the fall of East Germany, Tenbrock took courses in the area of adult education and works to this day in that field. His employer is a private firm that offers courses to youth and unemployed adults who are trying to get into the workforce. He is quite satisfied with his line of work and keenly interested in the broader issues surrounding the field of education, which leads him to the conclusion that the current German education system is disastrous. He is relieved that his children were already out of school when the Wall fell.

Over the past decade and a half, the intelligent, articulate Tenbrock has assisted those on the fringes of society to a better life. He has for the most part left his service in the Stasi behind him and accommodated himself to the new reality. Still, from time to time, he grows frustrated with the united Germany and considers the possibility of emigrating. It is indeed ironic that the very one who prevented so many people from leaving East Germany now considers the new environment so stifling that he wants to leave, and thinks it is the most normal thing in the world to want to leave a country in which one is no longer comfortable.

### Markus Schram–The Enamored One[77]

Markus Schram is one of a handful of Stasi officers interviewed who did not move after 1989, preferring the confines of his top-floor apartment in a typical East German prefabricated apartment building in Zehdenick. Crossword books are piled neatly on the coffee table. He is a friendly sort who smiles often, not at all self-conscious about his two shiny gold incisor teeth, which had been made by one of Tenbrock's informants. When I mentioned toward the end of our interview that we had been talking for nearly four hours, the fifty-six-year-old former law student[78] shrugged, smiled and said without a hint of insincerity: "I hardly noticed the time passing."

Joining the Stasi was an easy decision for Herr Schram. He signed on as informant "Ralf Hoppe," a name he took because he was a fan of the German actor by that name, and made it clear to his controlling officer Tenbrock that his long-term wish was to become a full-time Stasi officer. He had, in fact, been in the bodyguard division of the Stasi from 1968 to 1970 but was dismissed because he had committed theft at the workplace. Both his father and grandfather had been Communist Party members, and his wife was still in the party through 1989 and beyond, so involvement in the Communist Party had been a family trait for generations. Thus, ideology played a major role in Schram's desire to join the Stasi, but, as he candidly admitted, so too did money. His salary nearly doubled from 680 marks a month when he worked in the district government to his starting salary of 1,150 marks a month with the Stasi. He originally worked in the Department responsible for the economy where he focused on VEB Mikroelektronik, an important factory that outfitted the East German navy with electronics and employed some 1,600 people. In 1987, he played a crucial role in making sure that the father of the two boys shot in the back by a Soviet soldier while running away from a Soviet military base did not find out the details of his children's deaths.

One of Schram's fondest memories was the camaraderie around the Stasi office. Each morning, following a short bus ride from Zehdenick, Schram arrived at the office at 8 a.m. He and the other five officers in his section would chat over coffee before going over documents for a few hours and then picking up a "reasonably priced and tasty" lunch from the nearby city administration building. The Christmas office party at a rented hall was an annual highlight, and all staff were able to attend because a neighboring district office took care of guarding the Gransee Office. Schram truly relished his time in the Stasi, and at no time did he feel that the population loathed him. As a case in point, he brought up how pleasant his wife's co-workers were to him at her office parties because he was a "decent human being (*Mensch*)." Schram made a point of adding a touch of coziness to his office in the form of fresh flowers in a vase. Otherwise, the office that he shared with one other officer was fairly standard—two desks, a black telephone, and filing cabinets containing informant files and "a few bottles." Unlike other Stasi officers who adorned their walls with portraits of notable Communists like Wilhelm Pieck, Walter Ulbricht, and the founder of the Soviet secret police, Felix Dzerzhinski, Schram and his partner preferred to keep their walls blank.

In his eagerness to explain how Tamme, the leader of the district until 1985, was much more humane than the one who followed him, Schram claimed that all of those individuals who had been secretly investigated in personal surveillance operations and who the Stasi had determined to be innocent, were then informed by a Stasi officer that the investigation was over and that nothing more would come of it. It is, of course, absurd to believe that the Stasi would inform someone that they had secretly investigated them and all of their relatives and acquaintances for years, that they had tapped their phone and opened their mail and monitored their house. Why Schram would tell it in this way is puzzling, but perhaps his love of the Stasi caused him to want to portray the Stasi in the best possible light. Other aspects of his account also lacked sincerity. In response to a question about the use of informants in pubs (and there were thirty-five pubs in Zehdenick alone) for general surveillance duties, he answered: "We never thought about placing informants in pubs—but what a good idea!" and smiled broadly.

It is also unlikely that Schram refused his superior's request to write a report on everybody who lived in his apartment building. Schram claims that he refused on the grounds that "these were my neighbors," but it would be highly unusual for an officer to refuse a task handed down by a superior. The very fact that Schram's superior requested this is an interesting revelation about the extent of Stasi surveillance: the building was clearly not a sensitive economic or military site, nor was it common practice to investigate everyone in the neighborhood where a Stasi officer lived. This incident appears to be a case of a senior Stasi officer simply taking advantage of an opportunity to gather more information on ordinary people in the district.

Although there is no question that Schram was dedicated to the cause, he was also aware of some of the limitations of the Stasi. For one, the Stasi in his opinion had become too unwieldy. His economic branch grew from three officers in 1978 to six in 1989. He felt enormous pressure to recruit informants, a task that became more difficult as the 1980s wore on and the population increasingly turned its back on the regime. Schram was not the only officer to point out that the Stasi itself sensed the waning fortunes of the GDR in its difficulty in convincing individuals to become informants. Schram claimed to be under constant pressure from the director Töpfer to produce a "spectacular" victory in the economics field, such as the arrest of an out-and-out saboteur, but nothing in his eleven years of Stasi work came close to such a victory.

On December 18, 1989, Herr Schram handed in his Stasi identification card to the police officer guarding the district office. He now no longer worked for the Stasi, and the Communist cause in Germany for which generations in his family had fought was about to be swept aside with breathtaking speed. His life work, the countless hours of meetings with informants, the endless reports on the population, the professional upgrading, the day-in, day-out administration of his files was all for naught. When prompted on how an individual deals with the magnitude of an event such as the collapse of East Germany, Schram answered simply: "I came home and did a crossword puzzle." Perhaps it is very human to seek solace in the mundane when the revolution outside is too awful to ponder.

On New Year's Day 1990, Schram, the former secret police agent, became a regular worker in a factory in Zehdenick. After being let go in September as many former East German industries rationalized, he obtained work with low-level security firms responsible for guarding furniture warehouses at night. An inherent danger in this line of work was less that of catching criminals in the act than the nighttime driving on the dimly lit roads of the district. He was badly injured one night in a collision with a boar and afterwards worked only sporadically until the late 1990s. At that time he joined a company tasked with converting the former Soviet military base at Vogelsang into housing and entertainment facilities. Schram now collects unemployment insurance and anxiously awaits the age of sixty-five when he will receive a state pension.

### Werner Beuster—The Earnest One[79]

Unlike Tenbrock and Schram whose surroundings are comfortable, Werner Beuster's modest brick farmhouse has seen better days. Judging from the state of disrepair, the grimy carpets, and food left out on the counter, Werner Beuster has fallen on hard times. The spindly forty-eight-year-old Beuster gazes intensely in front of him as he talks. The only instance during the interview when he became animated was when a young girl, possibly his granddaughter, interrupted our conversation by throwing open the living room door and yelling "Caught ya!" Beuster sprang from his chair and chased the girl out.

Siegmund Tamme, the director of the District Gransee Stasi office, played an active role in recruiting Beuster for the Stasi, just as he had in recruiting Tenbrock, by personally convincing him that East Germany's socialist society was worthy of protection. Unlike Schram, neither Beuster nor Tenbrock originally conceived of a career in the secret police. Following his studies in agriculture, Beuster worked in the countryside around Cottbus before moving back to District Gransee, where he was to work on an agricultural collective but opted instead for the Stasi. Seeing as he would have made more money as the chair of an agricultural collective, financial incentive did not play a role in Beuster's decision to join the Stasi, but rather ideology was at the heart of his decision.

Although neither of Beuster's parents were in the Communist Party, he was a devoted Communist who believed that there were enemies trying to subvert the system from within. Even before joining, Beuster had heard stories of sabotage in the countryside, such as farm workers who improperly milked cows in order to render them incapable of giving milk. Beuster, eager to neutralize these enemies in the agricultural sector, was sorely disappointed after four years of monitoring the countryside that he had come across many cases of incompetence and laziness, but not one case of an individual who had knowingly tried to disrupt the regime. Beuster phrased it in a way that almost seemed as if he had been misled during his recruitment: "Sloppiness, procrastination—there was plenty of that. But not one person in agriculture was a conscious opponent of the regime." His shift to the monitoring of factories produced a similar reaction. Beuster frankly admitted that the young worker who had been secretly pouring water on the equipment in the micro-electronic plant in Zehdenick so that the production process would be brought to a halt was simply lazy—not anti-Communist.

Although Beuster grew disillusioned with the constant search for phantom regime opponents, he nevertheless justified Stasi work on the basis of its hunt

for former leading Nazis and war criminals. After describing the Stasi's successful apprehension of the war criminal Heinz Barth who had been living in
Gransee from the end of the war (and who still lives there), Beuster rested his
case: "Our work was important. On the basis of this example [Barth] I can make
it crystal clear to anyone, *to an-y-one*, why the Stasi was necessary." For emphasis,
he added: "And you know what? He was still using Nazi newspapers as lining in
his sock drawer when we arrested him."

Beuster experienced firsthand the pressure from above to produce reams of
reports based on meetings with informants. He was dedicated to his job and
therefore did not feel it a hardship to recruit more and more informants to fulfill
quotas; he felt the need to recruit them in order to do his job properly. But the
district director himself became frustrated with Beuster as his reports from informants' meetings contained little information of value; the director even threatened that he might have to start meeting with the informants himself. Beuster
shot back that he was welcome to do so, as he would see that the problem lay
with the informant, not the controlling officer.

In certain aspects, Beuster's accounts dovetailed with those of Tenbrock. Both
were frustrated with the endless situation reports that they were required to
forward to the party, and today, like Tenbrock, Beuster doubts that the party
officials so much as glanced at them.[80] As much as Stasi officers like to blame the
party, however, to a certain extent the Stasi was also responsible for the reams
of information being produced. In return for permission to travel, for example,
a businessman would be required to write a report about what occurred on his
trip. Out of fear that a fellow-traveler might be similarly tasked, the businessman wrote extremely lengthy, detailed reports, lest he miss something reported
by a colleague and be denied future travel privileges. In other aspects, however,
Beuster sees a much more pervasive organization than did Tenbrock. Beuster
had no informants who were card corpses, believing that every informant on
his roster *could* provide valuable information even if they were not presently
offering information of consequence. He also addressed the issue of "secondary
individuals" who appeared in monitoring operations, calling them "products of
chance" (*Zufallsprodukte*) and emphasizing that every single name, regardless of
how it was discovered, was of interest to the Stasi. Beuster summed up the Stasi
approach to societal surveillance: "There was nothing that we weren't interested
in." The Stasi's index card system of cataloguing East Germans, the backbone
of its surveillance apparatus, involved writing notes on each card whenever a
person came to the attention of the Stasi, even if the instances were years apart.
A one-off brush with the Stasi might be dismissed, but if an individual's card
had a number of entries, they would be looked into more closely. Beuster's
metaphor for the Stasi index card system is poignant: "Out of the mosaic of
information on the card, we were able to form a picture of the individual."
For example, if an individual had said something against the regime once, and
twenty years later his son wanted to join the army officer corps, he might be

allowed to do so. If, however, the father had several entries on his card, if there had been a *pattern* of suspicious behavior, the son could very well be denied entry to the officer school.

Beuster, a former avid soccer player—so much of one that the Stasi requested he cut back because of frequent injuries—is still physically active, yet he appears frail, exhausted. Like other Stasi officers, he emphasized that the life of a secret police officer involved punishing hours: "I ran between twenty and thirty informants. I couldn't meet with them during the day because they had full-time jobs, so I began my meetings with them around 7 p.m. By the time I met with a few informants, it was the middle of the night and I had to be back in the office for 8 a.m." There was no question that, at a certain point, a law of diminishing returns came into play as whatever the most efficient ratio of informants to officers was, was surely passed once this number ran into the thirties. In the case of a high informant/officer ratio and the extreme hours required to run them, historians are provided with a telling case of the practical limitations on a state's desire for broad control. There simply were not enough hours in the day to meet with informants—in 1987 the Perleberg district office had an average of 7.6 meetings a day with informants, assuming meetings took place every single day of the year[81]—yet every year the district raised its target for informant recruitment. Totalitarianism, as Martin Malia has suggested, manifests itself much more in the desire for total control, rather than in its actual implementation, which—for reasons like the above, or the unpredictability of societal reaction—will always be less than the ideal.[82]

Siegmund Beuster was lying in a hospital in November 1989 following a routine operation when he found out that the Berlin Wall had fallen. In spite of the unrest throughout the land in that summer and fall, he was genuinely surprised when he heard the news. Released a few days later, he went to the district office to find the People's Police securing the building against attempts by Stasi personnel to destroy documents or access weapons. Beuster was disgusted that the same police officers who worked hand-in-hand with the Stasi had changed allegiances so quickly, many of them going on to uninterrupted police careers in the new united Germany. Clearly angry, Beuster said: "The fact that so many of our police officers willingly worked for the new system leaves a bitter aftertaste. I have to tell you."

After a brief stint as a locksmith, Beuster retrained as an entry-level tax specialist but did not continue in that line of work. He now collects unemployment, like his former colleague Schram. Although Beuster grew disenchanted with the Stasi, he expresses no remorse nor does he believe that the Stasi was the sinister organization that is sometimes portrayed. Especially because of his belief in the "rightness" of the Stasi's hunt for former Nazis, Beuster did not keep a low profile after unification nor did he change his phone number or address as many did. One even gets the sense that Beuster would have enjoyed the opportunity to engage fellow East Germans in discussion of his Stasi past:

"There was not a single day, not even immediately after the fall of the Wall, that I feared going in to my favorite pub in town."

## DISTRICT PERLEBERG

### Reinhard Kuhlow—The Repentant One[83]

The soft-spoken Reinhard Kuhlow sits in the examining room of his physiotherapy practice, colored posters of sinewy knee ligaments and muscles adorning the walls. He has worked hard to reestablish himself after the fall of the Wall, shedding his Stasi past and embarking on a three-year physiotherapy course. Some of his former informants come to him for treatment at his successful practice on the main square.

After briefly considering taking up studies at Humboldt University in Berlin in order to become a German teacher, Kuhlow, like Werner Beuster in the Gransee Office, joined the Stasi in part to counter what he thought were the efforts of opponents in the countryside to scuttle food production in the GDR. After reviewing Kuhlow's report cards from junior high school and the report by an informant who had been a childhood friend of Kuhlow, officer Alfred Pielach asked Kuhlow to join the Stasi. The Department of Personnel and Training made Kuhlow's transfer from the agricultural collective to the Stasi easy for him by securing him an apartment and arranging his transfer with the chairman of the agricultural collective. Almost immediately, however, Kuhlow became disenchanted with the Stasi. He found the ninety-plus minutes to copy out his pledge to work for the Stasi a sign of things to come, that he was joining an organization that was more interested in fueling its own bureaucracy than in undertaking concrete tasks to safeguard the GDR against legitimate threats. He never worked in the agricultural sector but instead had to cover the major factories in Wittenberge, the rayon mill and the sewing machine factory, the importance of which caused the Stasi to open a small substation of the Perleberg office in Wittenberge. In 1989, Kuhlow was promoted to captain and director of the Wittenberge substation and its complement of five officers.

Kuhlow today speaks in harsh terms about the manner in which the Stasi operated: "There was something sick about monitoring every small local festival. That's not what I signed up for, for useless reporting and these endless reports on the mood of the population." He talked of the many operations that went on for years, Stasi officers observing and writing up reports on a suspect long after it had become clear that the individual was not engaged in any oppositional activities. Kuhlow is still in disbelief that he "never met an actual enemy of the state" and kept returning to the phrase "paper tiger" to describe the Stasi, an organization obsessed with reports on the population and on potential opponents, an organization that equated bursting filing cabinets with increased national security. On the key issue of whether there was blanket surveillance in the GDR, Kuhlow replied simply: "The desire was there" and singled out the earlier district director, Tilse in particular, for "seeing enemies everywhere." The only real success of the Stasi, according to Kuhlow, was pointing out laziness and sloppiness in key factories, a task that need not have fallen to a secret police. All others were simply trumped-up victories.

Unlike most officers in the Perleberg office, Kuhlow welcomed the change of leadership in 1985 from Tamme to the domineering Ryll, in part because he had had several run-ins with Tamme. One in particular included an embarrassing incident when Tamme emptied Kuhlow's garbage can in front of his co-workers to "prove" that Kuhlow was sloppy with the Stasi's sensitive documents. Kuhlow liked the fresh approach that Ryll brought; he recalled how Ryll had saved him from a party sanction in 1989 (at a meeting of the Stasi collective) for speaking out that his father was over seventy and no longer seemed able to find imaginative solutions to problems, and that he suspected it was the same for those in power in East Germany.

For Kuhlow, the true nature of the organization that he worked for came to light in the final days of 1989 when he, as leader of the Wittenberge substation, locked up the small Stasi branch office for the last time. To his astonishment, he was not able to do so easily because the locks on the outside of the building had been sealed. The doors could be locked only from the inside. In other words, the Stasi did not lock others out; they locked themselves in their own building.

As the regime collapsed, Kuhlow joined other Stasi officers in feeding documents to the district office's coal fireplace. On the outside, Kuhlow worried for his family, believing that the crowds (which Kuhlow refers to as the "mob") would harm his wife or teenage children, fears that were not allayed by a teacher who verbally humiliated his son because of his father's association with the Stasi and generally made life unpleasant for him.

Kuhlow's story has elements of tragedy—the well-intentioned, slightly naïve youth who joins an organization to fight for the greater good, quickly becomes disillusioned, and is unable to leave because, as he candidly admitted, he needed the money in order to support his young family. His personnel file confirms what he says about his disenchantment. In 1984, his salary was reduced from 700 to 650 marks a month because of his "inability, or lack of desire, to follow through on operational procedures." Kuhlow is the only one of the Stasi from this district to enter into a profession after the collapse of East Germany and is, by far, the most remorseful of the Stasi personnel interviewed. As the conversation came to a close, Kuhlow's anguish about his past was palpable: "It is strange for me to talk about this," he said as he shook hands and averted eye contact.

## Anne Klenk—The Ambivalent One[84]

Frau Klenk was a rarity for the Stasi: a woman in operational duty. Klenk decided to leave her job as a secretary with the railroad outfitting works in Wittenberge to join the Stasi for a variety of reasons, including money and other privileges such as more food stamps, more vacation days, and more attractive vacation resorts than other employers in the GDR. She does not discount the role that ideology played, as she was predisposed to the GDR's message that it was the "peaceful" Germany. Recruiters for the Stasi, whether they were dealing with full-time workers or with informants, often turned to this refrain about East Germany in order to recruit, spinning their recruitment pitch in terms of an invitation to help maintain world peace in light of an aggressive West bent on nuclear annihilation.

Like the other officers we have met, Frau Klenk was initially pleased with her work. She enjoyed her colleagues, found the secretarial work challenging, and believed in the importance of protecting industry from saboteurs. Around 1980 she was approached to work in the powerful evaluation branch in the District Perleberg office, a branch that was the nerve center of the Stasi. It was here that case officers sent their reports from informants and other sources to be evaluated for a future course of action. Those five or six officers in the evaluation branch had a comprehensive view of all activities undertaken by the Stasi, and recommended to the district director an approach based on this information. Frau Klenk worked in the travel section of the analysis and evaluation branch, responsible for background checks on anyone in the district who wanted to travel to the West whether for a special family occasion, a conference, or as part of their job. She was one of very few district employees permitted to see the sensitive card catalogue that contained personal information on district residents, a privilege that was not accorded the run-of-the-mill officer. Echoing Beuster's comments about "making a picture out of a mosaic," Klenk looked for patterns of behavior as captured on the index cards to decide whether she would recommend that the person be allowed to travel. Being written up for having been a "rowdy" twenty years ago would not necessarily prevent an individual from traveling West, but several instances of similar behavior would.

In the course of her new duties, Klenk became overwhelmed with the sheer volume of information that the Stasi collected on an individual in order to determine if they could visit a relative in West Germany, even for a short time—informants' reports, police reports, recommendations from the work place, the card catalogue. And then daily meetings with the leader of the district to discuss her recommendation. As she was talking, a thought dawned on her: "Can you imagine if East Germany were hosting the World Cup? We would have to investigate every athlete, masseur, coach, and waterboy. We would have gone crazy!" She shook her head: "Nein. Nein" as if to say that the thought of it were too awful to contemplate.

In the mid-1980s she became disillusioned with her work, questioning why the Stasi had to check into the backgrounds of every athlete or factory boss heading West and whether this was really the job of a Ministry for State Security. Although she says the Stasi was not in a position to blanket monitor the population, she used the identical phrase to Reinhard Kuhlow when describing the Stasi approach to blanket societal surveillance: "The desire was there." These revelations combined with the stress of her work caused her to consider leaving the Stasi. At one point, she asked to return to her secretarial position, but her request was denied. The fall of the Berlin Wall turned out to be her deus ex machina.

Today, Frau Klenk breathes a sigh of relief that she happened to be on vacation when the Wall fell. Although this meant that she did not have to deal with the groups of citizens who monitored those going in and out of the district office, she nevertheless was concerned lest the crowd turn violent. As she explains: "I was deathly afraid during that time. I worried that they would line us up and shoot us and our families. My son was a teacher and I worried what they might do to him." After being turned down for several secretarial positions after 1989, which she attributes to discrimination against her Stasi past, she joined the accounting division of the French car manufacturer Renault in the town where she lives. She was proud that her previous training had prepared her for private sector work as well: "We were disciplined, industrious, and reliable. These were qualities that my new employer appreciated as much as my old one." For the past fourteen years, Frau Klenk has worked in the same office and still gets together for coffee with former Stasi secretaries. She sees the current negative publicity about the Stasi more as a function of present politics than historic reality. With a trace of satisfaction, she says: "As the economic situation in the Federal Republic continues to deteriorate, the government looks for scapegoats. It's no coincidence that the Stasi keeps coming up." This, at least, is more tastefully phrased than another officer who, echoing a similar sentiment, complained: "In 1937, it was the Jews. Now it's the Stasi."[85]

### Antje Müller—The Ambitious Socialite[86]

Even at age fifty-two, Frau Müller does not look out of place wearing the trendy clothes of a teenager. The attractive former secretary sits in her conservatory and looks out over the frog pond in her back yard, evidently pleased with the life that she has built for herself. She was born in Poland, where her father was working in agriculture before moving to Germany while she was still a young girl. Barely eighteen when she became a secretary in the Perleberg Stasi office, she was once chided by her colleague Rudolf Schulze that she made a lot of work for him because she came from a large family and he had to investigate every relative. The veil of secrecy around the Stasi meant that she had little idea of the nature of the work she would be doing. She was not even aware that the abbreviation MfS stood for Ministry for State Security. Müller was not alone in not knowing in advance what type of work she would be engaged in since the Stasi was, after all, a secret police. Although some expected to be involved in cloak-and-dagger activities, the majority who joined the Stasi in District Perleberg tended to envision investigative police work similar to that undertaken by the regular criminal police. It would be safe to say that no one joined the Stasi for the endless, mundane reporting on the population that occupied the lion's share of an officer's day.

Frau Müller was taken aback by the gravity of the initiation process. She was required to swear an oath at a mass swearing-in ceremony in Schwerin and was immediately whisked away to a two-week intensive course on Marxism-Leninism, the history of the GDR, and the history of the Soviet secret police. Although women in the Stasi were not permitted to carry weapons, a few times a year they had to practice firing a gun and undertake some light outdoor physical fitness activities. Müller soon came to love the comradery of the unit, looking forward to annual parties and flirting with her primarily male colleagues. "We were a great collective," she said.

Her job entailed typical secretarial duties such as retyping memos (the Stasi did not possess photocopy machines), transcribing, and other office duties. In 1981 she was promoted to the position of personal secretary to the district director, a move that was somewhat disappointing as she aspired to a more challenging job in the evaluation branch where Frau Klenk worked. To have been promoted to this branch, however, would have required additional training outside of the district, and the Stasi preferred that she stay close to home to tend to her children, an attitude that was pervasive in the male-dominated secret police.

Müller becomes somewhat evasive when the topic turns to societal monitoring and the shockingly large informant network. She admits that she did not really question what her colleagues were doing and repeatedly returns to the point that she was eighteen when she began working for the Stasi. Once in, it was difficult to leave. As a way of side-stepping the issue, she says that if the Stasi was involved in repression, then it was wrong for it to have been—without admitting that the Stasi was indeed an agent of repression.

Frau Müller too recalls the document destruction that took place in the fall of 1989. At one point, because of the limited capacity of the coal-burning fireplace in the district office, the Stasi began trucking the documents out to the woods nearby where, she thought, they might still lay buried. Frau Müller is an assertive, confident woman, and it is difficult to imagine her trembling in fear; yet the revolution of 1989 caused her to have an almost complete physical collapse. By her own account, she threw up only three times in her life because of stress and nerves—twice at the birth of her children, and once in November 1989 when the district leader sent the women of the office home. As she left the district office on her bicycle in the dark, she looked up to see rows of citizens lining the route, pointing their fingers. The minute she got home, she vomited.

After a short period of being without work, Frau Müller was hired by a West German billboard company that had opened up an office in eastern Germany. One of the company lawyers, she recalls, made it clear that she was unwelcome in the company due to her Stasi past. Nevertheless, she stayed with the company for seven years before personal circumstances caused her to look for other work. She had a series of secretarial jobs with a wood company, a call center, a lawyer's office, and even learned Swedish at one point because she thought she might relocate there (at least one of her former co-workers had gone this route). In 2004, looking for a new challenge, she bought the convenience store where she now works. In many ways, she finds this turn of events comical: "I sell cigarettes, tabloids, and lotto tickets—none of which I've ever been interested in!"

### Matthias Piekert—The Realist[87]

Of all the Stasi personnel interviewed, Herr Piekert is the only officer I could imagine with an iPod and Facebook account. He is forty-five but looks ten years younger due to his thick, jet black hair, jeans jacket, and energetic dog bounding around him. Piekert is bright and entrepreneurial, by day taking numerous calls on his cell phone from a former Stasi colleague with whom he works in a transportation company; by night reading weighty academic works, including Jens Gieseke's monographs on the Stasi (which he considers reasonable accounts). Piekert was only twenty-eight when the Wall fell and therefore one of the newest generation of Stasi officers. His only memory of East Germany was one with the Wall in place, an aspect of the regime that never bothered him because he did not care for travel.

Originally, Piekert thought that he would become an army officer like his father, but when approached by a Stasi contact in 1984 while he was in the army, Piekert reconsidered, even though he was not entirely sure what line of work he would be getting into. Like Frau Müller, he had heard of the Stasi but had no clear vision of what its duties were. He described his impression of the Stasi as "secretive but neutral." Although he believed in the regime, he admits that he joined the Stasi in part due to a sense of adventure, in spite of his recruiting officer's admonition that it wouldn't be "like James Bond."

Piekert worked in the Stasi department responsible for counterespionage (Department II). The only major site of interest in the district for enemy agents would have been the Soviet garrison in Perleberg that housed the latest Warsaw Pact equipment—Perleberg's location was a mere 9 miles (15 km) from the Cold War front. In his five years with the Stasi, Piekert never caught a spy, although he maintained a large roster of informants for this purpose. The crushing pressure from above to recruit informants and to meet with them frequently irritated the young Stasi officer, who also talked of having informants who were "card corpses." In order to fulfill recruitment quotas, some informants were recruited under pressure, and these were always the weakest informants, offering up banalities that barely satisfied their reporting role. Although his appearance was disarming, Piekert could be heavy-handed during the recruitment process. If an informant hesitated to join, he asked them threateningly whether they "supported peace or war." If Piekert determined that it was a lost cause, the candidate would be released without consequence. Alternately, Piekert might bring up some minor incident in the candidate's past—perhaps a brief conversation with a West German at a rest stop on the road from West Germany to West Berlin—to blackmail them in to informant work. Piekert considered this obsession with informants and their reports the greatest weakness of the Stasi: it led to poor quality reports on the population and distracted from duties of safeguarding economic and military sites. He complained that these duties should not have been at the core of a secret police: "We did the work of a regular police force, we did the work of a city administration, but we did little secret police work."

In many ways, Piekert's tasks were those that one imagines of a secret police officer—apprehending enemy spies—and thus he can be somewhat more objective on other aspects of Stasi work like the level of societal surveillance, which he was not involved in as such. He candidly admits that had he been asked to monitor and control the population, he would have done so with the same level of dedication and enthusiasm he approached his other tasks. In another comment that lends credence to Piekert's account, he said: "I was part of the system, so if repression took place, even though it was not in my branch, I bear some responsibility." That being so, Piekert's views on the level of societal monitoring merit close attention. Piekert claims that monitoring in the GDR was not "100 percent blanket coverage, but it was extremely high," and went on to say that if one considers the border controls, the Wall, and the Stasi, "the GDR had a perverted approach to security." It is interesting that this officer, who frankly accepted a certain degree of responsibility for repression although he himself was not personally involved in societal monitoring, and who was as objective an "outsider" as one could be while still a part of the Stasi, saw the Stasi as an instrument of "extreme surveillance."

Piekert recalls only one serious demonstration in 1989 outside the district office, which was diffused simply by ennui. Although somewhat concerned about the crowd, Piekert was put at ease by the fact that the Stasi's informants made up a portion of the demonstration. Nevertheless, in case things spiraled out of control, he and his colleagues armed themselves with fire extinguishers. Piekert feels compelled here to the right the record: "So many historians marvel at the peaceful conduct of the revolutionaries in 1989. The fact is that it didn't come to violence in the fall of 1989 because *both* sides exercised restraint."

Piekert relates a telling incident that reveals how both Stasi and the general public perceived each other. When the Stasi allowed members of the citizens movement to enter the Stasi building in the fall of 1989 after the Wall fell, one of the citizens asked to see the blood stains from the Stasi's victims. When Piekert responded mockingly that they used the pile of brown coal to cover the stains, some of the citizens started to move away the coal. Although there is no doubt that the Stasi was not engaged in murder in its later years, it nevertheless must accept some of the blame for this monstrous perception that permeated the population. The Stasi to a large degree cultivated the aura of sinister mystery around itself. In another district office, East Germans armed with shovels and pick axes demanded to be brought to the Stasi's torture chambers.[88]

As much as he realized that the Stasi as it then existed was coming to an end, he also remembers that many officers held a secret hope that the Stasi would continue in some fashion. These officers used the guise of document destruction to burn all of their problematic or tiresome files, but kept safe their informant files and similar documents, which they thought might be useful again in six months. Piekert is firm in his resolve that all of the Stasi documents should have been destroyed: "It's too bad that we didn't destroy all of the documents. It makes me sick today to see the difficulties that some informants run into because they worked for us. The truth is that many informants told us nothing. And many we pressured into working for us."

In the first few years after unification, Piekert thought about moving his family out of Germany, in part because of an incident that occurred in 1991 when he approached a pastor about allowing him to hunt on church lands. The pastor was aware that Piekert had been with the Stasi and responded that he "would talk to him from his position as pastor, but not as one human being to another." They ended up sitting down and having a drink, and talked for hours. In the end, the pastor followed the path of Solomon, neither permitting him nor refusing him to hunt on church property. Although he is self-assured, there is something about Piekert's conduct that suggests he is still conflicted about his past. He purposefully sought out the target of one of the Perleberg Stasi's long-running operations, the pastor, Dr. Woronowicz, although there would be no compelling reason for him to do so since he was not personally involved. It does not appear that Piekert intended to apologize for the Stasi's actions nor did he appear to seek catharsis. After an afternoon conversing with Piekert, the pastor offered the former Stasi agent two children's Bibles, which Piekert dutifully passed on to his children. Although he is not religious, Piekert was willing to allow his children to make this decision for themselves. He thinks that one of his boys has come to believe in God.

Late in our conversation, one fundamental difference between East and West Germany seemed to occur to Piekert: "I would admit that had things happened the other way, had East Germany taken over West Germany, we would have locked up every member of the West German secret service."

## Rolf Schwegel—The Spiteful One[89]

Of all the former Stasi officers who continue to live in District Perleberg, Herr Schwegel is the one who has the most contact with his former colleagues. This is not because he likes them—quite the contrary—but because, out of a sense of duty, he provides many of them with one of his farm-raised ducks at Christmas time. For a good part of the interview, Herr Schwegel went over the list of former

Stasi workers obtained online and alternatively ridiculed or hurled vindictives about each one. By the end of the list, it was not enough that an officer were "a poser" but the "biggest poser of all time," and this was the mildest form of rebuke. For practically every individual, he recalled some incident where they insulted him in one fashion or another. After Schwegel handed in his Stasi identification card in 1989 (he retired on schedule, luckily for him just before the revolution), his colleague said: "I guess I can't call you comrade anymore." Schwegel was exasperated and tried to explain that he was still in the party but had just retired from the Stasi. In fact, Schwegel's relations with his colleagues seemed to be a never-ending source of frustration.

Setting aside his mother's trepidations, Schwegel joined the Stasi in 1964 and worked in the very sensitive medical sector, monitoring in particular medical professionals who might have been considering fleeing the Republic. He was pleased with his informants in the medical world, all of whom met with him on a regular basis, unlike his unreliable youth informants. Over time he had built up a cadre of four informants in the Wittenberge hospital (one of whom was a nurse, one a doctor, the others he could not recall), three informants in the hospital in Perleberg, and one informant in the small medical center in Bad Wilsnack. Schwegel spent much of his time painting a realistic portrait of the medical situation in the GDR based on the informants' reports, and the portrait was sobering: faulty hydraulics causing operating tables to randomly rise and lower during operations, an acute shortage of rubber gloves, medical professionals seeking any opportunity to leave the GDR, and the like. Schwegel was enraged that the party never properly responded to his reports on the disastrous situation in health care. Even today, it still irritates him that after the fall of the Wall, former East German leader Erich Honecker disparaged the Stasi in a Moscow interview; Honecker said he never read the Stasi reports since they contained the same gloom-and-doom information as the tabloid West German *Bildzeitung*.

Given his focus on the medical field, it is perhaps understandable that Schwegel did not see the Stasi as an instrument of blanket surveillance, dismissing any notion of totalitarian rule with the simple observation that "there were villages in the district that I could care less about." As some of the evidence already encountered has suggested, however, the Stasi could not be so neatly compartmentalized. By virtue of Schwegel's physician informants, he was privy to information about patients (as was Tenbrock in the District Gransee office) regardless of which village they came from. Moreover, time and again informants changed their places of work or moved, and still they remained on the books even if their new location was originally one that did not factor into Stasi plans.

### Herr and Frau Paupst—The Committed Support Staff[90]

The Paupsts appear to be very comfortable in their apartment above a store in Perleberg, both with their surroundings and with each other. Although they do not sit beside one another on the couch, they show their deep affection for each other in subtle winks and in their constant apologizing when interrupting the other. Herr and Frau Paupst both worked at the district office in supporting roles, he as chauffeur for the district director and she on the cleaning staff.

Herr Paupst started with District Perleberg in 1970, not entirely sure what type of work the Stasi undertook, but happy to be the leader's chauffeur after his stressful stint with the border troops. As time went on, even though he was not in operational duty, Herr Paupst believed that he was contributing to socialism in his own way: "I stood behind the thing [socialism]. I worked for the Stasi out of conviction." He loved working on the cars in the district, and recalls fondly the very first car that he drove the leader in—an expensive Muscovitch. Later, he would drive an East German Wartburg (one step up from the ubiquitous Trabant), and the Russian-built Volga and Lada. In the latter years, regular officers shared the six Trabants that the office possessed, but prior to that most officers got around on either a moped or small motorcycle. In the late 1980s, as East Germany found itself crushed underneath its debt load, officers had to dip into the coffee fund in order to pay for gas for their business trips. If there were any question about the sensitivity of his job, it was answered in an incident shortly after his arrival when the district leader hit a post coming out of the underground parking. At the garage, a mechanic took the license plate from the leader's car, placed it on his own Trabant, and drove to safety in West Germany.

Because of the frequent trips around the district, and the longer rides to East Berlin, no other co-worker spent as much time with the district's leaders as Herr Paupst. He was inordinately fond of the earlier leader, Herr Tilse, "someone who you could really talk to, even about family problems." The leader confided in his chauffeur, but used the familiar "Du" only while in the confines of the car, gently reminding him that "the minute you get out of the car, you've forgotten everything we talked about." Tilse drove himself to work in the morning and reserved Herr Paupst's services for longer trips. Tilse would have a social drink from time to time but did not drink heavily, often asking Herr Paupst to come pick him up from a party function half an hour after his arrival under some trumped-up pretense of his being needed in the office. Tilse's successor, Werner Ryll, was the opposite personality, insisting on being driven to work every morning and wanting his chauffeur to report in on his whereabouts on a regular basis. He made a point of going to every occasion where alcohol was served, often leaving his chauffeur to wait for him in the car until dawn. Frau Paupst became animated when the conversation turned to Ryll's behavior, recalling her own earlier incident when Ryll turned down her request to spend a few extra days with her daughter as she gave birth.

What emerges from both Paupst's accounts is a Stasi collective that from 1985 on was increasingly dispirited due in large part to its drunken, uncompassionate leader, who pushed officers beyond capacity and reason. That the District Office had grown well beyond the original tight collective into a sprawling apparatus also contributed to bad overall morale. Christmas parties were no longer fun, the Paupsts recalled, because everyone had to rush back to work. "Ryll unsettled our district office," Herr Paupst summed up.

The Paupsts had little difficulty finding work after 1989. He works in a trucking company along with his former co-worker Piekert, and she is in custodial services at a local firm. The only incident that caused them any concern about their treatment in the new Germany occurred shortly after 1989. At that time, the couple lived in one of a cluster of seven or eight prefabricated high-rise apartment buildings, which had gone up in Perleberg fairly late in the GDR's history. By 1990 the general upkeep of the building was sorely lacking, which was perhaps understandable given the general chaos of the postrevolutionary spring. The lobby in particular was filthy. Herr Paupst put up a notice for the residents suggesting that they all chip in to clean up the lobby. Upon returning the next day, he found that a large "X" had been drawn across his notice and that somebody had scribbled: "Herr Paupst. The Red era is over!" The Paupsts promptly moved out.

### Bernd Lohre—The Unrepentant One[91]

As the individual tasked with tracking down those behind anonymous letters against the regime and behind anti-Communist graffiti, Bernd Lohre considered his job a very important one. It involved endless hours of pouring over writing samples (some obtained by fabricated essays in high schools) and comparing them to the unidentified letter. Lohre loved the thrill of the hunt and found it intoxicating when he was able to find the culprit among the tens of thousands who lived in the district.

Lohre did not originally plan on working for the Stasi, but had imagined a career in the criminal police instead. Although his father-in-law worked for the Stasi, he had little idea of what the job would entail, believing it might be detective work very similar to that of the regular police. He threw himself into his work and was quickly singled out for his successes in apprehending the authors of anonymous letters against the regime.

For Lohre, the real crux of Stasi work was the recruitment of informants, what he calls the "Alpha and Omega of operational work." Lohre was candid about the challenges that the Stasi faced in recruiting an informant. To penetrate the church, an institution against which the Stasi was "completely helpless," it was better to recruit an informant on the outside who would work his way into the church milieu. Otherwise, the Stasi would not trust the informant completely. Although on paper it appears that many informants worked for the Stasi out of conviction, many were indeed pressured into working for them; Stasi officers doctored their reports because a coerced informant was the least desirable for higher-ups. From the mid-1980s on, as the situation in the GDR deteriorated and popular frustration grew, it became almost impossible to recruit an informant out of conviction. The standard recruitment phrase that the individual would be assisting the GDR in maintaining global peace now fell on deaf ears.

Lohre believes that the recruitment of informants speaks to the manner in which the Stasi worked according to areas of priority (*Schwerpunkte*), rather than blanket surveillance of the population. The Stasi, he argues, reacted to situations and concentrated its efforts in areas where new crises seemed to be emerging. He said, for example, that if there were three hundred workers in a certain division of the rayon mill, and fifteen of them applied to emigrate, the Stasi would then actively seek out an informant to assess the situation in what had become an area of priority. Similarly, one night in the late 1970s there was a large brawl between police and youth in Wittenberge. During the questioning, the Stasi recruited twenty-three informants who were then required to monitor youth in the district. As Lohre said: "We asked ourselves the question: 'Where is it necessary to recruit an informant?'" He dismisses the concept of blanket surveillance as "ridiculous," pointing out that there was no way to monitor every nook and cranny of the district, yet at the same time he acknowledges that blanket surveillance was a term that one did hear around the office.

"I was not alone in noticing that the work we did in the late 1980s had little to do with state security and we were, after all, the Ministry for State Security." This refrain had been reiterated frequently enough in the interviews that it must be taken into account when addressing the history of the Stasi. There were many officers who were becoming disgruntled with the burgeoning tasks of the Stasi into areas of mundane background checks and securing parades. This is not to say that the Stasi personnel were quasi-revolutionaries;[92] most remained obedient and dedicated to the regime. They simply wanted to get back to a state where they "guaranteed peace in the country and defended against enemies." Of course, this idyllic past never really existed; from the 1950s the Stasi had taken on tasks that went well beyond a traditional understanding of national security, including broad societal monitoring. Lohre placed the blame for the expanded duties squarely on the shoulders of Erich Mielke ("who would sell his own grandmother") and his eagerness to demonstrate the prowess of "his" Ministry for State Security.

In the turbulent fall of 1989, Lohre feared the worst: "I was certain that I was going to be strung up on a lamppost. I told my children not to tell anyone where their father had worked. Because of the feelings against us, I was angry that the Ministry had transported our weapons to the regional office. Now we were defenseless." To this day, Lohre's children have denied that their father was a Stasi officer. Given the changed situation in the fall of 1989, the German-German border became congested and many former Stasi officers like Lohre joined the burgeoning ranks of customs officials. With the Stasi Files Law and vetting of individuals for previous Stasi involvement, Lohre was dismissed from his civil service position and for the next thirteen years worked in Wittenberge assembling furniture. In 2005 he stopped working because of his deteriorating health. As his wife has recently died, Lohre finds himself frequently alone, but he refuses to get together with former Stasi. "Nowadays," he says "I try not to talk about the Stasi."

## Horst Sauer—The Recruiter[93]

Horst Sauer avoids eye contact when he talks, and he often allows a hand gesture to substitute for the word he is not quite able to come up with. The widower appears nervous, frequently glancing out the window to the busy street outside. As one of the key recruiters for the Stasi, Herr Sauer spent more of his time outside the district office than in it. His was not the work of a typical operational officer—recruiting informants, societal monitoring, conducting surveillance operations—but it was nonetheless critical work, for he was responsible for making sure that the next generation of Stasi officers would be in place. Herr Sauer was a regular at the district recruiting office for the National People's Army, where he would sit with regular army officers when candidates presented themselves for duty, participating in the conversation only if the candidate had indicated that they would like to serve more than the required two years of service. For Stasi recruitment officers, this was a sign that the individual was dedicated to the regime. Herr Sauer would suggest to the recruit that he could serve his time guarding party and Stasi installations in Berlin as part of the elite Feliks Dzerzhinski regiment. Three years in this regiment provided the Stasi with an opportunity to determine whether the candidate would be suitable for full-time work with the Stasi. In response to a question about the relative ease or difficulty of obtaining recruits for the Stasi, Herr Sauer stated simply: "It was hard to recruit people." He also actively recruited from among the ranks of officers' children.

Although he considered much of his work "dry paper-pushing," he nevertheless believed in what he was doing: "I was convinced by the whole thing," he said almost bashfully.

## Rudolf Schulze—The Leader-in-Waiting[94]

Schulze's living room looks like a hunting lodge. Deer antlers and boar tusks adorn the dark panel walls, fur carpets lie in front of the cottage furniture. Hunting magazines and books about forests are neatly stacked on tables or on the shelves of the credenza that takes up the far wall. Somehow the plush bunnies leftover from Easter in the front entrance seem sorely out of place. Rudolf Schulze, a large man with short-cropped gray hair, answers the door in gray slacks and a turtleneck.

Schulze was recruited for the Stasi in 1967 while he was working customs at the German-German border; he was one of a number of Stasi officers whom the industrious leader of the district office, Herbert Tilse, recruited directly, a characteristic of Stasi recruitment that appears to be unique to the district level.

Certainly, it would be difficult to imagine a regional Stasi leader or one of the department leaders in the HQ in Berlin personally recruiting officers. Schulze admits that he was attracted to the Stasi in large part because of the salary and benefits. By 1978, as the Stasi began to devote serious attention to replacing the first generation of leadership, Schulze was earmarked to assume a leading function in the district. Part of his grooming involved working closely with the deputy district leader and reading sensitive materials reserved for leadership and future leadership cadres.

Schulze worked on counterespionage in Department II. Schulze's biggest headache was the twice-yearly exchange of equipment that the Soviets undertook at their barracks in Perleberg in order to make sure that this forward post of the Cold War would have state-of-the-art technology should war break out. In the final days of the Cold War, the Perleberg garrison received shipment of the ultrasecret T-80 Soviet tank. Schulze and his team made sure that the nighttime exchange of tanks and weapons took place beyond the eyes of locals and enemy agents.

Like Lohre, Rudolf Schulze believed that the Stasi followed the principle of area of priority in its approach to informant recruitment. He dismissed out of hand the suggestion that there were informants in pubs and restaurants, citing not the moral part of this equation but the purely technical aspect—pub talk tended to be exaggerated and unreliable. Stasi officers needed facts and proof, not malicious gossip. If the Stasi were to prosecute successfully, it needed more than just hearsay from a restaurant. Although there are incidences of the Stasi recruiting waiters and innkeepers in the past, by the latter years this was certainly the exception, not the rule. In truth, however, it was not entirely necessary. The Stasi was able to obtain its information from other gathering places like churches, dance halls, and offices.

At the same time, he complained that the party was paranoid, citing examples of local party officials who called the Stasi district office every time they heard the slightest rumor about something amiss in the district and berated the Stasi officers: "How is it you have no idea what is going on?" Schulze's disgust at his party superiors expressed itself in other instances as well. He complained that by 1988 the party told the Stasi not to bother reporting on the chronic problems in the rayon factory in Wittenberge since there was nothing the party could do about it. In one of the few instances when Schulze became animated, he railed against the party for not addressing the exodus and travel issues that had been brewing in the 1980s and which the Stasi brought to its attention on several occasions: "The party was helpless. It had *no answers.*" Although he may have been critical of his party superiors, Schulze was by no means an opponent of the regime: "The vast majority of the Stasi, including me, stood behind socialism."

## Klaus-Peter Schmid—Neighboring District Leader: The Ideologue[95]

As a lieutenant colonel, Klaus-Peter Schmid was the highest ranking Stasi officer interviewed for this project. He wears a blue vest and slippers, his thin white hair brushed back to reveal a widow's peak. His living room is humble. Throws cover the chairs, crystal, and model trains are on display in a cabinet. We talked over a lunch of chicken and white asparagus, the only choice of vegetable, given the spring season in which we met. Herr Schmid is remarkably fit for seventy-seven, although his chiseled, almost perfect wrinkles make him look older. His wife joined us for lunch but seemed reticent to talk until the topic turned to freedom to travel, when she opened up about the many marvelous places to travel in Eastern Europe. And the beaches of Bulgaria! Oh, the beaches! *Herrlich!* Magnificent! It really was no loss to have been confined to travels in Eastern Europe.

Herr Schmid's path to the Stasi was a typical one. He worked at a cement factory until 1954 when he joined the Stasi in the District Pritzwalk office, where he would return in 1964 as director after a brief stint as deputy director of the Kyritz office. For the next twenty-five years Herr Schmid guided the district office immediately to the east of District Perleberg. He portrays himself as a serene captain of his ship, above the fray and the day-to-day messiness of operational duty, keeping only a light hand on the tiller. Other district leaders, like those in neighboring Perleberg, should have been wise to adopt his soft approach to power, he suggests: "Today, Tilse and his wife sit trembling in their apartment. I never did. There was no reason to. Not one person in the district, *not one person*, said a cross word to me after 1989. You see, I never lost contact to the masses." This was so, he explained, because: "When I left my home at 7 a.m. heading to the office, I chatted with people along the way to get the lay of the land. I wished them a good day. I knew many doctors and police officers and would talk to them as well."

Schmid claimed to be suspicious of his officers who were running an army of informants, seeing an officer who had lost the personal touch. This latter statement is, of course, utter nonsense. In a bureaucracy driven by paperwork and bean-counting, in a system that built informant recruitment into the annual work plans of its officers, it is absurd to suggest that some officers would be allowed to eschew all this in favor of casual conversations with acquaintances. Even today Schmid is aghast that his neighbor, a police officer, with whom he often chats while the latter is out gardening, does not want to hear Schmid's tips on the population.

Schmid became most spirited—leaning forward, his weight on the arm of the sitting chair and his voice raised—when he discussed the greatest changes that he noted during his long tenure with the Stasi. He lamented the passing of the era when Stasi officers and informants worked for the cause of socialism rather than for a paycheck. "Where are the ideologues?" he thundered. "We should have been fighting for a cause. And *then* accepting money for the job." The current situation in Germany, to which he kept returning, was proof enough that the old East Germany had been on the right path: "Look around you—crime is rampant, criminals have more rights than victims, police cars drive around aimlessly until they get a call, and politicians do nothing. The other day, Jehovah's

Witnesses came to the door. I said I was an atheist. All you had to do was look at everything that was happening in the world to come to the conclusion that God did not exist. I invited them in nonetheless, and was very happy to talk to them."

## PERFECTLY ORDINARY PERPETRATORS?

For the most part, the composition of the Districts Gransee and Perleberg Stasi offices was in line with the larger Stasi. Over the years, the complement's average age crept up so that the typical Stasi operational officer was a male in his early forties. In the vast majority of cases, Stasi officers at the district level knew no other secret police existence than that of the district level, nor did they vault from the district to a higher position elsewhere, as one account suggests.[96] From this point of view, the Stasi in the districts was exceptionally insular. The Stasi out in the provinces was just that—provincial. Gransee and Perleberg officers had been trained predominantly in a trade and tended to enter the Stasi directly from their line of work. This evidence suggests that district offices were generally behind other Stasi units in recruiting members from the intelligentsia and middle classes, as the percentage of working-class recruits overall in the Stasi fell to 13 percent in the 1980s while it remained much higher in the districts.[97] Over time Stasi recruitment of full-time workers came to be based more on political reliability than on the strategic targets outlined in Stasi guidelines. The first recruitment guideline issued by the Stasi, the 1959 Directive on Recruitment, foresaw recruitment primarily from the army and the police, an approach that lasted (in theory if not in practice) until 1985 when new guidelines called for increased recruitment from those involved with industry.[98] In the end, however, the ideal recruit was a Communist-raised individual with relations in the Stasi, regardless of their previous place of employment.

The documents and interviews also demonstrate the totalitarian nature of the GDR in other ways beyond strictly that of surveillance. The Stasi, as many of the officers made clear in almost nonchalant asides, was enormously powerful; it had the ability to use the state and its apparatus for its own purposes. Officer Tenbrock arranged for his top informant's daughter to be admitted to medical school; Lohre instructed all teachers in the district to obtain writing samples for him. The Department of Personnel and Training exerted its enormous power in order to ensure the orderly acquisition of new recruits. It obtained employment for spouses, it took care of every detail in wrapping up duties with a previous employer, and, in a country with chronic housing shortages, it arranged for apartments for its new officers. Totalitarianism must be understood not as a state consistently exerting control over individuals, but doing so when it needed to. In Donnersmarck's movie *The Lives of Others*, this power to control the lives of East Germans was captured brilliantly (and, eerily, very similar to the real-life case above) in the scene involving the oppositional playwright

Dreyman's neighbor who, having witnessed the bugging of the apartment, is sternly warned by the Stasi Captain Wiesler: "Frau Meineke, a word about this to anyone and your Mascha will lose her spot in medical school tomorrow. Is this understood?"[99]

The Perleberg district office was considerably larger than its Gransee counterpart, and its officers in general better educated. Its employees were also slightly older. Although Perleberg employed more women than the Gransee office, including one in operational duty in the evaluation branch, the percentage of women in the Stasi at a district level was low in comparison to the Stasi overall, a result of the absence of mail monitoring at the district level where the lion's share of women in the Stasi were employed. Historians have explained the remarkably few women in leadership positions in the Stasi by the continuing gender bias in the Stasi leadership that women should tend families, not run informants.[100] Of the so-called "Fortune Two Thousand," the top Stasi positions, only forty-eight were occupied by women, and of these only four in operational branches.[101] Even though Erich Mielke appeared to emancipate women for Stasi work in his order of 1962 in which he emphasized that women in a socialist society were equal to men, the reality was that every Stasi worker had to be prepared to work longer than the mandated forty-eight-hour work week, something that would affect women disproportionately as they bore the brunt of the "double burden"—working and raising a family. As Jens Gieseke has written, Mielke felt he could not plan the Stasi's tasks around the opening times of day cares.[102] This view of women's domestic role was not limited to the Stasi. Even though the GDR in 1970 could point with justifiable pride to the fact that women were 34.3 percent of physicians, 53 percent of judges, and had obtained the world's highest percentage of female participation in an industrialized work force,[103] an employed woman still had to conform to a male-engineered ideal. Images of women in GDR magazines showed women in an earlier era working heavy machinery and later on as smartly dressed technical workers, but always as an employed woman *and* mother, who took care of meals and the home.[104]

In the Stasi, this double burden tended to be resolved by impeding promotion for women so as not to affect their traditional role as nurturer. Annual evaluations reflected the different criteria for men and women. Whereas men were judged on their performance of assigned tasks, women's evaluations commented on their "friendliness" and willingness to "pitch-in."[105] There may have been something particular about secret police work that caused the male leadership of the Stasi to think women ill-suited for the tasks, but their views were not entirely out of step with party policies that promoted both female employment and a higher birthrate, with the latter frequently taking precedence.[106] That Frau Müller's ambitions were thwarted by a similar attitude in District Perleberg implies that chauvinism penetrated into the smallest territorial unit of the Stasi, yet Frau Klenk, also a wife and mother, performed exceedingly well in her leadership position in the same office and was recognized repeatedly for her contributions. Why the experiences of these women in the same district office at the same time would be so different remains for the time being a mystery.

Neither leader of the district offices in the last years of the regime had any inhibitions about using the apparatus at his disposal to the fullest and demanding long hours from his employees. The abrupt, heavy-handed Werner Ryll in Perleberg succeeded in alienating the vast majority of his employees, while increasing societal monitoring. From the accounts of former employees, Hans-Jürgen Töpfer in District Gransee appears to be a less loathsome figure than Ryll, although he too was a dedicated Chekist who, in order to advance his own career, asked his superiors in 1980 to prevent his parents from traveling West. Although the district leaders were part of a larger Stasi that had been increasing societal monitoring since 1953, the combination of systemic factors and the role of personalities is nevertheless notable. At a district level, with its intimate relationship to the population and a relatively small contingent of operational officers, the leader made an appreciable difference in the operation of the Stasi and by extension in the lives of ordinary people in the district. Certainly, all officers interviewed talked of just how exhausting their job had become by the late 1980s, a confession that could mean only one thing in the context of East Germany—more societal surveillance, be it in the form of informant recruitment, background checks on travelers, or operational activity. There was, however, another critical way in which the district leader shaped the Stasi office under his command—in the recruitment process itself. Many officers were either handpicked by the district leader, personally known to him, or approached by him with an offer of employment, all of which suggests that the district leader played an important role in grooming the next generation of Stasi officers. At a minimum, it suggests once again that the Stasi in the districts was deeply insular and rooted in its immediate surroundings.

For many scholars, what motivated individuals to work for the Stasi is the most pressing issue for a more complete understanding of the officer corps and its conduct although, to be sure, this is not a debate that has the same urgency as that of perpetrators' motivations in the heinous crimes of the Third Reich. As the interviews have made clear, Stasi officers joined the ranks of the secret police for a variety of reasons—financial reward, fringe benefits, eagerness to serve the cause of socialism, adventurism, and, in many cases, false expectations that the work would be like that of a private detective. It is this point—that recruits were frequently in the dark about what their work would entail—that is often missed in scholarly treatments of the Stasi and which proceeds from the assumption that a recruit knew what to expect, an assumption that inaccurately magnifies the question of motive. As time went on, however, every single Stasi officer interviewed became disillusioned with his work—albeit to varying degrees.

For some, the Stasi had become involved in areas that had little to do with what they perceived as the mandate of the Stasi; thorough background checks on every person who applied to emigrate was surely the duty of some other branch of government. Endless reporting on the population and the years-long operations against individuals who exhibited no oppositional activity also irked many Stasi. Today, the vast majority of the Stasi personnel heap scorn on the party for the absurd level of surveillance and for the obsession with informants.[107] One former major said: "There really was no need to recruit new informants every year. I was tasked with recruiting so and so many informants, which was very difficult in such a small territory."[108] There was, as I have mentioned, a mathematical problem as well—you could not have everyone reporting on everyone. Although the party was indeed partially responsible for creating this state of affairs—the Stasi was an instrument that carried out instructions—the people who made up the Stasi must also accept responsibility for their direct role in surveillance, which Herr Piekert and Herr Kuhlow readily acknowledge. Several Stasi officers who engaged in honest reflection on their work for the GDR lamented that the Stasi had become an instrument of widespread repression.

Unlike Gerd Wiesler, the fictional Stasi captain in *The Lives of Others* who has doubts about the organization to which he has dedicated his life and sides with a prominent regime opponent, there is no sense in District Perleberg or Gransee that the officers were remotely close to treason. Although there was certainly frustration that the party had not addressed the issues that were bringing people to the streets,[109] Stasi workers remained loyal to the regime: they recruited informants, they ran operations, they hunted down authors of anonymous letters, they hid the truth about the cause of death from parents, they broke up engagements, they staged break-ins, and they made life unbearable for regime opponents. In spite of their inner concerns, in spite of their slight moral protest, in spite of their hostility toward their party bosses, they continued and indeed increased their exhaustive work of societal repression and, it should be emphasized, at no point did any of them indicate that they feared reprimand should they not fulfill their duties. In fact, it is striking how many challenged their superiors about workloads and the incessant demand for informants, all of which suggests that Stasi personnel continued in their posts for reasons other than fear of what might happen had they stopped participating in societal repression.

Perhaps predictably, the two reasons that many continued in spite of reservations were similar to those suggested for joining the Stasi—belief in socialism and a generous salary. Because salaries depended on rank, years of service, bonuses for operational successes, and responsibilities, it is difficult to generalize about Stasi salaries. However, a Stasi captain who ran informants, like the ones interviewed here, with ten years' experience, could expect a salary around 2,200 East German marks (Ostmarks) a month in the 1980s, more than double the average worker's salary in the GDR.[110] Yet a third reason for remaining with the Stasi emerges from the interviews: the camaraderie of the collective. The district office was not only where officers ran informants and deciphered handwriting, but also where they shared coffee with colleagues, held Christmas parties, flirted, and united against a domineering boss, a closeness that other officers remember as unique to the district level.[111]

In turning to the question of totalitarianism, Martin Malia's approach resonates strongly with the history of the Stasi in Districts Gransee and Perleberg: "Totalitarianism does not mean that such regimes in fact exercise total control over the population; it means rather that such control is their aspiration."[112] Several officers stated in no uncertain terms that the Stasi strove for blanket surveillance of society, which has an unmistakable "totalitarian" undertone to it. "The desire was there" was a refrain that several Stasi officers repeated. Herr Beuster formulated it differently but the message was the same: "We were interested in everything," and went on to draw the analogy of using the card catalogue system to form a complete picture of an individual from the "mosaic" of information available. Even those Stasi officers who deny the existence of blanket surveillance acknowledge that the term itself was "in the air" in the hallways of the Stasi office. One of the first Stasi memoirs to appear after the fall of the Wall, well before the renewed debate on totalitarianism took hold in the historical profession, discussed the Stasi's ambition to "blanket monitor and observe the country"[113] at the latest with Order 2/85 in 1985.[114] Another early interviewee claimed that every "man and mouse" was monitored.[115] To suggest, as some officers have done, that blanket surveillance could not have existed in East Germany because revolutionaries were able to take to the streets is to confuse blanket surveillance with political repression.[116] The latter requires active engagement at a political level, something that was lacking in 1989.

As several officers commented in their interviews, Stasi officers recruited informants in areas of priority rather than to haphazardly monitor society. At the same time, what seemed a neat and tidy compartmentalized process on paper looked decidedly less so in practice, as informants changed locations and workplaces and were rarely let go. In other words, an argument that points to the Stasi's emphasis on areas of priority in order to undermine the totalitarian concept misses the crucial point that the areas of priority approach *itself* held the potential for much broader societal surveillance. In addition, the areas of priority encompassed societal areas that covered the overwhelming majority of the population.

Former Stasi officers in a fascinating "insider" account have squarely addressed the question of blanket monitoring vs. areas of priority, arguing that the Stasi had precisely defined areas of society that it was instructed to monitor. Leaving no room for uncertainty, the authors write: "All in all, there never was blanket monitoring and surveillance of GDR citizens by the Ministry for State Security,"[117] yet by their own admission it was impossible to be "exact" in the surveillance of the areas of priority, and the increased duties assigned to the Stasi in the 1980s vastly expanded its purview. The Stasi became, according to the insiders, a tool to manage a population increasingly disgruntled by the party's ineptitude. In a statement that rings with candor, the former Stasi officers acknowledged that they were becoming involved in widespread control of society: "With the transfer of an increasing number of duties to the Stasi, to the Ministry of Interior, and to other state departments, duties that should have been more properly taken care of at a political level, the party attempted to make up for its own political deficiencies by downloading to other agencies: These agencies were to keep societal response to party decisions in check, and make larger, more negative reactions to political decisions easier to control."[118]

The idea that the Stasi had increasingly become a substitute for a failing political system was raised in several of the interviews for this chapter. Stasi personnel were angered by the party's failure to address deficiencies in the medical sector, things such as inadequate supplies or faulty equipment, or the exodus of East Germans, issues that could not be resolved by an increased number of informants. In the end, perhaps the party's greatest error was to believe that political problems could be solved with police methods.

The interviews also challenge the standard interpretation of informants as a barometer of regime support, in particular the notion that the Third Reich was more "popular" than East Germany: many Germans spontaneously denounced to the Gestapo whereas the Stasi needed to groom an army of semi-professional informants. Just as Eric Johnson's works have helped to show that this approach does not address the complexity of Gestapo-society relations,[119] so too is a redress of the significance of informants in East Germany necessary. Stasi officers confirmed a finding that the Stasi was more reactive than originally thought, due in part to the number of "irregular collaborators" and "casual employees" or contact persons (*Kontaktpersonen*) (see chap. 4) who provided information to the Stasi in a manner not dissimilar to that of Third Reich denouncers. The fact that Stasi officers found it increasingly difficult to recruit informants toward the end of the regime also helps revise the idea that East Germany's unpopularity was evidenced in the need for many informants. At different times in East Germany's history it *was* easier to recruit informants because of a certain support of the regime. By the latter half of the 1980s, however, it seemed that no amount of appeal to serve the "better Germany" could win over a potential informant.

For such a large organization, one might expect that the personnel would represent a cross-section of East German society or, at a minimum, many different personality types. The Stasi personnel who agreed to be interviewed were, however, remarkably similar. In general, they were subdued, considerate, matter-of-fact (perhaps even humorless) individuals; none of them bristled at any questions nor were they testy. Only Frau Müller, the district leader's secretary, could be said to be animated. None of them became agitated in the course of the interview, nor did they look particularly uncomfortable. Apart from Herr Kuhlow, who expressed profound remorse, these were individuals who had a clear conscience.[120] That their work might have been in some fashion morally reprehensible seems not to have occurred to them, echoing the sentiments of a former leader of the Stasi office in District Treptow in East Berlin who claimed that the use of informants was for him never a moral question, but simply a question of national security.[121]

With an open admission that I have come to know these individuals, making it harder to be objective, it is difficult to know how to categorize full-time Stasi workers. The term "perpetrator" seems far too harsh and, given its association with the Nazi era, inappropriate.[122] These Stasi workers are a blend of bureaucrat and front-line case officer, often spending countless hours in the office pouring over paper work, directives, and reports, but also working outside the precinct engaging in surveillance, meeting informants, and psychologically harassing opponents into submission. They are certainly not the "desk murderers" of Raul Hilberg's infamy, nor are they harmless paper tigers. They occupy some middle ground of an individual who had the ability to control the life opportunities of their fellow citizens, often in heavy-handed ways, but whose conduct was in no way reminiscent of the "ordinary" men who made up the infamous Police Battalion 101. The term that the Federal Commission for the Stasi Files uses to describe those who worked for the Stasi, both full-time and as informants, is *Begünstigste*, or "those advantaged by their association with the Stasi," a passive term that insufficiently captures the fact that they acted upon other people. Given that the same commission uses the term *Betroffene*—"the affected ones," to describe Stasi victims, it might be more appropriate to consider Stasi officers not as "perpetrators" or "advantaged ones" but rather as "affectors of lives."

With the exception of Klaus-Peter Schmid, the committed ideologue who berated the newer generation of Stasi officer for their lack of commitment to the cause of communism, none of the Stasi officers interviewed were chest-thumping patriots or bloody-minded. Even those who were critical of certain aspects of its work chose to focus instead on the "good" that the Stasi did, like catching foreign spies, protecting the economy, or hunting down former Nazis. These are not blind ideologues who adopted a mantra of "my Stasi, right or wrong"; they are the furthest thing from fanatical. They generally supported the cause of socialism, albeit without the revolutionary fervor of the war generation—which was true in other branches of the state apparatus[123] and in other East European states. Even in the Soviet Union, home of the Communist revolution, the typical functionary in the postwar period was "no longer the Communist believer and enthusiast of the 1930s, but the careerist who might not believe in the Party or its goals but carried out its orders nonetheless."[124] There was a sadness to many of the interviewees, bordering on shock that their ideology, which had been taught to them as scientifically, demonstrably better than capitalism, as favored by history, as not simply a truth but *the* truth, had been swept away in the blink of an eye. Before saying anything about his time with "the Firm" Officer Tenbrock set the stage with his lament: "I'd like to say at the outset that you cannot dedicate your life to something and then suddenly turn on it." Another Stasi officer phrased it this way: "The thought that it was all for naught is almost too much to bear."[125]

After 1989, the younger Stasi officers adapted to the new Germany to varying degrees whereas the older ones seem to have withdrawn somewhat. That sense of belonging, both to a collective and to a historical moment, has vanished, leaving the Stasi personnel to conduct their lives almost exclusively in their family circles. This was made clear to me when one Stasi officer drove me to the train station and on the way we passed Herr Kuhlow, the Stasi-turned-physiotherapist and a long-time colleague, riding his bicycle. My driver did not acknowledge him in any way, except to turn to me and say: "He was one of ours. But we don't talk anymore."

# 3

# THE CANDIDATE
## Stasi Informants

WITH THE SWEEPING REVOLUTIONS OF 1989 that toppled, almost in an instant, the dictatorships of East-central Europe, it appeared as though the files of seven secret police organizations would be opened, a prospect as important to regime victims as it was enticing to scholars in both the West and the East. Apart from the opportunity to investigate the sensational, including the involvement of the Bulgarian secret police in the attempted assassination of Pope John Paul II, Stasi support of the PLO, or the use of X-rays by the Romanian Securitate (secret police) to sterilize regime opponents, file access would allow for a historical understanding of Eastern Europe's most important instrument for societal control. But the lofty expectations for file access were, for the most part, dashed. As neo-Communists came back to power in several countries, and as ordinary citizens increasingly worried about their past appearing on the evening news, access to the files in many cases shrank, or was never granted in the first place.[1] Some members of parliament argued that the fragile new democracies needed time to develop before they could undertake a reckoning with the past.

At the heart of the discussion around file access was really only one issue: the role of informants. It was by no means clear to any decision maker that there was merit in revealing the hundreds of thousands of betrayals contained in the labyrinthine archives. Because of the potential for the documents to rupture families and friendships, some in East Germany, including the influential minister of the interior, Peter-Michael Diestel, and even members of the Citizens' Movement involved in the round-table talks, argued for a complete destruction of the documents. Others who shared this opinion feared worse: reprisal murder. East Germans involved in the Citizens' Movement who stormed the secret police buildings in December 1989 and January 1990 were determined, however, that the files would be opened, no matter how painful. The first freely elected members of the East German parliament, some of whom had themselves been in the Citizens' Movement, agreed, and granted almost complete file access.[2]

This turns out to have been a wise decision indeed. The files have, to be sure, caused friendships to end and families to be ruined, but in general the files have proven that the family remained a sanctuary against an invasive state presence. No one has been murdered or physically harmed as a result of the files, not even in the southern industrial city of Halle, where the list of informants was published for all to see—an illegal act.[3] As a result of daring decisions by both the East German and subsequently all-German parliament, East Germany's secret police files are the most open secret police files in history, and with more than five million applications to view the files already (the overwhelming majority by private East Germans, rather than academics, inquiring about their past), there is good evidence that file access was broadly desired.[4] How long this state of affairs will continue remains to be seen. Debate rages in Germany today between politicians who want the files transferred into the federal archive system, and those who wish to maintain the Stasi files' special status.[5]

Once recruited, informants gave themselves cover names like those of students anonymously entering chat rooms—Cherry, Max, Ram, Angel, Machine, Artist, Sugar. Several of these cover names are part of the German landscape: "Notar," the alleged cover name of Gregor Gysi who led the revamped Communist Party after 1989 and is still the German Left's great hope; "Sekretär," the cover name of Manfred Stolpe who, despite his Stasi association, went on to become premier of Brandenburg and a minister in the federal government, and "Margarete," the alias of the renowned East German author Christa Wolf.[6] Although the cover name has a certain James Bond flair to it, the Stasi was eager to dissuade informants from the notion that a cover name was a necessity because of the Stasi's various engagements in underhanded activities. Rather, Stasi officers encouraged their informants to think of cover names in terms of a "working name" or "pseudonym."[7]

Given their prominence in the debate around file access, their staggering numbers (there were nearly twice as many informants as regular Stasi workers), and their prominent role in societal monitoring, it seems wise to consider how the Stasi found and worked with informants. Let us return to our quiet districts in East Germany where the Stasi agents were active, as they were throughout the country, in seeking out, recruiting and running ordinary Germans to monitor society. In the vetting and recruitment process, the Stasi always referred to a potential informant as "the candidate."

## THE NUMBER OF INFORMANTS

If there were documents from Gransee and Perleberg that contained information on the number of informants the Stasi employed in any given year, they have fallen prey to the file destruction that took place in the fall of 1989. A few significant documents on this question have survived, including end-of-year reports on the informants in District Perleberg for 1984, 1985, 1987, and 1988, along with some telling documents from Gransee. It is not possible, however, to trace the size of the informant net in these districts from inception to end.

It is important to distinguish the different categories of informants. Although the media commonly employ the generic "IM" to signify a Stasi informant, there were in the 1980s six types of Stasi informant, each with concrete roles and responsibilities. At first blush the various acronyms can be confusing (IMS, FIM, IME, GMS, IMB, IMK), but the roles of each can be categorized fairly neatly.[8] The first five types of informant were individuals who monitored society in some fashion, whereas the last category (IMK) represented an individual who provided his house keys to the Stasi so that a case officer could meet his informant away from the informant's work or home, in return for a token monetary sum or perhaps a coal delivery. The owner of the premises was not permitted to be in the house when the meeting took place. These conspiratorial dwellings were vital to the Stasi given the inherent difficulties in meeting with informants at the local Stasi branch, at the informant's workplace or, as sometimes occurred as a last resort, in parks or cemeteries. In an interview, Rolf Schwegel recalled with a certain fondness how he frequently rode his motorcycle out to secluded parkland for what he termed "field and forest" meetings with his informants.[9]

The number of conspiratorial meeting places was astonishing. The Potsdam branch of the Stasi archive had a map of the city of Potsdam on one wall, but it is almost impossible to make out the city beneath the forest of push pins that indicate a conspiratorial dwelling. The Stasi took the identification and acquisition of conspiratorial meeting places very seriously. Prior to approaching a candidate, the Stasi drew detailed maps of the area around the dwelling, more often than not had obtained a basic layout of the apartment, knew roughly where the furniture was located, how many entrances it had, and the backgrounds of everyone else who lived in the building.[10] The IMK was a passive informant who did not report on others, yet without these types of informants the entire system would have been difficult to run. It might be helpful to separate out the IMK from the other informants in order to distinguish between "passive" and "active" informants, as some historians do,[11] and indeed the Stasi itself tended to do so in order to determine the number of informants available for monitoring, but for the purposes of understanding the level of societal involvement with the Stasi, the IMK must be taken into account. A final point about the categories of informants is worth mentioning: they were fluid. A regular informant could be "downgraded" to an IMK or other category, and vice versa.

In the last few years of the regime, the total number of informants in District Perleberg hovered around six hundred. By the time of the Stasi's collapse, there was in District Perleberg roughly one informant for every seventy-six people between the ages of eighteen and sixty-five.[12] Stasi documents, it should be remembered, reveal the number of informants at any given time, not the aggregate number who had ever worked for the Stasi. If one desired an indication of societal involvement in the Stasi, a useful ratio might be that of current and *former* informants to population, which would certainly be more than one informant for every seventy-six pre-retirement adults.

The number of Stasi officers who ran informants in District Perleberg decreased slightly over these years, from twenty-three in 1984 to eighteen in 1988. Considering that the number of informants remained steady, the constant refrain from officers that their workload increased over time rings true.

Another interesting statistic, since it reveals much about the Stasi thought process, is the number of meetings that took place between Stasi case officers and their informants. That the Stasi even recorded this number reveals the Stasi obsession with frequency of meetings. There were roughly seven meetings between informants and their case officers taking place on any given day in the late 1980s. Out of these meetings came a striking level of paperwork. In almost every year of the late 1980s, informants generated more than five thousand reports on the district.[13]

On a document from 1985, the leader of District Perleberg, Herbert Tilse, scribbled a note in the margin that provides historians with excellent insight into the nature of Stasi work. The document was a statistical report from the first three months of 1985 on the frequency of meetings with informants. Tilse circled all of the cases where officers were meeting less frequently than in 1984, and wrote: "After careful examination of informant work in our district, I have determined that our goal of every informant-running officer working with ten capable informants has not been reached. The officers do not apply themselves sufficiently, and are not forced to do so by their department heads."[14] This document contains twenty tabs, one for each officer that ran informants, with pull-out spread sheets of when they met with informants, and to what end the informant's information was put (overwhelmingly just societal observation, and much less related to a specific operation).

For the Stasi, it was a numbers game—the size of the informant roster, the frequency of meetings, the number of reports. It is no wonder that Stasi officers felt enormous pressure to hold meeting after meeting with informants and to increase the number of informants, rather than to focus on the *quality* of reporting. Senior Stasi officials at the district level believed that the sheer size of the informant net combined with exhaustive meetings would secure the area. Several Stasi officers in the districts stated in no uncertain terms how this relentless push to acquire more informants caused them to despise their superiors. Matthias Piekert, for example, referred to a "sick" obsession with informants and complained bitterly about informants recruited for no other reason than to boost the roster. This practice, he thought, was the Stasi's lethal weakness.[15]

In the regime's final decade, District Perleberg revealed itself typical of the overall Stasi in the informant areas of gender and the use of minors. In 1988, of twenty-five informants recruited, three were women, and two were under the age of eighteen. For 1987, there were twenty recruits (no women, one under eighteen), 1985—twenty-four recruits (four women, one under eighteen), and 1984—twenty-two recruits (three women, two under eighteen).[16] District

Perleberg's informant net was approximately 85 to 90 percent male and comprised between 5 and 10 percent minors.[17]

District Gransee residents were subject to a greater informant presence than were District Perleberg residents, a surprising finding given its small size and its general incompetence. In 1988, there was roughly one Stasi informant for every sixty-six people between the ages of eighteen and sixty-five in District Gransee.[18] This is an astonishing level of surveillance, and one unmatched in Eastern Europe.[19] (For instance, a university the size of Harvard with roughly 20,000 students hypothetically placed in District Perleberg could expect to have 263 informants on campus, certainly at least one in every large lecture class. If it were in District Gransee, there would be 303 informants.)

Whereas District Perleberg witnessed a slight increase in the number of informants, the trend in District Gransee was downward. This might be explained in a number of ways. First, the trend in the overall number of informants in the GDR was slightly down (from 111,000 in 1983 to 108,000 in 1989, IMK excluded), a result in part of instructions issued in 1979 to improve the quality of the informant net.[20] In the region of Potsdam, in which Gransee was situated, the overall informant complement dropped by nearly 11 percent. With reference to Gransee in particular, there is also a good possibility that the drop in informants was due to the by then well-known inefficiency of this branch. The District Gransee office had the fewest informants of any of the fifteen districts in the region of Potsdam, even compared to districts of a similar size like Belzig, Kyritz, Pritzwalk, and Wittstock,[21] and was below the regional average in almost every other "operational" category.[22]

A final possible explanation for the decline in the number of informants in District Gransee is the most interesting of all: an increasing number of East Germans were refusing to become informants, or were ending their association with the Stasi. Several Stasi officers mentioned that they found it more difficult to recruit informants in the final years of the regime than in earlier ones. As one made clear: "I used to be able to say to a candidate: 'You'll be supporting the German Democratic Republic.' Towards the end, that just didn't wash anymore."[23] One study has suggested that one in ten East Germans in the region of Potsdam who were approached for Stasi work declined. Some made clear their refusal on grounds that they did not support the state, others because of health or family issues, which could have been convenient excuses.[24] What remains unclear is why this would have been more prevalent in Gransee than in Perleberg where the informant roster remained fairly stable.

## STASI CONDUCT WITH ITS INFORMANTS

In its nearly forty-year history, the Stasi laid down five directives regarding informants, and none in its last twenty years. Although the directives illustrate a progressive desire for a more refined approach to recruiting and running informants, they do not diverge from the central tenet of informant work: the informant was the most important weapon in the regime's fight against "the enemy."[25] The initial two sets of guidelines reveal a secret police organization both still somewhat raw, as illustrated in its crude approach to recruitment whereby coercion bordering on blackmail was accepted and even promoted, yet already mature beyond its years. The 1950 directive, which appeared only seven months after the establishment of the secret police, contained information on the screening, recruitment, and running of informants, and already there was a classification of informants into "secret co-workers," defined as those who had contact with enemies; "informants," defined as those who were in a position to provide general information, such as waiters, inn owners, and insurance agents; and "individuals who maintained conspiratorial dwellings."[26] Although these categories would be refined over the years, the broad parameters for types of informants was set in 1950. Given the level of detail contained in this first directive, there can be little doubt that KGB advisors had a hand in its authorship.[27]

In Perleberg, the Stasi began its search for what were initially called "V-Men" (*V-Männer*) or "Trusted-Men," even before the Stasi was officially founded. Karl Ehmann, a Communist who had served time during the Nazi era in three notorious prisons (including Berlin's Columbiahaus) because of his political affiliations, would prove to be one of the very first informants recruited in the district. The bald, divorced, fifty-year-old former salesman who was on the verge of marrying a woman fifteen years his junior came to Perleberg—in part because of his divorce and because of the opportunity to work at the tractor-lending station of an agricultural collective. As early as this recruitment, which spanned the six months from December 1949, the Stasi had a strategy for vetting that would be a characteristic of Stasi work henceforth—the use of official sources in determining whether the candidate would be a suitable informant.[28] The Stasi was interested in particular in the individual's personality, relationships, and workplace conduct.[29] Debauchery, adultery, tendencies to alcohol—these were all vices that the Stasi wanted to know about its potential informants. It is one of the great ironies of Stasi history that the Stasi sought information on whether the candidate was clean, morally upright, and respectable, so that they could be put to work finding out intimate details on their neighbors.[30]

In this case, a member of the local branch of the Communist Party knew the candidate (a fellow party member) and offered the Stasi an assessment of him.[31] Shortly thereafter, Karl Ehmann did what was required of secret informants, an act that has been so damning for those who in the past twenty years have tried to deny working for the Stasi: He handwrote (these are seldom typed) his declaration of willingness to work for the Stasi, he signed and dated it, and he chose a cover name that he would use in his dealings with the Stasi. Karl Ehmann became informant "Bird." Only in rare cases, including that of Gregor Gysi, were informants permitted to forego the written commitment to cooperate with the Stasi. Ehmann's commitment was as follows:

> I declare myself prepared to fulfill to the best of my knowledge and con-science, the duties given to me by representatives of the Ministry for State Security, as, being a Communist Party member, I recognize the political necessity of this work. Since I recognize this importance, I also feel obliged not to mention this matter to anyone, not even to family members. If I do not abide by this, I am aware that I can be brought to justice.[32]

Bird proved a mediocre informant. He was eminently suspicious of a book-keeper at the tractor-lending station because he had daily telephone conversa-tions with a female, who, the informant admitted, was likely the man's wife. After Bird was fired from the tractor-lending station because he used company letterhead to try to obtain six light bulbs for his apartment, he found employ-ment at the decrepit rayon factory in Wittenberge. Over the next four years, Bird authored more than one hundred reports on the factory and on the nearby Viskose Basement Pub. In 1954, with Bird now employed at a community col-lege in Wittenberge, the Stasi ended its association with the informant because he simply did not have enough insight to provide useful information. In Stasi jargon, it was said that he "lacked perspective."[33]

The case of Bird provides insight into the nature of the Stasi. Bird was origi-nally recruited because he worked at a sensitive site—a machine-lending station that housed agricultural equipment vital in the building of the new Communist state in the countryside. Bird soon left there, however, and moved on to a fac-tory and community college. Considering that he no longer fulfilled the original reason for his recruitment, the Stasi might well have broken off contact when he left the machine-lending station, but it chose not to do this until years later. Targeted recruitment had given way to blanket surveillance.

A tip by an official at the river port in Wittenberge initiated the recruitment of Kurt Wollschläger, a candidate of interest to the Stasi because several co-workers with whom he was acquainted were critical of the regime, and because he was separated from his wife, an advantageous situation, the Stasi claimed, since he would be in a position to frequent bars in the evening. The Stasi sought evalu-ations of his personality from a party official at the port, who provided a forth-right assessment that he was collegial but clumsy and slow-witted, so much so that he had to be demoted to secretary. The case officer sought other opinions too; his current landlady said he was quiet and polite, but a previous employer had little recollection of the candidate. Despite the candidate's membership in the Nazi party from 1942 to 1945, and despite the fact that he was judged of mediocre intellect, the Stasi decided to recruit him because of the need to deal with suspected grumbling at the Wittenberge river port.[34] The recruitment was initially to take place at the housing office of the district council, where the can-didate would be engaged in a discussion of the severity of the housing situation in the West. If he responded positively to the officer's comments, the officer would reveal his Stasi association and attempt to recruit the candidate.

But between the formulation of this plan and the actual meeting, the candidate changed jobs, becoming a schoolteacher. The Stasi responded accordingly, abandoning the initial "housing" approach to recruiting him and instead bringing the conversation to the manner in which West Germany was "abusing" East German youth, although the exact form of this abuse was not stated. At the recruitment, the candidate did not respond as hoped. He appeared sympathetic to the case officer's pronouncements, but when the officer revealed his Stasi association, the candidate balked. When the candidate asked the Stasi officer why he had singled him out specifically for recruitment, the officer answered that the Stasi were interested in "only the best."[35] Flattered, the candidate joined the Stasi, choosing the less-than-threatening cover name "Snuggles."

The moment of recruitment was a poignant one that required preparation, an appropriate setting, a cover story, and, perhaps most importantly, a reading of how the candidate was responding to the tenor of the meeting. It was to be, as an early directive phrased it, a work of art.[36] In describing the all-important recruitment meeting, Matthias Piekert explained how he kept several cards up his sleeve to be played depending how the meeting unfolded. Most candidates agreed to become informants on the initial request. If they wavered, however, Piekert would remind them in blunt terms of some infraction, however minor, from their past. Very rarely did candidates then have the courage to refuse.[37]

Another of the initial wave of recruitments from District Perleberg demonstrates how Stasi officers had several strategies at the ready to seal the recruitment. Officer Stein was to pose as a member of the local government council's agricultural branch and invite the candidate in to discuss his work. The plan was to begin the conversation with a discussion of the importance of farmers with large land holdings (of which the candidate was one) since they were responsible for feeding the population. Stein was then to bring the conversation around to the fact that there were people in East Germany who wanted to bring down the regime by secretly introducing diseases into the livestock. Stein hoped that this ruse would be sufficient to convince the candidate to work for the Stasi, but if not Stein would turn to coercion. The candidate's wife had been caught with pamphlets from a West Berlin-based anti-Communist group, the Fighting Group Against Inhumanity (KgU), and she would be brought to trial if he did not agree to collaborate.[38] Stein did not have to resort to coercion since the candidate freely agreed to work for the Stasi. The new informant, "Angel," might well have thought that spying on behalf of the Stasi was not as glamorous as he had hoped—part of his duties entailed reporting on the supply of manure in the district.

As early as 1953, the Stasi leadership was concerned that a failure to identify suitable candidates coupled with a reliance on heavy-handed methods of recruitment was leading to an informant net of those who "spoke out of both sides of their mouth," and of "provocateurs."[39] The fact of nearly one million East Germans taking to the streets in more than seven hundred cities and towns in June 1953 could, of course, hardly have inspired confidence in the informant net.[40] In an effort to bolster surveillance, Secretary of State Security Ernst Wollweber undertook something unheard of for the head of a secret police in late Stalinism: he crisscrossed the country on a public speaking tour to drum up support for the Stasi. In January 1954 he spoke at a Berlin brake factory; in February at a steel sheet plant in Berlin-Adlershof and the Weimar administration school; in April at a factory rally in Ludwigsfelde; in August at the factories H. F. Werk Köpenick and Leuna Werk Walter Ulbricht; in September in the House of German-Soviet Friendship in Köpenick; and in December in Mansfeld.[41]

The result of this and similar recruitment efforts was an informant net that doubled in size between 1953 and 1955 and even led to internal concerns that at this pace "every second East German citizen" would soon be or have been an informant.[42] Such an undertaking certainly brought with it excesses. In the revised guidelines of 1958, Erich Mielke, the minister of state security, makes clear that Stasi officers were to focus on recruiting candidates through conviction rather than coercion, claiming that the latter had often led to failures that "damaged" the Stasi.[43] The case of a Wittenberge informant who was blackmailed into informant work on account of his SS past but proved a poor informant was evidently not a lone case.[44] Overall, the handling of informants was to be professionalized. In previous directives, meetings with informants were to be held "preferably" in specially designated informants' dwellings; the frequency was now changed to "normally." The security of sites within the GDR became paramount rather than penetration of the many anti-Communist groups operating against the GDR from West Germany. Informants were to be developed not only through surveillance tactics but politically, to the point that "he would even be prepared to give his life for the cause."[45]

Following the collapse of the regime, Stasi officials still thought of informants in these terms, calling them "unofficial co-workers" in the true sense of the words and "political co-fighters."[46] Former Stasi officers are still fiercely protective of their informants. One said to me at the beginning of our interview, without knowing precisely what aspect of Stasi work I would be asking about: "Under no circumstances will I reveal the names of my informants." It seemed important to him that I understand that he still talked to his former informants. They were not his friends, he clarified, but they still greet each other on the street, even the ones whom he pressured into informing.[47]

A new category, the Secret Lead Informant (*Geheimer Hauptinformator*—GHI), an informant who ran other informants, first introduced in 1953, was expanded and codified in the new directive, perhaps as a result of difficulties in grooming these special informants. The remarkable case of Paul Wittkowski was one of the earliest of this new type of informant. During the war, Wittkowski, a Jew, worked in Wittenberge until he was drafted into the Wehrmacht by some bureaucratic slipup. After the war, as a factory worker at Wittenberge's margarine plant, he was recruited as informant "Ram" and was, by all accounts, an excellent informant. He reported promptly for meetings with his case officer. He delivered exhaustive reports on his work colleagues: One worker appeared at the plant wearing Western-style shoes, another was drunk. In town, a woman had supper in a restaurant with a man who was not her husband.[48] In six years, Ram delivered more than one hundred reports. These were, of course, not without repercussions for the targets. In a few cases, based solely on Ram's reports, the Stasi recommended to party officials in the factory that certain workers be dismissed.[49] His performance netted him the occasional cash bonus, sometimes DM 10 for a particularly good report, other times DM 40 for a sustained period of good work.[50]

Two years following his recruitment, Ram's case officer recommended that he be promoted to senior informant and put in charge of five other informants. This was the beginning of the end of his time with the Stasi. Overwhelmed by the work involved in administering his charges, Ram became sluggish, rarely meeting with the informants under him. Despite prodding from his superiors, Ram proved incapable of handling his increased responsibility, leading to his eventual dismissal by the Stasi.[51]

Partly as a result of the Grand Coalition in West Germany and increased ties between East and West Germany, the Stasi undertook another expansion of the informant net in the late 1960s. The guidelines of 1968 were to assist during the transition. Stasi officers were instructed to be selective in their choice of candidate and to widen the scope beyond the "easy" targets of party members, something that was difficult to implement. By 1979 District Gransee was still reporting that 31 percent of its informants were in the party although their party association, which would have been known to the public, made them ill-suited to uncover popular sentiment.[52] In an effort to bind the informant more closely to the Stasi and to deepen the apprenticeship, informant reports were to be written rather than oral, and a new category of informant was introduced, the Societal Co-Worker for Security (*Gesellschaftlicher Mitarbeiter für Sicherheit*—GMS), an informant who reported on society in general, rather than working a specific case. It was hoped that these duties could then be shifted away from the overburdened regular informants.

A few years after Guideline 1/68 had been put in place the Stasi began updating it. In 1979, after five or so years of revision, the Stasi released new, and what would turn out to be the last, guidelines for running informants. Again, the informant net was to be updated, modernized, and improved. Erich Mielke reiterated that coercion was the least desirable manner to obtain an informant and emphasized a pressing need for an improvement in the quality of information received from informants.[53] Reflecting this emphasis, the leader of district Gransee called on his subordinates to improve their work with informants, in particular "increasing the amount of relevant information."[54] Other aspects in the latest guidelines aimed to refine the informant net. Spot checks and using informants to monitor other informants were to ensure greater accuracy.[55] Meetings with informants were to take place only in the homes of other informants. Unlike the guidelines of the 1950s, which provided simple examples and real-life incidents as illustrations of what not to do, the 1979 guidelines are written in a sophisticated manner, reflecting the higher educational qualifications of the officer corps and the generally matured work of the Stasi.

In keeping with the new guidelines, informant recruitment became more systematic and methodical. Recruiting an informant after a chance encounter in the street, as had happened in Wittenberge in 1952,[56] was much less likely in the later years of the Stasi. So too were instances like the officer who, to save time, attempted to recruit three informants at one meeting, already undermining the basic tenet that no one else was to know the informant's identity.[57] At the end of every year, the leader in the district developed a plan for the following year and outlined the number of informants to be recruited in any given area—such as church, economy, or youth. As a 1976 proposal for recruitment stated: "According to the yearly work plan, an informant is to be recruited from within the circle of mid-level medical professions at the medical clinic in Wittenberge."[58]

This is not to say that a detailed outline of where informants were to be recruited always translated into an orderly recruitment. An exasperated Erich Mielke complained: "You can't just recruit any old unofficial employee and check later what role he can fulfill."[59] In the earlier period, recruitment frequently occurred on the first meeting with the candidate, whereas the last decades reveal a Stasi that met with candidates on several occasions before the actual recruitment offer was made.[60] Handwritten commitments were more explicit and demonstrated the territorial nature of the Stasi, as in the case of a minor recruited by the Perleberg Stasi: "I [name blacked out because the individual is a minor] dedicate myself voluntarily to work with the Ministry for State Security. I will dedicate my entire strength toward the security of the GDR. I am aware that I am not permitted to discuss my work here with any other third person, nor with other state instruments like the People's Police or Justice. I will inform the MfS of all occurrences among young people."[61] In its last year, the Gransee Stasi was at work developing a new and complex system of information gathering for its top informants.[62]

The system of informants running other informants was also much developed by the later years. After eight years as an informant, Rudi Gerth of Perleberg was promoted and placed in charge of eighteen to twenty informants—a shockingly large number and considerably more than the five or six informants per lead informant foreseen in the 1953 guidelines.[63] Informant "Reini" was charged with securing the southern half of District Gransee, including all factories, agriculture, youth, and Soviet military installations, and for his outstanding contributions to the GDR, he was awarded the bronze "For Loyal Service" medal on the twenty-third anniversary of the founding of the GDR, and the same award, but this time in silver, six years later.[64] Reini dedicated his life to the Stasi, even continuing to work for it after a heart operation and doctors' explicit orders to stop work. When he finally entered a center for lung disease on a long-term basis, the Stasi reluctantly ended its association with him. Due to his immense commitment to the Stasi over the years, the Stasi paid him a disability pension.[65]

The Reini case also provides insight into the Stasi's place of importance within the GDR. The Stasi requested that a local factory in Potsdam pay Reini's salary after the Stasi had inserted him into the plant. The salary of seven hundred Ostmarks a month proved burdensome to the plant, which requested that the Stasi absorb the expenses of its informant. Since the sum was also too steep for the District Perleberg Stasi office, the regional office paid for the informant's salary. Nevertheless, it is significant that even for a few months the Stasi was able to have a factory pay for an informant's presence.[66]

Somewhat surprisingly, none of the guidelines on informants deal with a "lower" category of individual who collaborated with the Stasi, known as a "contact person," a type of casual employee, usually someone able to offer information to the Stasi by virtue of their job, like a school principal or factory boss. The primary differences between a contact person and an informant were that a contact person was not given major cases to work, nor did that person sign a commitment, nor did they receive the occasional monetary bonuses paid to regular informants. These individuals were nevertheless crucial for Stasi work. One of those interviewed praised his contact persons as much more reliable and useful than his informants.[67]

In sum, the Stasi refined its work with informants over the years. In the last decade of the secret police, informants were sent off to Stasi colleges for instruction on informant-running, on party directives, and on the global march toward Communism.[68] They were put in charge of dozens of other informants, were recruited in elaborate operations that frequently took months, even years, and were classified along a spectrum of six categories (as opposed to the initial three categories). Not to be forgotten is the enormous increase in the number of informants that accompanied these changes. From approximately 15,000 informants in 1951,[69] the Stasi grew to 173,000 by the time the Berlin Wall fell.

## BLANKET SURVEILLANCE?

Former Stasi officers have suggested that claims of blanket surveillance in East Germany have little basis in reality but are rooted instead in the politics of the day. Leaving little room for misinterpretation, one group of leading Stasi officials has written: "Our priority targets were by no means imprecise or elastic, and therefore did not lead the Stasi to use its instruments in a blanket fashion— as is frequently [...] put forward by those with a political agenda."[70] Historians have also highlighted the Stasi's "targeted" surveillance of certain sites (such as important factories) or specific groups (the church),[71] and have generally discarded the term "blanket surveillance" because of its suggestion of a complete and seamless surveillance that never really existed in practice. There can be little doubt that members of a church group were more likely to be under surveillance than those not involved, but we must not lose sight of the fact that the Stasi engaged in widespread general surveillance, nor that the untidy implementation of "targeted" surveillance invariably led to broader monitoring.

Many of the informants recruited in these districts had no targeted task other than reporting on ordinary East Germans. The Perleberg Stasi, for example, identified Wittenberge's Restaurant Koym as a site for the placement of an informant. Unlike the factories in the district or the machine-lending stations that were important sites for the economic development of East Germany, Restaurant Koym was simply a social gathering place. Margarete Ratzlaff, a thirty-two-year-old secretary in the Glowen police office, was recruited as an informant when she proved willing to talk to (unbeknownst to her at the time) a Stasi officer on the street about the restaurants' patrons. Although she was originally recruited to monitor the restaurant and the police station where she worked, she did neither because she found work as a typist at the sewing machine factory in Wittenberge. Although her reports on work colleagues contained scathing personal information, the Stasi let her go when it discovered her relationship with a married man.[72]

In the 1960s, the Stasi in District Gransee recruited a man on a disability pension (someone with "much free time," as the Stasi phrased it) to report on conversations on the streets and in bars. His disability was a result of nerve damage he suffered at Auschwitz, where his parents were murdered because they were Sinti (gypsy).[73] Since he was a member of both the local fishing society and the volunteer fire department and repaired small items like umbrellas and musical instruments, he had a variety of societal contacts.[74] Informant "Peter" reported on conversations he overheard in two local restaurants that he frequented, The Lindendorf, and The City of Gransee: A woman complained that the government had promised the citizens of East Germany that it would build houses; instead it built a wall;[75] one person showed around the restaurant photos of his trip to West Germany; a retired man complained that his car was requisitioned in 1945 and never returned to him; someone else bragged that they had a television that could pick up West German channels.[76] On the church square, a person stood in front of a poster of East German leader Walter Ulbricht, clicked his heels together, and gave the Hitler salute.[77] He overheard someone on the street tell a joke: "Olympic Silver Medal winner Gaby Seifert was in Ulbricht's office. For her fine performance at the Olympics, Ulbricht granted Seifert one wish. 'I wish that you would tear down the Wall,' Seifert replied. Ulbricht answered: 'I'm very sorry my child, but I can't do that. We'd be the only two left here.' "[78]

Informant Peter asked his own daughter to obtain information on youth in town who might be hostile to the regime, something that the Stasi had encouraged him to do.[79] Finally, at the age of seventy-two, and having provided details on hundreds of random individuals for more than twenty-three years, Peter was retired from Stasi work.[80]

Whereas many younger informants were, by and large, unmotivated and simply did not report, informant "Emil" was zealous. He reported when groups of teens gathered on the market square in town. He reported television antennas on houses that were pointing to West Germany. He reported all occurrences at the local movie theater where he worked, including when rowdy teens whistled and yelled, and when two young people with long hair who he had not seen before attended the 5 p.m. showing. In another instance, he sheepishly apologized to the Stasi that he had accidentally cut out the wrong part of a movie as he had been instructed to do. He was supposed to cut out a scene where a wreath is laid down in honor of those who died in the 1968 "Prague Spring," but instead he accidentally cut a scene where a wreath is laid at the World Games in Sofia. "Fortunately," he wrote, "only thirty people were there for the showing."[81]

Emil also duly reported a calculator game making the rounds. The game went as follows: On a calculator, multiply 1976 by nine, because the ninth Party Congress of the SED took place in 1976. Multiply this number by 1980, the year of the next Party Congress. Add to this number the telephone number of East German leader Erich Honecker, 30 11 55, and then turn over the calculator for the answer: SCHEISSE [shit]! (35513475)[82] Emil's case officer brought this game to the attention of Lieutenant Gaeth with a request for him to investigate the matter further.

By far the most fascinating of Emil's reports related to an incident that took place in 1977, when a freak accident might have caused the world to come within a hair of nuclear war. During a thunderstorm, a bolt of lightning struck the Soviet army base in District Gransee and caused two rockets to launch—Blitzkrieg in a literal sense. Fortunately, the rockets were heading east, as a westward direction would no doubt have provoked instant retaliation. People in the district heard of what had happened and began outrageous rumors that hundreds were killed.[83]

None of the information reviewed in these cases could be classified as "targeted" surveillance, nor can market squares, movie houses, and restaurants be considered "priority areas" in any reasonable sense. The fact that Erich Mielke issued guidelines in 1979 calling for the acquisition of more "relevant" information suggests that this widespread monitoring had become common practice, yet there is every indication that the Stasi continued to engage in broad surveillance. In a 1985 review of several districts in the region of Potsdam, including District Gransee, the officers conducting the review wrote that there was "insufficient use of informants while at home and in their free time, of their contacts and associations."[84]

Over the years, an obsession with the acquisition of informants set in, leading the Stasi on many occasions to take on people of limited ability, in frail health, criminals, and even those who had once proved incapable of informant work.

One informant who monitored an agricultural collective in District Gransee was incompetent and generally not up to the task of informing, yet the Stasi refused to drop him from the roster. After he had been with the Stasi four years, his case officer wrote: "His intellect is weak. The same can be said of his general understanding of things. Nevertheless, he can, with appropriate guidance, become a good unofficial co-worker."[85] In the next five years, the informant had no contact with the Stasi. Still, the Stasi refused to give up on him, using a phrase almost identical to that of five years earlier: "Although the informant has limited abilities, he can still be developed."[86] Finally, in 1971, after fifteen years of sub-par informant work, the Stasi demoted him to the lowest level of informant, a GMS, but still did not terminate its relationship with him.[87]

In another case, informant "Magnolia" stayed on the active roster of informants after he had had a heart attack.[88] And another, a former French legionnaire who served time in prison because he had been beaten up by the husband of a woman he was seeing became an informant but was released when he blew his cover. A few years later, the Stasi took him on again.[89] In one recruitment, an informant already working for the Stasi said in his evaluation of an informant candidate that he was not suitable because he was an alcoholic who had already been fired from several jobs, but the case officer mentioned none of this when justifying to his superiors the need for the informant.[90]

Informant Snuggles was another example of maintaining an informant, no matter how weak. Snuggles's case officer recorded a litany of complaints about him. He was meek, he had no opinions of his own, he was lazy. He made excuses for the lack of information in his reports. Things reached a breaking point in January 1956, when Snuggles informed the Stasi that he no longer wanted to be an informant because he was a Christian and he would rather suffer than cause others to suffer.[91] The Stasi officer responded coolly, not with truncheons or crowbars as one might expect from Gestapo officers, but with refined, casual coercion. The Stasi officer simply asked how long Snuggles wanted to remain a teacher, a question that caused the candidate to become "visibly nervous" and in the end to agree to continue to work for the Stasi.[92] Snuggles's work did not improve, however, leading to a meeting with the district leader at which the informant broke down and said: "It is this simple. I cannot spy on people."[93] Unmoved, the Stasi said it would still be "keeping in touch" with him until it was able to find another informant in the area.[94]

Snuggles, who was recruited to monitor grumbling at the Wittenberge river port but soon thereafter became a teacher, is yet another example of maintaining an informant even though the justification for the informant no longer applied. There were many others. A female informant was recruited to monitor the doctor's office where she worked. Within a few months, she fell ill and entered the hospital for an extended period. Once she left the hospital, she could no longer work and spent her days tending her child who had tuberculosis. Unbeknownst to the informant, the Stasi monitored her house to see if the child was indeed ill or whether she had concocted the story to bring an end to her collaboration.[95] Rather than releasing the informant, the Stasi requested that she report on a group of housewives in her neighborhood.

A secretary at a medical facility remained an informant ten years after the physician she was to monitor had fled to the West.[96] Informant "Silvana" was kept on to monitor the Ravensbrück memorial site when she became a secretary there, although she was originally scheduled to monitor a factory in Fürstenberg. Her scathing reports on the site director's alleged incompetence were partly responsible for his dismissal. It is difficult to imagine a scenario whereby a Nazi memorial site (and a small, thinly staffed one at that) could be considered a pressing target for surveillance, leaving one to accept that Stasi reluctance to release informants led to significantly wider surveillance than the original targets. (As an aside, Silvana encountered a "dreamy" Canadian professor on a vacation in Bulgaria, and was instructed to keep in touch with him for information on the Canadian academic scene. It turned out to be not as interesting as the Stasi thought.)[97]

Early in 1971, the sewing machine plant in Wittenberge was on the verge of unveiling a new generation of sewing machine, illustriously named the ROBOTRON 3000. The Stasi wanted an informant in the research and development branch of the plant in order to monitor the final stages and launch of the new machine. In leafing through his files, Stasi officer Schmidt noted that the Stasi had had an informant in that section from 1961 to 1967 but that this informant was let go because he did not have the proper "mind-set" to continue working with the Stasi.[98] Specifically, his reports were subjective, he had few contacts, he was a loner, and he rarely showed up for the pre-arranged meetings with his case officer. Undaunted, the officer recruited the candidate, who readily agreed to work for the Stasi again, signing a commitment that differed from his first. In 1961, the candidate wrote:

> I, Johannes Beil, born on May 17, 1934, declare that I am willing to voluntarily work for the Ministry for State Security. I will not mention my association to any other person, including my own relations. I will provide my reports in writing and sign them with the name "Sinus."[99]

In 1971, the commitment read as follows:

> I, Johannes Beil, declare that I am willing to continue my association with the Ministry for State Security that began in 1961. I will use my knowledge to prevent sabotage, espionage and other enemy actions. I will take seriously the appointments arranged between us and do my utmost to keep them. I will sign my reports with the name "Walter."[100]

The new commitment reveals Beil's previous inability to keep his appointments.

Predictably, this informant was as weak the second time around as he was the first, and for the same reasons. He was still a loner and found it difficult to talk to others, and to make matters worse, he was soon transferred and now had no contact whatsoever with the ROBOTRON 3000. One might reasonably assume that at this point, the Stasi would have dropped this abysmal informant, but it kept him on. In 1983 the Stasi complained that since his wife's death he was dressing sloppily, that he was drinking too much, and that he was not keeping his appointments with the case officer. The Stasi still did not release him.[101] As far as can be determined, he was still working for the Stasi when the regime collapsed in 1989.

In contrast, "Udo" and "Joseph Nöcker" were among the most reliable, long-serving, and powerful Stasi informants. In 1955, Christian Kupke, a twenty-year-old biology student at teacher's college in Potsdam, came to the attention of the Stasi when an informant at the school alerted the Stasi that he was a potential informant. Since it did not have an informant in the biology department (of which the Stasi was suspicious because it participated relatively poorly when the regime called for help with the harvest), and because the candidate was a member of the Free German Youth and well liked by his fellow students, the Stasi followed up.[102] On October 24, 1955, Christian Kupke entered a room at his college ostensibly to discuss career options with a representative of the Ministry of the Interior. The Stasi agent awaiting him engaged him in a general conversation about his department and about the university before bringing the topic around to the regime's need to be vigilant in the face of attempts from the West to subvert the GDR.[103] Kupke needed little convincing and immediately signed on as "Udo," the name of a friend he had once had. For his first assignment Udo was given three weeks to author a report on the social background of his fellow students and on anyone who traveled to West Berlin.[104]

When Udo informed the Stasi about his aunt, who taught at the Hochschule für Politik in West Berlin, a university attended by many students who had fled the GDR, the Stasi asked Udo to contact his aunt with the idea that she herself might become an informant.[105] Udo was to endear himself to his aunt by learning home repair and then undertaking small repair jobs in her apartment, for which, the Stasi made a point of telling him, he was not to charge.[106] Despite his efforts, the aunt was tight-lipped about her school and did not indicate support for the GDR. She was not invited to be an informant.

In 1957, the last year of Udo's studies, the Stasi had little contact with him because he spent most of his time in the library studying for his finals. After leaving the university, Udo became a teacher at the Polytechnisch Oberschule (POS) in Zehdenick and was therefore taken over by the District Gransee office, something that did not please Udo, as he felt that there would be little for him to report on there. The Stasi assured him that this would not be the case. After his arrival in Zehdenick, Udo married and became the father of two children. His wife was aware that he worked for the Stasi. By 1961 he had risen to the position of associate director of the technical college and continued to be a model informant. He authored copious reports on the reaction in the district to the building of the Berlin Wall and on attitudes of voters that he gleaned as a volunteer at polling stations.[107] Udo, a large man with a high forehead and large glasses, was a gregarious, warm, and exceedingly popular teacher. As Stasi officer Hoffmann phrased it: "Because of his open conduct in public, his love of his job and his spotless lifestyle, the informant relates very well to his students. He understands how to develop these contacts for our purposes."[108]

Udo's reports on his own students lack lurid details but nevertheless were an odious breach of trust. He reported on a female student who was beginning to adopt (unspecified) Western manners. A male student was reported to be a "lout," a "big mouth," and a "real handful."[109] Udo even passed on information obtained from his children, including that pupils in his son's first grade class had shown photos of churches to the class. No doubt with a certain amount of pride, Udo reported that "his son knew enough to report this to the teacher." The teacher did not take any action against the pupils, so the Stasi began to monitor her.[110] Based on a conversation with his older boy who was in the seventh grade, Udo informed the Stasi on students who used the Hitler salute with each other. When one teacher was let go without notice for speaking of the West German election in a way that "confused" students, Udo, according to the Stasi, "worked hard" so that the students would understand why the teacher had been let go, informing the students not only of the teacher's political failings but also his "moral" ones.[111] Those students who had been planning on sending a thank-you card to the teacher decided against this course of action once they heard these details. In the 1980s, Udo, who was an avid photographer, took a picture of each of his students and made a montage. When one student asked why a certain student was missing, Udo said that the student would explain this to the class himself, and the student got up in front of the class and said that his mother had applied to leave East Germany.[112]

Udo's power over his students was vast. One of them hoped to study marine biology at the University of Rostock, but Udo requested the Stasi prevent his studies in this field since he suspected that the student would eventually use research in international waters as a pretense to flee the GDR.[113] Udo also asked for Stasi assistance in expelling a twelfth grader at Udo's next school, the Dr. Salvador Allende school in Gransee, in part because he wore a Stars-and-Stripes scarf to a Free German Youth event.[114] Udo had already reported to the Stasi that this student should not be allowed to become a fighter pilot because of his political unreliability. In Udo's thirty-four-year career as an informant, he had authored hundreds of reports on students, fellow teachers, voters, and ordinary residents of the district, and had affected the life chances of many of his students. Recruited in 1955, he was still reporting for the Stasi when the regime collapsed in 1989.

As part of a targeted effort in the 1970s and 1980s to prevent the exodus of medical personnel, the Stasi recruited Dr. Rolf Schiefer (cover name "Josef

Nöcker"), director of the Gransee District Hospital, into informant work. Dr. Schiefer was a man of impressive physical stature who would be brought down, ironically, by something very small. One Stasi officer recalled Schiefer's children dancing around him as they tried desperately to prevent wasps from landing on him. He had been stung twice before, both stings resulting in cardiac arrest, and the third time would no doubt have been fatal. He was, nevertheless, an exceedingly valuable informant, and his case officer admitted frankly that Nöcker had made his career. On several occasions, the officer received major awards for the information that Dr. Schiefer had supplied.[115]

Dr. Schiefer, a native of Leipzig, was born in 1931 and brought up by his mother after his father's death on the front in 1945. Even as a medical student at Karl-Marx University in Leipzig from 1951 to 1956, his commitment to Communism was clear, as his nickname, "Red Schiefer," indicated. Following a short stint with the Barracked People's Police in Greifswald, he moved to Heringsdorf, where he took over the surgical division.[116] At the impressively young age of thirty-five, he sought out and won the position of director of the Gransee Hospital in 1966, an unassuming facility nestled in tall pines on a hill overlooking Gransee, a very un-hospital-like building that resembles a villa. Although he left the Communist Party in 1963, he remained a firm believer in the GDR. By 1975 the Stasi was anxious to have an informant in the medical sector in District Gransee, primarily to prevent medical professionals from escaping but also because of the strategic position of the hospital. It had a special surgical unit for victims of car crashes off the nearby Transit route F96 to West Germany. Dr. Schiefer would therefore be in a position to provide the Stasi with information on suspicious accidents involving Westerners or people in transit to and from West Germany.[117] Officer Oschim worried initially that Dr. Schiefer would not agree to work for the Stasi, as he had refused to sign an oath while with the People's Police in Barracks, but Oschim's worries proved unfounded; Schiefer signed his commitment after a two-hour discussion with the handlers who had come to the hospital to recruit him.[118]

Informant Nöcker's position proved invaluable. He provided information on one of his patients who claimed to have contact with a group that helped physicians leave East Germany. In another instance, he reported on a surgeon who did not wash properly before and after surgery. Despite repeated disciplinary measures, the surgeon did not mend his ways. The Stasi intervened, collecting evidence against him (in the aptly named Operation Polyp) and turned the file over to the justice department, which banned him from the operating room for a year. The Stasi's original suggestion of a life ban was rejected for fear that he might escape to the West, where he would be celebrated as a martyr.[119] One of Schiefer's patients was an electrician who worked at the home of the war criminal Heinz Barth, also a target of a Stasi operation because of war crimes he had committed during World War II in Czechoslovakia and France.[120]

The manner by which the Stasi took care of its prized informant provides historians with insight into the extent of the Stasi's power in state and society. In early 1978 a power struggle erupted in the Gransee hospital when the city council, for unknown reasons, sought to remove Dr. Schiefer from his position. It was, of course, vital that the Stasi maintain him in his advantageous post, causing the Stasi to go over the head of city council and thwart the attempt at his removal.[121] In another instance, the Stasi obtained a spot in Humboldt University's medical school for Dr. Schiefer's daughter.[122] The Stasi also facilitated Schiefer's frequent trips to West Berlin, where he was being treated for his life-threatening wasp allergy. As a result of all of this Stasi assistance, Schiefer was loyal: "A close, trusting relationship developed between us and the informant. One of the reasons for this is the Ministry for State Security's influence in maintaining his current position in the hospital, in facilitating his treatment in West Berlin, and in bringing about the admission of his daughter to medical school."[123]

The following year, however, the Stasi became concerned about Schiefer's loyalty. Since he was often in West Berlin, and since he was investigating West Berlin–based groups that aided medical professionals wanting to leave East Germany, the Stasi became concerned that he himself might flee. In 1983, the Stasi placed a microphone in the wall of a Stasi office and secretly recorded one of Schiefer's oral reports. The recording was then sent to Berlin for voice stress analysis, and the results suggested Schiefer was telling the truth.[124] Within a few years, however, the Stasi worried that Schiefer was starting to manipulate them. When he was finally transferred to a hospital in Berlin, the Stasi ended its association with him, a somewhat surprising fate for an informant who had proved so valuable over the years.[125]

## LIMITATIONS OF THE INFORMANT NET

East Germany was a place of pervasive surveillance, and one that over time moved toward even more complete monitoring of society, yet the nature of the informant net dampened the regime's totalitarian ambitions. A system based on amateur informants was bound to have weaknesses. The element of coercion in the Stasi's recruitment of informants lays bare one of the most fundamental weakness in the Stasi and provides historians with a contrast to the conduct of the secret police of the Hitler era. Robert Gellately in particular has emphasized how *little* coercion was necessary for Gestapo officers because ordinary Germans readily provided them with information on other Germans.[126] Thus, the Gestapo possessed a much smaller roster of informants than the Stasi did. The Stasi seems to have been well aware that in many cases, their candidates would not freely work for it. Informant cases from the Perleberg and Gransee districts demonstrate that some East Germans were not inclined to offer up information to the Stasi without prompting or a certain degree of coercion.

Thus the paradox: informants who were obtained through coercion were, quite simply, unwilling informants, and this fact was not lost on the more reasonable Stasi officers. Lieutenant Tenbrock of the Gransee branch was extremely reluctant to take on an informant unless he or she had agreed to work for the Stasi of their own conviction.[127] It was understandable, then, that many Stasi officers chose the easier route of recruiting from the Communist Party, even though this was generally frowned upon because the general public did not usually talk openly to party members.

Many of the key elements in the use and limits of coercion in the Stasi's dealings with its informants were clear in the exceptional case of Paul Bindig, alias Informant "Schulz." According to another informant, Bindig, an employee of the margarine factory in Wittenberge, despised the GDR and vented his frustrations with colleagues at work, complaining about the poor pay and the regime's ridiculous claims to be a "workers' and farmers' state."[128] The Stasi immediately recognized an opportunity to penetrate a group of opponents, but here was an individual who would clearly not volunteer for the Stasi. Bindig's past provided the Stasi with the element of blackmail it needed to recruit him as an informant.

On August 18, 1955, a Stasi agent summoned Bindig to an office in the plant where he worked. The Stasi officer proceeded to engage the candidate in a conversation about the current political situation, before bringing the topic around to the candidate's role during the Third Reich. After repeated denials, the candidate finally confessed that he had been in the SS and had worked at the Sachsenhausen concentration camp. Officer Behr informed the candidate that he could avoid arrest if he agreed to work for the Stasi. Bindig signed his commitment at the same meeting.[129] Although Behr planned to use the candidate's past as required to make sure he fulfilled his informant duties, he never really needed to. The informant did not have as much opportunity as the officer had thought to interact with others from the factory, since most of his work entailed shoveling coal alone outside the factory fences, and the informant was, according to the Stasi, "of limited intelligence."[130] What is perhaps most fascinating about this informant case is not that the Stasi exhibited odious behavior in employing a former SS concentration camp guard as an informant, but that the Stasi was interested in him because it hoped he would report on enemies of the current regime, not, as one might think, to locate fellow SS members in the GDR.[131]

If Stasi officers considered coercion a less-than-ideal manner of recruitment[132]—although one they did not hesitate to use—a series of positive incentives was no guarantee of a reliable informant. "Nelly," for example, came to the Stasi's attention because she regularly visited West Berlin to be with her two-year-old son, who was seeking medical attention, and because she was acquainted with a couple that the Stasi suspected was working with the Investigative Committee of Free Jurists, an anti-Communist group based in

West Berlin. Nelly's tips helped lead to the couple's arrest and a sentencing of, respectively, six and eight years in prison. For her reporting, Nelly was awarded substantial monetary bonuses and, much more importantly, the Stasi arranged that her brother, who had been sentenced by the Soviets to twenty-five years in the East German prison in Bautzen, be released early.[133] Shortly after her brother's release, both Nelly and her brother fled to West Germany, which caused the Stasi to pay a visit to their parents. They claimed to have no previous knowledge of the defection but were able to provide the Stasi with a current address. The Stasi then wrote to Nelly in the West with veiled threats for her to get back in touch with them:

> Dear Margot!
> I understand that you've arrived safely. I'm doing well, and hope you are too. I can also let you know that your son is doing well.
> It is really too bad, dear Nelly, that we weren't able to talk before you left. I hope, though, that you'll make sure we can talk soon. Although your circumstances don't permit us at the moment to see each other, I hope that you won't forget about an old friend and that you'll write to the address below. You too are certainly thinking about what you mentioned to me on several occasions
> I'll sign off now wishing you all the best, and hoping that you will write to me in the next few days. Otherwise I'll be very mad.
> Yours,
> Karl

There is no evidence that Nelly responded.

The Stasi was also prey to normal human physical frailties, although it must be noted that the number of instances of serious health-related issues in the informant files leads one to wonder if this was more than mere coincidence. In the case of informant "Cherry," for example, the Stasi called for more pressure on her to deliver better information, and several months later she checked into the Wittenberge hospital because of a nervous breakdown.[134] "Sugar," a waiter in Wittenberge, had an existing nervous condition that Stasi work appears to have exacerbated. As Stasi officer Berndt summarized at the recruitment: "Because of his nerve affliction, we have to be very careful when talking with him. Otherwise he gets so nervous and frightened that he could bring on a complete nervous breakdown."[135] After months of reporting, he begged the Stasi to release him because his nerves were "totally shot."[136] The Stasi granted his request. One informant became so distraught that he came to believe that the Stasi was spying on him, that his wife and all his friends were in the employ of the Stasi. His case officer dismissed the informant because he was "hallucinating" about the Stasi being everywhere.[137]

Young informants were perhaps the most problematic to deal with. They were tentative about the nature of the work and prone to expose their Stasi association.

Contrary to claims made by former Stasi officers,[138] the Stasi did indeed recruit some minors for informant work, their youth and uncertainty partially visible in the handwritten commitments that bear the hallmark of a shaky, unsure hand compared to the commitments of the older informants.[139] In one case, the Stasi recruited a seventeen-year-old twelfth grader from Wittenberge in the office of the school principal. Clearly distraught, he said that he could not become an informant because this would require lying to his parents, to which the Stasi officer replied: "It's not lying if they do not ask you directly if you work for us. You will conduct yourself as you always have, and that way they won't ask, and you won't have to lie." Immediately after his recruitment, the candidate told his parents that he was recruited as an informant. The parents were livid and, remarkably, phoned the district Stasi leader and told him in no uncertain terms that he should be ashamed for recruiting a minor. Since the youth was now clearly of no further use to the Stasi, he was released and his file sent to the archives.[140]

The relationship to a twenty-four-year-old recruited to monitor a theater in Zehdenick where rowdy youth had occasionally gathered got off to an inauspicious beginning. The candidate arrived at his first appointment with the Stasi having had two beers and a cognac but, he claimed, "not drunk."[141] Hoffmann, the case officer, was shocked at his tipsy informant and warned him that it must not happen again. The informant's commitment was loaded with grammatical errors, including repeated mistakes in "I am" (*Ich binn*, instead of *Ich bin*). This was not the result of his drinking beforehand, the informant stated, but grammar was not "his thing."[142]

Informants were not simply passive recipients of orders, but in many cases demonstrated a remarkable manipulation of the Stasi. Informant "Max" from Mellen was recruited to monitor the local agricultural collective, which had been founded against the wishes of most farmers. The Stasi was quite impressed with this thirty-one-year-old informant, praising his dedication and debating whether he should be promoted. Their trust in him was such that they allowed him to travel to West Berlin in early 1956 to monitor a week of environmental events. Upon his return, he was twice awarded cash bonuses of DM 40, but only two months later, informant Max left East Germany permanently for West Berlin, taking nine others from his home town with him.[143] There can be little doubt that Max used the information he had gathered in West Berlin while conducting Stasi work to organize this major escape.

It would be an exaggeration to say that the informant tail was wagging the Stasi dog, but certainly one is struck by the manner in which some informants used their relationship with the Stasi for personal ends. Informant "Tabacco" almost never provided information on his co-workers nor did he always fulfill the tasks assigned to him; instead he reported on "factory issues that were important to him personally."[144] If a task that the informant was doing at the workplace as part of his job was distasteful to him, an informant might well report to the Stasi that it was dangerous.[145] Stasi informants also reported on workplace rivals or other individuals who had wronged the informant in some way. The informant network had a built-in element of denunciation for personal gain, although the 1979 guidelines, which called for greater verification of informant reports and monitoring of informants with other informants, went some way toward curbing these incidents.

Having informants run other informants, a practice that was becoming more common in the last decades of the regime in order to relieve some of the burden on the regular officers, proved difficult to administer. Informant Ram, for example, had simply collapsed under the pressure of running his five informants, but his case was not unique. In the small riverside town of Havelberg, informant Max was put in charge of three other informants, all of them, like him, in the local police detachment. He proved incapable of obtaining valuable information from his informants, despite the urging of his case officer.[146] Some informants resented working for a fellow informant and simply refused to do so.[147]

Max's case also provides insight into the manner in which the Stasi was hamstrung by the real-life situations of its informants. Max met with his case officer on June 16, 1953, the night before the revolution that came within a hair of toppling the regime. He did not suggest anything amiss. In the week following the revolution, Max worked around the clock trying to stabilize the region and arrest the revolutionaries, so that when he met with his case officer he had little to report since he had been focused exclusively on his police work. The next meeting with his case officer was postponed because the officer had had to be admitted to the hospital. It was two months before Max could provide any reasonable information to the Stasi. At this point, however, he was due for his three-week vacation. Although the Stasi was in the middle of an operation to investigate a member of the police force, they did not meet with this key informant because he was away on vacation.[148]

## INFORMANTS AND THE LIVES OF OTHERS

The archive that the Stasi had had built in its sprawling headquarters complex in the East Berlin neighborhood of Lichtenberg was made out of reinforced concrete in expectation of vast documentation. The six million personal files that sit in those archives were created by tens and eventually hundreds of thousands of informants reporting day in and day out on East German society for the forty years of its existence. Stasi officers after 1989 tried to portray informants as fulfilling a public function, much like those who provide tips in the Crime Stoppers program, of "keeping everyone safe."[149] The documents tell another story. For their part, informants have defended their actions saying that their reporting was banal and nonincriminating.[150] That much of this information today does indeed appear banal is beside the point. As Werner Beuster observed, many "ordinary" reports over the course of time helped the Stasi form a "mosaic" of an individual, and surveillance of an individual was frequently extraordinarily long. A 1993/94 survey of East Germans who had viewed their Stasi files revealed an *average* time under informant monitoring of nine years; the longest was thirty-six years.[151]

There were real-life consequences to people in Districts Gransee and Perleberg from the actions of informants—students denied the opportunity to study marine biology at the university, teachers and factory workers dismissed, and the Ravensbrück memorial site director fired. Longtime, respected informants like Udo or Nöcker held a great deal of power over other East Germans, their word frequently taken at face value by the Stasi. In short, informants' reports on individuals were not simply idle gossip that ended up in some labyrinthine archive and forgotten. Societal surveillance in the GDR was never strictly a passive act.[152] On another level, there was something insidious in the very act of reporting personal information to a secret police to vet and store. Even now, it must be an eerie feeling for people who live in Districts Gransee and Perleberg today to know that many of their most intimate family secrets sit in binders on spindly metal shelves in a nondescript building on the outskirts of town.

There was in the Stasi an institutionalized obsession with informants. The district leadership monitored carefully the number of informants and meticulously recorded the frequency of informant/officer meetings. According to one officer, Stasi officers were reprimanded for not meeting with informants frequently enough, a statement borne out in the documentation.[153] Moreover, the Stasi maintained informants long after the original reason for recruitment had expired. One study has found that nearly 78 percent of informants were *not* involved in working a specific case.[154]

The recruitment of informants involved many others in the repression apparatus. The Stasi relied heavily on official sources, frequently party members in factories or school principals for tips about recruitment, or about an individual once identified as a candidate, but who had pulled in others in their assessments: friends and family members of informants, landlords, teachers, and the like. The sheer act of recruiting 173,000 informants—perhaps 600,000 in total in the GDR's history—must have involved a staggering number of ordinary Germans.

There were serious limitations to the Stasi's reliance on an amateur informant net to secure the district. It was extremely vulnerable to an informant changing his or her place of work. Operations had to be put on hold if informants fell ill, got pregnant, went on business trips, or were transferred. Informants were ordinary people...and spying does not come easily to everyone. Some simply never quite accustomed themselves to informant work, or could engage people in conversation in a way to tease out appropriate information, in spite of the Stasi's best efforts to train its informants. Some had a crisis of conscience. Even the Stasi noted that some of its informants were too "cowardly" to admit that they no longer wanted to work for the Stasi, and so tried to force their own dismissal by fulfilling their duties poorly or not at all.[155] Other informants took advantage of their Stasi association for personal gain. All of these issues were well known to the Stasi, which, through its informant guidelines, continually refined the informant network and tried to limit its deficiencies. The pervasive informant system was totalitarian in intent, if inefficient in practice.

Despite the challenges of this vast army of part-time informants, Stasi officers could scarcely imagine doing their jobs without them. Two officers admitted that immediately after the Berlin Wall fell, they destroyed huge amounts of Stasi files but protected their informant records. In case the Stasi should rise again, they wanted to have the informant net operational as quickly as possible.[156]

In one of the last recruitments in District Gransee, a Stasi officer pondered the recruitment of Klaus Hoffmann. He wrote down the candidate's name in the middle of the page and drew arrows, like a spider in a web, leading between him and various individuals in the district—an acquaintance in Falkenthal, someone in Marienthal, a teacher in Gransee. In total, the Stasi thought he had contact to at least eleven "operationally interesting" individuals.[157] What might happen to the lives of those others depended very much on the officer's next move.

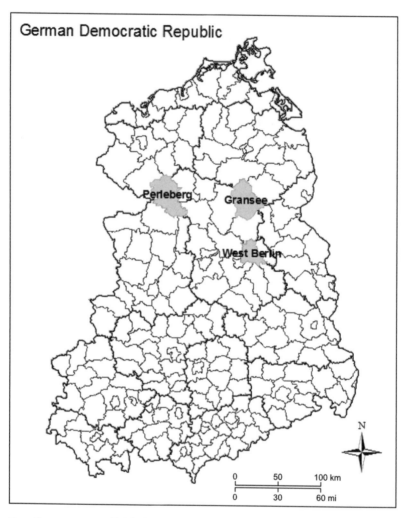

East Germany was divided into 217 districts, and the Stasi had an office in everyone. *Map by Jonathan Kitay*

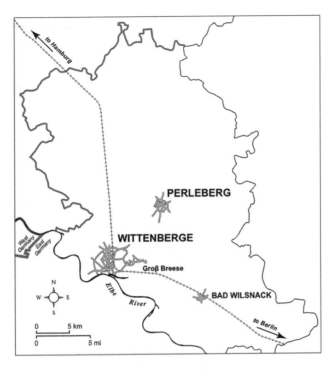

District Perleberg. *Map by Barry Levely*

District Gransee. *Map by Barry Levely*

The former District Gransee Stasi office, today a retirement home. Stasi officers conducted their day-to-day business here but always met with their informants elsewhere. *Photo by Gary Bruce*

The former District Perleberg Stasi office, today a branch of the local hospital. Demonstrators gathered outside this building in the fall of 1989 and shouted at Stasi workers. *Bundesbeauftragte für die Unterlagen des Staatssicherheitsdienstes der ehemaligen Deutschen Demokratischen Republik Außenstelle Schwerin*

The statue of Roland stands guard over the city of Perleberg. During the revolution, East Germans demonstrated on the market square where it is located. *Photo by Gary Bruce*

Perleberg's city hall (left) and St. Jacob's Church. The Stasi monitored the church's minister, Gottfried de Haas, and his family for much of the 1980s. Thousands of people crowded into the church during the revolution to hear opponents speak out against the regime. *Photo by Gary Bruce*

A homemade quasi-submarine abandoned on the shore of the river by a would-be defector. In one of the more prominent failures of the Stasi in District Perleberg, the Stasi scoured East Germany for years trying to find the perpetrator. *Bundesbeauftragte für die Unterlagen des Staatssicherheitsdienstes der ehemaligen Deutschen Demokratischen Republik, Ministerium für Staatssicherheit, Bezirksverwaltung Schwerin, AOP 13/88*

A helmeted Stasi officer (barely visible at left) tests out the quasi-submarine. After several test runs along the river, the Stasi determined that the perpetrator abandoned his quest because water was pouring in the open hole at the top. *Bundesbeauftragte für die Unterlagen des Staatssicherheitsdienstes der ehemaligen Deutschen Demokratischen Republik, Ministerium für Staatssicherheit, Bezirksverwaltung Schwerin, AOP 13/88*

Werner Ryll led the District Perleberg office from 1985 until its demise in 1989. Former employees heaped scorn on his heavy-handed manner. *Bundesbeauftragte für die Unterlagen des Staatssich erheitsdienstes der ehemaligen Deutschen Demokratischen Republik, Ministerium für Staatssicherheit, Bezirksverwaltung Schwerin, KuSch 1160*

The Nazi war criminal Heinz Barth listens to testimony at his trial in 1983. Finding Barth, a chance discovery from a routine vetting, was the most successful operation in District Gransee's history. Barth was sentenced to life in prison for crimes against humanity committed in France and Occupied Czechoslovakia. *Bundesbeauftragte für die Unterlagen des Staatssicherheitsd ienstes der ehemaligen Deutschen Demokratischen Republik, Ministerium für Staatssicherheit, Bezirksverwaltung Potsdam, ZUV 66*

# 4

# IN THE LINE OF SIGHT
## Targeted by the Stasi

ON A RELATIVELY COOL NIGHT in 1980 two middle-aged men, Sebastien and Dietrich,[1] stumbled into a farmer's field near the hamlet of Meuß, north of Wittenberge, struggling with an old wooden cart containing a package weighing nearly two hundred pounds. In the distance behind them were the parallel rows of stocky red brick villagers' houses, only stingily allowing for the cobblestone street to run between them. They had planned for this night a long time, and chose the evening very carefully. Hovering between 20° and 30°F, the night air was ideal for what they had in mind. In the pitch black they unpacked the cart—a table top, parts of a bed frame, a large metal ring, rope, a propane gas canister, and nearly 5,000 square feet of material stitched together, partly by hand, partly on an old Singer sewing machine. The immediate task at hand was straightforward—breathe life into the empty, crinkled sack spread out before them like a relief map, step into the homemade basket, and lift off in their balloon, designed mostly from the colored illustrations of the Montgolfier brothers' wobbly balloon in children's books they had borrowed from the Martin Andersen Nexö library in Wittenberge. Once aloft, a favorable wind was to float them over the border with West Germany that ran down the middle of the Elbe River some 8 miles (13 km) away, over a brickyard, and on to safety in West Germany. The two must have known that in those early morning hours, the sound of air being pumped into their balloon would have carried great distances, so they made haste.

Years of planning ended in twenty minutes.[2] The balloon did not fill, most likely because of their amateurish stitching job. Now began a race against time. Since their wives had dropped them off at their summer farmhouse where the balloon materials had been stored, the two men attempting to flee East Germany had to cart everything back to the summer house, hide it in the basement, and walk back to Wittenberge before daylight. Two strangers walking along rarely traveled country roads during the day would have aroused suspicion from the all-seeing villagers. After jogging most of the way, with the singular thought that they should have been in West Germany, both men arrived back at their homes that night in 1980 after their adventurous evening. The task ahead was no less adventurous: They would have to be sure that the Stasi did not find out about their attempt to leave the German Democratic Republic.

Dietmar Benecke was twenty years old when he began working as a full-time Stasi officer in 1969. Not particularly good-looking, he was balding with long sideburns, a goatee, and a thin mustache. Benecke had spent the year prior to his arrival with the Stasi in the Feliks Dzerzhinski regiment, which was responsible for guarding Stasi installations and was a common recruiting ground for future Stasi officers. Benecke's time with the Stasi earned him mixed reviews. On a personal level, he was boastful, gossipy, and an adulterer, but at the same time his work for the Stasi had netted him several honors, including the euphemistically titled Bronze Medal for Honorable Service to the National People's Army, an additional two days vacation, and a total of 2,000 Ostmarks in bonuses.[3] After his nine years as a Stasi officer, Benecke's penchant to boast landed him in serious trouble. One night, in an ill-advised attempt to impress his drinking companions at the local pub, Benecke rattled off dozens of Stasi secrets, the kind of behavior that was almost impossible to go unnoticed by the Stasi. Benecke was stripped of his position and sent to prison for four years.[4]

After three years of monitoring Benecke in prison, the Stasi pushed for his early release so that he could return to the Stasi as an informant. They even gave him 3,000 Ostmarks to furnish his new two-bedroom apartment in Wittenberge.[5] The former Stasi officer became informant "Axel" in April 1981.

Axel had not been to Wittenberge since his prison term, and he looked up his aunt when he returned to town. She was delighted to see her nephew, and after several conversations, mentioned that her other nephew, Dietrich, had thought about escaping from East Germany by balloon.[6] Eager to investigate this tip, Axel paid a visit to his cousin Dietrich in Wittenberge in December 1981. Dietrich was the oldest of three children, worked as a locksmith in a factory in Potsdam, and lived with his second wife, a kindergarten teacher, on Maxim Gorky Street in Wittenberge. Her new place of employment was a considerable improvement on the rayon factory where she had worked for years. They were the doting parents of a two-and-a-half-year-old daughter and spent much of their time at their modest country farm house in Mesekow, north of Wittenberge, which they had bought with their good friends the Putzke family. According to Axel, Dietrich adored his dog and became misty-eyed when his friends pointed out that he would need to prepare himself for the dog's eventual death.[7]

The cousins had not been close growing up, a fact that was revealed by Dietrich's surprise at seeing Axel appear on his doorstep, but Axel brushed off his cousin's response by saying that it was a long overdue visit on his part. Axel began complaining about East Germany and expressed his ardent wish to live in Hamburg. Dietrich's wife, Anne, immediately took Axel's bait and said that both she and her husband had thought about leaving East Germany for years, ever since a report on West German television about a couple who had successfully left East Germany by balloon. Anne showed here, at first glance, a surprising level of comfort with a stranger, but Axel was family, after all—and ultimately, Anne did not tell him at this point that the couple had, in fact, constructed a balloon in an attempt to flee. Anne was skeptical about the reports on West German television about the successful balloon flight out of East Germany, as the reporters had indicated that the balloon was constructed from stitched-together bedsheets. She thought that there simply were not that many sheets available for purchase in the GDR.[8] Dietrich, too, confided in the informant. Although initially nervous about talking to his cousin after such a long absence, Axel laughed off any fears that Dietrich might have, claiming that he could not possibly be a Stasi informant since he had gone to jail for betraying his former employer. Reassured, Dietrich told Axel about his desire to leave East Germany because of its stifling atmosphere and travel restrictions.

Dietrich's motives were much like those of many other reasonable, ordinary individuals who attempted wild escapes from the GDR. A visit to the Checkpoint Charlie Museum, which chronicles many of the attempts to flee East Germany and is a highlight for many North American tourists in the German capital, leaves one struck by the sheer bravado of it all—the man who married a woman in the West who looked like his wife in East Berlin and then returned to East Berlin to fetch his real wife, murder the new one, and drive back to West Berlin; crop duster flights to safety where the pilot had never flown before; homemade submarines. The people who undertook such risky enterprises were generally not young males thirsting for adventure, but were often ordinary, thoughtful, family-oriented individuals driven to life-risking extremes by a stifling environment. In the widely acclaimed novel *Krokodil im Nacken* (A Crocodile Breathing Down My Neck), Klaus Kordon depicts the protagonist Manfred Lenz as the prototype of the individual who tried to escape East Germany. It was not in the heat of the moment that Lenz decided to escape with his family through Romania, fully cognizant of the risks involved for his wife and two young children, but after years of quiet contemplation, of finally and reluctantly listening to the "crocodiles" of his conscience who reminded him daily that only in another environment could he become the writer that he had always wished.[9] Dietrich, likewise, comes across not as a reckless adventure-seeker but as a man who has calculated that the enormous risk was worth it for a better life in the West.

When Axel reported his findings to the Stasi, the district office immediately launched a Personal Surveillance Operation (OPK) against Dietrich called OPK Balloon, with the intention of monitoring Dietrich and his family for future attempts to leave East Germany. Such an operation began when information came to the Stasi, often although not exclusively through its network of informants, that aroused sufficient suspicion that an individual was "negatively" inclined toward the state. In practice, there was no predicting what would constitute sufficient suspicion, for although all OPKs had to be approved by the district leader, the trip-wire for the commencement of one varied from officer to officer. Nevertheless, the opening report for all OPKs contained the same basic information, beginning with everything that was already known about the person to be monitored—license plate number, home and work addresses, names of family members, and his "morality." The Stasi officer behind the operation then justified in detail why it was necessary to place the individual under surveillance and requested the resources to carry it out, almost always a combination of telephone taps, mail monitoring, and informants.[10]

Dietrich had made it clear in his conversations with Axel that he was still considering ways of leaving East Germany. He talked of imitating the home-built submarine attempt of a few years earlier, and had also mentioned a motorized hang glider. Axel speculated that Dietrich's habit of holding his breath underwater while taking a bath was likely practice for a water-based escape from East Germany, perhaps swimming the Elbe River or even the treacherous Baltic Sea.[11]

At a party over the Christmas holidays, nearly three weeks after Axel had drifted into their lives, Dietrich and Anne made the mistake of confiding in him that Dietrich had tried to escape East Germany by balloon back in 1980 but that the plan had to be scuttled when the balloon failed to fill with air. They told Axel that Dietrich and his friend Sebastien were to fly to West Germany by balloon, and then apply under provisions of the Helsinki Conference on Human Rights to have their wives join them in West Germany. Dietrich confessed that he wanted to try to escape anew—and wanted Axel to help him—but to do so, he had to know that he could trust Axel completely.[12]

In light of this new information, the Stasi upgraded the operation from an OPK to the next level, the highest that the Stasi had at a district level—Operational Case (*Operativer Vorgang*—OV), which generally entailed a greater degree of monitoring and a shift from passive observation to active involvement. Moreover, an OV laid the groundwork for criminal prosecution. OV Balloon called for the gathering of information on the individuals with an eye to prosecution for an imminent attempt to flee the GDR, something that was punishable under Paragraph 213 of the East German legal code, using an array of monitoring—Dietrich and Anne's phone was to be tapped, their mail opened, an observation post established outside the apartment, Axel was to keep close tabs on the suspects, while informant "Wedel" controlled peripheral friendships. Stasi officer Dieter Giese, whose duties included checking with the local libraries for books that had been borrowed on balloons or on flight in general,[13] did indeed determine that Dietrich had taken books with titles like *Man Conquers the Air*, and *What Happened to the Great Inventors?* out of the local library.[14]

It is a curious feature of the Stasi and its place within the East German legal system that information from its informants could *not* be admitted into a court of law, yet this was the most prolific source of information for the secret police.[15] If the Stasi had been alerted to illegal acts by an informant, it had to find some other way to bring this information to light so that it could be admitted as evidence. One option was to use a party member or senior functionary in a workplace who could have overheard the same information, or seen the same act, as an informant. Most cases were not this easy, however, and sometimes the case could not be brought to trial due to insufficient evidence—even when the Stasi knew the individual in question was guilty. Although it is true that the Stasi could indeed operate outside the law[16]—house searches, for example, were regularly conducted without a warrant—it did not do so where the submission of informant evidence was concerned, for one of the overriding priorities for the Stasi was the protection of the informant's identity. Stasi officers were fiercely protective of their informants.[17]

As a case in point, one officer from District Perleberg, who grew a beard after 1989 so as not to be easily recognized, stood up in front of the assembled officers at the last staff meeting of the District Perleberg office, as demonstrators were gathering in the streets, and asked not what would become of them but rather what was being done to protect the informants.[18] Even today, most Stasi officers will not reveal the names of their informants.

To return to the case at hand, how, then, could the Stasi prove that Dietrich and Sebastien had planned to leave the GDR without using Axel's information? The Stasi turned to one of its preferred strategies: a staged break-in.[19] Stasi officers would break into the farm home that contained the materials used back in 1980 for the attempted escape, then have another Stasi agent "happen" upon the scene and call the local police. In responding to the call, the police would find the balloon materials, contact the Stasi, and instruct the Wittenberge police detachment to arrest the owners of the house.[20] At 10:40 p.m. on March 25, 1982, Stasi agents entered the farm house near Mesekow. There, amid the mess of old men's shoes, a fading Department of Health brochure titled "Your Health," construction material, playing cards, and an air mattress, they found the equipment that had been used on that unlucky February night in 1980— rope with carabiners, a propane tank, and other balloon materials.[21] Six people were arrested as a result of the staged break-in—Dietrich and Anne, Sebastien and his wife, and the co-owners of the farmhouse, the Putzkes. Always on the lookout for new informants, the Stasi suggested to Frau Putzke that she work for the Stasi, but she refused.[22] As the ringleader, Dietrich was sent to jail for three years and six months. The young father of a three-year-old daughter would miss many of those early milestones in a child's life, not the least of which was the first day of school—which, in Germany, a country that identifies itself as a "Land of Education," is an occasion of tremendous significance. Dietrich's co-conspirator, Sebastien, was sentenced to two years and eight months. Their wives and the co-owners of the farm house were exonerated.

OV Balloon was the most famous case in District Perleberg's history, one that was used as a teaching tool for new recruits to the district.[23] Twenty years after it was first sent to the archives, Stasi officers who were normally very placid became animated. "Finally," one recalled "we had something interesting to deal with!"[24]

## STASI OPERATIONS AND DAY-TO-DAY ACTIVITIES

Operations like OPKs and OVs were the backbone of Stasi activity at the district level and, along with telephone and mail monitoring, formed the pillars of Stasi surveillance. One year before its collapse, the Stasi initiated 7,000 OPKs and roughly 4,500 of the more sophisticated OVs. Former Stasi officers have claimed that more than 70 percent of these operations targeted individuals who were planning to physically harm another person, and thus were noble undertakings done for the safety of East German citizens.[25] The archival record does not support this claim. When the Stasi archives were opened in the 1990s, more than one million East Germans were revealed to have been the subjects of Stasi operations.[26]

The number and quality of operations against individual East Germans and the recruitment of informants determined the degree to which the district was "successful," and these became the Stasi's performance measures. If a district launched just a handful of OPKs in any given year, rather than fifteen to twenty as expected, the regional office would severely reprimand the local office. The Stasi also offered a "carrot," rewarding districts for above-target operational duty. Every year in Region Schwerin, district offices competed for the Dr. Richard Sorge Banner, a coveted award named after a German who spied for the Soviets in the 1930s and 1940s, given to the most active district office in the region based on its operational activity. The successful district office received a sizable award of 3,000 Ostmarks, which was usually spent on a party for the entire collective.[27] Stasi officers received generous bonuses for launching an OPK, and an even more generous one if the result were deemed a success, which, to the Stasi, was a range of outcomes apart from criminal prosecution, including recruitment of the target as an informant, or removal of the threat through intimidation. In 1988, the Stasi had on the books 19,169 OPKs and roughly 5,000 OVs. Of those OVs concluded in 1988, only 28 percent led to a criminal proceeding,[28] but again, this should not be interpreted as failure of the Stasi, which was often equally pleased if the operation led to the acquisition of an informant instead of an arrest.

Erich Mielke replaced the earlier screening cases—straightforward background checks on suspects combined with rudimentary surveillance—with the more sophisticated OPK in 1971; this element of Stasi work was now to be integrated into the annual planning process of every district office. Mielke's justification for the increased formality was the standard refrain of a threat from imperialist powers and domestic resisters bent on undermining the system. In the important Directive 1/71, Mielke called for the "targeted use of the Ministry for State Security's power, especially its informant apparatus, in the surveillance of certain individuals."[29] His emphasis on the informant apparatus is noteworthy, and certainly came to be the foremost feature of every operation. Directive 1/71 also called on the Stasi to evaluate systematically the information obtained in an OPK to determine if an informant might be recruited from those under surveillance, a point illustrated in the Balloon operation and one that is worth emphasizing: the search for informants was part and parcel of the OPK, not a chance by-product.[30] No one was immune from having an OPK laid down against them, as Mielke made clear: "Fundamentally, anyone who is on the territory of the GDR, permanently or temporarily, can be placed under operational personal surveillance, as long as there is evidence of it being necessary."[31] In practice, however, the limitation to the territory of the GDR did not always apply, as the Stasi frequently ranged into West Germany during OPKs.[32]

When Erich Mielke updated the guidelines for an OPK in 1981, he highlighted the role of the OPK in monitoring for *potential* criminal activity: "Given their preventative nature, OPKs are to contribute to the prevention and timely uncovering of negative-enemy behavior."[33] Accordingly, OPKs were also to have firm timelines in which to expose the oppositional behavior and, although in practice some OPKs dragged on for years, there was nevertheless a sense of urgency around them. Ideally, the informant who tipped the Stasi off about an individual was also to be employed on the OPK so that there would be seamless operational surveillance.[34] This was a primary reason why the Stasi was frustrated when the tip to launch an OPK came from an official source such as a party member rather than one of their own informants. Since the OPK aimed primarily to determine whether the individual in question was an "enemy" of the state, it is not surprising that Mielke's 1981 guidelines called for informants to monitor the target's activity in his neighborhood, at the workplace, and in his free time.[35] How and with whom he spent his time naturally provided clues to the Stasi as to the type of individual it was dealing with, but by extension also brought others into its purview. OPKs were never confined to the one individual in question but sprawled to encompass all those with whom the target of the operation was in contact. The OPK was, then, not a surgical strike against a potential regime opponent but a blunt instrument that surveyed a number of individuals.

If there were sufficient suspicion from an OPK that the individual in question was engaged in, or planning on, a political activity that ran counter to the laws of the GDR, the Stasi upgraded the operation to an Operational Case (OV), the highest level of Stasi operation.[36] OVs differed from OPKs in several ways. First, an OV was to hold a relatively decent possibility of leading to a criminal prosecution, rather than simply a preliminary investigation as was the case with OPKs. Erich Mielke outlined in a directive from 1976 that a suspect could be involved in any number of activities that would permit an OV, including treason, attempts to escape from the GDR, sabotage, bribery, terrorism, disparaging of the GDR, and the organizing of anti-state groups.[37] According to a leading authority on the Stasi, the catalogue of potential offenses was so wide that an OV could likely have been justified against every East German at some point in their lives.[38]

Second, an OV required substantial information in order to be initiated, and as such was almost exclusively the result of a previous OPK. And finally, an OV was not simply passive observation but required informants to be infiltrated into the person or group's immediate surroundings with the purpose of disruption.[39] As was the case with OPKs, the informant was the Stasi's most important tool in an OV although the Stasi strove to have only its finest informants working at this higher level. Not simply run-of-the-mill informants, OV informants (because of the more invasive nature of OV work) were described by Mielke as "courageous, upright, duty-ready, loyal, and tightly bound to the MfS."[40]

Although the Stasi strove to initiate formal operations against individuals, much of its day-to-day work involved mundane, preliminary investigations to determine whether there were grounds for a formal operation. There were, for example, literally dozens of incidents at the environmentally catastrophic rayon mill in Wittenberge that the Stasi investigated, usually without turning them into OPKs. In 1982 the Stasi investigated a pig farmer who was dumping manure into the Elbe upriver, contaminating the water supply of the plant, an annoying but by no means revolutionary act that the Stasi investigated without a formal operation.[41] Stasi attention was also drawn to any remotely oppositional act—like pulling down posters in the factory that blared socialist slogans, which caused the Stasi to dust the posters for fingerprints, or drawing mustaches on posters of party functionaries, which the Stasi investigated by monitoring employees in possession of blue markers.

The Stasi also systematically followed up on bathroom graffiti (including the rather original "I'm seeking a Communist").[42] The appalling environmental devastation that the plant caused was something the Stasi kept an eye on, but there was little it could do about it apart from inform the party. In 1988, that factory alone produced the equivalent pollution of a city of 400,000 and was responsible for 40 percent of all emissions in Region Schwerin.[43] Fearing that panic would ensue if the director of the plant foundry ordered his employees to wear masks to protect against the vile emissions, he instead opted against such a course of action even though the concentration of carbon disulfide was dangerously high.

Other run-of-the-mill duties that fell to the Stasi were monitoring Western visitors to the sewing machine factory in Wittenberge and the enormously time-consuming task of investigating the background and acquaintance circle of every person in the district who had applied to visit the West, or whose job required travel to the West. General reports on the mood of the population also fell to the Stasi.

## STASI OPERATIONS, 1950s–1970s

When asked about the biggest changes he had seen in the Stasi during his twenty-five years as a secret police officer, Klaus-Peter Schmid immediately responded, angrily, that employees in "the Firm" were no longer the patriots of the founding years but were nine-to-five office men.[44] On many scores, Schmid was right.

Some (although certainly not all) of the initial revolutionary exuberance had given way to mundane bureaucracy and paperwork—but also to a much more efficient Stasi. Operations from the 1950s, that turbulent decade in which the Stasi was founded, reveal a relatively crude approach, executed by officers who were single-minded, inflexible, and to a large degree not as well educated as some of the later officer corps,[45] and a poorly developed informant system much smaller than in later years. The Stasi surgically targeted overt regime opponents. By contrast, in the 1980s the Stasi was a refined secret police outfit with a variety of surveillance techniques, spy-labs, and a well-developed informant system at its disposal. The gargantuan apparatus spilled over into many societal sections in its search for an ever-widening category of enemies. Its vast network of regular officers, informants, official sources, and part-time helpers, combined with enormous pressure from the party to know everything of significance in the land, meant that the Stasi and society became mutually entwined. Because of the Stasi's influence throughout East German society, an examination of any particular aspect of East Germany needs to include the Stasi in order to be complete. Setting the Stasi aside in order to address a "positive" aspect of the GDR such as health care can lead to a distorted view of East German history.[46]

In the Stasi's first decade, operations were called "screening cases" rather than the more familiar OPK of the later years. One screening case that stands out from District Gransee was "Storm," which dealt with the investigation of a horse-breeding society. In 1957, the local police detachment brought to the attention of the Stasi a society that looked as if it might be a haven for former members of the Nazi party and its paramilitary arm, the SA.[47] The police were suspicious that all of the approximately sixty members of the society wore identical outfits—black pants, white shirts, red ties. The fact that this was a fairly large organization was advantageous to the Stasi since it made it easier to penetrate with an informant, which the Stasi successfully did four months later. Informant "Hans-Dieter" immediately reported that the executive of the group was merely a front for the real brains behind the society, several individuals with ties to a pre-1945 group called the "Black SS Knighthood." His key piece of evidence here was a speech by the president of the society that seemed "too intelligent" for that individual.[48] As he was on the verge of making a breakthrough in the case, Stasi officer Meyer waited impatiently in a conspiratorial home at 3:00 p.m. on April 10, 1958, for Hans-Dieter but the informant never showed up. The following day, Meyer discovered that his key informant in this case had fled to West Germany.[49]

Hans-Dieter had, however, contributed to Stasi surveillance by reporting on the families and friends of a number of the members of the group. The number of people in the line of the Stasi's sight had grown significantly beyond the original target group. Two years after the operation had begun, the Stasi appeared very confused—none of the accusations against the group seemed founded, the members had at no time spoken out against the regime, there did not appear to be a behind-the-scenes leadership, and the group did not even wear a "uniform" as the police had initially stated.[50] To top things off, the informant who had supplied much of this information had fled to the West. Still, the Stasi would monitor the group for another year before bringing the operation to a merciful end because "there were no signs whatsoever that the group was against our state in any form."[51]

The Jehovah's Witnesses, because of their pacifist stance, were a focus of the Stasi early in its development. They boldly refused, for example, to participate in the initial East German election of 1950.[52] As early as 1954, the Stasi in District Gransee was conducting a screening case against the group (which was upgraded to a full-fledged OV the following year.) The three main targets of the operation elicited little sympathy from the Stasi even though one of the targets had spent eight years in the partially female-run Ravensbrück concentration camp for women, and another had spent nine years in a camp because he had refused to serve in the Wehrmacht.[53] Apart from the three key figures, OV Truth encompassed twenty-three others under surveillance. The Stasi was frustrated by its inability to penetrate this closed society with an informant. Their best hope was informant "Bärbel," whose mother and sister regularly took part in the Jehovah's Witnesses meetings. Since Bärbel was consistently denied membership in the group,[54] the Stasi tried to disrupt the group by sending anonymous, threatening letters to them in the hopes of sowing seeds of distrust that would cause the entire group to disintegrate. The Stasi also considered using a construction worker who often repaired the house where the Witnesses met to eavesdrop on conversations.[55] Since these measures produced no significant results, and since the monitoring had not revealed major anti-state activity by the group or an increase in the size of the group, the Stasi closed the file.[56]

Unlike the later years when Stasi officers had to fully justify the laying down of an OPK or an OV, it took remarkably little in the 1950s for the Stasi to initiate an operation against an individual. A vague tip from a police officer sufficed in the above horse-breeding case. In another operation, a lawyer reported to the local Stasi office that a seventy-year-old client of his suspected his cleaning woman was a spy because she often sat by the train tracks as Soviet troop transports rumbled through the district.[57] She also seemed to be spending time with an "unsavory" character who worked for the German Railway Company. Stasi officer Schmidt talked to the lawyer's client and to the party secretary at the train station. Having determined that there was something suspicious, the Stasi launched a screening case against the woman and for the next year investigated her, the individual at the railway company, and the people in their acquaintance. Perhaps predictably, this file turned out to be a case of the seventy-year-old manipulating the Stasi to his own ends. He had wanted a physical relationship with his much younger cleaning lady and became enraged when she refused and began dating the railway worker instead. The Stasi was to exact revenge on his behalf, a conclusion that the Stasi also reached.[58] Remarkably, the District

Gransee Stasi office was blasé about the fact that it had been manipulated for private ends and undertook no action against the man who had tricked his lawyer into reporting to the Stasi.

On a tip from a party member that a physical education teacher in Zehdenick was continuing to meet with former high-ranking Nazis, the Stasi undertook some light duties to investigate the individual, and then launched a full-blown screening case.[59] The Stasi was enormously suspicious that the teacher had left his house in torrential downpour, and assumed that there must have been a pressing meeting he wanted to attend. (It turns out that he had supervisory duties, which he could not miss, at the school ). Two years after launching the operation, the Stasi looked further into the person who had tipped them off and concluded that she knew the physical education teacher very well, and had often had run-ins with him. The Stasi concluded: "Since surveillance of the person in question has not revealed any enemy activity and since the tip was provided to us in part for personal reasons, [screening case] Nr. 15/57 should be sent to the archives."[60]

The Stasi of these districts in the 1950s mirrored broader patterns in East Germany of a relatively small organization, which focused primarily on easily identifiable opponents of the regime and was highly dependent on spontaneous denunciation. In 1955, 30 to 50 percent of all Stasi OVs were started as a result of an anonymous tip.[61] This fact has generally gotten lost in the scholarship on the Stasi, which is heavy on the latter years of the organization when the Stasi oversaw a much larger network of groomed informants. Historians frequently contrast the Stasi and Gestapo (and, as a corollary, the Nazi and East German regimes) on the issue of denunciation. One of the richest finds of recent years with regard to the Gestapo has been the fact that the Gestapo was much more dependent on denunciations from ordinary Germans than previously thought. The Gestapo was not on every corner, as many had believed, but ordinary citizens willing to denounce their neighbors were.

As time passed, there was a clear shift in the way that the Stasi used denunciations in its everyday work. In the initial years, the Stasi did rely to a large extent on random, spontaneous denunciations from the general public, whereas the final years of the regime were marked by a Stasi that responded almost exclusively to tips from its cultivated informants and its contacts, including leading factory functionaries and officers of the regular police. Spontaneous denunciation as such, in marked contrast to the Third Reich, had ceased.

During the Stasi's period of brisk expansion from 1957 to 1971, it also began to operate differently, moving away from its founding ideology of confronting class opponents and beginning to take on functions not normally associated with a secret police—functions related to behind-the-scenes guiding of society, to infiltration of state and bureaucracy on a mammoth scale, to the development of a sprawling net of informants, agents, and spies. Certain operations of the 1960s in Districts Gransee and Perleberg demonstrate both the leftover methods of an unrefined secret police and the beginnings of the more sophisticated apparatus of the latter years. In OV *Maler* (painter), an individual at the Wittenberge vegetable oil processing plant was investigated for his verbal support of Alexander Dubcek's Prague Spring in neighboring Czechoslovakia. The Stasi instructed an informant to search the suspect's wallet, which he kept in his coat pocket in his work locker. The informant found a piece of paper with a series of numbers and letters as follows

```
X     12/3     02,30
P      6—4
X=R-X 3 m
Koord. 11/1b
       7/a-x
Pail. X 12/4, 3, 7, 5     115°, 89°, 37°
```

Believing this to be code for a dead-letter box, the Stasi forwarded the cryptic note on to Berlin, but the cryptanalysts there were unable to break what was in all likelihood a harmless form of personal math shorthand.

The file for OV *Maler* contains a flowchart outlining the connections that he had to twenty-four people in town—all of whom were placed under surveillance in the course of the investigation. As the operation moved into its fifth month and as the Stasi had yet to find enough incriminating evidence on the suspect, Stasi officer Pippig, in yet another blunt approach typical of the earlier years of the Stasi, instructed his key informant to take the suspect out for drinks in the local pub. The Stasi had previously arranged that the barkeep would hand out free beer as part of an upcoming beer competition so as to entice the suspect to have too much to drink and incriminate himself. In the end, the suspect was indeed arrested.[62] Missing documentation prevents researchers from knowing why he was arrested and whether he was convicted.

Citizen reactions to the "protective border measures" of August 13, 1961, as the Communist Party termed the Berlin Wall, caused a small flurry of Stasi activity in these districts. In Wittenberge, the Stasi apprehended an eighteen-year-old student who had laid hundreds of flyers at people's doorsteps urging them to "Think about Berlin" and vote against the unity list in the upcoming elections. The student, who had the bad luck of being spotted at Peace Square by a party member while distributing his pamphlets, received a jail sentence of one year and four months.[63] A worker at the rayon factory in Wittenberge was also investigated by the Stasi for speaking out against the Wall. If he expressed remorse about his statements when confronted by the Stasi, he was to be allowed to continue in his job because he was a skilled employee. If he stood by his statements, the Stasi was to arrest him.[64] The concluding report does not reveal his fate.

By the 1970s, even outlying rural districts like Gransee were becoming more professionalized in their operations. OV *Student*, an extensive operation in

1977/78 conducted by the Gransee Stasi office, exemplifies the "new" Stasi. The documentation on the operation that sits in the Stasi archive today in Berlin fills six bursting file folders, and more than 1,570 pages—more than any given volume of the *Encyclopaedia Britannica*. The student in question was a twenty-year-old architecture student who had become pen pals with a prisoner in West Germany in 1975 via the BBC program "Friday Club." The two fell in love and exchanged gold engagement rings through the mail a year after their correspondence had begun.[65] Although the Stasi never learned what the prisoner had done to earn jail time, the case officers were aware that he had received four years and that he was due to be released in May 1978.[66] The basic goal of OV *Student* was simply to prevent the student from leaving East Germany illegally to be with her fiancé. Informants were used, as usual, to monitor the student, but the Stasi also attempted to break off contact altogether by sending her a letter ostensibly from the prisoner in the West. Years later, the Stasi officer who drafted the letter stated matter-of-factly that he had authored the letter himself, taking great care that it sound genuine. Upon receipt of the letter, in which the prisoner claimed that his fiancée was just one of the many girls that he wrote to in East Germany as part of a general West German prisoner pastime, the female student became very upset, to the point of wanting to break off the engagement.[67] The Stasi officer behind the fabricated letter took it as a compliment that his forgery was so good the recipient did not doubt its authenticity. The prisoner, however, was eventually able to convince the student that he was not the author of the letter.

Things turned more serious when the prisoner suggested that they take a hotel room in East Berlin after his release and try to get her pregnant. She could then apply on humanitarian grounds to leave East Germany.[68] At 7 a.m. on October 29, 1977, at the Berlin Wall crossing point on Heinrich-Heine-Strasse, the student stood waiting to see her fiancé for the first time in her life. In the Stasi files on this operation, grainy black-and-white pictures taken with a zoom lens show an elegant woman nervously checking her watch. She waited in vain for two hours before taking the subway back home. Following her failed attempt to meet up with her fiancé, Officer Gaeth confronted the student directly, telling her that she would lose her place in architecture school if she did not break off contact with the prisoner.[69]

The student agreed to end her relationship. Following her final letter to her fiancé, the prisoner responded with several letters of bewilderment, all of which the Stasi intercepted.[70] Two months later, comfortable that she no longer had contact with the prisoner, Gaeth approached the student about another topic: whether she would work for the Stasi as an informant. She agreed on the spot and took the code name "Franziska Linkerhand" after the novel by Brigitte Reimann.[71] Although the Stasi had caused her anguish, her reaction should not be baffling. Ralf-Dieter Gaeth had exhibited on several occasions the power that he wielded—he could prevent her further studies, he controlled her mail, he had halted the entry of her fiancé into East Germany, he had had her stripped of her identification card and replaced it with a PM 12 card (Pass- und Meldewesen [Passports and Registration]) that restricted her ability to move about East Germany. To a twenty-one-year-old student, the Stasi officer must have appeared as someone with far-reaching powers, someone not to be denied. It would be an error to think that the student had agreed to become an informant out of conviction. She must have believed that to refuse to do so would have had serious repercussions for her. Since she spent most of her time in Weimar at the architecture school, District Gransee transferred her files to the District Weimar office, and her fate remains unknown.

Operation *Student* in particular offers an opportunity to dispel the version of informant work offered in "official" histories of the Stasi, whereby informants were recruited strictly for a specific task rather than as a general attempt to augment the informant roster. The 2002 volume *Die Sicherheit* (Security), a work written by former Stasi officers, argues that "informants were recruited neither to build up a swollen reservoir of conspiratorial assistants nor to meet quotas, but rather exclusively to help with concrete assignments."[72] In this operation, the architectural student was recruited for no other reason than that the controlling officer recognized an opportunity to recruit an individual into Stasi work who, because of her experience with the organization, was likely to agree.

## OPERATIONS IN THE 1980s

The larger, multilayered, and generally more refined Stasi operations of the 1980s in Districts Gransee and Perleberg stand in sharp contrast to the operations of the earlier era. For both districts, the plurality of operations in the 1980s (more than 40 percent for each district) dealt with monitoring individuals who had applied to leave East Germany, an issue that the Stasi never satisfactorily resolved. The catalyst for such an operation was the above-board application of an East German citizen to leave East Germany, an act that was indeed legal in East Germany but overwhelmingly led to a denial unless the applicant was a senior citizen. Between 1977 and 1988, 121,000 East Germans emigrated legally.[73] The bureaucratic term for a would-be emigrant was *Antragsteller auf ständige Ausreise* (AstA), or "applicant to permanently leave the country." In 1989, many East Germans put a capital *A* in masking tape in their car's rear window. This was required by law for those just learning to drive, called *Anfänger* (beginners), to signal to other drivers one's lack of experience on the road. In the last days of the regime, however, putting an *A* in one's car window became a protest act. Many experienced drivers adorned their rear windows with the *A* to indicate they were an "Applicant" to leave East Germany. Given the proliferation of these window signs in 1989, and the fact that at least some of them were legitimate, there was little the police could do. It is worth making clear here that these were not individuals who had applied to visit the West temporarily for an important family occasion such as major birthdays or funerals—the background screening of which also fell to the Stasi—but to leave East Germany permanently.

An application to emigrate from East Germany was a red flag to the Stasi of an opponent of the regime and someone who might look to illegal means to flee East Germany if their application was not approved. In the case of the unoriginally named OPK *Zahn* (tooth), a female dentist and her husband, a food engineer, applied to emigrate to West Germany in 1984 and were, as a consequence, placed under surveillance. Unbeknownst to the dentist, her husband had been an informant for the Stasi for two years in the 1970s, and he greatly feared reprisal from her should she find out. Some of the first measures to be undertaken in OPK *Zahn* were standard fare for the Stasi—monitoring of the individuals' mail (letters to and from the couple were steamed open, the contents photocopied, and the envelope ironed shut), establishment of observation posts around the couple's home, obtaining samples of their handwriting, and, most importantly, employing informants (in this case, informants "Andrea" and "Pluto") to find out as much as possible about their interest in leaving East Germany or, alternatively, what they planned if their application were to be rejected.[74]

As several cases have demonstrated, informants played the most important role in monitoring suspect individuals in OPKs and OVs, far beyond the importance of telephone or mail monitoring. Much like white blood cells, informants were to locate bodies harmful to the well-being of the corpus and disseminate information about their presence to the immune system. In the cases of applicants to emigrate, the Stasi instructed its informants to encourage the applicant to withdraw their application; this was the easiest solution to the perceived problem. Informant Pluto, for example, had been a longtime friend of the couple (he had met the husband back in high school) and invited them over for a pleasant night of rummy, per the instructions of his controlling officer.

Pluto was able to determine that the wife was upset because the regime forced her to work in a hospital rather than take over her father's dental practice. In a sad case of putting her husband on a pedestal he did not deserve, she believed that the real reason she was not permitted to take over the clinic was that her husband had refused to work for the Stasi.[75] In the course of the conversation, Pluto obtained the names of several individuals with whom the couple had contact, names his case officer then forwarded on to the regional level. Indicative of the power of the informant, Pluto recommended to the Stasi that the dentist not be awarded her father's practice since he did not believe that it would cause her to withdraw her application to emigrate.[76] Phone monitoring had revealed that the dentist called her sister and her husband in East Berlin. The Stasi then began a file on this couple, too, and asked the regional Berlin Stasi office for any information on them.[77] Informant Andrea, responsible for monitoring the dentist at her workplace, reported to the Stasi that the dentist had complained about the GDR to her patients, even going so far as to say that the GDR was similar to the Third Reich.[78] By June 1984, about five months after the operation had begun, the Stasi knew that the couple had postal or telephone contact with two sisters and one aunt in West Germany, a fellow dentist in Wittenberge, and three other East German citizens. Within a few months, the number of individuals in the operation who were "secondary people," as the Stasi termed it, rose to thirty-four.[79] OPK *Zahn*, just like the search for informant candidates, soon ballooned to touch many more individuals than the initial couple in question.

Two years after the operation had begun, the Stasi was frustrated that there still were no grounds to prosecute the couple. They were determined to follow through with the application to emigrate and had made no signs of preparing to leave the GDR illegally. Undeterred, the Stasi simply changed the focus of the operation, looking to obtain a conviction for slander or defamation of the GDR.

Meanwhile, the private life of the couple deteriorated as they desperately waited for permission to leave East Germany. In April 1986, the husband quit his job and began checking on a daily basis with the local council to see if his application had been approved. Within a year, his wife had quit her practice, and the couple had sold their house to a local veterinarian. Encountering dead ends at every turn, they wrote ceaselessly to anyone who might be able to help. In 1986 and 1987, they wrote nearly fifty letters to the local council asking for updates on their file and drawing attention to the wife's deteriorating health as her nerves frayed waiting for news. They wrote to the East German leader, Erich Honecker, on three occasions, letters in which the utter anguish of the couple is palpable: "In our powerlessness, our despair, and our mercy, we turn to you. We ask you to intervene on our behalf."[80]

Driven to desperation, the husband entered the district council office in Perleberg and said he would not leave the building until he had an answer on his application. At that point, he had been waiting about four years. Following his arrest by the Stasi, the husband calmly explained to his interrogating officer that he did not consider it a crime to want an update on his file after four years, nor did he consider it a crime to want to leave East Germany.[81] The husband was sentenced to ten months in jail in Cottbus for the public disruption he had caused at the council office.[82] In a strange twist, the closing on the sale of the house was postponed because of the jail sentence, but the veterinarian was in the process of moving into the house and pressured the Stasi to remove the family. In order to appease the veterinarian, the Stasi released the husband from jail and relocated him in the West. Shortly thereafter, his wife and daughter joined him for the new life in West Germany that they had been seeking for so long.

What is frustrating for a historian of the Stasi is the lack of patterns or predictability in its conduct. OPK *Transport*, for example, is a case that is fundamentally similar to OPK *Zahn*, both in content, in the era it occurred, and in the district: A husband and his wife applied to leave East Germany in 1985. Both worked in the health sector in important jobs; she was a nurse at the Wittenberge hospital, he drove an ambulance. Both became belligerent as time went on, appearing at the council office in Perleberg on a regular basis, writing letters to local officials, and at one point threatening to look for a "public" solution to their quandary. She quit her job.[83] Five months after the start of OPK *Transport*, the couple was permitted to emigrate to West Germany, where she found work as a nurse and he as an ambulance driver.[84] Unlike the first case, where the husband ended up serving jail time for his contentious attitude, this couple was simply allowed to leave. There is no good explanation why the fate of the two couples was so different.

Stasi operations that attempted to coerce East Germans to withdraw their applications to emigrate exhibited a high tendency to use contact persons and irregular collaborators, a logical course to pursue given that family members in particular could use their influence to the Stasi's advantage. Understandably, most would-be emigrants had conflicted feelings about leaving friends and family behind. It was not uncommon for the Stasi to approach an applicant's mother to urge the applicant to reflect on her increasing need for care, or to have a close friend or co-worker relate what a loss it would be to him personally if the applicant were to leave East Germany.[85] In instances where the applicant did not have stable family relations or work environment, the Stasi turned to more creative methods of locating collaborators who could exert pressure on the individual to remain in East Germany. In OV *Treffpunkt* (meeting place), the Stasi used the former cellmate of a twenty-one-year-old applicant to leave East Germany to convince him to withdraw his application.[86] Their efforts failed.

The focus of attention for Stasi officers in District Gransee was the more than twenty Soviet and East German military installations housed in the district. The Stasi constantly feared that the area was overrun with spies eager to glimpse the latest military hardware of the Warsaw Pact. From 1983 to 1986, for example, the Stasi investigated an innkeeper who mentioned in passing that he thought a new rocket base was being built in the district. Mail monitoring, the slipping-in of an informant as waiter, and three years of monitoring his friends and relatives revealed nothing out of the ordinary.[87] Even more revealing of the tension surrounding these sites was OPK *Observant*, in which a West German couple was investigated because they had visited her in-laws on a regular basis in East Germany, and on two occasions had been spotted with binoculars near a Soviet military base. When approached by the police, the couple replied that they were interested in their family's nearby property, and in particular whether there were still catfish in the pond.[88]

Locals revealed in casual chats with undercover Stasi officers that there had not been fish in the pond in ages, and that a catfish was far too large for that pond anyway—sufficient evidence for the Stasi to believe it had a been fed a bogus cover story. One of the Stasi officers assigned to the case rapidly became an expert on catfish, voraciously reading the only academic monograph on the subject. The officer wrote, in all seriousness: "Jozef Mihalik in his publication on catfish writes that it is the largest fresh water fish in Central Europe, and can achieve 3 to 5 meters [9–16 ft] in length. This conclusively demonstrates that no fish of this size can live in the 30 cm [12 in] deep pond and thus the claim by the West German citizen to want to see if there are catfish in the pond must be viewed as a cover story for observing the military site."[89] After a year of observing the couple's visits to East Germany, and continuing talks with fishermen in the area, the Stasi admitted that there was no evidence of espionage and sheepishly acknowledged that a "fish very similar to the catfish" had inhabited the pond for decades.[90] Apparently, the last thing that the Stasi thought to do was inspect the pond for fish.

The most significant operation related to a military base began in the quiet of a June 1987 night in the countryside near Gransee. It was this operation that proved so exhausting to Markus Schram, encountered in chapter 2. A German teenager by the last name of Baer climbed a wall and was 16 feet (5 m) within the boundaries of a Soviet military installation when a Soviet guard in a watchtower spotted him. The nineteen-year-old guard entering into the last hour of his twelve-hour shift shouted at him first in Russian, then in broken German: "Stop. Be shot." The boy scurried over the wall as the soldier fired a warning shot into the air, and ran into the woods. The Soviet soldier gave chase. Feigning fatigue, the boy dropped to his knees in front of the soldier, at which point the fleeing suspect's brother jumped out of the woods and tried to grab the guard's AK-47. The soldier fired. The first bullet ripped through one boy's upper thigh, and he dragged himself several feet before dying. According to the Soviet soldier, he shot the second boy in the throat in self-defense and killed him instantly. A short distance from the bodies the Stasi found a moped and some tools, suggesting that the reason for the boys' interest in the installation was to secure parts—either by theft or barter—for the moped.[91] The boys had been regulars at the military base, often collecting scrap metal and waste from the kitchen.

Fifteen minutes after the shooting, the Soviet commander telephoned the police station at Gransee about the incident, and by 7:00 p.m. a doctor from town had pronounced both boys dead. The official autopsy conducted at a nearby army hospital revealed a damning inconsistency in the soldier's story. Although the first boy did indeed die from blood loss as a result of the bullet wound to his thigh, the bullet in the second boy was found wedged near his upper teeth on the left side of his mouth, and the entry hole clearly was in his back. Without mincing words, the doctor reported: "The entry hole found in the corpse of [name blacked out] contradicts the testimony of the Soviet guard, who claimed that at the time of firing the victim was facing him."[92]

Unknown to most Western researchers during the Cold War, the Stasi was responsible for damage control in the face of disasters. When an Interflug flight carrying a Mecklenburg school group crashed in 1985 just shy of East Berlin's Schönefeld airport, for example, the Stasi was first on site. Töpfer, the leader of the District

Gransee Stasi office, was on the scene within twenty minutes of the shooting at the Soviet base. At eight the next morning, the Stasi held a meeting at which all members of the district office were informed of what had happened and ordered to keep in close contact with their informants to monitor the district. The Stasi called for immediate mail monitoring of the relatives and acquaintances of the victims, as well as blanket mail monitoring of the cities of Gransee and Fürstenberg for at least eight days, and longer in the immediate area of the shootings.[93]

Even before the formal OV *Vergeltung* (retaliation) began, the Stasi met with high-level contacts from the area to explain what had happened at the Soviet base. The leader of the Soviet military base was informed on a continual basis of Stasi activities. The Soviets agreed not to frequent some of the pubs in town, nor to walk the streets in groups. Of course, the Stasi was extremely concerned with tracking the progress of gossip about the event, duly noting four days after the occurrence that word had leaked out to the towns of Zehdenick and Gransee and into the countryside, and bars filled with chatter about the event, most of it highly disparaging to Russians, including a common refrain of "If you are our friends, why do you shoot us?"[94] In one case, a twenty-one-year-old with a troubled past and fortified with alcohol accused a restaurant owner of being a Russian friend, spitting at him: "Don't you know that they've shot two Germans?" The youth brawled with police as they moved in on him and his friends, amid his taunts of "I don't know why I paid dues in the German-Soviet Friendship League—I guess for the coffins of the boys." The young man was sentenced to one year and three months in jail for rowdy behavior.[95]

The extent to which the Stasi orchestrated the funeral service for the Baer brothers provides insight into the manner in which ordinary Germans were co-opted into the system of repression on an ad hoc, frequently involuntary basis. (Although the names have been crossed out in the Stasi documents as required by German law, they have since become common knowledge and can therefore be used here.)[96] In order to keep the father of the boys under tight control on the day of the funeral, the Stasi arranged with the funeral director that Herr Baer would not be able to inspect the bodies too closely during visitation. (The parents had divorced well before 1987 and the mother had moved away, leaving the father of the teenagers as the focus of the operation.) An informant had already investigated the background of the hearse drivers who would transport the bodies and of the workers assigned to dig the graves. The issue of whether the sons had been shot in the back had not gone away, and the Stasi took great care to cover up the Soviet soldier's conduct. An informant reported that the father had discussed with the parish priest who would be conducting the funeral service whether it might be possible for the priest to inspect the body. In reviewing the plan for the day, the Stasi also noted that after the service at noon and prior to the reception, there would be a period of roughly thirty minutes when the caskets would be unsupervised, and could present an opportunity for the father, or others, to inspect the corpses.[97]

In the end, the father was not able to inspect the bodies closely enough during the service to see the entry wound—thanks to the combined efforts of 110 Stasi officers, 74 police officers, and an undetermined number of informants and "irregular collaborators."[98] In addition, the number of individuals whom the Stasi monitored apart from the father is noteworthy—the hearse drivers and grave diggers, the parish priest who gave the eulogy, and the mortuary assistants who prepared the corpses for viewing. Informant "Cordula Peters" reported that the eulogy did not contain any provocative references, stating simply that the two boys had died "tragically."[99] Perhaps as the final insult, Herr Baer was instructed as to what would appear on the gravestones.[100]

Four weeks after the incident, the Stasi was shocked to find that West German radio, television, and newspapers carried the story of the shootings, including the widely read tabloid *Bildzeitung*, which stated: "At a barracks of the Soviet forces in Germany, near Fürstenberg, a 16- and 19-year-old were shot. They wanted to trade for scrap metal as they had in the past." By using informants, the District Gransee Stasi were able to determine that the father's sister-in-law, who lived in West Germany, had provided information to the West German press on what had occurred.

At this point, the Stasi began OV *Vergeltung* against Herr Baer in order to prevent him from retaliating against the Soviets, whether verbally or physically, and to stop him from talking to his sister-in-law in the West about the incident. The backbone of the Stasi's approach to this "issue" was per usual—it would employ informants from the population to monitor the individual, as well as official contact persons. The lead informant in this operation was "Troll" (the most troubling aspect of this name is that the informants always freely chose their own cover names). Informant "Werner" monitored the target at the work place; informant "Sunshine" (clearly, a happier disposition) was in contact with the sister-in-law who lived in Berlin. The Stasi also saw in the Herr Baer's boss an individual who could exert appropriate pressure so that he did not speak disparagingly about the Soviets or the GDR.

Töpfer, the head of the district Stasi, ordered the father's telephone monitored, stating that all information describing, interpreting, or commenting on the incident was of interest.[101] The Stasi also intended to closely monitor his sister-in-law's upcoming visit, including searching his apartment, making a copy of his apartment key, and creating an observation post across the road.[102] The goals of the operation as articulated by the Stasi were straightforward—to prevent the "abuse" of the Herr Baer by "enemy mass media" and other enemies, and to influence him in such a way that he act negatively neither toward the Soviet forces in Germany nor the GDR overall.[103]

A year of monitoring revealed little enemy behavior. Herr Baer was behaving himself in public and indeed, he was delighted that he was able to get a car more quickly than normal, something that the Stasi had arranged. His second wife's pregnancy was also at the top of his thoughts. The boys' graves had not been a focus of public demonstrations. Nobody, apart from family members, dropped by to express their condolences on the day following the burial. Mail and telephone monitoring had not revealed any particularly noticeable comments by the target or his acquaintances.[104] By August of the following year, the Stasi in the district felt comfortable enough to close the file. Informant Troll, in his many personal conversations with the target, had determined that the father had come to terms with the death of his sons and was focusing on his new baby, which had arrived in January. The father's sister-in-law in West Germany was a woman of modest intellect, according to Troll, who had met her on several occasions in 1988 when she visited the father and was therefore unlikely to be in contact with enemy agencies in West Germany. Informant Werner echoed much of informant Troll's conclusions, completely ruling out any act of revenge on the part of the father. The one-year anniversary of the incident passed without public notice. As a result, the operation was formally closed, with the proviso of placing an informant in the Fürstenberg area on the anniversary, keeping an eye on the graves, and monitoring the mail for another six months.[105]

Methodically and skillfully, with a clinical focus on the job at hand and not the moral nature of what had occurred, the Stasi had kept secret from the entire population of District Gransee, and especially from the father, that a teenage boy had been shot in the back while running away from a Soviet soldier during peacetime. Moreover, this operation provides a clear example of how many in East Germany were drawn into the repression system against their will. The Stasi relied not only on its own officers and informants but on the occasional cooperation of those in a variety of positions—from factory bosses to funeral home directors to police officers to teachers—who otherwise had no dealings with the Stasi. In other words, the repressive apparatus of the Stasi cannot be measured solely on the basis of its official workers and informants. This other category of individual, it should be emphasized, was not the contact person—the "official" source to whom the Stasi turned on a regular basis—but often a one-off or irregular contact. In some cases, the personal friends of Stasi officers, or the casual acquaintance on the street, delivered information to them.[106] The long-serving leader of the district next to Perleberg recalled fondly that "he never lost contact to the masses"[107] and prided himself on the fact that people on the street would often let him know what was going on in the district. Setting aside for the moment whether his relationship to the population was as rosy as he suggests, he does alert historians to the fact that Stasi personnel had their own informal networks, which could be tapped for official purposes. In the case of OV *Vergeltung*, the funeral home director and the parish priest become—briefly, unwillingly, informally, but not inconsequentially—agents of the secret police.

Similarly, the effect of the Stasi reached beyond the target of an operation. "Secondary" individuals who found themselves with even a loose connection to the subject of a Stasi investigation were monitored and recorded in the card catalog. To come under surveillance of the Stasi in East Germany, one might have only a few degrees of separation from the target of one of their operations. The dentist and his wife were the focus of OPK *Zahn*, but there were thirty-four other people that the Stasi investigated in the course of the operation. In OPK *Meister*, an additional twelve came under surveillance. In OV Retaliation, all residents of Fürstenberg and Gransee had their mail monitored for a period of time. The "secondary people" were the collateral damage in the Stasi's world and were not limited to surveillance operations—they were also investigated when anyone applied to visit the West (some 40,000 East Germans a year visited the West from 1973 to 1982),[108] or applied for jobs that would bring them in contact with the West, like truck drivers. The Stasi also investigated the circles of friends, family, and acquaintances of every informant candidate and every would-be Stasi officer.

## THE ISSUE OF COLLABORATION BEYOND INFORMANTS

To monitor any suspect, the Stasi relied on informants, mail monitoring, and telephone tapping, but another key source of information in OPKs and OVs was "official" sources such as factory bosses or police officers. These individuals are sometimes referred to as *Partner des operativen Zusammenwirkens* (POZW, Collaborative operational partners) but more frequently as *Kontaktpersonen* (contact persons). In modern human resources jargon, these individuals would be considered "casual employees," with the important distinction that they generally did not receive payment for their efforts.

One of the saddest limitations of the Stasi Files Law that was promulgated by the all-German parliament in 1991 was that it barred former full-time Stasi employees and registered informants from public office, but did not address the issue of contact persons. One former Stasi officer complained bitterly—and no doubt rightly—that it was unfair that he was banned from employment after 1989 with the public sector, indeed was vilified in the streets, because he had been a full-time Stasi officer, while his contact in the local police detachment who telephoned him on average five times per day with tips about individuals was allowed to continue as a police officer in the united Germany. These contact persons presented a challenge to senior Stasi officers who were unsure whether to classify them as informants, who would then be subject to specific directives. In 1989, Erich Mielke was forced to take a stand: "Contact persons are not informants.... We know of cases, however, where contact persons are employed in OPKs, or where their work differs from that of an informant only insofar as one is registered, the other not."[109] It was Mielke's wish that informants be used on a regular basis while contacts were to be used much more sparingly.

Beyond the registered informants and the nonregistered contact persons lies a third category of collaborator, a category that might be conceived of as "irregular collaborator." Former Stasi officers, in their highly illuminating two-volume defense of the Stasi, tangentially refer to this form of assistance to the Stasi when they write: "It is beyond doubt: Every intelligence service depends primarily on information obtained by its informants and other 'tip-givers.'"[110] Although these tip-givers capture a certain type of collaboration in this category of informant, it does not fully describe individuals who performed a task or rendered a service, rather than provided information to the Stasi, like the funeral director in OV *Vergeltung*, whose involvement with the Stasi was limited to providing a specific service once, for a clearly defined purpose. This category would be defined by its lack of regular contact to the Stasi, and as such would have the weakest ties to the Stasi while still forming part of the repression apparatus. Although the number of registered informants is extremely high (173,000), this number does not include contacts[111] nor "irregular collaborators." It is worth stating this point explicitly: the Stasi's network of unofficial cooperation reached far beyond the well-researched registered informants (IMs) to include contacts and irregular collaborators.

Several operations should help illuminate these various forms of participation with the Stasi. School principals and teachers formed an important category of contact persons for the Stasi because they were so closely involved with East German youth. Even in the 1980s, high school students were being investigated by the Stasi at the first sign of oppositional behavior. Franz Lehmann was a ninth grade student in District Gransee who, in his class on German culture, drew a picture of "the Future City," as was required of all students in class. With colored pencils, Lehmann, a mediocre artist, drew three city streets heading off to the horizon that ended in front of three clearly labeled buildings: a prison, a bordello, and a nuclear power plant. This negative view of the future was even more suspicious to the teacher because draped across all three streets was a banner that read: "FC [football club] Union, German Champion," even though Berlin Dynamo FC was the soccer team of choice for the party. The teacher insisted that the student draw another, more proper, vision of the future. This time the cityscape was dominated by prisons and large piles of trash. After having gone to the Stasi's local office to inform them of the incident, the school principal was told that the teaching body should continue as usual. The Stasi would handle the case.[112]

Stasi officer Werner Oschim followed up with still more contacts, including the party secretary in the school and the student's teacher, in order to form a fuller picture of the suspect. Oschim determined that the student dressed in punk style (chains, safety pin as an earring, short hair, neck scarves), had no real group of friends, watched West German television, and was lacking ambition. He was proud of his father, who had opposed the regime. Oschim concluded on this, in his view grim, situation: "The task now with [name blacked out] is to save whatever there is left to save, to limit his influence on other students and to restore harmony to the school."[113]

The following spring, Lt. Ralf-Dieter Gaeth of the Stasi intervened directly, sitting Lehmann down for a serious chat. Lehmann did not hide the fact that he despised the lack of freedom in the GDR, that he would like to visit West Germany and possibly stay there, and that he liked to push his teachers to get a reaction. Soon, however, Lehmann ran into trouble with the law and was sentenced to two years and six months at a youth detention facility. (Due to privacy considerations, historians are not allowed to know what offense the youth committed.) As his sentence drew to a close, the Stasi approached Lehmann with a request to become a Stasi informant. Lehmann agreed in July 1987.[114] Although not totally naïve, the Stasi was nonetheless so obsessed with the desire to recruit informants that they took aboard someone who was much more an opponent than collaborator. "In the first phase, the motive for his unofficial cooperation was thirst for adventure," wrote Stasi officer Bracklow, who continued, "Furthermore, the informant saw in his close ties to the Ministry for State Security the opportunity to avoid being sent to jail again."[115]

The newly minted informant soon became involved in oppositional church activities and the embryonic environmental movement in the district, taking on a leadership role and helping to produce five issues of an underground newspaper. The local Stasi office was delighted by his reports on these groups and provided him with a 100 Ostmark bonus. It took the regional office in Potsdam to point out that the informant was using his links to the Stasi to protect these movements, not to destroy them, and ordered District Gransee to call off its association with him.[116]

In the early 1980s OPK *Sänger* (Singer) monitored an individual who had twice been arrested for attempting to flee East Germany and had now applied to leave legally. The Stasi approached several contacts to find out more about the individual and to attempt to influence him to withdraw his application. These included the party chairman at the factory where he worked, the head of the Internal Affairs Department on the city council where Singer had applied to leave East Germany, the mayor, a co-worker, and the subject's mother. As instructed, the mother tried to convince her son not to leave East Germany because of her failing health. The son responded that she looked to be in great shape. She also mentioned to her son her concern that the Stasi had been visiting her ever since he applied to emigrate, and she told the Stasi that the more she talked to her son about it, the harder his views became.[117] Because he refused to withdraw his application, the Stasi admitted defeat and resettled him in the West: "Our aim for this operation— the withdrawal of his application to emigrate—could not be obtained."[118] Singer went on to live in West Germany, where he would be able to do more than just "eat, sleep, and work," as he phrased it.[119]

In this case the fact that the individual was a loner, former prisoner, and poor worker caused the Stasi to look to resettlement rather than to more actively pursue the case. It was also fortunate for Singer that he did not contemplate leaving East Germany illegally, for the Stasi treated those cases differently. An operation that was conducted side by side with OPK *Sänger* was OV *Treffpunkt*, concerning a twenty-one-year-old male who was planning on leaving East Germany illegally. The suspect was a troubled youth who had spent time in group homes in Halle and Dessau and had turned to criminal activities as a teen, stealing cars and attempting to flee East Germany. For the latter offense he spent ten months in jail in 1980 and, once released, was neither permitted to leave District Gransee without police permission nor to spend time at two popular restaurants in town.[120] The suspect continued to write to a friend in West Germany who had escaped East Germany through the mountainous region in Saxony along the Czech border by stowing away on a cargo train that crossed the border at 2 a.m. Given his past and recent mail monitoring, which had revealed his interest in a renewed escape attempt, the Stasi began OV *Treffpunkt* and turned to an irregular collaborator, the former cell mate, for assistance. The Stasi located the cell mate and instructed him to come to District Gransee and talk with the suspect. Since the suspect was out of town when the cell mate arrived, he struck up a conversation with the suspect's girlfriend, who confirmed that he was planning on leaving East Germany illegally.[121] When taken into custody for questioning, the suspect stated categorically: "I will try over and over to leave the GDR and if I can't do it legally then I will try by illegal methods. I would also like to add that I won't shy away from the use of force and if need be of weapons to leave East Germany."[122] The confession was sufficient for the Stasi to turn the case over to the local police to begin the prosecution process.[123]

## BREAKING AN OPPONENT

The Stasi did not always seek to arrest regime opponents. Frequently it was enough simply to scare them to the point where they stopped their activities. Alternatively, the Stasi could have them removed from a position of influence at work, or the Stasi could pressure them into becoming informants. It would be an error, then, to measure the effectiveness of the Stasi on arrests alone.[124] Although the former could be ad hoc measures, the Stasi followed, from the 1970s on, a formal strategy of limiting the oppositional impact of an individual in society who was not technically engaged in illegal conduct and therefore could not be sent to jail. This strategy is known as *Zersetzen*, translated as "to undermine," "to subvert," or "to break down," and involved unsettling the targeted individuals, often by spreading rumors about them that would ruin their reputations and cause great personal distress, or by sowing seeds of suspicion in a group.[125] There was also a certain amount of psycho-terror, such as phone calls in the middle of the night. Many affected by the Stasi referred to *Zersetzen* as "punishment without verdict."[126] Mielke defined *Zersetzen* as the "exploitation of differences among enemy forces, directed in a manner that results in the splintering, paralyzing, disorganizing, or isolation of the forces so that their activities are considerably reduced, or even halted altogether."[127]

Although the tactic had been used in the past, as in the operation against the Jehovah's Witnesses in District Gransee in the 1950s when the Stasi sent the group anonymous letters to spread distrust among the members, it became the primary tool of the Stasi with the introduction of Guideline 1/76 in 1976, which outlined in some detail specific methods to break down an opponent.[128] That the directive came out at this point is a result of détente producing some international goodwill toward the GDR, which the regime did not want to damage by employing brutal repression against domestic opponents, and of the fact that in 1975 East Germany had signed on to the Helsinki Final Act, which called on signatory states, in very public fashion, to safeguard basic rights. In reflecting on these constraints, Mielke said to his assembled colleagues: "You know that, for political as well as operational reasons, we cannot immediately arrest all enemies.... We know these enemies, have them under surveillance, and know what they are planning."[129]

*Zersetzen* always took place within an OV. Gossiping in a pub that an individual was an adulterer or an alcoholic was a preferred Stasi method to undermine its target, but Stasi officers might also post anonymous notices on trees in the town with the same message. The first leader of the Stasi Archives after the fall of the Wall had been himself a victim of *Zersetzen;* his wife received anonymous letters about his (fabricated) extramarital affairs. If the Stasi really wanted to inflict damage on the person's reputation, it would spread a rumor that the individual in question was a Stasi informant. In essence, the Stasi aimed to isolate the individual through the spread of false information and rumors, the origins of which the individual was never to know. This method of repression was much more subtle than the terror and torture methods of the Gestapo (and even of the Stasi in the 1950s), but it was nevertheless insidious.

Unlike Third Reich forms of repression such as concentration camps or the death penalty, of which one was fully cognizant when embarking on resistance activity,[130] this was a refined, bureaucratic, behind-the-scenes repression. Even until the collapse of the East German regime, many victims of *Zersetzen* had no idea who was responsible for the sudden downward spiral in their lives. In order to describe this phenomenon—at once intrusive yet subtle—Hubertus Knabe has coined the term "quiet repression,"[131] a more accurate term than Clemens Vollnhals's "gentle totalitarianism," since many of the Stasi's actions were not gentle at all.[132] Somehow the description used by O'Brien, the antagonist in Orwell's oft-cited *1984,* does not resonate with the Stasi of the same year, when O'Brien tells the naïve Winston Smith: "If you want a picture of the future, imagine a boot stomping on a human face forever." An imagined East German future could be better likened to the toxic black cloud in Don Delillo's *White Noise* that hovers ominously in the distance, always threatening, always unsettling, a constant potential threat.

In Perleberg and Gransee, there are no cases of *Zersetzen* that involve this odious defamation of a person's character, but there are two notable examples of OVs that made use of *Zersetzen* in order to limit the impact of certain regime opponents. The first comes from District Perleberg, where the Stasi had been frustrated for years by the presence of the oppositional superintendent of the Church District of Havelberg-Wilsnack. Ulrich Woronowicz, a Lutheran minister, was a forthright, determined, and thoughtful individual who engaged in a range of resistance behavior that was just shy of being illegal. He helped would-be emigrants with their applications, visited political prisoners, and delivered barely disguised criticisms of the regime in his sermons. He told his parishioners, for example, not to be afraid even "as the enemy sits among you."[133]

In another instance, referring to the large-scale building projects that the regime was undertaking—the Palast der Republik in Berlin, the TV tower, large apartment buildings—Woronowicz reminded his listeners that God punished the builders of the Tower of Babel.[134] Throughout most of the 1980s the Stasi monitored Woronowicz in OV *Brille* (glasses)—Dr. Woronowicz does indeed wear glasses—an operation that ran to more than one thousand pages of reports and employed twenty-seven informants. Even at the time, Woronowicz was aware that he was the subject of surveillance, as he noticed the cars that followed him and the distinct clicking on his telephone line. As a result, Woronowicz developed the habit—which continues to this day—of keeping his telephone calls as brief as possible. After years of the Stasi painstakingly influencing the church council against Woronowicz, the council was scheduled to meet on November 9, 1989, in order to pressure Woronowicz to resign from his position. On that day, of course, the Wall fell, and the seven-year operation collapsed.[135]

There was an important aspect to this case that remains unexplained. In the early morning hours of a fall day, Dr. Woronowicz, an avid cyclist, mounted his bicycle to return home after a long day at the office. It was about 1:30 a.m. As he rounded a darkened corner, a man clad in black shoved a pipe in his wheel spokes and launched Woronowicz from the bicycle, badly injuring him. Naturally, Woronowicz suspects that the Stasi was behind the attack, but there was no reference to it in the lengthy documentation on his case, and none of the Stasi personnel interviewed later, be they officers or support staff, had any recollection of the event. Granted, Stasi personnel could have been hiding the truth, but the cleaning staff and secretaries would have had no reason to lie, and they certainly would have gotten wind of such an attack on a prominent minister if one of their colleagues had been responsible. More to the point, this incident does not fit with the manner in which the Stasi operated in the 1980s—it was too noisy, too brash, not "quiet" enough as Knabe reminds us in his description of the regime. *Zersetzen*, the preferred strategy for the 1980s, was much more subtle.

This is not to say, of course, that the Stasi never behaved so aggressively. Historians have uncovered Stasi documents from the 1980s for the planned murder of prominent opponents Rainer Eppelman and Ralf Hirsch (which did not take place), and the death of Matthias Domaschk at the hands of the Stasi in 1981 remains unexplained.[136] Nevertheless, these are the exceptions that prove the rule. As Mielke himself said in 1984: "If we weren't here in the GDR—I'm going to tell you this honestly—if I were in the happy circumstance of being in the Soviet Union, I would have a few of them shot."[137] The individual who dealt Pastor Woronowicz that blow remains a mystery.

An operation from 1988 in District Gransee that dealt with an anarchist who was meeting on a regular basis with youth involved in the church offers another example of *Zersetzen*. Fearing that he would bring the youth over to his way of thinking, and given that his ties reached to environmental groups such as the Environment Library in Berlin, a center of a burgeoning oppositional movement,[138] the Stasi launched OV *Anarchist*.[139] The person in question had established a "Federation of Anarchist Communists" and intended to publish a newsletter and hold meetings with youths not only in the area but around Berlin, Oranienburg, and Frankfurt/Oder as well.[140] He had already held a "Tolstoy evening" to discuss the great author's position on various issues, including anarchy. This was reason enough for the Stasi to bring him in for interrogation and to warn him that further activities would land him in violation of East German laws on building anti-state groups.

The Stasi now arranged for his employer to transfer him to a district on the outskirts of Berlin. But three months later, the Stasi noted that he was still distributing anarchist pamphlets, this time in District Strausberg near Berlin, and that his informal meetings (occasionally held at his apartment), were being attended by various youths from District Gransee.[141] One of the first orders of business for the Stasi was to arrange that the lead member of the group be called up early for military service in order to disrupt the group.[142] It is not clear why this measure failed—perhaps the suspect was unfit for military service.

In the middle of that eventful summer of 1989, Stasi Major Bracklow reported that the use of *Zersetzen* tactics had successfully neutralized the target of OV *Anarchist*—but his level of confidence is truly astonishing, given the flimsy manner in which the target was brought under control. It was not the threat of jail or the denial of a future career that the Stasi lorded over the target, but the disappointment of his mother. Twice the Stasi visited the target's house in the presence of his mother and discussed his various activities, making clear that he was on the verge of arrest. An informant had already alerted the Stasi to the fact that the target was very close to his mother and that if she were aware of his anarchist activities, she would be sorely disappointed. Furthermore, the mother would be mortified if her coffee group found out she had a son in jail. Since she was not aware of the full extent of her son's activities, the Stasi revelations dismayed her. Stasi officers reported that she was visibly upset to learn that he was organizing anarchist meetings. The son, in turn, vowed to give up these activities. Thus, proceeding on the assumption that his mother would keep her wayward son in check, the Stasi closed the case.[143]

In early autumn 1989, however, shortly before the fall of the Wall, an informant reported to the Stasi that the suspect in OV *Anarchist* had not entirely given up his oppositional behavior. Major Bracklow immediately paid a visit to his mother, questioning her ability to keep her twenty-seven-year-old son in line. She promised to talk to him, but added: "Things here can't go on the way they are"[144]—a common refrain of East Germans in the summer of 1989. With the fall of the Wall there was no need for the mother to have that talk with her son.

In the course of this operation, and under a pretense that remains unclear, the Stasi had the "anarchist" read aloud an article from the party daily *Neues Deutschland* in order to obtain a sample of his voice, which was sent to the central archive in Berlin for safekeeping. Transcribing these and similar tapes, some of which can be played only on obsolete, hard-to-find equipment, has proven to be an enormously time-consuming task of the archivists who work in the Stasi archive today. Although the Stasi archive is predominantly paper, the amount of other media, including tapes, disks, photos, and scent samples, is also staggering.

Arrest, quiet measures to deal with a problem, *Zersetzen*, and intimidation were all possible outcomes of an operation, but so too was Stasi failure. The Stasi was by no means all-powerful, and it often failed to find the perpetrator of an offense. From 1963 to 1967, the Stasi investigated swastikas that had been painted on a men's washroom in the rayon factory in Wittenberge but were unable to locate the culprit.[145] One of the most spectacular Stasi failures occurred in District Perleberg in the 1980s. Early one morning, a citizen of the district was out for a walk along the sandy embankment of the Elbe when he spotted a curious metal object sitting by the river, the waves lapping at its wheels. The object was about the size of a reclining chair and had a cockpit with gauges and wires. In their report, the officers referred to it as a "boat-like flotation device." Clearly, this was a homemade quasi-submarine (it was not able to submerge; the top of it floated a few inches above the water's surface) that had been abandoned by someone trying to cross the Elbe to West Germany. Stasi officers surmised that the waves on the Elbe, a river that can be wild depending on season and rainfall, caused water to pour into the hatchless top and scuttled the effort. Some of the tin used in the construction of the device was relatively rare and should have made efforts to locate the perpetrator relatively easy, but investigations in factories where it could be obtained produced no leads. After seven years of dedicated investigation and the involvement of almost every regional Stasi office, the Stasi admitted failure and sent the files to the archives.[146]

## CASE STUDY: OPERATIONS TO FIND AUTHORS OF ANONYMOUS LETTERS

The Stasi spent considerable resources trying to determine the origins of anonymous letters to local government agencies. The files of three operations, OV *Wachs* (wax) from 1970, OV *Impressionist* from 1981, and OV *Schreiber* (writer) from 1987, as well as conversations with a former Stasi officer employed in this field, reinforce the conclusion that the secret police became increasingly sophisticated, entwined itself fully into the society by numerous and varied relationships, and held sweeping powers that suggest totalitarian elements to its work.

Bernd Lohre, who ended his career as a major in the District Perleberg Stasi office, specialized in locating the authors of anonymous anti-regime letters. He trained in Potsdam in handwriting analysis, including small, letter-size writing as well as larger graffiti writing. He reflects today on how time-consuming his job was, for he had to sift manually through original writing samples to determine a match to the writing in question, including handwritten applications for identification cards (which almost every East German had). Other handwriting samples that the Stasi could access were the CVs or resumes of prisoners (East German authorities demanded handwritten CVs from prisoners so that they would have both a writing sample and a record of where the individual was at various points in their life), letters confiscated by the Stasi, or student essays.[147] Lohre approached his task scientifically, fascinated by the challenge of finding the needle in the proverbial haystack. The fact that some of the people he found were youths who received three-year prison sentences hardly concerned him. "Saying malicious things about the regime," as he explained, "was a crime under the laws of the GDR."[148]

The Stasi employed a bewildering array of resources to determine the authorship of letters, often completely disproportionate to the mundane statements contained in any given letter. These letters were never, for example, accusations of someone's complicity in murder or a death threat, but rather often innocuous anti-regime statements that would go unnoticed in most societal systems. Letters and envelopes were sent to Department OTS-Abt 32, a special department of the Stasi in Berlin with sophisticated lab equipment, for analysis of the saliva on the stamps and the flaps that gave clues to gender and blood type. Typing a letter instead of writing it by hand was no guarantee of avoiding the Stasi, as it employed agents to analyze typed text, paying particular attention to the *V* and the *L*, which were often give-aways as to what brand of typewriter had been used. Stasi officers in this branch could tell at a glance whether the letter was produced on an Optima, Erika, or Olivetti machine.[149]

Lohre's first encounter with an anonymous letter took place in 1970 in OV *Wachs*. During one of the common spot checks of mail, a postal worker opened a letter and found the following: "To the finder: Vote for the NPD [a neo-Nazi party], the only party of greater Germany! Down with the Russians! Heil Hitler!" The letter was signed by "The Black Candle." The postal worker withdrew the letter from circulation and forwarded it to the Stasi office. Based on a test of the saliva on the letter, the Stasi determined that the author was a young man, likely between the ages of eighteen and thirty. The Stasi therefore requested writing samples of every youth in Wittenberge—something that involved every high school in the district issuing a trumped up essay-writing assignment. Only six days after OV *Wachs* began, Lohre matched the handwriting of a sixteen-year-old student to the anonymous letter. Stasi officer Pippig was baffled that the perpetrator was a quiet, polite student who participated enthusiastically in socialist youth groups and whose father was in the party. Nevertheless, he was arrested and sent to prison for two years.[150] What is remarkable about this case is the number of individuals who became accomplices of the Stasi, unwittingly to be sure. Every teacher in Wittenberge contributed in some way to locating the student who wrote the letters. In this particular case, one might be inclined to think that their participation in the search was justified, given the odious nature of the letter. But these teachers did not know the content of the writing, and it could just as easily have been benign comments against the regime.

This point was made clear in another operation, one beginning on the morning of September 17, 1981. During a routine sorting of the mail, a postal worker spotted two suspicious postcards, withdrew them from the mail, and presented them to Captain Hoffmann of the Stasi. The first postcard was addressed to the SED leader in Gransee and contained the poem:

> We plead to the Russian authorities
> Tanks, Rockets, Military Police
> Construct peace without weapons.
> No one ever hears these words.[151]

The second postcard was addressed to the district co-operative store in Gransee and had but one line: "Sparrows sing it from Dannenwalde to Gransee, [name blacked out] spies for the Stasi."[152] The crooked handwriting in old German script seemed to match that on previous postcards, ones that were investigated inconclusively back in 1977 when the Stasi suspected two individuals of sending oppositional postcards. That operation had been archived in 1980, but would now be revived.

The necessary detective work would be undertaken by informants and regular Stasi officers, including those in the Technical Field Operation (Operative-technische Sektor [OTS]) of the Stasi, a technologically well-equipped, semi-independent department that was part forensic lab and part private detective outfit. It was here that the postcards were to be sent for handwriting analysis, in particular to determine whether the handwriting on the postcards matched the earlier cards, or matched that of a variety of individuals in the store, including the primary suspect from the 1977 operation who had avoided arrest because of the lack of evidence. The lab was able to determine that the writing was similar to the postcards of the previous operation, but was not able to match definitively the handwriting of the primary suspect from 1977.

In addition to lab work, the officer in charge of the investigation sent a list of twenty-three questions to an unnamed contact at the co-op store about certain individuals, including whether they had said anything about the Solidarity movement in Poland, whether they were able to write in old German, and whether they possessed a typewriter.

The final element of the investigation was to search the primary suspect's home. On May 15 at 9 a.m., five Stasi officers entered his apartment while the suspect was in a prearranged meeting at work. As a precaution, a Stasi agent was in his car in front of the apartment building equipped with a walkie-talkie to alert the agents in the building if need be. The Stasi arranged for the suspect's female partner to be occupied at the local party headquarters, and a retired woman on the same floor would be distracted by a visit from her son, a retired Stasi agent. The apartment directly across was empty. Lieutenant Oschim outlined the types of materials for which the agents should be on the lookout—store-bought postcards, samples of handwriting, any written materials that contained content similar to that of the postcards, materials in old German script, literature related to Rudolf Bahro, the former SED member whose arrest in 1977 for criticism of the regime provoked international outrage.[153] Every room, closet, and drawer was thoroughly searched. Written material, including letters, receipts, recipes, and brochures were found in the shelves in the living room and photographed for comparison purposes. After an hour and a half the search team left the apartment, careful not to leave any hint that they had been there. The head of the operation was convinced that there had been no evidence of their presence.[154]

At 10:30 a.m. on June 22, 1982, Stasi officers arrested the suspect and brought him for interrogation to the regional Stasi office in Potsdam. He yelled at the Stasi officers from the time of his arrest, spat, and protested his innocence. On the same day, charges were filed against him as the suspect behind five anonymous postcards, three from 1977 and the more recent two from 1981. During the questioning, the suspect was uncooperative, refused to speak, and refused to provide a handwriting sample in old German script. On top of this, the house search had not turned up any damning evidence. Frustrated, the Stasi officers repeatedly tried to make the suspect speak so that he might incriminate himself, but he refused to communicate with them. A criminal studies professor from Humboldt University examined the suspect and informed the Stasi that it was unlikely that the individual would change his mind.

All this was somewhat disappointing to the officers, who were forced to admit that due to a lack of evidence the preliminary proceedings against him should be dropped.[155] Still, the Stasi was defiant: "Although the preliminary proceedings did not lead to a conviction of the suspect, Department XX/2, Department IX of the Potsdam office, and the District of Gransee are all of one mind, that the individual in question is the originator of the anonymous writings." The Stasi confidently predicted that the individual would not continue with his writings, as his brush with the Stasi would surely have scared him, and the case officers also noted with satisfaction that no societal harm had come of the events.[156]

A final example of Stasi operations against authors of anti-regime letters comes from 1987. The leader of the People's Solidarity Club in District Perleberg received a shocking anonymous letter responding to her article in the local newspaper, the *Schweriner Volkszeitung*, boasting of the humane treatment in the prison system in East Germany. The discontented anonymous letter-writer lashed out at her: "I am a former prisoner and I have experienced first-hand the inhumanity of the SED system....Mistreatment à la Fascism still exists in the GDR today. There are indeed concentration camps."[157] For the Stasi, the biggest clue to the author's identity was the seldom-used phrase "à la." Accordingly, Stasi informants were instructed to keep their ears out for that telling phrase. While the letter was sent off to a lab for analysis, the Stasi also gathered writing samples of all those in the city who had applied to leave East Germany.

Within a few months of opening the operation, the Stasi set a trap by having an article printed in the local paper that discussed suicide in West Germany in a fairly provocative fashion. The anonymous letter-writer took the bait and wrote to the newspaper stating that many in East Germany also contemplated suicide. He did not include his name, but the writing was identical to the first letter, thus providing the Stasi with two pieces of evidence that they were able to match with the files in Schwerin. The Stasi then identified the suspect based on writing samples that had been obtained back in 1985 when he had sent threatening letters to his second ex-wife (something that netted him jail time).[158] It is, unfortunately, unclear what sentence the author of the letter received for his comments that East Germany still had concentration camps.

## FILES WITHOUT VICTIMS?

For years immediately after the collapse of East Germany, it seemed that the evening news was somehow incomplete without another sensational revelation that a high-profile East German had been a Stasi informant. In a country that had become far too accustomed at using abbreviations as a shorthand for villainy— SS (*Schutzstaffel*—protection squads), SA (*Sturmabteilung*—storm troops), KZ (*Konzentrationslager*—concentration camp)—a new abbreviation began making the rounds: IM, the abbreviation for "unofficial co-worker" of the Stasi. The letters entered into everyday conversations, often uttered in disgust. Although our understanding of informants is now more complex, at the time IM became synonymous with the person whom Dante deemed the worst of traitors—the individual who betrayed friends and family. It is time that KP (*Kontaktpersonen*) assumed its place beside IM and accordingly to revise our view of the Stasi as a strictly proactive secret police to one of a secret police that frequently reacted to spontaneous tips from those in privileged positions in East Germany as well as from its informants.

During this period of frenzied IM revelations, there was a group of individuals who must have been relieved that IMs had become a lightning rod for public scorn. The Stasi depended almost equally on contact persons, those many individuals in positions of authority who collaborated with the Stasi, as it did on its regular informants to monitor society. As much as senior Stasi officials were exasperated with the organization's dependence on their contacts,[159] they should not have been surprised. It was much easier for Stasi officers to wait for tips from a school principal, for example, than to engage in the lengthy process of grooming student informants. In the waning years of the regime, at least 40 percent of Stasi monitoring operations in District Perleberg were launched based on tips from contact persons and mail monitoring—not from the vast informant army.[160]

One step further removed along the spectrum of association with the Stasi was the amorphous category of irregular collaborators who either rendered some service for the Stasi, like the funeral home director in OV *Vergeltung* or the high school teachers in OV *Wachs* who had their students write essays in order to obtain samples of their handwriting, or who provided information to the Stasi, like the acquaintances of Stasi officers. The Czechoslovak security service, the StB, had a category of informant called "occasional informant," and it might be helpful to think of irregular collaborators or contact persons in those terms.

Although former Stasi officers would have us believe otherwise, the Stasi did not use these varied informants to monitor only those individuals who fell within its stated priorities. When the head of the regional office came to District Gransee in 1985 to oversee the transfer of leadership from Tamme to Töpfer, he addressed the entire complement of the secret police outfit in Gransee during which he reiterated the Stasi desire to work according to priorities: "The Priority Principle means that we first address those tasks that are the most important for the security of the GDR."[161] Priorities were, however, sweeping. As he went on to say: "This requires that we be informed in a timely manner about everything that is important for the assessment of the political-operational situation in the District. All informants...are to be mobilized to provide information to us."[162]

In a scene reminiscent of Hitler's speech to the Reichstag where he read out Franklin Roosevelt's letter asking Hitler to guarantee the security of so many countries that the Reichstag deputies start to laugh uncontrollably, the visiting senior Stasi officer then outlined his priorities: the twenty-three military bases in the district, economic installations like the electronic plant in Zehdenick and the rail network, societal sectors like youth, the medical sector, and the church milieu, and securing the elections set for the following year. Quite apart from the fact that these "priorities" would encompass the vast majority of the district's population, the Stasi could not address these areas in a surgical manner—it was too big and prone to sprawl, and society too complex to be boxed into tidy categories. Working according to predetermined areas of concentration might have been an ideal, but the reality was much closer to blanket coverage. To borrow a phrase from Robert Service, which he applied to the Soviet system, the Stasi exhibited "totalizing practices" in its day-to-day work.[163]

The "secondary individuals," those who were not the main targets but who were investigated in the course of an operation, reveal the all-encompassing nature of the Stasi. They were all subject to, at the least, minor investigation.

This was true not only for formal operations but also for routine investigations of applicants to visit the West, of informant and regular officer candidates, of East Germans designated for border service, of those who had to travel outside of the country as part of their job. "Secondary individuals" were, on the one hand, a welcome bonus to the Stasi. As a Stasi officer from District Perleberg made clear: "All departments can improve their work on secondary individuals who become known to us during an [operation]."[164] On the other hand, the ever-widening circles of surveillance began to overwhelm the apparatus. Wolfgang Schwanitz, the leader of the short-lived Stasi successor, the Office for National Security, stated frankly after the fall of the Wall that surveillance had spiraled out of control: "The number of individuals we were screening was far too large. This led to an unsustainable expansion of the Ministry's work."[165]

At its heart, the Stasi was an organization that monitored society for those who, in Rosa Luxemburg's phrase, "thought differently." Stasi officers worked tirelessly to insure that a disruption to the socialist order—be it anti-state graffiti, the establishment of groups that did not conform to the SED's worldview, defections, or whatever form it might take—did not occur. *Verbeugung* (prevention or hindering), is a term that the Stasi used ceaselessly in its documentation.[166] Driving back to his country home after touring District Gransee in 2006, Lieutenant Tenbrock expressed his exasperation with the law enforcement agencies of today's Federal Republic of Germany who wait for "something bad to happen" before investigating. "We investigated," he commented "before the crime was committed, not after."[167]

In order to differentiate the two German dictatorships of the twentieth century, the German philosopher Margherita von Brentano wrote: "The Third Reich left behind mountains of corpses. The GDR left behind mountains of catalogue cards."[168] She is correct, of course, that Nazi Germany's murder of Jews and other racial "undesirables" had no parallel in East Germany. On another level, however, she has engaged in a certain sleight-of-hand. The vast numbers of East Germans on those catalogue cards were spied upon and unknowingly had their lives altered by secret police agents whom they never encountered. Those who have viewed their files and become aware of the unseen controlling presence may well wonder at the authenticity of their lives. Opponents who were methodically "broken down" by the Stasi's quiet tactics feel the effects to this day.

It was precisely these quasi-criminal measures employed by the Stasi that frustrated so many regime opponents who tried to bring former secret police agents to justice after 1989. Although the Stasi held sway over a future career, dashed relationships, ruined reputations, and coerced collaboration—could any of this be successfully prosecuted in a court of law? And if it could be, would it not be somehow laughable to sentence a member of the largest per capita secret police in world history for spreading rumors? This longing to have justice served but being unable to do so is captured nowhere more brilliantly than in Julian

Barnes's fictional *The Porcupine*, where the young lawyer Peter Solinsky fails at every turn to come up with a suitable charge against the ousted leader Stoyo Petkanov. Faced with the prospect of Petkanov walking away, Solinsky becomes the very individual he despises. He fabricates evidence to convict Petkanov of a charge appropriate to the bitterness of East Europeans who suffered under the system—murder of his own daughter. In reality, however, a judicial failure does not mean the absence of a crime. The East German dictatorship left behind much more than card catalogues.

# 5

## THE STASI IN
## EVERYDAY LIFE

DR. WERNER HOFFMANN STUDIED MEDICINE at Humboldt
University in Berlin from 1954 to 1960 before interning until 1963 at the hospital in Fürstenberg in District Gransee. The hospital had been the site of Oskar
Minkowski's breakthrough discoveries at the end of the nineteenth century linking the pancreas to diabetes and ultimately paving the way for the discovery
of insulin. His time in Fürstenberg counted toward his compulsory *Landjahr*,
a year in the countryside required of all new physicians. In 1962, one year after
the construction of the Berlin Wall (which made previously available western
medicines nearly impossible to obtain) and while still tending to the medical
needs of villagers and miners from the southern GDR who had a union holiday retreat near Fürstenberg, Dr. Hoffmann began his specialization in internal
medicine at the regional hospital in Schwerin.

While vacationing on the Black Sea, Eastern Europe's Riviera, in a resort
that had been one of Stalin's favorites, he happened upon a high-ranking
administrator in the Wittenberge hospital who arranged for his transfer there.
It was by no means a demotion from the larger city of Schwerin, as the hospital in Wittenberge (housed in what had been during World War II a factory
for bomber optics) was roughly the same size as that of the regional capital
and allowed for greater opportunities for advancement. Five years later he was
promoted to senior physician in charge of the rheumatism division. Within the
decade, he had become one of the very few surgeons in the GDR who could treat
people who suffered from rheumatism in their knuckles, a surgery that was in its
infancy in the West as well.

His first misgivings about the regime came in 1972 when the position of chief
of medicine opened up in nearby Bad Wilsnack. Although the position called
for expertise in rheumatoid arthritis, Dr. Hoffmann was passed over in favor of
a younger physician who had no experience in treating rheumatism but was a
member of the Communist Party. He also found himself in a constant battle
with the party over who would be permitted to take the healing waters in Bad
Wilsnack, his preference being for those seriously ill, the party preferring to use
the few spaces available at the spa as a reward for loyal party members.

Hoffmann knew that in order to one day become chief of medicine he would have to join the Communist Party, and so in spite of what he had seen, he joined the SED in 1974. He was promoted to chief of medicine of the Wittenberge Hospital in 1978. Financially, this was a good decision. In this position he earned 2,500 Ostmarks a month, nearly twice the average wage in the GDR of 1,280 Ostmarks but, remarkably, on a par with Stasi wages, where the *average* wage for Stasi officers in the regional administrations was 1,700 a month. But the Stasi employees also enjoyed an advantageous tax situation, extra vacation time, exclusive vacation resorts, and generous bonuses.[1] Joachim Abraham, for example, who was a Stasi major, received a bonus of 5,000 marks in 1981 for twenty-five years of service, the equivalent of two months' salary for the top surgeon in the district.[2] In other words, surgeons and high-ranking Stasi officers in the district offices earned roughly similar salaries.

Dr. Hoffmann's position required him to be responsible for every aspect of the hospital, from the care of patients (with 615 beds and anywhere from fifteen to twenty-eight physicians, the hospital was quite large) to ordering rubber gloves to ensuring broken windows were replaced, and that there was sufficient coal for heating. Particularly time-consuming was his preparation of an emergency plan for the hospital in the event of war, which included securing it against biological weapons, doubling the number of beds, protecting the water supply, and guarding entrances and exits.

Shortly after his appointment, the urologist on staff attempted to flee the GDR while vacationing in Romania. Although he was a colleague and close friend of Dr. Hoffmann, the escape attempt caught Wittenberge's chief doctor completely by surprise. Months later Dr. Hoffmann and his wife were awaiting a flight to Bucharest at Schönefeld airport in East Berlin when two Stasi officers arrested them and escorted them through the airport, past the ticket counters, and into waiting vans. He and his wife were transported separately to Alexanderplatz in Berlin, where they were accused of preparing to flee the GDR, just as the urologist had. In the initial whirr of events, the surgeon had difficulty comprehending what was happening. When his interrogator asked him if he knew where he was, Hoffmann answered that he believed he was in police headquarters. The Stasi officer looked at him squarely and, scanning his face for any reaction, said: "No. You are at the Ministry for State Security." Hoffmann was still not terribly nervous because he felt he had a card up his sleeve that would immediately end the interrogation. When he calmly informed the interrogating officer that he was a comrade, a party member, the Stasi officer barely contained his laughter and answered: "Do you have any idea how many comrades we've arrested?"

Later that night the surgeon and his wife were transported to the Stasi prison on Demmlerplatz in Schwerin. During the trip from Berlin, a Stasi officer held a gun at Hoffmann as he relieved himself in a bush at the side of the road. There was little indication from the Stasi's actions that they were dealing with a talented, unassuming surgeon who had committed no crime. As he was being led along the hallway of the prison, the Stasi officer accompanying him turned to him and said that if he called loudly enough, his urologist friend would be able to hear him, a statement that out of the entire ordeal grated on him the most and still visibly angers him. Further questioning failed to turn up anything untoward in the couple's actions, and the couple was released. At 2:00 a.m. they were driven back to their apartment.

The following day two Stasi agents appeared at his office and reimbursed him, down to the penny, for the vacation in Romania that they had prevented him from taking. (The Hoffmanns bought a color television with the funds.) They then asked him to become an informant. Given what he had witnessed of the Stasi, its far-ranging powers, its audacity, its self-assurance of its place in the regime, its disregard for party membership, Dr. Hoffmann felt he had no choice but to go along with what seemed to be more of a demand than a request. Every four weeks, Stasi officers went to his office and received reports on the general situation in the hospital. Hoffmann painted a bleak picture of an insufficient supply of rubber gloves and coal, of operating tables with malfunctioning hydraulics that caused the tables to randomly move during surgery, of lacking and sub-par gastroscopes and ultrasound equipment (which Hoffmann described as "horrendous, like using a Stone Age ax"), of an overburdened staff—all of which fell on deaf ears. In his two decades as chief of medicine, none of the complaints he brought to the Stasi produced any changes to the working environment in the hospital.

One cannot help but wonder what the cost in human terms would have been had the fall of the Wall not headed off the impending health-care catastrophe. In 1990 the minister of health in the first freely elected government in East Germany's history stated candidly that the health care system was in an "existential crisis."[3] This is, however, not to take away from the personal dedication of people like Hoffmann, who today exhibit an understandable professional pride in their work; although the technology was second-rate, he and his staff worked tirelessly to provide a high level of care and to educate the public about pressing issues like diabetes, alcoholism, and obesity.

Today, Dr. Hoffmann believes that his ordeal that night with the Stasi was an elaborate operation to turn him in to an informant, to give him good reason to fear the consequences of refusal. Even though his controlling officer denied in an interview that this was the reason behind the operation,[4] it is nevertheless telling that the surgeon believed the Stasi was capable of conducting such an operation for that purpose. When asked at interview about the intelligence he passed on to the Stasi, Dr. Hoffmann referred only to the information he provided on medical supplies and equipment, but it would have been highly unusual for the Stasi not to have asked him for information on the political reliability of his co-workers. Preventing the escape of medical professionals to the West was one of the primary concerns of local Stasi officers, who were clearly annoyed by the urologist's attempted flight to West Germany. Perhaps Hoffmann limited his discussion to less inflammatory subjects of his reporting. His suspicions of a far-reaching Stasi were nevertheless confirmed after unification when he learned that his secretary, head of human resources, and the head of hospital administration were all Stasi informants.

Hoffmann continued in his position through the process of German unification until 1994, when his relationship with the Stasi was made public and he was let go. Like the many others thrown out of work, the gifted surgeon spent his days at the local unemployment office, but, at the age of fifty-eight, few employers were willing to hire him. He taught for a brief time at a nursing school before taking early retirement, and now spends his days as a volunteer at one of the most successful travel agencies in Germany; in keeping with a long-time German medical belief in the healing powers of thermal waters, he advises clients on appropriate spas and retreats for their particular ailments. Although Hoffmann is not unhappy with how things turned out—it is difficult to imagine this eminently serene man allowing anything to eat away at him—he would be within his rights to be irked by the unfairness of it all. Many physicians who had informed for the Stasi took up lucrative practices in western Germany following unification where no one questioned their past. Even those who stayed in what had been East Germany frequently remained in their posts, for the very good reason that doctors, regardless of their past, were hard to come by.[5] Dr. Hoffmann, and by extension East Germans who suffered from rheumatism, was just unlucky.[6]

For the last decade or so of East Germany's existence, Dr. Hoffmann's life was entwined with the Stasi, and its effect on him carried over long after East Germany disappeared. The question of how, precisely, the Stasi affected ordinary Germans, the manner by which even those who did not have a direct encounter with the organization internalized its presence, and the overall impact of the Stasi on society are questions vital to an understanding of life in the dictatorship, yet very little has been written about repression in daily life. Jens Gieseke has rightly stated that "the quest for the commensurate place of the secret police and its direct and indirect presence in the overall picture of GDR society is still in its infancy."[7] The points of contact between ordinary East Germans and the Stasi, there where East Germans "bumped up" against the East German dictatorship, to borrow a phrase of Sheila Fitzpatrick, were numerous and varied. It would not be an exaggeration to state that every East German citizen has a "Stasi story," either personally or that of a close acquaintance. Some of the brushes with the secret police were mild, some were harrowing, but all of them reveal a life that was anything but "ordinary."

The former East Germans (for simplicity, referred to here as East Germans) who agreed to be interviewed for this book were contacted primarily through local newspapers. The *Märkische Allgemeine Zeitung* and the *Gransee Kurier* ran ads in the winter of 2006 indicating my interest in talking with residents about the experience of daily life in East Germany. These newspapers also ran stories on me and my research, and asked for citizens to contact the newspaper if they were willing to be interviewed. In addition, several members of local cultural associations answered the interview request that had been passed on by the clubs' executives. Three talented senior history students from Viadrina University served as my contacts in Germany and arranged the interviews for the spring. In an unexpected twist, a former resident of one of the districts, who now lives in Kitchener, Canada, was alerted to my project by a friend who had seen the newspaper article. My efforts were not intended to produce a representative sample in a qualitative sense—it is open to debate whether respondents to newspaper ads can ever be "representative"—but rather to gain insight into dictatorship through individual biography. In this sense, I was pleased that respondents came from a range of professions, including physicians, teachers, grocery store clerks, agricultural workers, pastors, and state officials.

One of the challenges of oral history is that human memory is not a still photograph of a bygone era but a never-ending collage of images, constantly tweaked by the circumstances of the present. East Germans are not the people of Pompeii; they were not preserved for the rest of time for future study but continue to be influenced by what has happened since the demise of East Germany, which, in this case, can be a politically stable but oftentimes tumultuous and very public reckoning with the past. For our topic in particular, oral history is tricky in that the Stasi has been such a news item in Germany that East Germans have become unsure about what they knew about the Stasi at the time, compared to what they have learned since. For example, the widely used abbreviation for a Stasi informant, IM, is a bureaucratic acronym used by the Stasi internally that today has entered the popular discourse, yet was not used by ordinary Germans during the GDR, who tended to use *Spitzel* (spy, but in a pejorative sense similar to "narc") to describe a Stasi informant.

The Stasi remained fundamentally mysterious, its size and methods of operations unknown to most East Germans. It was precisely because the Stasi worked "in the dark," as the first federal commissioner for the Stasi Files, Joachim Gauck, phrased it, that legislation banning former members of the repression apparatus from public positions after 1989 targeted strictly Stasi personnel, rather than the regular police or party who were also involved in repression but worked in the open.[8] A consistent discrepancy in the accounts of the East Germans interviewed relates to the presence of the Stasi in society. Most interviewees expressed surprise at the enormity of the Stasi that was revealed after 1989, yet based on experience they strongly suspected that the Stasi had many informants. They discussed their fears of informants at the workplace, at restaurants, on trains, and in other public places, yet they do not seem to have drawn from this the obvious conclusion that there must have been a vast network of informants in place. One wonders if the disbelief that East Germans today express at the size of the Stasi is more a consequence of the shocking media images of the endless Stasi files and the revelation of "sensational" informants (like the Olympic figure skater Katarina Witt), rather than a reflection of their own life experience, which would have suggested a very large secret police presence. Where East Germans may be making more of a distinction is in the surprise that they, themselves, were spied upon. East Germans seem to have known that there were informants, but were not aware at the time that these same informants could be authoring reports on them. As one subject of Stasi surveillance said about the ubiquitous Stasi presence: "Of course we all knew it, we all knew it. But each one of us thought that he wasn't personally affected."[9] Of the East Germans interviewed, at least half had been subject to Stasi surveillance, which they determined by viewing their files after the collapse of the regime. The number of people in the interview group who had been watched by the Stasi could have been even higher, however, since to date many of them have chosen *not* to view their files, making it impossible to know if they had been monitored.

East Germans interviewed for this project recall their country as a land of contrasts. Even though they genuinely despised the Stasi and the Berlin Wall, many of them made clear that there was much about the former German Democratic Republic that they enjoyed. Several interviews emphasized that the GDR was a land of "simplicity," where prices of most goods were not only consistent over the course of years but were the same "from the Baltic to the Czech border";[10] a country where insurance was straightforward, doors left unlocked, and one's place of work secure.[11] Restaurants always had enough food and drink, even if not necessarily what people were looking for.

Two physicians, although frustrated by the lacking latest technology in the health sector, generally supported the East German approach to health care, which designated physicians for assignment in underserviced areas of East Germany and trained physicians in specialties currently not adequately covered.[12] On balance, both believed that the health care system was decent, a sentiment echoed by East German patients. The director of a food co-operative recalled how thrilled he was with the GDR's health care after breaking a leg while working on a pipeline in Russia and being subjected there to "medieval" treatment.[13] The education system also tended to be universally praised. Day care spots were plentiful, and elementary school instruction was rigorous. One interviewee stated that she would much rather "have a conversation with a five-year-old East German than an eight-year-old West German."[14]

Praise of the social net even came from an East German who had to abandon her lifelong dream of becoming a kindergarten teacher because the party's economic planning called for her to be a poultry farmer instead.[15] She protested but then came to, in her words, "arrange" herself with the regime. Indeed, she became somewhat of a local celebrity and was publicly recognized for her remarkable dedication to blood donation. In the span of roughly thirty years, she donated blood more than 120 times. In sum, with the exception of one out-and-out victim of the Stasi, none of those interviewed universally disparaged the

GDR. They tended to support the idea of the GDR, if not its implementation in practice, yet at the same time they stated in no uncertain terms that they had no desire to see the GDR return.

At least a partial answer to this apparent paradox likely lies in the experiences that the East Germans interviewed had with the Stasi. Almost all of the interviewees had encountered the Stasi at one point or another in their lives, but these experiences varied greatly. At one end of the spectrum were tangential encounters that served as reminders of the Stasi's presence even if nothing further came of it. A former worker at the MBZ factory complex in Zehdenick remembered clearly that workers would be pulled from the factory floor to talk with Stasi officers in an out-of-the-way room on site.[16] A grocery store clerk recounted how her brother came from West Germany to attend their mother's funeral, but since her other brother was in the East German army "suddenly there were two guys following" the family.[17] One woman's husband was approached by the Stasi to initiate contact with his sister who had fled West. She remembers telling her husband after the Stasi visit: "Espionage? Oh no. Oh no."[18] It is, of course, difficult to know what long-term consequences a one-time encounter like this would produce for the family, but it would certainly serve to confirm a notion that one would be wise to factor the Stasi's presence into one's conduct.

A more direct form of encounter involved one-off information gathering about another individual. An architect related how he was obliged to fill out a Stasi questionnaire about the employees working on his building project.[19] A kindergarten teacher in Gransee remembered a Stasi officer coming to her school to talk to her about her husband's application to visit West Germany on business. The officer suggested that she should encourage him to visit another relative on the same trip who worked for the powerful Siemens corporation, the unwritten assumption being that he would then be able to engage in industrial espionage.[20] A high school teacher was asked for his assessment of certain students whom the Stasi was considering for recruitment.[21] Similarly, a physician recalled a Stasi officer appearing at the hospital to ask her to provide information about a colleague who had applied to leave East Germany permanently.

In all of these cases, the individuals cooperated with the Stasi for fear of the consequences if they did not. Revealing a sense that the Stasi held power that went beyond the confines of its secret police work, the physician admitted that she feared for her husband's employment and her child's educational opportunities if she refused to cooperate.[22] On a less serious but nonetheless revelatory note, the physician's curiosity about how a colleague was able to acquire high-end antiques was satisfied when it was revealed after the collapse of the GDR that he had been a Stasi informant. Although neither the architect, the physician, the clerk, the high school teacher, nor the kindergarten teacher had any further dealings with the Stasi, for a moment in time they became—hesitatingly, unwillingly—complicit with the repression apparatus and fell into the "irregular collaborator" category that was essential for the Stasi to conduct its work.

These two underlying themes of East German-Stasi interaction—being unwillingly recruited into the repression apparatus, and the sense that the Stasi was able to control life opportunities for oneself and one's family and friends—are echoed in the experiences of an innkeeper in Zehdenick. Apart from the busy, blinking video lottery machine on the bar, the inn on the main street looks much as it did during the GDR, gold-stained windows giving a warm tinge to the dimly lit dining room of carved benches and booths. Herr Niemann assumed ownership of the inn in 1982 after a decade of shift work a local factory. Although there was an expectation that he would turn a modest profit, the state made it difficult to do so by virtue of the fact that it determined the price of food and drink. During his seven years as innkeeper, the prices did not once change: a meal of schnitzel and potatoes cost 3.60 Ostmark, a beer 1.60. Because Niemann's inn was one of only three in the district where foreign guests were permitted to stay overnight, the Stasi met with him on a regular basis, asking about the movements of the foreigners. Niemann dispatched this duty with a bare minimum of information, offering only vague details about directions they went in when they left the hotel and approximations of times they returned.

A more serious encounter with the Stasi, however, took place toward the end of the regime. One day, he complained loudly in his restaurant that his application to visit his aunt in West Germany on the occasion of her sixtieth birthday had been refused. The following day, Stasi officers met with him in a back room of the inn and warned him that his business permit would be taken away if he continued to complain about the denial of his visa. Although it was never fully clarified, Niemann believes that it is no coincidence that the following week he received a bill for 6,000 Ostmark in back taxes, revealing again a common belief among East Germans that the Stasi had unfettered access to information in all government ministries. Niemann considers it a personal affront that an organization of Stasi veterans is permitted to exist in the new Germany.[23]

The only individual interviewed who was a target of a Stasi operation was Dr. Woronowicz, the parish priest who was at the center of Operation Glasses in which the Stasi attempted to orchestrate his dismissal. In contrast to the first decades of the GDR, when the regime depended on the Protestant church for its nurseries, senior citizens' homes, hospitals, and other charitable organizations, the regime in the 1970s and 1980s took systematic measures to limit the church's role in society, not the least of which was the introduction of the *Jugendweihe* (youth ordination), a secular equivalent to confirmation that soon far outstripped the religious ceremony in popularity.[24] Since 1989, the Lutheran church's political position of coexistence or, at it phrased it, of a church *in* socialism, has earned it scathing reviews from several historians who view the church as having colluded with an atheistic regime and provided the regime with legitimacy.[25] And, given that fifteen million of seventeen million Germans in eastern Germany in the immediate post–World War II period adhered to Protestantism, it is primarily the Protestant churches that have been the focus of debate.

The interviewees who were involved with the church, however, could hardly be accused of collusion. Because of Woronowicz's oppositional—yet, it must be emphasized, legal—activities such as providing assistance to would-be émigrés from East Germany and visiting prisoners, the parish priest was targeted for "disruption" (*Zersetzen*) by the Stasi. The Stasi first attempted to ruin his reputation among his parishioners, but the rumors Stasi officers initiated fell on deaf ears due to Woronowicz's impeccable credentials and evidently moral lifestyle. It then attempted to remove him from his position by infiltrating the body that oversaw his church, an effort that likely would have paid dividends had the Wall not fallen in the interim.

Woronowicz became accustomed to being followed by strange cars, to hearing clicks on the telephone line, and to having his conversations at work reported on by one of the many informants he assumed were monitoring him. (In fact, twenty-seven Stasi informants were employed against him.) Woronowicz never encountered the Stasi directly, and he claims not to have feared what they might do to him, a claim that rings true given how self-assured the soft-spoken Lutheran minister is and given his decades-long record of tireless opposition to the regime. As is frequently the case with resisters, however, Woronowicz worried that his actions would have adverse effects on his family, both in terms of health and life opportunities, a concern that was borne out. Woronowicz's children were prevented from obtaining the *Abitur* necessary for university, and his wife suffers from high blood pressure, a result, Woronowicz is convinced, of the family's long, stressful relationship with the secret police. Certainly, there were real, long-term mental health consequences similar to post traumatic stress syndrome to having been a Stasi target and which are being treated in dedicated clinics in Germany today.[26]

Despite the constant surveillance, Woronowicz remarks today on how his life was not dramatically altered by the investigations against him, although this would certainly be a different refrain if the Stasi had succeeded in removing him from his position. In many ways, his was a symbiotic relationship with the Stasi; his lifework tended to be oriented toward negating the effect of the Stasi on other people's lives and assisting them in navigating around it. Individuals who came to him wanting to flee East Germany, for example, were told to apply to emigrate legally, for "they must never know the truly brutal methods the Stasi employed."[27] In this respect, the manner in which Woronowicz conducted his life was not altogether different from individuals who were not the target of a Stasi operation but who simply assumed and accepted its presence in their lives. Following the collapse of the East German regime, Woronowicz continued his work on behalf of the regime's victims by founding an organization called Forgiveness in Truth, which, he hopes, will help them deal with their anger toward their repressors.

Although they were not the targets of special operations as Woronowicz was, the experiences of Jürgen Heiser and Detlef Jung, both associated with the church, reveal the challenges for even mildly oppositional East Germans. As a parish priest for thirty-eight years at the church in Groß Breese, Herr Heiser was a typically long-serving clergyman. He was only the twentieth priest in the parish since the Protestant Reformation in 1517, translating into an average tenure of roughly twenty-five years for each minister. Herr Heiser rarely voted in GDR elections—something that the Stasi would have assiduously recorded—and he encouraged his sons to avoid the Free German Youth. Because they were the sons of a regime opponent who did not partake in the mass organizations of the party, the boys were forbidden to pursue higher education although they were, in their father's words, "very smart."[28] Herr Heiser resented especially the strictly controlled school curriculum, lobbying fruitlessly to have it include religious instruction. (Today he finds it delightfully ironic that in 1989 Erich Honecker and his wife sought refuge at a Lutheran minister's house near Bernau because no party member would take in the deposed East German leader.)

Heiser was never entirely free of the Stasi. He could hear the clicking on his telephone as the Stasi's rudimentary tapping technology kicked in. The organist at his church was an informant, a fact that she freely admitted to him, explaining that she agreed to work for the Stasi in return for permission to travel west (which, in fact, the Stasi never granted), and he was aware of informants in his congregation, one of whom spoke Plattdeutsch (low German, a northern dialect) and could inform on him. On the one or two times a year Heiser gave a sermon in that dialect, he dared to be somewhat more oppositional, given the paucity of native speakers of that dialect in his town.

The most shocking Stasi-related incident for Herr Heiser occurred in 1974 when a young man from Groß Breese went missing. When his body was discovered in the Elbe, the regime claimed that he had drowned while attempting to escape, but residents of the area had it on good authority that he had been run over by a Stasi motorboat. It sickened Heiser to give the funeral oration without being able to mention the mysterious circumstances of the young man's death. In 1998, the Stasi officials involved in the incident were tried in a court set up in Schwerin's Demmlerplatz, ironically the former Stasi regional headquarters, and were found innocent. In order to provide a modicum of solace to the family after what was in Heiser's view a horrendous miscarriage of justice, he helped arrange for a memorial panel to be placed alongside the riverbank where the young man lost his life.

Spurred by this incident and others involving the Stasi, Heiser gave a sermon to a crowd of nearly 10,000 demonstrators in Wittenberge on January 15, 1990, in which he denounced the Stasi's presence in society, and he received a vibrant round of applause when he said that churchgoers were fed up of having their license plate numbers recorded by Stasi agents. Although he was sure that he would be arrested for his comments—even though they came over two months after the fall of the Wall—the regime took no action against his disparagement of the secret police, which convinced him that the Stasi in its revamped form, as the Office for National Security, had, once and for all, lost its teeth.

As much as his life and the lives of other East Germans were under constant Stasi surveillance, there is an urgency in Herr Heiser's plea not to misunderstand this state of affairs as evidence of a cowering or trampled people. He stresses that there was still "civic courage" in the GDR and that he refused to let the ubiquitous monitoring rule his life. As an example, he relates an incident in 1986 when he requested from the mayor that he become volunteer fire chief for the district, knowing full well that the party would not want a minister to occupy this position. Heiser was delighted when the SED installed a more "reliable" fire chief because his aim all along was simply to have the long-vacant position filled. Heiser takes pride today in claiming that societal monitoring in the GDR did not turn him into a "yes-man," but it is difficult to know if his claim is meant as criticism of those who succumbed and accommodated themselves to the regime's ubiquitous presence, or whether he is sympathetic with those who did not swim against the stream, knowing the serious consequences to his family from his life as a regime opponent.

Herr Jung, another interviewee who was a member of the church in his youth, became the object of Stasi interest when he was seventeen years old. Following a youth meeting in East Germany, he received a letter from a West German church youth group requesting that the two groups establish contact. Unbeknownst to him, the Stasi had intercepted the letter and immediately employed three informants to monitor him. His file would grow over the years to include eighteen informants and some three hundred pages. Herr Jung is remarkably even-handed when discussing the informant reports on him, claiming that most are "banal, boring, or naïve." At this point in the conversation his sister, who had joined us on the patio, added that many informants were likely *protecting* individuals with their purposefully generalized reports. It is, however, difficult to imagine that all eighteen informants were "protecting" Herr Jung, or that his entire file offered up banalities.

Although it is true that informant reports did not always accurately reflect their subject, as Timothy Garten Ash demonstrated in sometimes hilarious fashion in his own case,[29] informers today frequently cite the banality of the information to defend their own actions.[30] This is not much of a defense. Stasi officers did not consider any information commonplace, but rather all part of a composite image it worked tirelessly to form about East Germans. Furthermore, there had to be some element of personal information in the reporting for it to have any air of authenticity, a fact that required the hardly defensible position of information-gathering on someone the informant knew and then, unbeknownst to that individual, passing that information on to a state authority.

An unrelated run-in with the Stasi recounted by Herr Jung reveals the power of the organization in society. While looking for a bank robber, the Stasi took Herr Jung off the streets and kept him in a Stasi holding cell overnight without any communication with his family. His sister frantically called police stations to try to locate her brother, but to no avail. Although he was released the next day and was not injured in any way, the incident raises questions about the image that he and his family would have of the Stasi and how this might affect their conduct in society. As an organization with sweeping powers and one which was by every indication "above the law," the Stasi caused East Germans like Herr Jung to lead as inconspicuous a life as possible. One final aspect of Jung's life is worth recounting: He and his pregnant wife spent their wedding night in prison after an evening stroll accidentally brought them into a restricted zone near the border with West Germany.[31] It was in part because of this incident that he was throughout his life, as he says, "on his guard."

Apart from the Stasi presence, East Germans noted the fact of "dictatorship" primarily in two other venues, travel and television, the latter not to be underestimated because it was the most popular home pastime in East Germany.[32] For several individuals, travel restrictions were the most visible manifestation that the state they lived in was a strictly regulated one. Contrary to what is often assumed in the West, East Germans could legally emigrate to western countries, something that became marginally easier following the regime's signing on to the Helsinki Final Act in 1975.[33] Although it was a lengthy and complicated process, and one that overwhelmingly led to a denial of the request, East Germans could apply to emigrate to the West (and usually this meant to West Germany). Between 1977 and 1988, 121,000 East Germans emigrated legally.[34] Given the difficulty of the procedure, thousands of East Germans attempted high-risk measures of escape—the Stasi prevented fifty-four attempts to hijack airplanes out of East Germany between 1962 and 1973—or opted for the easier route of remaining in the West while on an officially sanctioned visit.

While the cases of roughly 900 who died at the Wall and the German-German border while trying to escape are fairly well known, the 1,000 who were injured at the same locations, the 175 who died swimming or otherwise navigating the treacherous Baltic Sea to Denmark or Sweden, and the staggering 72,000 who were jailed for their failed attempts remain in the shadows of historical scholarship. The Stasi was the primary instrument for investigating individuals who had applied to leave legally as well as those who attempted the illegal exodus known as *Flucht*. Applications to emigrate to the West were by no means a new phenomenon in 1989, although there was marked increase at that time. In 1980, 2 percent of East Germans applied to emigrate; by June 1989 that number had risen to 12 percent.[35]

Restrictions on travel to West Germany for major family events like funerals, anniversaries, and significant birthdays were for many East Germans particularly irksome. A history teacher from Wittenberge recalls how his trip to West Germany in 1954 to attend his mother-in-law's wedding was the last time he was permitted to visit the Federal Republic until his mother developed terminal cancer in the 1980s, even though he had applied on several other occasions. The strictly controlled visas also proved impossible for the teacher's children to obtain. Despite his best efforts, his children never had an opportunity to meet their grandparents.[36] A kindergarten teacher from the small village of Neuglobsow echoed these thoughts, observing that the "most bothersome" aspect of the GDR was the travel restriction, something she would have experienced more than others, as travel to West Germany was all but forbidden for kindergarten teachers until late in the regime.[37] A grocery store clerk who remembers that her informal interrogation by a party member upon her return from a trip to the West soured her on future travel across the Wall, is today evidently making up for lost travel time, recounting enthusiastically her recent trips to Ireland, Egypt, and Marrakech.[38]

Others, however, did not appear particularly inconvenienced by the travel restrictions. Kristina Vogt, who had been forcibly removed from Poland at the end of World War II, was in many ways the very symbol of the "workers' and peasants' state." She was part of the generation that undertook the backbreaking work of rebuilding Germany at the end of the war, a task that fell disproportionately to women. Although the *Trümmerfrauen* (rubble women) have entered public memory as the classic image of gritty Germans determined to rebuild their country, this urban phenomenon had a lesser-known counterpart in the countryside, where nearly one quarter of farms were run solely by women because their husbands and/or sons had died in the war or were in a POW camp in the Soviet Union (most of whom returned only in 1955).[39] A destroyed infrastructure and lack of farm implements were chief among the challenges she faced.

Sitting across from me at a flimsy table in the vestibule of the farmhouse, rusting implements propped up against the window, Frau Vogt, weathered from the years of hard agricultural labor, said that travel was for her simply not an issue,[40] almost to suggest that on any given day in her adult life, the pressing needs of the farm would have taken precedence, that she always had better things to do. As if to underlie the point, at the conclusion of our interview the septuagenarian rose and, grabbing a farm tool, hurried back to work in the barn. Although the regime's travel restrictions—and their ugly manifestation in the Berlin Wall— brought many East Germans to the streets in 1989, Frau Vogt reminds us that a certain segment of the population, as in any society, were content to stay close to home. This is not to suggest that those who desired a glimpse of life on the other side of the Wall were adventurous *Wanderlusters*, but simply to acknowledge that some East Germans, especially if they did not have relations in the West, did not desire to travel—either in Western or Eastern Europe.

In 1997 in Eisenhüttenstadt, at the launch of his book on opposition in East Germany, the former pastor and now eminent historian Ehrhart Neubert was forced to correct his declaration that watching West German television was a "tolerated form of opposition" with the hasty qualification "only in the last decade."[41] Residents of this town would have been particularly sensitive to his comments given that it was home to the only antenna erected in the GDR to jam television broadcast frequencies from the West. In 1970 a dentist in the area used a magnifying glass to try to burn down the wooden tower on which the blocking device rested; he was sentenced to eight years in prison.[42] Several of Eisenhüttenstadt's inhabitants who were interviewed for an oral history of Stalin's massive industrial "model" city in East Germany, which grew up out of the countryside almost overnight—the town was originally called Stalin City—recalled threats of arrest from Stasi officers for watching western television, a refrain echoed by several interviewees.

Otto Dachs recalled that, in the 1970s, employees of the German post office drove around Perleberg looking for houses with rooftop antennas pointing westward. At one point, a man showed up at his front door with a handheld apparatus, said, "You are watching western television," and confiscated the device attached to his TV that enabled him to receive the western TV signal—nicknamed by East Germans the "mousetrap." The man warned Dachs that if he were caught watching western TV again, his name would be published in the newspaper. Even prior to this incident, western TV had been an issue for Dachs. A classmate of his was suspended from their school for claiming that he would push off his roof anyone who tried to take his antenna to prevent him from watching western television, even if it meant that they would fall to their death. Dachs's support of his friend led to his suspension too.[43] A teacher recalled that following the building of the Berlin Wall he was required to visit all parents of children in his school and instruct them not to watch western television. In any case, as a teacher in the GDR one had to commit to watching exclusively East German television.[44] One interviewee remembered his concern about watching western television while his future daughter-in-law was visiting the family for the first time. She initially left the room when it was on but later grew accustomed to it.[45]

From the regime's point of view, the danger of watching western television lay not in the soap operas or the evening dramas, nor exclusively in the news, which provided a different worldview, but also in the momentous achievements in the West. Neil Armstrong's small step onto the moon on July 21, 1969, was broadcast live in West Germany, but could be watched only furtively in the GDR.[46]

What the Stasi presence meant for the general conduct of East Germans in their daily life is difficult to capture. Two interviewees claimed that they continued to speak their minds in public, criticizing various aspects of the GDR, although, to be sure, not about taboo subjects such as the Politburo members, East German elections, or the Soviet presence. Most of the interviewees, however, expressed much of the sentiment described by historian of the Stasi Hubertus Knabe, that trust, spontaneity, and sense of one's self were badly damaged by the Stasi's presence.[47] Interviewees, even one who said that he did not fear expressing his opinion of the regime, reported that they were circumspect in restaurants because of the possible presence of informants.[48]

In the workplace, East Germans assumed the presence of an informant although they could never be sure who it might be. A Wittenberge teacher believed there to be three or four informants in the teaching complement; the director of a box-making factory assumed that his bookkeeper, whom the party insisted he take on, was secretly working for the Stasi—an assumption that was confirmed when the archives opened.[49] East German citizens constantly made a judgment about an individual to whom they were speaking and censored their information accordingly. In a remarkable revelation, one respondent's wife reported how she constantly whispered to her friends and family "quiet, quiet" when in public places, *and still does*. Fearing even today that the Stasi has not completely disappeared from the East German landscape, she reprimands her husband for being too critical of East Germany in public. East Germans also practiced self-censorship in other, more private areas, including mail and telephone, where it would be very unlikely for East Germans to speak openly for fear of Stasi interception.

In general, East Germans interviewed here did not fear the Stasi every minute of every day, but they did acknowledge leading a more cautious life because of its presence. They were selective in whom they confided, most switched off the West German television station if there was a knock at the door, they kept to neutral topics in restaurants, and none dared criticize the regime while at work. Although he was referring to the 1950s, the Polish dissident Czeslaw Milosz's view of East European society contains a timeless essence:

> It is hard to define the type of relationship that prevails between the people in the East otherwise than as acting, with the exception that one does not perform on a theater stage but in the street, office, factory, meeting hall, or even the room one lives in. Such acting is a highly developed craft that places a premium upon mental alertness. Before it leaves the lips, every word must be evaluated as to its consequences.[50]

When prompted about what, precisely, they feared from running afoul of the Stasi, few had a concrete answer. Prison sentences or physical harm were not at the center of their concerns, but rather a general sense that their lives would be harmed in some way by running up against the instruments of repression, that their children might not be able to pursue higher education, that they might be demoted, that permission to visit western relatives would not be granted, that waiting times for cars or housing would be extended. These fears were well grounded, since repression in the GDR in the later period manifested itself precisely in the molding and control of life-opportunities for East German citizens, rather than the blatant use of force that characterized the earlier period.[51] East Germans may not have been simply ruled, passive objects of the state, but the stick the state wielded over one's life chances and those of one's family certainly set boundaries for their agency.

If caution bordering on fear, and a general sense of keeping a low profile, were part of the East German experience, what is one to make of the often repeated refrain that East German society was more mutually supportive than the "cold" Germany of today? Even Dr. Hoffmann seems conflicted about this aspect, claiming at one point in the conversation that he had felt part of a broader collective in the GDR. He later chastised himself, saying this closeness was a mirage given the Stasi's ubiquitous presence. The idea that there was a sense of community in East Germany that has since evaporated is common in some circles of East Germany today. In 1998 this sentimental view of the country peaked with the widely publicized story of a widower in Brandenburg found mummified in his living room chair in front of the television in his apartment. He had been dead for four years. Newspapers throughout the region lamented that such a tragedy would not have been possible in East Germany, where there was more of a sense of a shared humanity (*Menschlichkeit*).

Stefan Wolle dismantled this rosy view in a scathing counterexplanation of why a body would have been discovered much sooner in the GDR. Due to the housing shortage, someone would have noticed the mail piling up or the plants wilting on the balcony and could well have tried to inquire at the housing office if the apartment were available or, as frequently happened, simply moved in and thereby presented the housing office with a fait accompli. The custodians of the apartment building, who not only kept up the building but also recorded guests who visited longer than three days and collected funds for solidarity projects, were frequently the first point of contact for Stasi investigations; they certainly would have noticed a missing renter. Finally, either the Stasi or the police would have investigated anyone whose participation in society (usually in the form of employment) suddenly dropped out of sight.[52]

Joachim Gauck has also suggested that the perceived solidarity in East Germany was a result of having to help each other survive an oppressive state.[53] If an East German today were asked how she managed to get by, given the chronic shortages of items like car parts or items to repair a leaky faucet, her immediate answer would be "Vitamin C" (connections) (in German, *Vitamin B [Beziehung]*), knowing someone who could procure the desired part, or, as East Germans would say, someone who could "organize" it. This peculiar source no doubt played a more significant role than simply obtaining spare parts, however, as it provided individuals with a sense of network, of being "propped up" in a human sense as well. A physician from District Gransee perhaps said it best when reflecting on the nature of solidarity in East Germany: "In dictatorship as in war," she observes, "people come together in difficult times."[54]

## ACTING ON THE EAST GERMAN STAGE

Although the reaction to encounters with dictatorship, and especially with the Stasi, depended on the individual and the nature of that encounter, it is noteworthy that these East Germans did indeed recognize that they took the Stasi into account in their everyday lives. This often took the form of self-censorship, a constant care of what one said to whom. One does not detect from East Germans' reflections on their past that they were gripped by a paralyzing fear, in the psychological sense of the word—although one interview subject did say she "was always afraid"[55]—but rather a deep resignation that one was not the master of one's own destiny, that to run afoul of the Stasi, even unintentionally, was to sacrifice power over one's life and the life opportunities of family members.[56] This latter point has been borne out in an exhaustive study of 576 East German political victims, 73.4 percent of whom said that their own oppositional activities brought negative consequences to family members who had not been involved in opposition, ranging from demotions to denial of travel permits to denial of higher education to children, and finally to, for many, years-long observation by the Stasi.[57]

To be sure, these fears did not relate solely to a loss of income, although that element cannot be underestimated, but it carried with them a wider fear that must be seen within the context of dictatorship: that of being ensnared in the repression apparatus.[58] To come into contact with the Stasi in even the mildest form would cause an East German to mentally search his past for whatever transgression, no matter when committed or how slight, for the content of every conversation and with whom they had it, for whatever it might be that the Stasi could now use against them.[59]

In a landmark study of thirty individuals affected by the Stasi, Babett Bauer argues that East Germans' unease regarding the Stasi presence tended to materialize after the first encounter with them, but once it did, it remained a permanent feature in their lives. Many East Germans who were not engaged in oppositional behavior but who had simply run across the Stasi in some fashion, and therefore did not "expect" a run-in as dissidents might, were so shaken that they launched themselves headlong into East German life. They became model employees and active participants in their neighborhood associations so as to reduce the chance of any further encounter with the regime's structures, something that might be termed a "pragmatic loyalty." Others withdrew from society and sought refuge after their encounter in the sanctuary of private life.[60] What remains unclear in Bauer's account is the definition of an "encounter" with the Stasi that would spark a life-long defense mechanism against not only the secret police but its assumed accomplices—workplace supervisors, the party, mass organizations. To varying degrees, these encounters would have caused East Germans to internalize the Stasi's presence. At some level, as Bauer so eloquently concludes, repression bored into "the body's wrinkles and the brain's mechanisms."[61]

Setting aside those who were directly repressed by the regime, many of the individuals interviewed claimed to be supporters of the GDR's societal system, even though they had had some encounter with the instruments of repression.

Most of these were ordinary citizens who could hardly be characterized as utopian dreamers. Brigitte Reimann, the author of the popular book *Franziska Linkerhand*, a passionate plea for the socialist city as a living place of communication that was published after her premature death in 1973, is one of the better-known examples of this sentiment. She believed in the GDR although she too had become entangled in the secret police apparatus. As she herself admitted, the Stasi manipulated her into informant work.

In her capacity as "Catherine" and in contrast to the vast majority of informants, Reimann did not sign a formal agreement—she reported on the artistic and literary community until she denounced herself to the Literary Circle of which she was a member, thereby rendering her useless to the Stasi.[62] She was bullied into Stasi work, blackmailed into more intrusive spying in order to free her husband who had been jailed after a fight with the police, betrayed friends and colleagues, and yet remained firmly committed to the GDR. How does one explain this paradox? Like many other East Germans, Reimann saw "good" in the GDR and an ideal that far outweighed its imperfect implementation.

The attempt to separate the "good" from the "bad" in East Germany is indeed at the heart of much recent literature on the country, although these are not attempts to resurrect the country or its system.[63] Nevertheless, there seems to be a feeling that one can separate out positive, humanitarian projects conducted by East German citizens and by the state from the harmful, repressive aspects of the regime. This was not, after all, the Nazi regime, where a murderous, racial ideology went hand in hand with the repression apparatus, and whose society was infused with its odious thought.[64] Even the admittedly impressive advancements in cancer that took place under the Nazi regime, from which postwar generations of Germans (particularly women) benefited, were conducted within the framework of protecting the "German genus."[65]

Historians of East Germany can point to many humanitarian accomplishments of the GDR that rested beyond negative aspects of ideology, including widening access to education to workers' and farmers' children, recycling initiatives, and, one frequently cited as a model accomplishment that the new Germany would do well to emulate, the *Poliklinik* system of medical care, which gathered under one roof medical professionals, labs, and radiology facilities. These might be considered similar to the medical clusters, or outpatient mini-hospitals that one finds in many Canadian and American cities, which can deal with most medical issues short of major surgery. Up to forty physicians and two hundred nonmedical staff provided medical care in *Polikliniken* for a wide range of issues, from immunization to counseling for people questioning their sexuality.[66] In fact, more than half of East German doctors worked at these outpatient clinics. Although the severe shortages of medicine and modern equipment cannot be denied, it is also true that this organization of the medical system was advantageous and offered a decent level of health care. Many of those who worked in it were compassionate and dedicated.

Repression, however, cannot be sifted out of the health care system. One senior physician maintains that all clinic directors had some involvement with the Stasi.[67] Hospitals were also heavily penetrated, as evidenced by Dr. Hoffmann's experience and the story of informant Nöcker from chapter 2, but these were not isolated incidents. The regional hospital in Magdeburg-Altstadt had thirty-one informants, two of whom were high-ranking physicians in the director's office.[68] The Stasi could determine who went to medical college in the first place, actively recruited informants at medical school, made sure that medical professionals did not flee the country, and used heavy-handed methods to recruit even top surgeons as informants. Roughly 3 to 5 percent of all physicians in the GDR were Stasi informants at the end of the regime, a participation rate significantly higher than the population at large.[69]

The Stasi's aggressive recruitment of informants out of medical colleges (oftentimes of students under the age of eighteen) paid off in that half of those adult students recruited remained as informants once they became practicing physicians.[70] From a secret police perspective, doctors were ideal informants not only for the information that they could provide on the medical sector, but also because they encountered East Germans from all walks of life in the course of their day. Although the Stasi rarely sought out a doctor to provide information on a specific patient, once the doctor became an informant they frequently reported on their patients. One recent study estimates that 25 percent of doctor-informants broke the oath of secrecy, and thus GDR law, in reporting to the Stasi on their patients' health, personal situation, and politics.[71] "Honecker's health care" may not have been "Hitler's highways" but neither did East Germany's social initiatives exist as an oasis immune from a repressive dictatorship.

Orlando Figes's masterful account of daily life in Stalin's Soviet Union, *The Whisperers*, makes plain that the Communist Party orchestrated mutual surveillance on a grand scale, even to the point that unrelated families lived together in communal apartments in order for citizens to more easily monitor each other. This, for Figes, is unique to the Soviet Union: "While the totalitarian regimes of the twentieth century sought to mobilize the population in the work of the police, and one or two, like the Stasi state in the GDR, managed for a while to infiltrate to almost every level of society, none succeeded as the Soviet regime did for sixty years, in controlling a population through collective security."[72]

The cult around Pavlik Morozov, the boy who denounced his father to the authorities as a kulak (a well-to-do farmer) and was lauded as a hero of the Soviet Union, illustrates the extent to which the state demanded vigilance from ordinary citizens in policing for enemies.[73] Private life, it was hoped, would come to an end. In many ways, the experiences of those interviewed here differ significantly from this "ideal" of a mutually monitoring society; there was in East Germany no cult of Morozov or forced living with strangers. Most East Germans were not burned by the sun of that revolution. In that they were prudent and exhibited deep concern for life opportunities, but did not experience a paralyzing fear of the gulag, East Germans cannot be thought of as "whisperers," but they did become, over the course of years, very good "actors."

# 6

# THE DOWNFALL

IN OCTOBER 1989, the residents of Wittenberge began emptying their cupboards of candles. Armed with this unvanquishable weapon they went first by the hundreds, then thousands, and eventually tens of thousands to the Lutheran church, which had been holding peace services every Monday, and then marched to the T-34 Soviet tank monument outside city hall, where they left their burning candles. Following East Germany's collapse the tank was taken away and replaced by a plowshare, but that display was of short duration. It too was removed and the site itself turned into a garden. There is no longer a single public reminder of the revolution that toppled communism in East Germany in Wittenberge, or in any of the towns in Districts Perleberg and Gransee.

When East Germans took to the streets in those two districts in the fall of 1989, it was the first time in anyone's memory that these sleepy towns had experienced any kind of serious disturbance. There were no major incidents during the Hitler years; the uprising of 1953 somehow bypassed the area. Thousands of people joined anti-regime protests in towns that unlike Berlin or some of the southern industrial centers had never given the regime any cause for concern. The revolutionaries out in the provinces, whose story is infrequently told and hardly memorialized, partook in the march of history as much as their better-known counterparts in larger centers.[1] That they were able to reclaim the streets in this strictly controlled society shocked the participants themselves.

## THE MAY 1989 COMMUNAL ELECTIONS

East German elections were always extravagant affairs. Bands played while local dignitaries shook hands with voters headed toward the booths to exercise the "first duty of a socialist citizen," and officials greeted first-time voters with bouquets of flowers. The communal elections of May 7, 1989, were conducted with equal fanfare, but their approach meant that the Stasi in District Perleberg spent most of the spring 1989 working to secure the electoral success of its political superiors, the Socialist Unity Party (*Sozialistische Einheitspartei Deutschlands—SED*).[2] "Symbol 89" was the code name given to the Stasi operation to secure the communal elections throughout East Germany, an operation that involved careful monitoring of individuals who might disrupt the election—such as church officials or applicants to emigrate from East Germany—and the use of informants to monitor societal discontent that could lead to nonparticipation at the election.[3] Stasi informants identified 370 individuals who planned to protest the election by not voting, and pointed to a lack of apartment space, poor roads, and supply problems as key factors behind potential nonparticipation in the election.[4] As the Stasi already had information on 582 individuals, including Jehovah's Witnesses, former criminals, and church leaders, none of whom were likely to participate (and in some cases had not for years), secret informants had uncovered in advance 370 of the 1,068 individuals (or 35 percent) who ended up not casting a ballot, an impressive performance.[5]

To an outsider, the results of the elections were an astonishing success for the ruling SED, reporting an endorsement of the election unity lists of 98.88 percent. Behind the scenes, however, the Stasi was well aware that even in the strictly controlled GDR, the population in District Perleberg had voiced dissent in the election. The official number of nonvoters at the election was a staggering 165 percent higher than at the last election in 1986.[6] Specialized workers (*Facharbeiter*) and factory workers comprised the lion's share of nonvoters. Unlike elsewhere in East Germany where individuals wrote letters of complaint about the falsified results, ministers voiced disapproval in sermons, and demonstrators took to the streets—as was the case of the 1,000 strong protest in Leipzig—no such protests took place in Districts Perleberg and Gransee.[7]

Many residents of District Perleberg who refused to cast their ballots on May 7, 1989, did so because of immediate standard-of-living issues. East Germans in the county of Reckenzin complained of not having access to the city water supply. The building site manager for the factory VEB Meliorationsbau threatened not to take part in the election because he had been waiting twelve years for a telephone.[8] Some residents protested vociferously that the only restaurant in their area had been closed for years for repairs; others complained that they could not obtain fresh fruit after 4 p.m.[9] In the lead-up to the election, citizens were called upon to put in writing to their city councils issues that they would like addressed. In Region Schwerin, 1,715 did so, including 246 from District Perleberg. The key issues in these letters, according to the Stasi, were lack of proper living accommodations, damage to the environment, lack of telephones, poor roads, and lack of building supplies.[10]

The Stasi prepared a special report on the situation in the city of Wittenberge, the industrial center of District Perleberg, which suggested that for some in the district, immediate living standard issues in and of themselves were not the sole factor behind discontent, but rather the party's ceaseless propaganda that glossed over the dire situation. The Stasi admitted that the situation in District Perleberg was considerably worse than neighboring industrial centers like Güstrow, and worse than the region in general.[11] Wittenberge could no longer meet the bread needs of the population, causing the local authorities to import 12,000 rolls (*Brötchen*), a staple in any German diet. The bread was brought in weekly from five surrounding districts, which, according to the Stasi, affected their freshness and appearance. The Stasi did not foresee much improvement in this area until a large bakery had been built in Perleberg, an improvement not scheduled until 1994.[12]

Important factories like the rayon factory (VEB Zellstoff- und Zellwollewerk), the sewing machine factory (VEB Nähmaschinenwerk Wittenberge), and the vegetable oil refinery (Märkische Ölwerke) were often shut down due to a lack of spare parts. The Stasi grimly reported: "It must be admitted that without support from the region, it will not be possible to solve the problems of the city of Wittenberge."[13] Given the precarious situation there, the Stasi recommended a swift response to the dire supply problems. What is noteworthy, however, is that this lack of material goods was often coupled with a distrust of the regime. Stasi appraisal of the popular mood suggest a population exasperated by the party's lies about overly fulfilling economic plans.[14] Deep popular anger resulted from the contradiction between regime propaganda and actual living conditions.[15]

The Stasi documents for District Gransee are not as plentiful on the May 1989 elections as one would like, but those of the Communist Party suggest that housing issues preoccupied the electorate. The majority of the 274 *Eingaben* (petitions) that East Germans sent to state authorities in the lead-up to the election landed in the housing branch of the district council. Considering that the trying housing situation of the immediate postwar period lay nearly forty years in the past, the complaints around housing were fully justified: one person requested an apartment with a bathroom, another complained of still having to live with his ex-wife because no other apartment was available, a family of four hoped to move out of their one-bedroom apartment, a married couple with a child were still living with their parents, a family of four requested an apartment with more than two rooms.[16]

In order to address the complaints about material goods that were evident at the election, the SED in District Gransee vowed to raise production of consumer goods by nearly 20 percent over 1988 figures; it boasted of increases in certain goods in the district that had already taken place: 3,000 more children's sandals, 2,500 more babies' shoes, 44 more sofas, 110 more easy chairs, and 22 more stools.[17] In the end, however, despite legitimate housing and material concerns, the elections in District Gransee were less contentious than other places in the GDR although it is worth noting that the district did have the only electoral district in the country that did not endorse the unity list, a result in large part of an abusive and roundly despised mayor.[18]

## EXODUS

On July 26, 1989, the director of the rayon factory in Wittenberge settled down to breakfast in his Linz hotel, where he planned to conduct business with an Austrian firm. He became upset that his director of technology was late. As a member of the SED, a graduate of the Karl Marx University in Leipzig, a reliable factory colleague since 1978, and the father of four sons, the director of technology was an unlikely candidate to flee to the West during a routine business trip, but this is precisely what had happened. For days afterwards, bewildered co-workers gossiped about the defection.[19] This case represents a high-profile defection from the district and one that the Stasi investigated inconclusively, but the exodus, both legal and illegal, of East Germans from all walks of life was becoming a Stasi concern in Perleberg in the summer and fall of 1989.

When Hungary began rolling up the barbed wire that formed the Iron Curtain between Hungary and Austria in May 1989, East Germans vacationing in Hungary on the summer break from school used the opportunity to flee to the West.[20] By late summer, roughly 1,600 East Germans had fled their country in this manner—on August 19 alone, 661 East Germans fled to the West through Hungary. Although a few days later an East German, Kurt Werner Schulz, would be shot in a scuffle with a Hungarian border guard,[21] in general the whole scene was taking place remarkably peacefully.

The permeation of the Iron Curtain between Hungary and Austria was having consequences in District Perleberg hundreds of miles to the north. The leader of the Stasi in Region Schwerin sent out an urgent memorandum to all district Stasi leaders, reminding his subordinates that all those who were applying to leave East Germany—even for a holiday—must be reported to the SED secretary for the area, and he advised them to be ever vigilant of increased attempts to leave East Germany directly.[22] Furthermore, all those who were applying to emigrate from East Germany were to be monitored by informants in order to prevent public protest. Informants were also to be used against those who were planning to travel to Hungary.[23]

Concern for "legal" emigration caused Werner Ryll, the leader of the Stasi for District Perleberg, using a Stasi tactic in place since the 1970s,[24] to command those in positions of authority, such as factory bosses, to apply pressure on employees to withdraw their emigration applications.[25] The tactic met with limited success, as some simply left illegally. By August 16 Perleberg District had lost twenty-six citizens to illegal emigration, and a cluster of five others were holed up in the West German embassy in Budapest awaiting permission to leave.[26] Within a few months the numbers of those illegally leaving the district rose. By the end of September, 110 individuals had left, three-quarters of them via Hungary. These individuals ran the gamut from waiters to doctors and nurses to employees of the German Railway, the sewing machine factory, and various construction sites. Following the orders of Erich Mielke, head of the Stasi, district Stasi officials held daily meetings with the regular police to find out who had applied for a travel permit to Hungary.[27]

In District Perleberg, 1988 had seen a total of eighty-nine applications to emigrate, involving 193 people (as families applied on a single application). By June 20, 1989, the District Council had already received seventy-five applications to emigrate for 171 people. Forty-four of these applications had already been approved, and the individuals had left.[28] Although we do not have the breakdown of these numbers for District Perleberg, we do have them for the Region Schwerin, in which Perleberg was situated. A variety of social backgrounds was represented in the applicants from Region Schwerin—15 percent were in industry, 7.4 percent in agriculture, 5.8 percent in the construction industry, 13.2 percent in commerce, and 12.3 percent from the health field.[29] Residents of Wittenberge represented 65 percent of the total emigration applications for District Perleberg. More than 60 percent were between the ages of twenty-five and forty. Stasi officers themselves seemed to be at a loss to explain the exodus among this segment of the population that had few material concerns, as they outlined in a report to the district leadership summarizing the situation in the land: "The following characteristics are typical of those applying to leave East Germany: All had a comfortable standard of living. They were average to very good workers at their work places. They participated actively in social functions of the workers' collective and in their neighborhoods. None of them gave any cause for concern."[30]

As had been the case for most of the 1980s, the number of Perleberg residents applying to emigrate was a focus of Stasi work in the district, as revealed by the number of operations (OVs) targeting individuals who had filed applications. In October 1989 the District Perleberg Stasi had five OVs underway (code named *Tendenz* (Tendency), *Täuscher* (Phoney), *Taxi*, *Brille* (Glasses), and *Stoma*). OV *Tendenz* and OV *Brille* were long-running investigations of two prominent Lutheran ministers; the others dealt with individuals who had applied to leave for the West. At the same time the Stasi was actively at work on the lower category of operation, the OPK (*Operative Personenkontrolle*—Personal Surveillance Operation). In May, there were forty OPKs underway, of which nineteen dealt with applicants to emigrate.[31] By October, the Stasi was involved with fifty-one OPKs, eighteen of which had been initiated during the year—only three more than in 1988 and fewer than the twenty-three which the Stasi initiated in 1987 (keeping in mind that the year 1989 was not yet over). There was, in fact, no appreciable increase in the number of high-end Stasi operations initiated in 1989, although one might have expected a dramatic increase in Stasi monitoring given the increasingly volatile situation in the Soviet bloc and the exodus.[32] In sum, the District Perleberg Stasi was no more operationally active in 1989 in the exodus arena than it had been earlier in the 1980s.

Although the Stasi was increasingly concerned with those who left the GDR illegally—and certainly some of the eighteen new operations (OPKs) in 1989 would have dealt with these individuals or their families—the situation was not catastrophic. As late as three weeks before the opening of the Berlin Wall, fifty residents of District Perleberg had occupied West German embassies in Prague and Warsaw, 107 left via Hungary, and thirty-three remained behind on a sanctioned visit to West Germany—in total, a mere 0.3 percent of the population. Naturally, those who had applied to visit Hungary, and who had also applied to emigrate, were denied travel permits.[33] By early October, the East German government had banned travel to the last permitted Soviet bloc country, Czechoslovakia.

If the bleeding of citizens to the West was of mild concern to the Stasi in District Perleberg, it was even less so in District Gransee where, by the end of April 1989, only forty-eight people had applied to settle permanently in West Germany, half of whom were dependents of adults who applied.[34] Exodus was hardly a factor at the communal elections in May.[35] Even in September, with an increasing number of East Germans applying to leave or departing through Hungary, only nine people in District Gransee applied to leave permanently, and up to that point in the year, only six had left the GDR via Hungary.[36] Those who applied to leave tended to be in their twenties and thirties.[37] A high-ranking Stasi officer who visited District Gransee in the late summer of 1989 indicated that the pressure on the District Gransee Stasi from would-be emigrants was "comparatively low," but warned the officers to be on the look out for applicants to emigrate who might consider collective action such as occupying churches, demonstrating, or storming embassies.[38]

## OPPOSITION GROUPS

The ponderous St. Jacob's church in the heart of Perleberg sat quietly through most of the years of the GDR, its spacious interior sparsely populated during church services with perhaps forty to fifty die-hard churchgoers, almost all of them over the age of fifty. In 1989, however, the mammoth edifice would not be large enough to hold the two thousand demonstrators who gathered for an evening service. With pews filled beyond comfort, six hundred demonstrators had to listen from the market square.

Werner Ryll, the leader of the Stasi in District Perleberg, became increasingly concerned throughout 1989 with the networks that church officials were developing, particularly around an environmental theme. Nowhere is this demonstrated more clearly than in the elaborate Stasi OV *Tendenz* against Parish Priest Gottfried de Haas of Perleberg and his family.

In 1984, the District Perleberg Stasi recruited one of the most successful informants in its history, Frank Pleß, code named Informant "Robert," a man who had been married for three years and had a child. Robert's illegal activities (which, due to privacy considerations, are not divulged to researchers) drew him to the attention of the Stasi and, in return for avoiding a prison sentence, Robert agreed to inform for the Stasi. Lt. Bernd Besenbiel of the District Perleberg Stasi office was excited at the prospects of Robert because he was still young enough to monitor the situation among the youth of the district.[39] A year after his recruitment, Robert was assigned to the Protestant Youth Group (*Junge Gemeinde*), where he came in contact with the parish priest, Gottfried de Haas of Perleberg, someone who had already been written up in Stasi files for his interest in building up the youth group's presence in the district. By 1986, Robert's case officer could write with some degree of satisfaction that Robert had penetrated the group and, equally importantly, had built up a "personal relationship" with de Haas.[40]

The astonishing result of Robert's longtime friendship with the de Haas family—he and de Haas's son, Joachim, had become fast friends—was that this Stasi informant was one of the handful of individuals present at the highly secret establishment of an oppositional environmental group. By 1987 the de Haas family was holding regular evening discussions on environmental issues. In 1989 Joachim, through his church contacts, had established a link with a Berlin group founded in 1988 named "Arche-grün-ökologisches Netzwerk" (The Ark Green Ecological Network) and wanted a Perleberg branch of the group. Robert was not only a founding member of the Perleberg branch of the Ark Green Network but also elected to the coordinating committee. The election took place in the living room of an Ark Green Network higher-up of the Berlin branch responsible for all East Germany.[41] On his trips to Berlin, the Stasi informant would often stay overnight at the flat of this same individual, one of the key figures overall in the movement. Robert and the three others in the Perleberg group actively took part in environmental actions, such as photographing the environmental damage caused by Soviet troop movements in the area, writing to city hall to request more trees be planted, or asking Greenpeace to send two million letters to East Germans about the environmental degradation in East Germany. Every aspect of these actions was duly reported back to the Stasi by Robert.

As a result of this information, in 1987 the Stasi upgraded the operation against Gottfried de Haas and his wife who, according to the Stasi, was the "dominant" member of the family, from an OPK (which had been underway since 1985) to OV, the highest level. The catalyst for the increased attention was the interest in the environmental movement combined with de Haas's understandable church contacts across the GDR, and even to West Germany.[42] Robert not only spied on the environmental groups but spent the next two years securing church documents and letters that would reveal de Haas's contacts. By February 1989 Besenbiel had grown more concerned about the Ark Green Network group in Perleberg because it had started to move into the political sphere.

One evening toward the end of the month, Joachim and the three other network members met in Joachim's apartment and drafted a letter to party leader Erich Honecker requesting that diplomatic relations with Iran be broken off due to the recent call by Ayatollah Khomeni for the execution of Salman Rushdie as punishment for his book *The Satanic Verses*.[43] Robert questioned the merit of the idea but could not push too hard without arousing suspicion. Lieutenant Besenbiel accordingly ordered that Robert make sure that no further environmental groups be established in the district. In a manner similar to the approach against applicants to emigrate, he suggested that the current Ark

Green Network group in Perleberg be subsumed under the regime's "policy of employing appropriate societal organizations to monitor a group"—a telling reference to the regime's use of a variety of instruments to monitor and guide society.[44]

In a meeting about OV *Tendenz* with his superiors in Schwerin, the head of Department XX (responsible for opposition in East Germany) stated that the Ark Green Network did not seem to him to be an enemy organization yet, and that OV *Tendenz* should be continued with an eye to reducing the group's size.[45] In addition, in order to control the regular evenings sponsored by the church on environmental issues, Ryll ordered the placing of "positive" individuals at meetings to balance out the number of opponents and to support "the security organs when the necessary dispersal of the gathering takes place." He also called for the placing of experts at these meetings to counter opponents' arguments about the environment. Finally, Ryll authorized the removal of the churches' photocopying permits if oppositional activity continued.[46]

Besenbiel recommended that Robert be awarded for his splendid work the service medal of the National People's Army on the fortieth anniversary of the Stasi—an anniversary that never came because of the intervening fall of the Berlin Wall. On October 24, 1989, Robert authored his last report for the Stasi, in which he reported on a spontaneous demonstration by some six hundred residents of Perleberg who had gathered in the streets yelling "Gorby! Get rid of the Stasi! We are the people!"[47] With that, his five years of Stasi work came to an end.

In many ways the opposition in District Gransee in 1989, and the Stasi's fight against it, were remarkably similar to that in District Perleberg. Several Stasi operations targeted Protestant ministers in the district who had long been involved in raising awareness about the environment but whose activities increased in 1989, along with the response of the population. In 1987 and 1988, churches in Menz, Zehdenick, and Neuglobsow had hosted environmental "information days" with exhibits and slide-shows about environmental devastation taking place in the GDR. Of particular concern to the Stasi was the involvement of younger people in these events and the burgeoning network of environmentalists beyond the district. The Stasi was especially interested in the *Umweltbibliothek* in Berlin, an environmental library and hub for opponents, which had been established in 1986. The Stasi's raid on it in 1987 caused opponents throughout the country to unite. Although the Stasi was mindful of opponents involved in environmental activities in Gransee, the numbers involved were quite small: The three environmental protection days in Neuglobsow in 1988 attracted a total of about fifty people.[48] In his 1989 plan, the leader of the Stasi in Gransee called for the recruitment of two informants under the age of eighteen with links to the church, in addition to the regular recruitment of informants, in order to counter the influence of the church among youth.[49] The Stasi believed that the vast majority of its problems with oppositionals would vanish if it could limit the church as an oppositional "home."[50]

Also like District Perleberg, the Stasi in District Gransee had a star informant in the church milieu. The informant "Cordula Peters" (whose real name is Karola Meineke) was twenty-five years old when she was recruited in 1986 with the task of monitoring church activity. In fact, her handwritten pledge to work secretly for the Stasi is a rarity: it states specifically that she will engage herself in helping the state "put through" its church policies, whereas the vast majority of pledges remained purposely vague on the type of work the informant would be engaged in.[51] Cordula Peters was diligent in her duties: in the space of three months, she authored reports on nineteen individuals involved with the church; she ranked the ten Protestant ministers and three Catholic priests in the district on a scale of one to four (one was progressive and loyal, four was "conservative" and presumably disloyal). All Roman Catholic priests received threes, and most of the Protestant ministers also tended toward the disloyal end of the spectrum); she monitored the "environmental Sundays" hosted by the church in 1989 and was the lead informant in Operation Representative (OV *Vertreter*) against the parish priest in Menz; she attended the funeral of the Baer brothers who had been shot by a Soviet soldier and reported word for word what the presiding minister said about the incident (see chap. 4). The Stasi twice rewarded her for her hard work with a generous bonus of 250 marks awarded on March 8, International Women's Day. Her copious reporting did not come to an end until November 2, 1989.[52]

## PERLEBERG'S 750th ANNIVERSARY CELEBRATIONS

During the week of August 18–27, 1989, Perleberg celebrated the 750th anniversary of its founding. One might indeed be tempted to sympathize with the Stasi personnel who, on top of their already exhausting duties, now had to deal with street musicians and entertainers. The festivities, which included parades, rock concerts, and street performers, were expected to attract as many as thirty thousand visitors to the town. An elaborate police plan to secure the festivities, including parking control and general crowd security, was coordinated with the local Stasi branch.[53] Fearful of the celebrations turning into public demonstrations against the regime, the head of the Perleberg Stasi office launched Operation City Jubilee 89, to be under his direct supervision. A high-ranking subordinate, Lieutenant Colonel Fluch, put in place a special committee of seven, including himself, to coordinate the efforts.

Individuals who had been denied the right to emigrate (seventy-one in total) formed one of the foci of the operations, perhaps spurred on by one individual's claim that he was going to burn himself publicly for having been denied exit to the West.[54] Stasi informants tailed him incessantly during the week of celebrations. Apart from operations under way, Fluch called for the use of informants against anyone who threatened violence during the festivities, against former criminals, and against members of the church or other "hostile-negative" groups.[55] Informants were also to monitor tourists in the area, a delegation from Preetz in West Germany seeking partner-city status with Perleberg, journalists, and key installations of the people's economy. Informants in the post office were to be trained to respond to anonymous calls threatening violence. Individuals suspected of wanting to escape over the border were also to be monitored.[56] A handwritten note outlined the venues that various informants were to cover. Informant "Alex," for example, was to monitor youth dances, informants "Albert," "Max Krause," "Beate," and others were to cover the parade.[57] Four informants were assigned to cover the farmers' market, four to the rock concert in a town square, and two to an evening indoor concert.[58] In total, sixty-five informants were employed in operations prior to and during the festivities.

Overall, the eighty celebrations took place largely without incident, although Werner Ryll was aghast that the band Rockhaus from Berlin came on stage to the theme music of the West German evening news.[59] Operations designed to monitor those who had been refused an exit visa, and those who planned to visit the West were by and large successful. Close informant monitoring meant that these individuals did not undertake actions against the regime. Those affiliated with the church were also quiet during the celebrations. Gottfried de Haas, the target of OV *Tendenz*, was closely monitored through informants. Although flags (both East German and of the city of Perleberg) were torn down during the festivities and de Haas had arranged two public visits to his church, both of which were relatively well attended,[60] Ryll nevertheless sang the praises of his informants, who conducted their work with "energy, discipline, and personal devotion."[61] Given this extreme level of Stasi involvement in local celebrations and monitoring of possible opponents who might disrupt the events, and its deep penetration of oppositional groups and individuals, the Stasi proved itself an instrument of control that reached far beyond the bounds of a "normal" securing of a public event.

## THE LAST DAYS

Public demonstrations in District Perleberg remained small and nonthreatening until the third week of October 1989, some six or seven weeks behind the major centers of Leipzig, where large, regular demonstrations were being held from the beginning of September, or in Dresden, where ten thousand people clashed with security forces on October 4.[62] Unlike in Leipzig, where there was a brief but visible Stasi presence at the big demonstration of October 9 before the Stasi retreated into the night, the Stasi in Perleberg remained invisible during the revolution.

The first major demonstration in the district occurred on October 20—several days after the party had shoved Erich Honecker into retirement and placed Egon Krenz at the helm. Eight hundred people attended a meeting in the Lutheran church in Wittenberge to hear two female representatives from the

Berlin-based opposition movement *Neues Forum* (New Forum).[63] This meeting was followed quickly by similar ones in Bad Wilsnack (five hundred in attendance) and in St. Jacob's Church in Perleberg (also five hundred).[64] Three days later, two thousand showed up for a meeting at St. Jacob's Church in Perleberg led by Frau de Haas, and finally, on October 27, in the last major demonstration in the district before the Wall fell, three thousand people crowded into the Lutheran Church in Wittenberge, these latter demonstrations similar in size to those in much larger cities like Erfurt, Rostock, Magdeburg, and even the regional capital of Schwerin, where five thousand protested on October 23.[65] It is estimated that in the last week of October, nearly half a million East Germans took to the streets.[66]

The meetings in District Perleberg revolved around the opposition platform of *Neues Forum* and various other problems in East Germany. Of these problems, the supply situation and the SED-controlled media topped the list, but other issues came out in discussion including poor medical facilities and lack of freedom to travel. The Stasi judged that support for *Neues Forum* came from youth, medical professionals, the teaching corps, and workers in large factories.[67] After the meetings, the demonstrators paraded through town in a peaceful fashion and placed candles at the steps of the party building. The nonthreatening demonstrations here contrast with those elsewhere in Region Schwerin, where the nervousness of the Stasi officer who penned the report in November 1989 on *Neues Forum* activities is almost tangible: "Demonstrations in district and region cities—almost without exception—file past SED and [Stasi] buildings [...] shouting 'Get rid of the Stasi pigs,' 'Strike them dead,' and 'The knives have been sharpened.'"[68]

In District Gransee, *Neues Forum* was informally founded under the guidance of the minister from Grüneberg on October 19, one day earlier than the first appearance of *Neues Forum* in District Perleberg.[69] Understandably, this new political group became the center of Stasi attention and elicited a memorandum from the regional Stasi director calling on the district offices to use "every means at their disposal" to gather information on this, the first nationwide political protest group in the GDR's history.[70] A few weeks later, about three hundred people attended a rally at a youth club in Zehdenick voicing complaints about the health care system (one person said you might as well bring a casket if you have to check in to the local hospital) and others calling for the dismantling of the Stasi.[71] At another gathering in a church in Zehdenick, protestors spoke about the environment and lack of freedom to travel.[72]

Residents of Gransee and Perleberg also angrily pointed out the unfair advantages of those East Germans with access to western currency, as they were able to shop at *Intershops,* which carried higher-end goods and a more plentiful selection.[73] This two-tier access to material goods is emerging in the literature as a source of discontent in the fall 1989 that was largely missed in works that appeared in the first decade or so following the revolution.[74] The last major demonstration in District Gransee, a gathering of one thousand people in a Gransee church, took place one day before the fall of the Wall.[75]

In those last days before the collapse of the Berlin Wall, there is a deep sense of foreboding in the Stasi documents from Gransee that the country stood on the brink of civil war. Normally, Stasi officers held a weapon but twice a year and that at the firing range. But in the fall of 1989 all Stasi officers were ordered to carry their personal weapons with them at all times and had explicit instructions to prevent attacks on Stasi installations by every means possible. There was also concern for attacks on their private residences.[76] On November 3, in the last memorandum of the long-serving minister for state security, Erich Mielke informed his officers that the party was undertaking everything possible for their protection.[77] Unlike the situation in Tiananmen Square, where the Chinese regime deployed tanks against opponents, a scenario that was increasingly unlikely in East Germany after the first successful demonstrations, it was probably not a robust military response by the regime that would have caused bloodshed but the quick trigger of a nervous Stasi officer. Even though the police frequently marched with demonstrators to prevent violence, one cannot help but think how easily events in East Germany could have resembled the violent revolution in Romania of a few weeks later.

After the fall of the Wall, the Stasi was renamed the Office of National Security (*Amt für nationale Sicherheit*), a short-lived outfit that attempted to style itself as a constitutional watchdog similar to that found in Western democracies. Most people in East Germany did not believe that the leopard had changed its spots. In late November, a group of citizens in Perleberg, including the mayor and Gottfried de Haas, met with Stasi representatives in the Stasi detachment. The citizens read aloud a letter that outlined their overwhelming fears in the past and demanded answers to a number of questions: Would the Stasi renounce the use of force? How many Stasi officials were there in the district? Would the Stasi open its building for inspection? The citizens also demanded that the Stasi stop monitoring citizens' meetings and bugging telephones. The branch director thanked the group for the letter and committed to a further meeting to answer the questions.[78] One physician who was among the demonstrators recalled the feeling he had on entering the building: "I was scared. But somehow most of my fear was already behind me."[79] A few weeks later, Stasi offices throughout the country were occupied by citizens concerned about the destruction of documents taking place. This was yet another unusual feature of the East German revolution: citizens occupying a still-intact secret police office had never happened before.[80]

## THE CROWD IN THE EAST GERMAN REVOLUTION

What motivated East Germans to take to the streets in 1989 has been a lightning rod for debate. Some historians have focused exclusively on the lack of consumer goods[81] while others have sought reasons beyond material considerations. Gale Stokes has written, "The reason so many wanted to flee East Germany was fundamentally not economic, however. They were fleeing a stifling sense of powerlessness, the regime's deadening insistence on capitulation, and the enervating denial of all possibility of idealism and hope."[82] Konrad Jarausch also argues that the lower living standards merely reinforced political frustrations.[83] Other historians speak to the relatively decent living standard in East Germany and point rather to "utter moral rot" of the regime[84] and to denied rights, including the lack of travel.[85]

From the evidence for Districts Perleberg and Gransee, it appears that any explanation of public pressure in the revolution of 1989 must take into account the failing trust between the population and the regime. It was often not solely a poor standard of living, but the combination of this with the overblown SED propaganda that eroded the legitimacy of the regime, and drove angry East German citizens to the streets. To be sure, there were also instances when standard-of-living issues alone caused hostility to the regime. A twelve-year wait for a telephone or a family of four living in a one-bedroom apartment was, for many, simply unbearable. Interestingly, the environmental degradation that caused the small underground group Ark Green Network to form in the summer of 1989 did not launch a discussion in the church meetings of late October. Perhaps the reason for this is that Perleberg was not a sight of major heavy industry and thus environmental issues were of less concern. It is worth recalling that the Ark Green in Perleberg never had more than four members, and that their activities were relatively benign. In contrast, the group in Region Halle filmed the horrendously scarred landscape around Bitterfeld and smuggled the tape to a West German television station where it was broadcast.[86] District Gransee, on the other hand, had several environmental groups and did witness popular discussion of the environment.

Failing trust is visible not only in Stasi documents that deal primarily with oppositional views in the population, but, remarkably, also in Stasi reports on those who *opposed* the drift toward revolution. Many were extremely concerned about developments in Poland and Hungary, supported China's use of armed force to confront demonstrators in Tiananmen Square, and generally approved of a more vibrant East German response to opposition at home.[87] How parents could risk taking their children on a wild journey through Hungary and into Austria was beyond many.[88] Some even went so far as to query why the regime did not counteract the flood of citizens by reporting on what had happened to those who ended up in the West. They expected that those that fled would be unemployed and dependent on soup kitchens and broadcasting this message might stem the tide.[89] Workers of the Wittenberge train station considered Hungary's opening of the border to Austria to be treasonous.[90]

Even those who sought a more robust SED response to the exodus criticized the SED for a lack of openness and honesty toward its own citizens. As one report, authored two days after the GDR had restricted East German travel to Czechoslovakia on October 3, 1989, noted: "Over and over citizens have expressed the view that people need to hear honest and open opinions."[91] Another report to the central agency in Berlin, analyzing the situation in the GDR, recommended that the SED retreat from its "propaganda of success." "The truth," the report suggested, "is easier to digest."[92] This point bears stating explicitly: Even hard-core supporters of communism, those who wanted a bloody suppression of the cheeky revolutionaries, wanted the regime to exhibit greater honesty. It should not surprise us that this motivation would also bring opponents to the streets. Failing trust should take its place alongside an abysmal situation in housing and material goods, anger at the two-tier access to consumer goods, denied rights, and political frustration as motives for public protest.

In assessing the balance between external factors, popular pressure, and regime implosion, the cases of Districts Gransee and Perleberg, away from the limelight of Berlin and Leipzig, suggest that the pressure exerted by the international situation—as manifested in the issue of exodus—was not a key factor in the revolution.[93] Strictly from a numbers point of view, not quite two hundred residents fled District Perleberg by October 1989, whereas one week in October in that district would witness demonstrations involving roughly six thousand people. One senior Stasi official candidly admitted that the pressure from the exodus file was "comparatively low" in District Gransee. Certainly, one is struck by the fact that the applicants to emigrate did not form a core of organized protests in either district, as was the case, for example, in Dresden.[94]

If one considers the chronology, the trigger for demonstrators in District Perleberg to take to the streets appears closely linked to the successful Leipzig demonstration of October 9, and even more so to the removal of Honecker on October 18. The first major demonstration in District Perleberg took place two days after Honecker's removal; in Gransee one day after. The closing on October 3 of the last country to which East Germans could travel without a visa, Czechoslovakia, passed relatively unnoticed. One resident of Wittenberge recalled specifically that demonstrations in that town commenced after residents witnessed the Leipzig demonstrations.[95]

From this, we may draw the conclusion that the experience of demonstrators elsewhere in the land, who did so with impunity, meant that Perlebergers and Granseers became bolder. An engineer from Wurzen summed up the feelings of many in East Germany: "I heard on the late night news that there were over seventy thousand at that demonstration in Leipzig and that it went off without incident. I poured myself one big Slibovic. I somehow knew that this was the end of the GDR."[96]

The flight of East Germans was not a major form of protest in District Perleberg as evidenced in Werner Ryll's work plan for 1990. His view of Stasi priorities is striking. He foresaw an elaborate plan to secure the rayon factory in Wittenberge that was undergoing technological upgrades. Roughly the same amount of the work plan is dedicated to the fight against "underground political activity," as Ryll called for more attention and resources to key operations aimed at hemming in opponents. Ryll envisaged a continuing effort to apply pressure on those who applied to emigrate to withdraw their applications and thus reduce the numbers leaving East Germany illegally. Stasi officers were to determine who had already left, then trace and monitor their relations and friends in East Germany. Ryll's calm projection of quarterly—not more frequent—reports on this subject for 1990, was issued *after* Hungary fully opened its border to Austria. In essence, Ryll called for no more serious measures against the exodus than in years past, and the place of exodus was not noticeably prominent in his work plan for 1990.[97]

It would be an exaggeration to say that the Lutheran church caused the collapse of East German communism, but it is difficult to imagine how the revolution would have taken place without it. The St. Nicholas church in Leipzig, home to the Monday demonstrations from which those huge demonstrations sprang, will assuredly take its place alongside other European buildings of revolutionary import—the Bastille, the Winter Palace, the Frankfurt Paulskirche. In Districts Gransee and Perleberg, churches provided leadership, infrastructure (public space, photocopiers, candles), organizational skills, and the perception of distance from the regime to manage and guide the demonstrators. More than the open border between Hungary and Austria, more than material concerns, more than failing regime legitimacy, more than popular anger toward the Stasi, the church was the regime's most vexing problem in 1989.

## 1989: A COLLAPSE OF THE FIRM?

Many see in the downfall of East Germany a delightful irony—a regime with an all-knowing, all-powerful secret police proved, in the end, as powerless to stop the collapse as the Wall did to prevent that final exodus. How could it be that a regime with a secret police nearly four decades in refinement was unable to halt the revolution? The answer to this riddle, for some, is Stasi incompetence.[98] However, the course of the revolution in these two districts should lead us away from the conclusion that the Stasi was inept, that myopic Marxist ideologues were gathering reams of the "wrong" information, or were not able to interpret the information properly. In many cases the Stasi officers gathered information from seasoned informants and passed the key elements of this information on to appropriate line departments, such as Department XX, responsible for internal opposition, and to the local officers responsible for information and analysis, who in turn fed the digested information to the analysis committee at the regional offices.

There is much in the documents to suggest a high degree of competency on the part of Stasi officers in their analysis of incoming information. In District Perleberg, they filtered the static of myriad complaints about the supply situation and consumer goods, to issue a special report on the abysmal situation in Wittenberge, and to draw attention to the negative effect of the regime's ceaseless propaganda. The local Stasi office indicated that the supply problems existed in large part because of an insufficient number of bakeries, poor cooling equipment in grocery stores, and improper cleansing machines in the brewery, not because of saboteurs and agents.[99] They also flagged the complaints of fundamental supporters of the regime. Their knowledge of Ark Green and the various other environmental groups in Gransee was up to date and comprehensive; the surveillance of would-be emigrants wide-ranging. Not everything in the Stasi reports is ideologically tainted, and as such it was indeed an important (though one-way) line of communication between the population and the party.[100] In short, the information-gathering apparatus at the district level continued to serve the Stasi well in 1989, as it had for the thirty-six years since the 1953 revolution.

Other historians have suggested that the Stasi "failure" in 1989 was not due to blind ideologues or basic incompetence but to internal Stasi questions about its raison d'être. In these accounts, certain Stasi officers suffer a profound crisis of conscience; like characters from a Victor Hugo novel, they suddenly question everything they thought to be undeniably true.[101] To be sure, there existed a certain bewilderment in the Stasi about developments in the GDR that required reassurance. In August 1989 the regional director gave a pep talk to the Gransee officers reminding them of the ideal for which they were fighting: "In spite of all the complications of the current situation, in spite of all the problems, we must never, as Communists and Chekists, lose sight of our great efforts to strengthen [our] socialist society. Focusing only on the negative side or, worse, giving in to fear, is unbecoming of a comrade. You should be vigilant and concerned but not pessimistic."[102] This should not, however, be mistaken for dissension in the ranks.

There is little in the documents to suggest that the Stasi was unreliable, let alone part of a conspiracy to overthrow the regime. In late August 1989, the Stasi and its informants undertook a major offensive against potential opposition during the Perleberg anniversary festivities, which drew glowing praise from the leader of District Perleberg. As late as October 4, the regional level was providing clear guidelines to the districts to penetrate oppositional groups and to render them harmless. In Hans-Hermann Hertle's *Der Fall der Mauer*, the most detailed account available on the fall of the Wall, the author takes pains to show that the Stasi did not open fire on the demonstrators of October 9 in Leipzig because they were overwhelmed by the demonstrators' numbers, not because they were afraid to shoot fellow citizens.[103] And indeed, on October 30, a mere nine days before the fall of the Berlin Wall, the Stasi issued to its officers what amounted to shoot-to-kill orders if demonstrators stormed Stasi offices.[104]

How then did the revolution come to pass? The refrain of Stasi officers about an old, paralyzed party that either ignored Stasi warnings or could not process the reams of information reaching it from its many sources (including its own party organization, police, and district council) turns out to have a ring of truth. The regular meetings of the SED leadership for Gransee and Perleberg from 1989 reveal a party oblivious to the developing anger in the streets. Following the communal elections of May in District Perleberg, in which the population had expressed discontent in a manner not seen in East Germany in forty years, the party leaders reported gleefully: "The election results are a clear indication of support for the policies of the party of the working class.... They are at the same time a resounding defeat for the enemies of socialism. Our communal elections have demonstrated the greatness, the maturity, and the superiority of our socialist democracy. The population's devotion and sense of belonging to its socialist Fatherland could hardly be more evident."[105]

One explanation for this kind of rhetoric in the face of evidence to the contrary may be the party's all-too-human tendency to give more weight to the rosy information coming to it from party officials, rather than to the more negative reporting from the Stasi and its network of informants. An internal party report claimed in late summer 1989 that discussions with the population on the twenty-eighth anniversary of the building of the Wall revealed that the "majority of our people agreed that the Wall should not be removed as long as the circumstances that led to its erection remain."[106] Other reports showed grassroots party members bewildered by East Germans escaping through Hungary: "Many comrades do not understand why young people want to leave for [West Germany], when the GDR guarantees them social security, employment, and the chance to become their own person"[107]—and even this kind of skewed information was frequently a short paragraph hidden within eight pages of updates on factory production.[108]

A shameless propaganda piece on East German television called "Human Trade," which "documented" West Germany's theft of East Germans in cloak-and-dagger operations, was said to have found resonance with many rank-and-file party members.[109] This kind of reporting simply could not have been helpful to a Communist Party that was trying to deal with issues of crisis proportion in late 1989. Stasi officers were correct that the party would have been better off listening to what Stasi informants had to say, rather than what the party's grassroots were saying. In fact, with the exception of an extraordinary sitting on October 9, the Stasi did not have a representative at meetings of the party leadership in Gransee throughout 1989.[110] The SED made the critical error, as political parties are wont to do, of confusing the views of its membership with those of the population at large.

In the scramble of October 1989, the Communist Party in District Gransee believed that the situation could be brought under control by calm dialogue and an increased party presence. From October 3 to October 31, for example, Horst Schultz, the secretary for agriculture in the district, was to have thirteen public functions, including attendance at a Free German Youth event, awarding prizes at a public ceremony, and participating in a membership meeting at several agricultural collectives.[111] In the very last communication from Dieter Schultz, the first secretary for District Gransee, to his superior Günther Jahn, the first secretary for Region Potsdam, Schultz acknowledges that the supply of the population with material goods required an "immediate solution" and that "a certain number" of workers and party members questioned the leadership of the party, yet this information is lost amid a sea of party platitudes and day-to-day administration that, by this point, should have been relegated to secondary consideration. The last phrase written by Schultz before the Wall fell, several weeks after a wave of demonstrations swept through Saxony, is almost painfully unaware: "We are convinced that in 1989 we will meet, and in some cases exceed, our quotas in the number of farm animals raised, and that in 1990 healthy and productive animal husbandry will guarantee meeting the tasks assigned by the party."[112]

Following the massive demonstrations in Leipzig and other major centers in October, the SED in Perleberg realized that power was slipping away, yet party officials still talked of reversing its fortunes. Gerhard Uhe, the first secretary of the party in District Perleberg, frankly admitted on November 1, 1989, that many East Germans opposed the party, the police, and the Stasi, and that the only way to win them back was through grassroots political campaigning, especially with the impending legalization of *Neues Forum*. For the first time in its history, East Germany's Communist Party would have to canvass like a Western political party. The first secretary talked about the challenges ahead for the SED: "We will begin in Wittenberge with an open forum on Sunday at 10 a.m. in the sewing machine factory. We have no idea how many will come out....I'm telling you this comrades because the real issue today is whether a socialist GDR will continue to exist. We must do everything possible to be victorious—hundreds upon hundreds of little acts with individuals."[113] As we now know, Gerhard Uhe was putting on a brave public face to cover what was for him the awful truth about the impending demise of East Germany. Six days after he authored this report, Uhe shot himself in the head.[114]

In our ongoing debates about the end of East Germany, it is important to remember the amazing speed with which the revolution descended on outlying areas, on, one might even be tempted to say, the more "typical" areas of East Germany. Günter Grass has pronounced in his majestic account of post-unification Germany, *Too Far Afield*, that 1989 was "not just any year." By the time 1989 had come to a close, that was certainly an appropriate description. What is remarkable is how uneventful 1989 was in outlying areas prior to October. For most of 1989 the Stasi simply did not judge the situation in the districts to be beyond its control,[115] a sentiment that was captured at the leadership level. On August 31, when Mielke inquired from the Region Gera representative whether the eve of another June 17 had approached, the representative answered: "It hasn't, and it won't arrive. That's what we're here for."[116]

One of the most fascinating conclusions from these rich records is that there is very little indication in outlying areas of an *escalation* toward revolution and mass demonstrations. The fudged communal elections results produced no protest, oppositional environment groups were small and under surveillance, residents were not stampeding to Hungary, and the Stasi office went about its work with, perhaps, slightly greater urgency but calmly nevertheless. In a report exuding confidence less than one month before the fall of the Berlin Wall, and only three days after the largest demonstration on East German soil since the revolution of 1953, the Stasi in District Perleberg stated categorically: "In our district, the state is secure."[117] When one reflects on the sudden surge of mass demonstrations and the corresponding collapse of state power, what comes to mind is a word well known to students of German history—this was a *Blitzrevolution*, a lightning revolution.

The Stasi was only as effective as its political masters. In embracing party information and ignoring negative reports, the party did not adequately respond to East Germans' legitimate concerns that could have headed off some of the anger that spilled onto the streets. Once demonstrators began taking to the streets in large numbers, and in particular the regime's decision not to confront the demonstration of October 9, 1989, in Leipzig, the pace of events, the *Blitzrevolution*, overwhelmed the party and its apparatus. Citizens throughout the country became emboldened by the example of the Leipzigers. That demonstrators were able to take to the streets in the fall of 1989 does not demonstrate that the regime was not a totalitarian state, or point to a conspiratorial Stasi, but rather it shows the inability of the party to interpret the deluge of information that came to it. The work style of the Stasi, which tended toward slow, plodding decomposition of enemies, would have had trouble adjusting to the rapidly changing environment, but it was clear that there was no political will for it to do so anyway.

Margaretha von Trotta's 1995 film *Das Versprechen* (The Promise) is a tragic, if somewhat kitschy tale of Berlin lovers separated by the Wall. One scene takes place on November 9, 1989, in which the sound of honking and commotion in the streets causes the protagonist to step onto the balcony of his shabby East Berlin apartment. When he inquires of his neighbor, also on a balcony, about the reason for the jubilation below, the neighbor responds: "The Wall is open!" Surveying the scene below him, the protagonist mutters under his breath: "Which wall?" Trotta captured in this scene a common sentiment of East Germans in the fall of 1989: that in spite of the year's turbulence, no one imagined the final end of East Germany. That the Berlin Wall with its guard towers and mines, its barbed wire, its dogs, its shoot-to-kill orders, that this bristling front of the Cold War that had been in place for twenty-eight years could, in an instant, no longer be there was too fantastical to be believed. One Gransee resident was at a stoplight when a radio bulletin announced that the Wall was now open. His son turned to him and said that they had to drive immediately to Berlin, to which the father laughed and told his son not to be so naïve, that clearly they were listening to some sort of radio play.[118]

# CONCLUSION

GYORGY DALOS'S *DIE BALATON-BRIGADE*, one of the most insightful novels about the Stasi, had the bad luck of appearing at roughly the same time as von Donnersmarck's movie *The Lives of Others*, and so did not make the impression in public that it might have. *Die Balaton-Brigade* has a similar story line to the movie, yet one that is far more nuanced. The story is told through a monologue delivered by the protagonist Joseph Klempner, a former Stasi officer, to his silent partner and the only one left in his life, his dog Hugo. Driven by his desire for the plum posting to the Balaton Brigade, the Stasi outfit that monitored East Germans at the popular vacation grounds on the shores of Lake Balaton in Hungary, Klempner obeys his superiors' request and reports to the Stasi on his own daughter's relationship with a Chilean living in West Berlin. Upon viewing her files after the collapse of East Germany, the daughter determines without much difficulty that the informer "El Padre" was her father and breaks off contact to him, in the process taking his only grandchild away. In addition, his wife left him. All that remains in his life is his dachshund, Hugo, but he too has a past. Klempner's bosses in the Stasi had instructed him to give the dog to his daughter as a peace offering after a fight they had had about her Chilean lover—and thereby to continue the surveillance on her.

Unlike Gerd Wiesler, the fictional Stasi captain in *The Lives of Others*, who has a crisis of conscience about the nature of his work (but not enough of one to prevent him from working for the Stasi), Dalos's character Klempner does not agonize over his past. Just as he knows what he did was wrong, he also knows that if the Stasi were still in place, he would serve it faithfully. And this is where Dalos is at his most brilliant. He does not ask the reader for sympathy for Klempner, who has lost everything because of his Stasi actions—Klempner himself accepts responsibility and does not seek pity—nor does he paint Klempner as the easy-to-despise villain. One reviewer has eloquently captured the essence of the book: Dalos, he says, "is convinced that a system like that of the Stasi would not have been possible without the participation of ordinary people. But how was it at all possible for ordinary people to work for such an outfit? Klempner's story offers an answer. That Dalos's main character is neither a sadist nor a fanatic, not even an evil person, does not make *him* more sinister, but rather the state that Joseph Klempner wanted to serve so unconditionally."[1]

There is no doubt that the GDR was maintained by the participation of ordinary people in state and society. Even though the dictatorship was one of pervasive surveillance, denial of basic rights, and widespread suffering of regime opponents, by no means were these all "bad" people. I would not categorize even those involved in the repression apparatus whom I met as "sinister." They are not the kinds of characters who populate the novels of Arthur Koestler, Ayn Rand, or Vassily Aksyonov. Indeed, the fact that they today for the most part lead quiet, normal lives in pleasant surroundings, with a network of family and friends, should lead our attention away from an inherent or unusual personality trait that caused them to partake in repression, toward the nature of a system that called on them to do so in the first place.

Ordinary East Germans engaged in the GDR: they took vacations, they joined neighborhood groups, they worked, and they participated in festivities. They also petitioned the regime endlessly with a myriad of complaints. Yet, in spite of committed socialists who wanted to reform the system, in spite of ordinary citizens who approved of the idea of the GDR in principle if not in practice, in spite of the millions of petitions that outlined the serious deficiencies in the GDR, there was no organized, public protest to reform the GDR until the fall of 1989, when it was far too late. Even in the factories, where workers and supervisors came to many informal arrangements on the shop floor, there was still no group effort to address the egregious deficiencies in industry or to exert political control. With the exception of 1953, the GDR never experienced strikes like those that plagued the Communist Party in Poland throughout its postwar history, especially in the early 1980s.[2]

Any explanation of the "unreformability" of the GDR must take into account both the nature of the regime and the nature of participation. The very fact that the secret police over time grew enormously and refined its methods is testimony that the regime was determined to prevent the kind of public demand for change that many East Germans expressed in private. The petitions (*Eingaben*) themselves, far from according East Germans "voice," amounted to a way to deny like-minded individuals from organizing protest, as was the case in the petition systems of the monarchs of old.[3] There was not a universal form of participation, but various kinds of it. For many, it was a pragmatic loyalty; for others it was, as Joachim Gauck, a former Rostock pastor and first federal commissioner for the Stasi files, phrases it, a "Fear-Accommodation-Syndrome."[4] With regard to the Stasi in particular, participation needs to be differentiated along gender lines; there were hardly any female informants, and no female operational officers to speak of. In contrast to Nazi Germany, which, as recent literature suggests, experienced enthusiastic participation from its citizens,[5] it is striking how little spontaneous adoration occurred in the GDR. May Day parades were contrived; celebrations for the founding of the Republic rehearsed.

In the course of its history, millions of East Germans also participated in the Stasi, whether as full-time workers, informants, contact persons, or irregular collaborators. In a secret police system that had expanded as massively as the Stasi had, and whose political masters were determined to know everything of importance in the country, it could not have happened otherwise. In the course of its duties, even its more "ordinary" ones like vetting, the Stasi drew East Germans into its purview. Vetting of informants, officers, applicants to emigrate, people who had applied to visit West Germany, and those who traveled west in the line of work required the collaboration of thousands of ordinary Germans. This is to say nothing of the targeted operations the Stasi conducted that ran into the tens of thousands every year. This book explores the history of two relatively small district offices of the Stasi. It is worth recalling that there were 215 others.

I have written a book about the Stasi because it was East Germany's most important instrument for societal control, but it was not the only one. The Communist Party could, and did, call upon a number of societal organizations to monitor and guide the population, including the only sanctioned trade union (FDGB), the Communist youth group (FDJ), the factory organizations of the party (GO), the police (including police "informants" [ABV]), educators, semi-formal, elected neighborhood governing bodies (*Hof- und Hausgemeinschaften*), newspapers (it was common practice for the editor of the regional newspaper to be at party secretariat sittings),[6] and, an organization often overlooked, the Agitation Commission of the Communist Party.[7] This committee organized public talks on communism and party work in factories and elsewhere, often with such awkward titles as "Joseph Stalin and the Soviet people were the best friends of the German people during the years of Hitler's tyranny and provided support and generous assistance for the German people in the years after 1945,"[8] staged local rallies, hung up banners in factories, broadcast the party message over loudspeakers in factory canteens and at the exits, authored and published brochures, and swept into factories and neighborhoods across the country to exercise damage control following periods of unrest like the revolutionary upheaval of June 17, 1953.[9] In earlier years, it organized "countryside Sundays," when thousands of factory workers were forced to give up their one day off to head into rural areas and convince farmers of the benefits of socialism.[10] These, too, contributed to totalitarianism in the GDR.

If ordinary people partaking in a repressive system led to the widespread societal control that came to characterize East Germany, then there is an important lesson in the East German experience for Western democracies. After all, the Stasi was a legally instituted organ of state and worked within the parameters of the GDR's constitution. If it was challenging, but not impossible, for the GDR to monitor broad sections of society through "old-fashioned" informants, it has become much easier in the computer age where every mouse click, Web page visit, and e-mail are easily recorded, and where people voluntarily offer up personal details on social networking sites. Several high-ranking Stasi officers have taken great pleasure in the turn of events in the West following

September 11, pointing out how those who criticized East Germany for putting security above individual freedoms are the very ones who now defend the USA PATRIOT Act or surveillance cameras in public places.[11] Few question that surveillance cameras have become part of our daily existence, yet there is little evidence that they keep us safer; they may help apprehend suspects, but they do not appear to prevent the crime in the first place, as the attacks on London's subways in 2005 and the most recent airline security breach in Amsterdam made abundantly clear. It is difficult to imagine, though, that the cameras will ever be taken down. There is in the United States an understandable desire to know the identities of airline passengers entering the country, yet in demanding the Passenger Name Records (PNR) from airlines prior to granting landing rights, U.S. authorities obtain other information too, including passengers' contact information, meal preferences, and disabilities. It is by no means clear at what point this information will be deleted, if ever.[12] That the subway stations in Washington, D.C., are covered with posters asking riders that if they "see something? say something!" does not necessarily lead us toward the surveillance state that was East Germany, but we must be ever cautious of a *system* that encourages ordinary people to partake in denunciation, repression, and surveillance in no small part because it widens the scope of who is considered an "enemy." That phrase attributed to Mark Twain still rings true: "To a man with a hammer, everything looks like a nail."

# Notes

## Introduction

1. Wolfgang Welsch, *Widerstand und MfS im SED-Staat* (Schwerin: Schmidt-Pohl, 1999), 95.
2. Interview with Dr. Jürgen Schmidt-Pohl, Warnemünde, September 25, 2005.
3. Jens Gieseke, *Mielke-Konzern: Die Geschichte der Stasi* (Stuttgart: DVA, 2001), 185.
4. Hubertus Knabe, *Die Täter sind unter uns* (Berlin: Propyläen Verlag, 2007), 113.
5. One earlier work discussed the role of the Stasi in the economy based on case studies of Stasi offices in chemical factories. Hans-Hermann Hertle and Franz-Otto Gilles, "Stasi in der Produktion," in *Aktenlage: Die Bedeutung der Unterlagen des Staatssicherheitsdienstes für die Zeitgeschichtsforschung*, ed. Klaus-Dietmar Henke and Roger Engelmann (Berlin: Links, 1995). Limited to 1989 is Günther Siegel, "Die Kreisdienststelle Mühlhausen des Ministeriums für Staatssicherheit der DDR im Herbst 1989," in *Mühlhausen 1989/1990: Die Wende in einer thüringischen Kreisstadt*, ed. Josef Aldenhövel et al. (Münster: 1993). Other studies of Stasi conduct at specific sites include Gerhard Kluge and Reinhard Meinel, *MfS und FSU: Das Wirken des Ministeriums für Staatssicherheit an der Friedrich-Schiller-Universität Jena* (Erfurt: Landesbeauftragter des Freistaats Thüringen für die Unterlagen des Staatssicherheitsdienstes der DDR, 1997); Frank Döbert, *Mit dem Ernstfall konfrontiert: Die Stasi und der VEB Carl Zeiss* (Geschichtswerkstatt Jena 3/96, 1996); Walter Schilling, "Die Bearbeitung der Landeskirche Thüringen durch das MfS," in *Staatspartei und Staatssicherheit: Zum Verhältnis von SED und MfS*, ed. Siegfried Suckut and Walter Süß (Berlin: Links, 1997), 211–66; and Steffen Reichert, *Unter Kontrolle: Die Martin-Luther-Universität und das Ministerium für Staatssicherheit 1968–1989* (Halle: Mitteldeutscher Verlag, 2007). Grit Löser's paper on District Frieber has unfortunately not been published: "Die Stellung der Kreisdienststellen im Gefüge des MfS, dargestellt am Beispiel der Kreisdienststelle Freiberg und deren Bearbeitung als Bestand" (PhD diss., Fachhochschule Potsdam, 1995).
6. John Schmeidel, *Stasi: Shield and Sword of the Party* (New York: Routledge, 2008), 17, 21.
7. As quoted in Martin Debes, *Durchdringen und Zersetzen:Die Bekämpfung der Opposition in Ostthüringen durch das MfS im Jahre 1989* (Manebach: Goldhelm Verlag, 1999), 12.
8. A useful overview of the Stasi files is found in Henke and Roger Engelmann, eds., *Aktenlage: die Bedeutung der Unterlagen des Staatssicherheitsdienstes für die Zeitgeschichtsforschung* (Berlin: Links, 1995).
9. For more on the controversy surrounding the Stasi Archive, see Gary Bruce, "Access to Secret Police Files, Justice and Vetting in East Germany since 1989," *German Politics and Society* 25, no. 4 (2008): 82–111.
10. Egon Krenz's claim after 1989 that the Stasi was a "state within a state" was primarily self-exculpatory. See Jens Gieseke's contribution in Friedrich-Ebert-Stiftung, *Im Visier der Geheimpolizei: Der kommunistische Überwachungs-und Repressionsapparat 1945–1989* (Leipzig: Friedrich-Ebert-Stiftung, 2007), 28.
11. As quoted in Knabe, *Die Täter*, 15.
12. RTL, "Die DDR Show: Von Ampelmännchen bis Zentralkomitee," Aug. 28, 2003, URL: http://www.stern.de/unterhaltung/film/512202.html?eid=512223.
13. Reichert, *Unter Kontrolle*, 87.

14. See for example the comments of Mary Beth Stein at the Apr. 30, 2007, Symposium held at the German Historical Institute, Washington DC; Steven Pfaff, *"The Lives of Others: East Germany Revisited?"* GHI Bulletin No. 41 (2007): 113.

15. Florian Henckel von Donnersmarck, *Das Leben der anderen: Filmbuch* (Frankfurt: Suhrkamp, 2006), 200–201.

16. Klaus-Dietmar Henke, "Zu Nutzung und Auswertung der Unterlagen des Staatssicherheitsdienstes," *VfZ* 41, no. 4 (1993): 575–87; Armin Mitter and Stefan Wolle, *Untergang auf Raten* (Munich: Bertelsmann, 1993).

17. Clemens Vollnhals, "Das Ministerium für Staatssicherheit: Ein Instrument totalitärer Herrschaftsausübung," in *Sozialgeschichte der DDR*, ed. Hartmut Kaelble et al. (Stuttgart:Oldenbourg, 1994), 514.

18. Ibid.

19. Sandra Pingel-Schliemann, *Zersetzen: Strategie einer Diktatur* (Berlin: Robert-Havemann-Gesellschaft, 2002), 16.

20. Hubertus Knabe, "Weiche Formen der Verfolgung in der DDR. Zum Wandel der repressiven Strategien in der Ära Honecker," *DA* 5 (1997): 709–19.

21. Thomas Lindenberger has criticized the Enquete-Commission for portraying the GDR in terms of victims and perpetrators and suggests that most GDR citizens did not see their own experience reflected in those categories. See Thomas Lindenberger, "Everyday History: New Approaches to the History of the Post-War Germanies," in The Divided Past: Rewriting Post-War German History, ed. Christoph Klessmann ( New York: Berg, 2001), 53.

22. It bears remembering that totalitarianism was an accepted concept by not only the Right but also the Left. The initial postwar years of the Social Democratic Party of Germany were dominated in large part by anti-totalitarianism. See Francis Fukuyama, *The End of History and the Last Man* (New York: Free Press, 1992). See also Mike Schmeitzner, "Der Totalitarismusbegriff Kurt Schumachers," in *Totalitarismuskritik von links*, ed. Mike Schmeitzner (Göttingen: Vandenhoeck & Ruprecht, 2007), 249–82.

23. Klaus-Dietmar Henke, "Aufarbeitung verstärken, Gedenken vertiefen: Grundsätzliche Bemerkungen zum Gedenken an deutsche Diktaturen," *DA* 40, no. 6 (2007): 1053. See also Grieder, "In Defense of Totalitarianism Theory as a Tool of Historical Scholarship," *Totalitarian Movements and Political Religions* 8, no. 3–4 (2007): 572–77. An approach that holds promise for comparative work is that which focuses on the *practice* of power. See for example Adelheid von Saldern, "Öffentlichkeiten in Diktaturen: Zu den Herrschaftspraktiken im Deutschland des 20. Jahrhunderts," in *Diktaturen in Deutschland- Vergleichsaspekte*, ed. Günther Heydemann and Heinrich Oberreuter (Bonn: Bundeszentrale für politische Bildung, 2003), 442–75.

24. Konrad Jarausch, "Care and Coercion: the GDR as Welfare Dictatorship," in *Dictatorship as Experience: Towards a Socio-Cultural History of the GDR*, ed. Konrad Jarausch (New York: Berghahn Books, 2000); Ralf Dahrendorf, *Der Moderne Soziale Konflikt* (Munich: DTV Verlag, 1994); Klaus Schroeder, *Der SED-Staat: Partei, Staat und Gesellschaft 1949–1990* (Munich: Hanser, 1998); Alf Lüdtke, "Helden der Arbeit-Mühen beim Arbeitem," in *Sozialgeschichte der DDR*, ed. Hartmut Kaelblre et al. (Stuttgart: Klett-Cotta, 1994). See also Mary Fulbrook, "Jenseits der Totalitarismustheorie?" in *German Monitor: The GDR and Its History: Rückblick und Revision*, ed. Peter Baker (Amsterdam: Rodopi, 2000), 36–42. Schroeder's criticisms are found in Klaus Schroeder, *Die veränderte Republik: Deutschland nach der Wiedervereinigung* (Munich: Ernst Vögel, 2006), 348–50.

25. Mary Fulbrook, *The People's State: East German Society from Hitler to Honecker* (New Haven: Yale University Press, 2005), 13.

26. A classic example of this approach is Richard Bessel and Ralph Jessen, eds., *Die Grenzen der Diktatur: Staat und Gesellschaft in der DDR* (Göttingen: Vandenhoeck & Rupprecht, 1996).

27. Martin Malia, "To the Stalin Mausoleum," *Daedalus* 119 (Winter 1990): 295–344. John Connelly has suggested that, in the East German case, the motivation for totalitarian control in the university sector was closely linked to the antifascist basis of the GDR:

"Rage born in the Nazi years combined with faith in state intervention and united anti-fascists with the partially nazified SED apparatus in an attempt to control the thinking of colleagues and students." Moreover, Connelly is correct to suggest that analyses of control in the GDR would do well to take into account the level of control in other East European states, rather than comparing East Germany solely to the abstract concept of totalitarianism. See John Connelly, *Captive University: The Sovietization of East German, Czech, and Polish Higher Education, 1945–1956* (Chapel Hill: University of North Carolina Press, 2000), 285.

28. Corey Ross writes of East Germans "not so much resisting or complying as extracting what they could from the circumstances." Corey Ross, *Constructing Socialism at the Grassroots* (Houndmill: Palgrave, 2000), 3.

29. Jeannette Madarasz, *Conflict and Compromise in East Germany 1971–1989: A Precarious Stability* (New York: Palgrave, 2003), 195.

30. Fulbrook, *People's State*, iix.

31. Madarasz, *Conflict and Compromise*, 192.

32. Jens Gieseke, "Die Einheit von Wirtschafts-, Sozial- und Sicherheitspolitik: Militarisierung und Überwachung als Probleme einer DDR-Sozialgeschichte der Ära Honecker," *Zeitschrift für Geschichtswissenschaft* 51, no. 11 (2003): 1011. An extremely thoughtful account of this phenomenon is Jan Palmowski, "Staatssicherheit und soziale Praxis," in *Staatssicherheit und Gesellschaft*, ed. Jens Gieseke (Gottingen: Vandenhoeck & Ruprecht, 2007), 253–72.

33. Thomas Lindenberger has explored the interrelation of *Eigen-Sinn* and *Herrschaft* in Lindenberger, "Everyday History," 44–55.

34. Thomas Lindenberger, "SED-Herrschaft als soziale Praxis, Herrschaft und 'Eigen-Sinn': Problemstellung und Begriffe," in *Staatssicherheit und Gesellschaff: Studien zum Herrschaftsalltag in der DDR*, ed. Jens Gieseke (Göttingen: Vandenhoeck & Ruprecht, 2007), 23–48. See also his *Herrschaft und Eigen-Sinn in der Diktatur: Studien zur Gesellschaftsgeschichte der DDR* (Köln: Böhlau Verlag, 1999), and *Volkspolizei: Herrschaftspraxis und öffentliche Ordnung im SED-Staat 1952–1968* (Köln: Böhlau Verlag, 2003).

35. Madarasz in *Conflict and Compromise* examines the compromises with four segments of society: women, youth, church, and writers.

36. See Jeffrey Kopstein, *The Politics of Economic Decline in East Germany* (Chapel Hill: University of North Carolina Press, 1997) and most recently Andrew Port, *Conflict and Stability in the German Democratic Republic* (New York: Cambridge University Press, 2007).

37. See especially Port, *Conflict and Stability* and Madarasz, *Conflict and Compromise*.

38. Mary Fulbrook, "Putting the People Back in: The Contentious State of GDR History," *German History* 24, no. 4 (2006): 609.

39. Peter Graf Kielmansegg, "Krise der Totalitarismustheorie?" in *Totalitarismus im 20. Jahrhundert*, ed. Eckhard Jesse (Baden-Baden: Nomos, 1996), 286–304.

40. Peter Grieder has forcefully argued for the applicability of the term totalitarianism for the GDR. See Peter Grieder, "In Defense of Totalitarianism Theory as a Tool of Historical Scholarship," *Totalitarian Movements and Political Religions* 8, nos. 3–4 (Sept. 2007): 563–89.

41. See David Ensikat, *Kleines Land, große Mauer: Die DDR für alle, die (nicht) dabei waren* (Munich: Piper, 2007), 180–81, and the comments of Joachim Gauck, first federal commissioner for the Stasi files, in *Opfer und Täter der SED-Herrschaft: Lebenswege in einer Diktatur* (Leipzig: Friedrich Ebert Stiftung, 2005), 40.

42. A committee of experts on GDR history has recommended to the German Ministry of Culture that it establish a History Cooperative "Dealing with the SED-Dictatorship," the focus of which would be aspects currently neglected: (1) Political dominance, Society, Resistance, (2) Surveillance and Repression, (3) Border and Division. See Martin Sabrow et al., eds., *Wohin treibt die DDR-Erinnerung?* (Göttingen: Vandenhoeck & Ruprecht, 2007), 41.

43. The surveys are summarized in Schroeder, *Die veränderte Republik*, 331–39.

44. Gieseke, *Staatssicherheit*, 13.

45. This translates into roughly one in fifty East Germans between the ages of eighteen and eighty working for the Stasi in some capacity. Friedrich-Ebert-Stiftung, *Im Visier der Geheimpolizei*, 12.

46. As quoted in Mike Dennis, *The Stasi: Myth and Reality* (London: Longman, 2003), 90.

47. Reichert, *Unter Kontrolle*, 15.

48. CSIS statistics are available in the annual reports, online at www.csis-scrs.gc.ca.

49. Volodymyr Semystiaha, "The Role and Place of Secret Collaborators in the Informational Activity of the GPU-NKVD in the 1920s and 1930s," *Cahiers du monde russe* 42, no. 2, 3, 4 (2001): 240.

50. Orlando Figes, *The Whisperers: Private Life in Stalin's Russia* (New York: Metropolitan, 2007), 258.

51. Fulbrook, "Jenseits," 42.

52. Gieseke, *Staatsicherheit*.

53. Lindenberger, "SED-Herrschaft," Hans-Hermann Hertle, Stefan Wolle, *Damals in der DDR: der Alltag im Arbeiter- und Bauernstaat* (München: Bertelsmann, 2004), 324. Emphasis added.

54. Thomas Lindenberger cancelled his subscription to *Horch und Guck* due to the review of Jens Gieseke, *Staatssicherheit*; Jochen Staadt, "Werkeln am Paradigmenwechsel: Die DDR als 'Konsensdiktatur'?" *Horch und Guck* 58, no. 2 (2007): 74–75.

55. Sheila Fitzpatrick, *Everyday Stalinism: Ordinary Life in Extraordinary Times: Soviet Russia in the 1930s* (Oxford: Oxford University Press, 1999), 14.

56. Yehuda Bauer, "Overall Explanations, German Society and the Jews: or Some Thoughts about context," in *Probing the Depths of German Antisemitism: German Society and the Persecution of the Jews, 1933–1941*, ed. David Bankier (New York: Berghahn, 2000), 16.

57. As quoted in Pingel-Schliemann, *Zersetzen*, 50.

58. Pfaff, "*The Lives of Others*," 114. David Ensikat echoes these sentiments: "For most others, the Stasi was not as big a deal as would be later claimed." Ensikat, *Kleines Land, große Mauer*, 95.

59. Rainer Eckert, "Schuld und Zeitgeschichte: Zwölf Thesen zur Auseinandersetzung mit der deutschen Diktatur," *Deutschland Archiv* 41, no. 1 (2008): 117.

60. Schroeder, *Die veränderte Republik*, 347.

61. An excellent introduction to the *Historikerstreit* is Peter Baldwin, *Reworking the Past: Hitler, the Holocaust, and the Historians' Debate* (Boston: Beacon, 1990).

62. Very little has been written in English about the Stasi. Edward Peterson's two books on the Stasi received universally negative reviews, *The Secret Police and the Revolution* (Westport, Conn.: Praeger, 2002) and *The Limits of Secret Police Power: The Magdeburger Stasi 1953–1989* (New York: P. Lang, 2004). Both Anna Funder, *Stasiland* (London: Granta Books, 2003) and John Koehler, *The Stasi: The Untold Story of the East German Secret Police* (Boulder: Westview, 1999) are loose, journalistic accounts. David Childs and Richard Popplewell's *The Stasi: The East German Intelligence and Security Service* (New York: New York University Press, 1996) did not make use of the Stasi archives. Dennis, *Stasi: Myth and Reality* is a helpful synthesis.

63. Katrin Dördelmann, "Aus einer gewissen Empörung hierüber habe ich Anzeige erstattet: Verhalten und Motive von Denunziantinnen," in *Zwischen Karriere und Verfolgung: Handlungsräume von Grauen im nationalsozialistischen Deutschland*, ed. Kristen Heinsohn, Birgit Vogel and Ulrike Weckel (Frankfurt: Campus Verlag, 1997), 190.

64. Sheila Fitzpatrick and Robert Gellately, "Introduction to the Practices of Denunciation in Modern European History," in *Accusatory Practices: Denunciation in Modern European History, 1789–1989*, ed. Sheila Fitzpatrick and Robert Gellately (Chicago: University of Chicago Press, 1997), 1.

65. Stephanie Abke, *Sichtbare Zeichen unsichtbarer Kräfte: Denunziationsmuter und Denunziationsverhalten 1933–1945* (Tübingen: Diskord, 2003).

66. Karl-Heinz Reuband, "Denunziation im Dritten Reich: Die Bedeutung von Systemunterstützung und Gelegenheitsstrukturen," *Historical Social Research* 26, no. 2/3 (2001): 219. Peter Fritzsche has demonstrated the many ways that Germans partook in

the Nazi dictatorship. Peter Fritzsche, *Life and Death in the Third Reich* (Cambridge, Mass.: Harvard University Press, 2008).

67. Robert Gellately, "Denunciations in Twentieth Century Germany," *Journal of Modern History* 68, no. 4 (1996): 933.

68. Robert Gellately, *The Gestapo and German Society* (Oxford: Oxford University Press, 1991).

69. See for example Vandana Joshi, *Gender and Power in the Third Reich: Female Denouncers and the Gestapo 1933–1945* (New York: Palgrave MacMillan, 2003). Stephanie Abke, *Sichtbare Zeichen unsichtbarer Kräfte: Denunziationsmuter und Denunziationsverhalten 1933–1945* (Tübingen: Diskord, 2003).

70. Eric Johnson, *Nazi Terror: The Gestapo, Jews, and Ordinary Germans* (New York: Basic Books, 1999).

71. Gellately, "Denunciations," 965.

72. Reuband, "Denunziation," 223. In the Soviet Union during the Great Terror, petty arguments and jealousies could often lead to denunciations. Figes, *Whisperers*, 264.

73. Fulbrook, *People's State*, 241.

74. *Opfer und Täter der SED-Herrschaft*, 101.

75. Gerhard Paul, *Staatlicher Terror und Gesellschaftliche Verrohung: Die Gestapo in Schleswig-Holstein* (Hamburg: Ergebnisse Verlag, 1996), 11.

76. Gieseke, *Mielke-Konzern*, 70.

77. There were 3,228 employed in trade, 5,845 in transportation and telecommunication, and 6,753 in the "non-production" sector. The above statistics were gathered from *Statistischer Jahresbericht 1956, Bezirke der DDR, Bezirk Schwerin* (Berlin:VEB Deutscher Zentralverlag, 1957), and from the *Statistisches Jahrbuch des Bezirkes Schwerin* (Staatliche Zentralverwaltung für Statistik, Bezirkstelle Schwerin) for the years 1982 and 1990. This publication did not appear between 1982 and 1990.

78. *Statistisches Jahrbuch 1990: Bezirk Potsdam.* (Statistisches Bezirksamt Potsdam, 1990), 21.

79. Annette Leo, *"Das ist so'n zweischneidiges Schwert hier unser KZ…" Der Fürstenberg Alltag und das Frauenkonzentrationslager Ravensbrück* (Berlin: Metropol Verlag, 2007), 32.

80. Ibid., 78.

81. Statistisches Bezirksamt Potsdam, *Statistisches Jahrbuch Bezirk Potsdam 1990*, 58–59.

## Chapter 1

1. Laurenz Demps, "Die Provinz Brandenburg in der NS-Zeit," in *Brandenburgische Geschichte*, ed. Ingo Materna and Wolfgang Ribbe (Berlin: Akademie Verlag, 1995), 619.

2. Ulrike Kohl, "Quellen zur Geschichte der NSDAP und ihrer Gliederungen in Berlin-Brandenburg," in *Jahrbuch für brandenburgische Landesgeschichte* (1999): 198.

3. Kohl, "Quellen," 202.

4. Dietrich Eichholtz, "Einleitung," in *Verfolgung, Alltag, Widerstand*, ed. Dietrich Eichholtz (Berlin: Volk & Welt, 1999), 8; Kohl, "Quellen," 207. These two works are the most important that have appeared since 1989 on the history of Brandenburg in the Nazi era. Laurenz Demps's chapter cited above is also an important contribution.

5. Demps, "Provinz Brandenburg," 624–25; Dietrich Eicholtz, "Soziale Umbrüche in Brandenburg 1943–1945," in *Terror, Herrschaft und Alltag im Nationalsozialismus: eine Sozialgeschichte des deutschen Faschismus*, ed. Brigitte Berlekamp and Werner Röhr (Münster: Verlag Westfälisches Dampfboot, 1995), 123.

6. Eicholtz, "Soziale,"123.

7. Gary Bruce, *Resistance with the People: Repression and Resistance in Eastern Germany, 1945–1955* (Lanham, Md.: Rowman & Littlefield, 2003), 187.

8. Eicholtz, "Soziale," 123–24.

9. Werner Krause, "Die Entwicklung des Granseer Schulwesens/Teil 25," *Gransee Zeitung*, June 29/30, 2002, 8.

10. Heinz Muchow, Hans-Joachim Eichel, Günter Rodegast, *Chronik der Stadt Wittenberge 1933 bis 1944* (Wittenberge: Eigenverlag der Stadtverwaltung Wittenberge, 1997), 1–10.

11. On voting patterns in the Weimar Republic, see in particular Thomas Childers, *The Nazi Voter* (Chapel Hill: University of North Carolina Press, 1983).

12. *Wittenberge: eine Chronik mit Bildern* (Nordhorn: BVB-Verlag, 2000), 62.
13. Gerhard Thiede, "Granseer Chronik 1918 bis 1945," unpublished manuscript, 360.
14. Muchow, *Chronik*, 1. Robert Gellately has argued that the concentration camps were well known to Germans, and that there was tacit support for their initial raison d'être. See in particular Robert Gellately, *Backing Hitler: Consent and Coersion in Nazi Germany* (Oxford: Oxford University Press, 2001).
15. Muchow, *Chronik*, 1.
16. Ibid.
17. Thiede, "Granseer Chronik," 382.
18. Muchow, *Chronik*, 2.
19. Muchow, *Chronik*, 5.
20. Muchow, *Chronik*, 3.
21. Muchow, *Chronik*, 19.
22. Thiede, "Granseer Chronik," 363-64.
23. Demper, "Provinz Brandenburg," 630.
24. Ibid.
25. Richard Evans, *The Coming of the Third Reich* (New York: Penguin, 2004), 238, 270-79.
26. Demper, "Provinz Brandenburg," 638-39.
27. Sigrid Jacobeit and Lieselotte Thoms-Heinrich, *Kreuzweg Ravensbrück: Lebensbilder antifaschistischer Widerstandskämpferinnen* (Leipzig: Verlag für die Frau, 1989), 13.
28. Thomas Glöwen, "Zwangsarbeit im Beutelager: das KZ-Aussenlager Glöwen," in *Havelberg: Kleine Stadt mit grosser Vergangenheit* (Halle: Mitteldeutscher Verlag, 1998), 169.
29. Fjodorovitch Karpenko, "Letter," in *Verschleppt nach Deutschland! Jugendliche Häftlinge des KZ Neuengamme aus der Sowjetunion erinnern sich*, ed. Herbert Dierks, (Bremen: Edition Temmen, 2000).
30. Irene Diekmann, "Boykott–Entrechtung–Pogrom–Deportation," in *Verfolgung, Alltag, Widerstand*, ed. Dietrich Eichholtz (Berlin: Volk & Welt, 1993), 207.
31. Diekmann, "Boykott," 209.
32. Yehuda Bauer, *A History of the Holocaust* (New York: Watts, 1982), 100.
33. Diekmann, "Boykott," 209.
34. Diekmann, "Boykott," 209-10.
35. Diekmann, "Boykott," 214-15.
36. Muchow, *Chronik*, 4; Armin Feldmann, "Das Städtische Lyzeum zu Wittenberge—Geschichte einer Schule," *Mitteilungen des Vereins für Geschichte der Prignitz* 5 (Perleberg 2005), 113.
37. Almuth Püschel,...*der Angeklagte ist Jude* (Potsdam: Brandenburg Landeszentrale für politische Bildung, 1998), 9.
38. Krause, Chronik-Blätter, "Die Juden in Gransee und die faschistische Pogromnacht," *Gransee Zeitung*, n.d.
39. Raul Hilberg, *The Destruction of the European Jews* (Chicago: Quadrangle Books, 1967), 23.
40. Thiede, "Granseer Chronik," 390.
41. Krause, "Zum 60. Jahrestag der Reichspogromnacht vom 9. November 1938," *Gransee Zeitung*, Nov. 7/8, 1998.
42. Krause, "War es Gottes Fügung oder nur ein seltsamer Zufall?" *Gransee Zeitung*, May 18, 1996.
43. Krause, "Die Zwangsberwirtschaftung während des Dritten Reiches" *Gransee Zeitung*, May 3/4, 1997
44. Demper, "Provinz Brandenburg," 660.
45. Helmut Bräutigam, ed., *Fremdarbeiter in Brandenburg in der NS-Zeit* (Potsdam: RAA Brandenburg, 1996), 17-20.
46. Hermann Kaienburg, "Zwangsarbeit für das "deutsche Rohstoffwunder," *1999 Zeitschrift für Sozialgeschichte des 20. und 21. Jahrhunderts* (Köln: SfS, 1994), 13-21.
47. Kaienburg, "Zwangsarbeit," 27.
48. Kaienburg, "Zwangsarbeit," 19.
49. Ibid.
50. Muchow, *Chronik*, 18.

51. Ibid.
52. Krause, "Die Entwicklung der Granseer Schulwesens" Teil 37. *Gransee Zeitung,* Sept. 21/22, 2002, 4.
53. Muchow, *Chronik,* 20.
54. "Disziplinierung durch Standrecht": Aus dem Tagebuch von Albert Hoppe, *Prignitz Kurier,* Feb. 11, 1995.
55. Demper, "Provinz Brandenburg," 665.
56. Muchow, *Chronik,* 21.
57. Thiede, "Granseer Chronik," 417.
58. Thiede, "Granseer Chronik," 418.
59. "Wagenburg auf dem Schulhof—der Flüchtlingsstrom wächst: Aus dem Tagebuch von Albert Hoppe," *Prignitz Kurier,* Feb. 9, 1995, 15.
60. "Heillose Verwirrung, Plünderung und kopflose Flucht: Aus dem Tagebuch von Albert Hoppe," *Prignitz Kurier.* Mar. 11, 1995.
61. Olaf Groehler, "Der Luftkrieg gegen Brandenburg in den lezten Kriegsmonaten," in *Brandenburg im Jahr 1945,* Werner Stang, ed. (Potsdam: Brandenburgische Landeszentrale für politische Bildung, 1995), 17–18.
62. Groehler, "Der Luftkrieg," 13–14.
63. Muchow, *Chronik,* 10.
64. Heinz Muchow, Hans-Joachim Eichel, Günter Rodegast, *Wittenberge im Jahre 1945: Eine Chronologie* (Wittenberge: Eigenverlag der Stadtverwaltung Wittenberge. 1998), 24.
65. Muchow, *Wittenberge im Jahre 1945,* 25–26.
66. Norman Naimark, "Die Sowjetische Militäradministration in Deutschland und die Frage des Stalinismus," *ZfG* 43 (1995), 294. Further details of rape in eastern Germany by the Red Army are found in Naimark, *The Russians in Germany* (Cambridge: Harvard University Press, 1995).
67. "Eine Pistolenmündung in Gesicht und Krieg gegen Frauen: Aus dem Tagebuch von Albert Hoppe," *Prignitz Kurier,* Mar. 25, 1995, 15.
68. Werner Krause, "Kinder waren die Helden von Gransee," *Gransee Zeitung,* May 6/7, 2006.
69. Groehler, "Der Luftkrieg," 32.
70. Krause, "Todesbotschaft zu Weihnachten," *Gransee Zeitung,* Dec. 24, 1997.
71. Muchow, *Wittenberge im Jahre 1945,* 37.

# Chapter 2

1. This is also a distinction for the Romanian secret police who, like the Stasi, were initially an instrument of terror before becoming, under Ceauşescu, an instrument of fear. Dennis Deletant, "Romania," in *A Handbook of the Communist Security Apparatus in East Central Europe 1944–1989,* ed. Krzysztok Persak and Lukasz Kaminsi (Warsaw: Institute of National Remembrance, 2005), 285. Stefan Wolle describes the ambivalent views of the Stasi as follows: "You trembled before the Stasi at the same time you mocked them." Hans-Hermann Hertle and Stefan Wolle, *Damals in der DDR: der Alltag im Arbeiter- und Bauernstaat* (Munich: Bertelsmann, 2004), 320.
2. Jens Gieseke, *Die hauptamtlichen Mitarbeiter der Staatssicherheit* (Berlin: Links, 2000), 12.
3. Some exceptions are Ariane Riecker, Annett Schwarz, and Dirk Schneider, *Stasi intim: Gespräche mit ehemaligen MfS-Angehörigen* (Leipzig: Forum Verlag, 1990); Gisela Karau, *Stasiprotokolle: Gespräche mit ehemaligen Mitarbeitern des Ministeriums für Staatssicherheit* (Frankfurt: Dipa, 1992); Christina Wilkening, *Staat im Staate* (Berlin: Aufbau, 1990); and Anna Funder, *Stasiland* (London: Granta, 2003). An illuminating memoir is Reinhardt Hahn, *Ausgedient: Ein Stasi-Major erzählt* (Leipzig: Mitteldeutscher Verlag, 1990).
4. In 1952, the national average of workers/district office was fourteen, with a distinct north-south divide. The south of the country had much larger district offices (Zittau had forty-four for example, Bautzen had thirty-one) than the north. District Gransee would not have been out of place in Region Schwerin, where the average number of workers in the district offices was seven. Gieseke, *Die hauptamtlichen Mitarbeiter,* 85–89.
5. Gieseke, *Die hauptamtlichen Mitarbeiter,* 88.

6. See Klaus-Dietmar Henke et al., *Anatomie der Staatssicherheit: Geschichte, Struktur und Methoden* (Berlin: BStU, 1996).

7. BStU-Potsdam, GVS PDM—193/89, June 27, 1989, Stellenplan der Bezirksverwaltung Potsdam, KD Gransee.

8. On the forerunner to the Stasi in East Germany, see Monika Tantzscher, "'In der Ostzone wird ein neuer Apparat aufgebaut': Die Gründung des DDR-Staatssicherheitsdienstes," *Deutschland Archiv* 31 (1998): 48–56; and Monika Tantzscher, "Die Vorläufer des Staatssicherheitsdienstes in der Polizei der Sowjetischen Besatzungszone," *Jahrbuch für Historische Kommunismusforschung* 7 (1998): 125–56.

9. Gieseke, *Die hauptamtlichen Mitarbeiter*, 124.

10. Even some works published after 1989 have continued the myth that the Stasi was the "Red Gestapo." See for example David Murphy, Sergei Kondrashev, and George Bailey, *Battleground Berlin: CIA vs. KGB in the Cold War* (New Haven: Yale University Press, 1997), 19. An early West German propaganda effort in this regard was Bernhard Sagolla, *Die rote Gestapo* (Berlin: Hansa Druck, 1952). Henry Leide's book demonstrates in scathing fashion that the Stasi had much fewer reservations about using former Nazis as informants. Leide, *NS-Verbrecher und Staatssicherheit* (Göttingen: Vandenhoeck & Ruprecht, 2005).

11. Gieseke, *Die hauptamtlichen Mitarbeiter*, 111.

12. Gieseke, *Die hauptamtlichen Mitarbeiter*, 535.

13. BStU-Potsdam, K3774, Kurt Körner, 63, Mar. 28, 1963, Einschätzung.

14. BStU-Potsdam, K531, Hans-Jürgen Töpfer, 29, Feb. 20, 1967, Abschlussbericht der KD Rathenow.

15. BStU-Potsdam, K531, Hans-Jürgen Töpfer, 82, Apr. 21, 1978, Beurteilung des Genossen Töpfer, gez. Verch.

16. BStU-Potsdam, K531, Hans-Jürgen Töpfer, 106, Aug. 12, 1985, Vorschlag zur Ernennung Töpfer zum Leiter der Kreisdienststelle Gransee mit Wirkung vom Nov. 1, 1985, 290. Nov. 18, 1980, Brief, KD Rathenow an VB Potsdam.

17. BStU-Potsdam, K3806 Eberhard Berndt, 29, Dec. 5, 1974, Einstellungsvorschlag, gez. Leiter der KD Luckenwalde.

18. BStU-Potsdam, K2503, Dietmar Hardt, 26, July 15, 1976, Vorschlag zur Einstellung, gez. Leiter der KD Zossen.

19. BStU-Potsdam, K1085 Karin Kuhlmann, 21, July 10, 1976, Einstellungsvorschlag, gez. Tamme.

20. BStU-Potsdam, K1082 Dietmar Köhler, 33, June 15, 1987, Einstellungsvorschlag, gez. Töpfer.

21. BStU-Potsdam, K3251, 32, May 5, 1987, Einstellungsvorschlag, gez. Leiter der KD Kwuster.

22. BStU-Potsdam, K1085, 21, July 10, 1976, Einstellungsvorschlag, gez. Tamme.

23. BStU-Potsdam, K3774 Kurt Körner, 11, Zusammengefasste Auskünfte (summary of information).

24. BStU-Potsdam, K198, Carsten Hoeltke, 34, May 8, 1989, Einstellungvorschlag, gez. Töpfer.

25. BStU-Potsdam, K1506, Hans-Jürgen Kämpfer.

26. Gieseke, *Die hauptamtlichen Mitarbeiter*, 267–68.

27. Gieseke, *Die hauptamtlichen Mitarbeiter*, 433.

28. Gieseke, *Die hauptamtlichen Mitarbeiter*, 338; and Henke et al., *Anatomie*, 48.

29. John Schmeidel, *Stasi: Shield and Sword of the Party* (New York: Routledge, 2008), 16.

30. BStU-Potsdam, K531 Hans-Jürgen Töpfer, 12. Undated Zusammengefasste Auskunft (summary of information).

31. Henke et al., *Anatomie*, 34.

32. BStU-Potsdam, K2002 Lothar Schrader, 114, Oct. 15, 1984, Vorschlag zur Ernennung des Hauptmann Schrader, Lothar, zum Referatsleiter des Referates Industrie/Territorial der KD Neuruppin.

33. Mike Dennis, *The Stasi: Myth and Reality* (London: Longman, 2003), 81.

34. Gieseke, *Die hauptamtlichen Mitarbeiter*, 421.

35. Gieseke, *Die hauptamtlichen Mitarbeiter*, 335.

36. BStU-Potsdam, K1082, Dietmar Köhler, 37, June 15, 1987, Einstellungsvorschlag, gez. Töpfer.

37. See for example BStU-Potsdam, K3392 Werner Oschim, and K1082 Dietmar Köhler.

38. Interview with Tenbrock, May 11, 2006.

39. BStU-Potsdam, K 3006–91, 98, Mar. 27, 1989, Brief.

40. BStU-Potsdam, K2002, Lothar Schrader, 64, Feb. 9, 1977, Beurteilung, gez. Schlögel, KD Neuruppin.

41. Interview with Müller, May 24, 2006.

42. BStU-Potsdam, K3251 Volker Ehmig, 91, Apr. 10, 1989, Aktenvermerk über eine durchgeführte Aussprache mit Ehmig.

43. BStU-Potsdam, K 2503. Dietmar Hardt, 7, 11, Zusammengefasste Auskunft (summary of information). Alcohol-related disciplinary issues at work amounted to about 25 percent of total offenses in the entire Stasi. Dennis, *Stasi: Myth and Reality*, 87.

44. BStU-Potsdam, K 1239 Lothar Strempel, 140, Apr. 12, 1985, Vorschlag zur Entbindung aus der Funktion Stellvertreter des Leiters einer KD, gez. Nikolaus.

45. Henke et al., *Anatomie*, 77.

46. Dennis, *Stasi: Myth and Reality*, 79.

47. Gieseke, *Die hauptamtlichen Mitarbeiter*, 537.

48. Armin Mitter and Stefan Wolle offer a different interpretation in *Untergang auf Raten* (Munich: Bertelsmann, 1993) of a secret police that continuously expanded from the revolutionary scare of 1953, rather than the expansion in bursts that Gieseke suggests. Jens Gieseke, *Mielke-Konzern: Die Geschichte der Stasi* (Stuttgart: DVA, 2001), 69.

49. Gieseke, *Mielke-Konzern*, 70.

50. Henke et al., *Anatomie*, 43.

51. BStU, ZA, HA KuSch, Abt Plan. 105. Uncatalogued material.

52. Gaps in the archival record do not allow for a complete reconstruction of the directorship of the District Perleberg Stasi office. As best as can be determined, Oberleutnant Mrowka led the office from June 1953 to December 1954. Norbert Skerra was leader from at least 1955 to 1957, but it is unclear who led the office until the appointment of Herbert Tilse in 1967. I am grateful to Herr Hoffmann of the Schwerin branch of the Stasi archive for piecing together this information based on a series of operational files, including AIM 8853, AIM 186/53, AIM 659/54, AOPK 952/88, AOPK 241/89, AOPK 298/89, AOPK 321/89, AOPK 605/89, AOPK 778/89, AOPK 41/89, AOPK 103/89, AOPK 298/89, AOPK 319/89, AOPK 745/89, AOPK 786/89, AOPK 795/89, AOPK 1026/89.

53. Interview with Herr Paupst, May 31, 2006.

54. Ibid.

55. Interview with Herr Piekert, May 23, 2006.

56. Interview with Frau Paupst, May 31, 2006.

57. Interview with Frau Müller, May 24, 2006.

58. BStU-Schwerin, Abt KuSch, 160, Werner Ryll, unpaginated. Nov. 10, 1967, Einstellungsvorschlag.

59. BStU-Schwerin, Abt KuSch, 160, Werner Ryll, unpaginated. June 14, 1967, IM Bericht über Ryll.

60. BStU-Schwerin, Abt KuSch, 105, Joachim Abraham, unpaginated.

61. BStU-Schwerin, Abt KuSch, 1464 Christiane Bleß, unpaginated.

62. BStU-Schwerin, Abt KuSch, 1249. Aug. 15, 1977, Plan zur Einführung in die politisch-operative Arbeit im MfS, gez. Tilse.

63. BStU-Schwerin, Abt KuSch, 249, unpaginated.

64. Interview with Frau Klenk, May 23, 2006, Wittenberge.

65. BStU-Schwerin, Abt KuSch 1115, unpaginated.

66. Gieseke, *Die hauptamtlichen Mitarbeiter*, 348.

67. BStU-Schwerin, Abt. KuSch, 412. See also BStU-Schwerin, Abt. KuSch, 1249.

68. Dennis, *Stasi: Myth and Reality*, 88.

69. Gieseke, *Die hauptamtlichen Mitarbeiter*, 278.

70. Gieseke, *Die hauptamtlichen Mitarbeiter*, 279.

71. Edward Peterson's account of the Stasi at a regional level does not discuss the careers or personalities of the Stasi officers in Region Magdeburg. Edward Peterson, *The Limits of Secret Police Power: The Magedburger Stasi, 1953–1989* (New York: P. Lang, 2004). One of the first accounts of the Stasi in English does not address the Stasi employees, although it does deal with the informants, David Childs and Richard Popplewell, *The Stasi: The East German Intelligence and Security Service* (New York: New York University Press, 1996).

72. See in particular Christopher Browning, *Ordinary Men: Reserve Police Battalion 101 and the Final Solution in Poland* (New York: Harper, 1992), 210.
73. Interviews took place Aug. 8, 2003 and May 11, 2006, in Häsen.
74. A brief description of the Barth case is available in Leide, *NS-Verbrecher*, 130–42.
75. Wilkening, *Staat im Staate*, 26–27, 155.
76. This is also a refrain in the interviews in Wilkening, *Staat im Staate*, 53–54.
77. Interview took place May 4, 2006, in Zehdenick.
78. BStU-Potsdam, K2986, 3.
79. Interview took place May 8, 2006, in Löwenberger Land.
80. The frustration with the party was not unique to the district level. See Childs and Popplewell, *Stasi*, 176.
81. See Bruce, "Wir haben den Kontakt," 367.
82. Martin Malia, "To the Stalin Mausoleum." *Daedalus* 119 (Winter 1990): 300–301.
83. Interview took place May 22, 2006.
84. Interview took place May 23, 2006, in Wittenberge.
85. Wilkening, *Staat im Staate*, 131.
86. Interview took place May 24, 2006, in Quitzow.
87. Interview took place May 23, 2006, in Wittenberge.
88. Wilkening, *Staat im Staate*, 69.
89. Interview took place May 31, 2006, in Wittenberge.
90. Interview took place May 31, 2006, in Perleberg.
91. Interview took place June 7, 2006, in Wittenberge.
92. One former Stasi officer in the Berlin evaluation branch ZAIG exaggerates when he claims that the Stasi would have led the revolution had the leadership been different. Wilkening, *Staat im Staate*, 26–27. In both *The Secret Police and the Revolution* and *The Limits of Secret Police Power* Edward Peterson suggests that there were many Stasi who sympathized with the revolutionaries.
93. Interview took place June 8, 2006, in Wittenberge.
94. Interview took place Apr. 28, 2006, in Wittenberge.
95. Interview took place May 6, 2006, in Neuruppin.
96. Schmeidel, *Stasi: Shield and Sword*, 20.
97. Dennis, *Stasi: Myth and Reality*, 81.
98. Henke et al., *Anatomie*, 17.
99. Florian Henckel von Donnersmarck, *Das Leben der anderen: Filmbuch* (Frankfurt: Suhrkamp, 2006), 43.
100. Dennis, *Stasi: Myth and Reality*, 80.
101. Henke et al., *Anatomie*, 55.
102. Gieseke, *Die hauptamtlichen Mitarbeiter*, 268–69.
103. Donna Harsch, "Society, the State, and Abortion in East Germany, 1950–1972," *American Historical Review* 102 (1997): 83.
104. Ina Merkel, "Leitbilder und Lebensweisen von Frauen in der DDR," in Kaelble et al, *Sozialgeschichte der DDR*, 376–77.
105. Renate Ellmenreich, *Frauen bei der Stasi: Am Beispiel der MfS-Bezirksverwaltung Gera* (Erfurt: Landesbeauftragte des Freistaates Thüringens, 1999), 47.
106. Donna Harsch, "Squaring the Circle: The Dilemmas and Evolution of Women's Policy," in *The Workers' and Peasants' State*, 151.
107. This is a refrain in several published interviews as well. See Riecker, Schwarz, and Schneider, *Stasi intim*, 12–13, 41; and Reinhard Grimmer et al., eds., *Die Sicherheit: zur Abwehrarbeit des MfS*, vol. 1 (Berlin: Edition Ost, 2002), 192–93.
108. Karau, *Stasiprotokolle*, 11.
109. Thomas Ammer and Hans-Joachim Memmler, *Staatssicherheit in Rostock: Zielgruppen, Methoden, Auflösung* (Cologne: Verlag Wissenschaft und Politik, 1991), 50–51.
110. Henke et al., *Anatomie*, 62.
111. Hahn, *Ausgedient*, 21.
112. Malia, "Stalin Mausoleum,"—300–301.
113. Hahn, *Ausgedient*, 34.

114. Hahn, *Ausgedient*, 90. Order 2/85 of February 1985 called for the "preventive disruption, exposure, and struggle against the political underground." Henke et al., *Anatomie*, 37.
115. Wilkening, *Staat im Staate*, 181.
116. Hahn, *Ausgedient*, 90; Wilkening, *Staat im Staate*122-23.
117. Grimmer et al., *Die Sicherheit*, vol. 1, 327.
118. Grimmer et al., *Die Sicherheit*, vol. 1, 266.
119. In particular Eric Johnson, *Nazi Terror: The Gestapo, Jews, and Ordinary Germans* (New York: Basic Books, 1999).
120. The only published interview of a former Stasi officer to reveal similar deep regret is in Riecker, Schwarz, and Schneider, *Stasi intim*, 204. The officer said that he felt "guilty. Morally guilty."
121. Karau, *Stasiprotokolle*, 81.
122. Perhaps unsurprising, no high-ranking SED members styled themselves as "perpetrators" after the fall of the Wall. See the important collection of interviews in Christian Jung, *Geschichte der Verlierer: Historische Selbstreflexion von hochrangigen Mitgliedern der SED nach 1989* (Heidelberg: Universitätsverlag, 2007).
123. See the discussion of the Bezirk party leaders in Mario Niemann, *Die Sekretäre der SED-Bezirksleitungen 1952–1989* (Paderborn: Schöningh, 2007).
124. Orlando Figes, *The Whisperers: Private Life in Stalin's Russia* (New York: Metropolitan, 2007), 472.
125. Hahn, *Ausgedient*, 15.

# Chapter 3

1. An excellent overview of file access in Eastern Europe after 1989 is Lavinia Stan, ed., *Transitional Justice in Eastern Europe and the former Soviet Union: Reckoning with the Communist Past* (New York: Routledge, 2008). See also Lavinia Stan, "Spies, Files and Lies: Explaining the failure of access to Securitate Files," *Communist and Post-Communist Studies* 37 (2004): 341–59.
2. For an overview of debates surrounding file access and the Stasi Records Law, see Gary Bruce, "Access to Secret Police Files, Justice and Vetting in East Germany since 1989," *German Politics and Society* 26, no. 1 (Spring 2008): 82–111.
3. Jens Gieseke, "Referat," in *Im Visier der Geheimpolizei: Der kommunistische Überwachungs-und Repressionsapparat 1945–1989* (Leipzig: Friedrich-Ebert-Stiftung, 2007), 35.
4. *Tätigkeitsbericht der Bundesbeauftragten für die Unterlagen des Staatssicherheitsdienstes der ehemaligen Deutschen Demokratischen Republik* (Berlin: BStU, 2001), 7.
5. Ilko-Sascha Kowalczuk, "Was den Stasi-Unterlagen im Bundesarchiv droht," *Frankfurter Allgemeine Zeitung*, Jan. 8, 2005.
6. Martin Debes, *Durchdringen und Zersetzen: Die Bekämpfung der Opposition in Ostthüringen durch das MfS im Jahre 1989* (Manebach: Goldhelm Verlag, 1999).
7. Barbara Miller, *Narratives of Guilt and Compliance in Unified Germany: Stasi Informers and their Impact on Society* (London: Routledge, 1999), 40.
8. More than half of all informants fell into the IMS category, the "classic" informant who was to report on a certain environment. The other categories represented more specialized tasks. See Jens Gieseke, *Mielke-Konzern: Die Geschichte der Stasi* (Stuttgart: DVA, 2001), 113. On the development of the categories over time, see Helmut Müller-Enbergs, *Inoffizielle Mitarbeiter des Ministeriums für Staatssicherheit* (Berlin: Ch. Links, 2001), 1:62.
9. Interview with Rolf Schwegel, Wittenberge, May 31, 2006.
10. BStU-Schwerin, AIM 444/56. See the maps and diagrams following p. 10 in that report.
11. See Müller-Enbergs, *Inoffizielle Mitarbeiter*, 3:53.
12. The following chart reveals the number of informants run by District Perleberg in several years in the 1980s for which data is available. The region of Schwerin, to which District Perleberg reported, also ran informants, some of whom were certainly present in District Perleberg. I estimated the number of regional informants in Perleberg by dividing the regional informants equally among the eleven districts. We cannot determine the exact numbers, but these may be considered a reasonable estimate:

| Year | Informants run by District Perleberg | Approx. number of Regional (BV) Informants in District Perleberg | Total Stasi informants in District Perleberg |
|---|---|---|---|
| 1984 | 345 | 238 | 583 |
| 1985 | 376 | 238 | 614 |
| 1987 | 377 | No data | |
| 1988 | 377 | 247 | 624 |

Source: BStU-Schwerin, KD Perleberg 10376, 10377. Untitled reports on Informants in KD Perleberg from Jan. 1 to Dec. 31, 1988, 1987, 1985, and 1984, and Helmut Müller-Enbergs, Inoffizielle Mitarbeiter: Teil 3, 835

13. Ibid. A summary of the number of informants in the districts in neighboring Region Neubrandenburg is found in Andreas Niemann and Walter Süß, "Gegen das Volk kann nichts mehr entschieden warden," in MfS und SED im Bezirk Neubrandenburg BF informiert 12 (Berlin: BStU, 1996), 69.
14. BStU-Schwerin, KD Perleberg 10377; Statische Berichterstattung für den Zeitraum 1.1–31.3, 1985.
15. Interview with Matthias Piekert, Wittenberge, May 23, 2006. See chap. 2.
16. BStU-Schwerin, KD Perleberg 10377; Statische Berichterstattung für den Zeitraum 1.1–31.1, 1985.
17. This was in line with the overall Stasi. Gieseke, Mielke-Konzern, 113.
18. The number of informants in District Gransee may be summarized as follows:

| Year | Informants run by District Gransee | Approx. number of Regional (BV) Informants in District Gransee | Total Stasi informants in District Gransee |
|---|---|---|---|
| 1978 | 227 | No data | |
| 1983 | 223 | 208 | 431 |
| 1984 | 247 | 205 | 452 |
| 1985 | 229 | 217 | 446 |
| 1986 | 142 | No data | |
| 1987 | 158 | Insufficient data | |
| 1988 | 199 | 215 | 414 |

Notes: A word of caution is necessary about these statistics: The totals from 1983 to 1987 do not include the GMS informant category, so the number of total informants in those years would have been higher than what appears here. In 1988, for example, we know that there were thirty-five GMS informants in the district. The sharp drop in the number of informants between 1985 and 1986, was a result in large part to the loss of nearly half of the informant roster in 1986 alone when a new director took office and "cleaned house." It was common for the Stasi to lose a certain number of informants in any given year, but the drastic drop in 1986 was exceptional.

Source: BStU-Potsdam AKG 240, Jan. 8, 1979, Kontrollbericht, p. 2; Müller-Enbergs, Inoffizielle Mitarbeiter: Teil 3, 791.

19. See the statistics on informants contained in Lukasz Kaminski et al., eds., *Handbuch der kommunistischen Geheimdienste in Osteuropa 1944–1991* (Göttingen: Vandenhoeck & Ruprecht, 2008).

20. Müller-Enbergs, *Inoffizielle Mitarbeiter*, 1:59.

21. BStU-Potsdam, AKG 1335, 10.

22. BStU-Potsdam, AKG 10542, Sept. 3, 1986, Hinweise zur Kreisdienststelle Gransee, von BV Potsdam, Auswertungs- und Kontrollgruppe.

23. Interview with Bernd Lohre, Wittenberge, June 7, 2006.

24. Roswitha Kaiser, "Stille Helden": Eine empirische Untersuchung über Verweigerungen und Ablehnungsgründe zur inoffiziellen Zusammenarbeit mit dem MfS am Beispiel der Bezirksverwaltung Potsdam" (Diplomarbeit, Fachhochschule Potsdam, 1997), 44–50.

25. Steffen Reichert, *Unter Kontrolle: Die Martin-Luther-Universität und das Ministerium für Staatssicherheit 1968–1989* (Halle: Mitteldeutscher Verlag, 2007), 131.

26. BStU-ZA, Sept. 20, 1950, Richtlinien über die Erfassung der geheimen Mitarbeiter, der Informatoren und der Personen, die konspirative Wohnungen unterhalten. GVS 9–50. This document is reprinted in Müller-Enbergs, *Inoffizielle Mitarbeiter*, 1:159–63.

27. Müller-Enbergs, *Inoffizielle Mitarbeiter*, 1:24–25.

28. Almost every instance of recruitment involved an assessment of the candidate by an official source such as factory boss, or local member of the Communist Party. See for example BStU-Potsdam, AIM 1852/69, 17; 27 Nov. 1958, Einschätzung, gez Sekr der BPO.

29. BStU-Schwerin, AIM 1378/80, 35; Nov. 11, 1968, Werbungsvorschlag, gez Kleiss-Schmid.

30. In virtually all cases of informant recruitment, other informants provided an assessment of the candidate's morality. See for example BStU-Schwerin, AIM 443/94, AIM 450/68, and AIM 247/73.

31. BStU-Schwerin, AIM 47/55; Mar. 4, 1950, letter.

32. BStU-Schwerin, AIM 47/55; June 22, 1950, Verpflichtung. Several informants were recruited even before the Stasi was officially founded. In those cases, the commitment does not refer to the Ministry for State Security, but contains vague phrasing about how the informant agrees to fight all enemies of the GDR. See, for example, AIM 138/55; Jan, 12, 1950, Verpflichtung.

33. BStU-Schwerin, AIM 47/55; Dec. 20, 1954, Beschluss über das Abbrechen der Verbindung.

34. BStU-Schwerin, AIM 444/56; Feb. 19, 1953, Vorschlag zur Anwerbung, gez. Prochnow.

35. BStU-Schwerin, AIM 444/56; June 3, 1953, Verpflichtungsbericht, gez. Stein.

36. Richtlinie 21, Nov. 2, 1952, repr. in Müller-Enbergs, *Inoffizielle Mitarbeiter*, 1:17. See also Miller, *Narratives*, 35.

37. Interview with Matthias Piekert, Wittenberge, May 23, 2006.

38. BStU-Schwerin, AIM 418/55; one of the few studies on this little-known group is Kai-Uwe Merz, *Kalter Krieg als antikommunistischer Widerstand: Die Kampfgruppe gegen Unmenschlichkeit, 1948–1959* (Munich: Oldenbourg, 1987).

39. BStU-ZA, 2.9;1953, Dienstanweisung Nr. 30/53 über die Erweiterung des Informatorennetzes und die Arbeit mit Hauptinformatoren.

40. Gerhard Ritter, "Der 17. Juni 1953," in *Volkserhebung gegen den SED-Staat: eine Bestandsaufnahme zum 17. Juni 1953*, ed. Ilko-Sascha Kowalczuk and Roger Engelmann (Göttingen: Vabdenhoeck & Ruprecht, 2005), 27. An outstanding work on the place of June 17, 1953, in German history is Bernd Eisenfeld, Ilko-Sascha Kowalczuk, and Erhart Neubert, eds., *Die verdrängte Revolution: der Platz des 17. Juni 1953 in der deutschen Geschichte* (Bremen: Edition Temmen, 2004). See also Gary Bruce, "The Prelude to Nationwide Surveillance in East Germany: Stasi Operations and Threat Perceptions, 1945–1953," *Journal of Cold War Studies* 5, no. 2 (2003): 3–31.

41. Gary Bruce, *Resistance with the People: Repression and Resistance in Eastern Germany, 1945–1955* (Lanham, Md.: Rowman & Littlefield, 2003), 234.

42. Müller-Enbergs, *Inoffizielle Mitarbeiter*, 1:36.

43. Oct. 1, 1958, Richtlinie 1/58, repr. in Müller-Enbergs, *Inoffizielle Mitarbeiter*, 1:212–13.

44. BStU-Schwerin, AIM 275/56; May 31, 1956; Beurteilung des GI Schulz, gez. Dannenberg.

45. Miller, *Narratives*, 44.

46. Reinhard Grimmer et al., eds., *Die Sicherheit: zur Abwehrarbeit des MfS*, vol. 1 (Berlin: Edition Ost, 2002), 353.
47. Matthias Piekert, Wittenberge, May 23, 2006.
48. BStU-Schwerin, AIM 586/56; vol. 2 contains many of Ram's reports.
49. BStU-Schwerin, AIM 586/56; Jan. 20, 1954, Bericht, gez. Behr.
50. BStU-Schwerin, AIM 586/56.
51. BStU-Schwerin, AIM 586/56; Dec. 14, 1956, Bericht zum Abbrechen der Verbindung, gez. Sternkopf.
52. BStU-Potsdam, AKG 240, Jan. 8, 1979, Kontrollbericht, 3.
53. Müller-Enbergs, *Inoffizielle Mitarbeiter*, 1:57.
54. BStU-Potsdam, AKG 240, Dec. 20, 1979, Schlussfolgerungen und Massnahmen der im Ergebnis durch die AKG durchgeführte Nachkontrolle.
55. Miller, *Narratives*, 15.
56. BStU-Schwerin, AIM 215/56. See the reports: Nov. 4, 1952, Vorschlag zum Informatoren, gez. Greulich; Jan. 3, 1956, Beurteilung des GI Siebert, gez. Prochnow; Feb. 7, 1956, Aktenvermerk gez. Prochnow.
57. Nov. 20, 1952, Richtlinie 21/52, reprinted in Müller-Enbergs, *Inoffizielle Mitarbeiter*, 1:174.
58. BStU-Schwerin, AIM 410/94; Apr. 16, 1975, Beschluss über das Anlegen eines IM Vorganges.
59. Miller, *Narratives*, 22.
60. BStU-Schwerin, AIM 410/94. See the reports by informants evaluating her character contained in this signature. See also BStU-Schwerin, AIM247/73; Mar. 28, 1973, Aktenvermerk, gez. Hohm.
61. BStU-Schwerin, AIM 1087/78, 12; Oct. 9, 1978, Verpflichtung.
62. BStU-Potsdam, AKG 1054, June 16, 1988, Bericht an BV Potsdam.
63. BStU-Schwerin, AIM 2682/80, 103–7; June 25, 1976, Einsatz- und Entwicklungskonzeptionen FIM Reini, gez. Oschim.
64. BStU-Schwerin, AIM 2682/80' June 6, 1978, Vorschlag.
65. BStU-Schwerin, AIM 2682/80, 483; Nov. 21, 1980, Abschlussbericht zum FIM-Vorgang Reini, gez. Oschim.
66. BStU-Schwerin, AIM 2682/80, 128; Mar. 17, 1967, Brief KD Gransee an BV Potsdam, Abt. 18, gez. Hoffmann.
67. Interview with Reinhard Kuhlow, Wittenberge, May 22, 2006.
68. BStU-Potsdam, AIM 2682/80, 113; Dec. 21, 1976, Schulungsplan.
69. Müller-Enbergs, *Inoffizielle Mitarbeiter*, 1:30.
70. Grimmer et al., *Die Sicherheit*, 1:264.
71. Roger Engelmann, "Eine Regionalstudie zu Herrschaft und Alltag im Staatssozialismus," in *Staatssicherheit und Gesellschafft: Studien zum Herrschaftsalltag in der DDR*, ed. Jens Gieseke (Göttingen: Vandenhoeck & Ruprecht, 2007), 175.
72. BStU-Schwerin, AIM 215/56. See the reports: Nov. 4, 1952, Vorschlag zum Informatoren, gez. Greulich; Jan. 3, 1956, Beurteilung des GI Siebert, gez. Prochnow; Feb 7, 1956, Aktenvermerk gez. Prochnow.
73. BStU-Potsdam, AGMS 885/85, 31–32; Apr. 2, 1974, Ermittlungsbericht zu Max Steinbach, gez. Mandel.
74. BStU-Potsdam, AIM 591/71, 32; Jan. 10, 1963, Vorschlag zur Anwerbung der Person Max Steinbach, gez. Schmidt.
75. BStU-Potsdam, AIM 591/71, 16; Sept. 20, 1963, Bericht.
76. BStU-Potsdam, AIM 591/71, 96;Nov. 6, 1965, Bericht.
77. BStU-Potsdam, AIM 591/71, 80; Mar. 10, 1966, Bericht.
78. Ibid.
79. BStU-Potsdam, AGMS 885/85, 169; Nov. 30, 1976, Treffbericht, and 189–90, May 16, 1977, Bericht über beabsichtigte Republikflucht von 4 Jugendlichen.
80. BStU-Potsdam, AGMS 885–85, 277. Abschlussbericht zur Archivierung des GMS Peter Reg. Nr. IV 1280/80.
81. BStU-Potsdam, KD GS 7, 64; Aug. 23, 1968, Treffbericht.
82. BStU-Potsdam, KD GS 7, 329; Jan. 13, 1977, Treffbericht.

83. BStU-Potsdam, KD GS 7, 48; Sept. 8, 1977, Treffbericht.

84. BStU-Potsdam, AKG 392, 5; June 10, 1985, Bericht über Ergebnisse der Untersuchungen zur Wirksamkeit der Arbeit mit IM/GMS bei der Durchdringung ausgewählter Schwerpunktbereiche und Zielgruppen des Gegners in den KD Gransee, Nauen, Oranienuburg, Potsdam und Rathenow, gez. Schweiger und Hielscher.

85. BStU-Potsdam, AIM 712/71, 65; June 22, 1960, Einschätzung der Zusammenarbeit des GI Paul, gez. Utln Lippert.

86. BStU-Potsdam, AIM 712/71, 66; Jan. 13, 1965, Einschätzung der Zusammenarbeit mit dem IM Paul, gez. Ultn Birkholtz.

87. BStU-Potsdam, AIM 712/71, 74; June 11, 1971, Abschlussberichte.

88. BStU-Schwerin, AIM 403/94; Feb. 17, 1982, Einschätzung des IMS Magnolie.

89. BStU-Schwerin, AIM 10/85; Apr. 26, 1972, Vorschlag zur Verpflichtung eines Kandidaten, gez. Doppert.

90. BStU-Schwerin, AIM 305/56.

91. BStU-Schwerin, AIM 444/56; Jan. 23, 1956, Bericht, gez. Pfeufer.

92. Ibid.

93. BstU-Schwerin, AIM 444/56; June 5, 1956, Aktenvermerk, gez. Pfeufer.

94. BStU-Schwerin, AIM 444/56; Jan. 7, 1956, Beurteilung des Kuschel.

95. BStU-Schwerin, AIM 598/56; Nov. 6, 1956, Bericht, gez. Schulz.

96. BStU-Schwerin, AIM 410/94; May 20, 1980, Begründung für die Ruckstufung des IMV Carmen in die Kategorie IMS, gez. Tilse See also the case of an informant hired to monitor a train station but who was then transferred to a military base BStU-Potsdam, AIM 293/58, 19; Aug. 20, 1958, Schlussbericht, gez. Ultn Wallert and Ultn. Schölzel, leader of the district.

97. BStU-Potsdam, 1321/89, vol. 3, 322; Jan. 19, 1982, Abschrift, gez. Silvana.

98. BStU-Schwerin, AIM 374/94; Jan. 13, 1971, Bericht über Bekanntwerden, gez. Schmidt.

99. BStU-Schwerin AIM 374/94; Jan. 13, 1971, Bericht über durchgeführte Neuverpflichtung, gez. Schmidt.

100. Ibid.

101. BStU-Schwerin, AIM 374/94; May 30, 1983, Konzeption zur Überprüfung des Patrioten Walter, gez. Futterlieb.

102. BStU-Potsdam, 1855/69, 19; Oct. 22, 1955, Betr. Vorschlag zum Geheimen Informator.

103. This was the era of a concentrated Stasi campaign against Western intelligence agencies and their associated groups. See in particular Karl Wilhelm Fricke and Roger Engelmann, *Konzentrierte Schläge: Staatssicherheitsaktionen und politische Prozesse in der DDR 1953–1956* (Berlin: Ch Links, 1998).

104. BStU-Potsdam, 1855/69, 25; Nov. 21, 1955, Durchgeführte Werbung, gez. Zörner, Drewnick, und Willkommen.

105. BStU-Potsdam, 1855/69, 43; Apr. 12, 1956, Auskunftsbericht.

106. BStU-Potsdam, 1855/69, 47; May 17, 1956, Perspektivplan, gez. Drewnick.

107. BStU-Potsdam, 1855/69, 70; Dec. 7, 1961, Vorschlag zur Umregistrierung des GI Udo zum GHI, gez. Hoffmann.

108. BStU-Potsdam, 1855/69, 103; Oct. 3, 1967, Auskunftsbericht gez. Hoffmann.

109. BStU-Potsdam, 1855/69, 80; Oct. 29, 1965, Treffbericht, gez. Reini.

110. BStU-Potsdam, 1855/69, 92; Feb. 11, 1966, Treffbericht gez. Reini.

111. BStU-Potsdam, 1855/69, 146; Mar. 19, 1969, Zusammenfassender Bericht über die Ereignisse an der EOS-Zehdenick und die damit im Zusammenhang stehende fristlose Entlassung der Lehrer (blacked out) aus dem Schuldienst, gez. Reini.

112. BStU-Potsdam, KD GS 64, 13; Apr. 28, 1986, Treffbericht, gez. Gerhardt.

113. BStU-Potsdam, KD GS 64, 120; Jan. 7, 1972, Bericht über den EOS-Schüler (blacked out), gez. Udo.

114. BStU-Potsdam, KD GS 64, 195–96; Oct. 4, 1976, Bericht über ideologisches Fehlverhalten des EOS-Schülers (blacked out) Information, gez. Udo.

115. Interview with Florian Tenbrock. Häsen, Aug. 8, 2003.

116. BStU-Potsdam, AIM 192/86, 63; Aug. 5, 1975, Ermittlung zur Person Herr Dr. Schiefer, gez. Oschim.

117. BStU-Potsdam, AIM 192/86, 167; Sept. 1, 1975, Vorschlag zur Verpflichtung Rolf Schiefer, gez. Oschim.
118. BStU-Potsdam, AIM 192/86, 176–78; Nov. 8, 1975, Bericht über die durchgeführte Verpflichtung, gez. Oschim.
119. BStU-Potsdam, AIM 192/86, 116; Apr. 17, 1979, Information zur OPK Polyp gez. J. Nöcker, taken down by Gaeth.
120. BStU-Potsdam, AIM 192/86, 353; July 27, 1981, Information zum Oradour.
121. BStU-Potsdam, AIM 192/86, 16; Dec. 1, 1978, Einschätzung der inoffiziellen Zusammenarbeit mit dem IMV Josef Nöcker, gez. Gaeth.
122. See also BStU-Potsdam, AIM 192/86, 101; Dec. 19, 1980, Brief, Leiter der Abt. 20, BV Potsdam an KD Gransee.
123. BStU-Potsdam, AIM 192/86, 118; Mar. 18, 1982, Einschätzung der inoffiziellen Zusammenarbeit mit dem IMS Josef Nöcker, gez. Gaeth.
124. BStU-Potsdam, AIM 192/86, 153; June 8, 1983, Brief, KD Gransee Leiter Tamme an HA II/3 in Berlin.
125. BStU-Potsdam, AIM 192/86, 271; Jan. 3, 1986, Abschlussbericht IMS Josef Nöcker, gez. Töpfer and Bracklow.
126. See in particular Robert Gellately, *The Gestapo and German Society: Enforcing Racial Policy 1933–1945* (Oxford: Clarendon Press, 1990). Eric Johnson has suggested that the Gestapo was more proactive than in Gellately's model, especially in the Catholic milieu. Eric Johnson, *Nazi Terror: The Gestapo, Jews, and Ordinary Germans* (New York: Basic Books, 1999).
127. Interview with Florian Tenbrock, in Häsen, Aug. 8, 2003.
128. BStU-Schwerin, AIM 275/56; July 25, 1955, Aktenvermerk gez. Behr; July 26, 1955, Ermittlung gez. Behr.
129. BStU-Schwerin, AIM 275/56; Aug. 18, 1955, Verpflichtungsbericht, gez. Behr.
130. BStU-Schwerin, AIM 275/56; May 31, 1956, Beurteilung des GI Schulz, gez. Dannenberg.
131. Stasi employment of former SS and war criminals is explored in Henry Leide, *NS-Verbrecher und Staatssicherheit: die Geheime Vergangenheitspolitik der DDR* (Göttingen: Vandenhoeck & Ruprecht, 2005).
132. Interview with Florian Tenbrock, in Häsen, Aug. 8, 2003.
133. BStU-Schwerin, AIM 19/56; Dec. 29, 1955, Abbrechen der Verbindung.
134. BStU-Schwerin, AIM 511/55; Jan. 4, 1955, Beurteilung des GI Kirsch, gez. Leutnant Bachmann.
135. BStU-Schwerin, AIM 707/55; July 11, 1955, Beurteilung, gez. Berndt.
136. BStU-Schwerin, AIM 707/55; Aug. 1, 1955, handwritten note by Sugar.
137. BStU-Potsdam, AIM 26/79, 59; Dec. 12, 1978, Einschätzung.
138. Grimmer et al., *Die Sicherheit*, 363.
139. BStU-Schwerin, AIM 62/55; July 15, 1954, Bericht, gez. Prochnow; AIM 791/52. July 8, 1950, Verpflichtung. See also BStU-Schwerin, AIM 1087/78, 12; Oct. 9, 1970, Verpflichtung.
140. BStU-Potsdam, 687/94, .71; Aug. 28, 1988, Aktenvermerk zum IM-Vorlauf des Gen. Oltn. Besenbiel.
141. BStU-Potsdam, KD GS 7, 21; Nov. 30, 1966, Bericht über durchgeführte Werbung, gez. Lt. Hoffmann.
142. BStU-Potsdam, KD GS 7, 21; Nov. 30, 1966, Bericht über durchgeführte Werbung, gez. Lt. Hoffmann; and Nov. 29, 1966, Verpflichtung.
143. BStU-Schwerin, AIM 421/56; Mar. 12, 1956, Bericht, gez. Prochnow.
144. BStU-Potsdam, AIM 1852/69, 30; Jan. 29, 1969, Vorschlag zur Umgruppierung and Oct. 26, 1967, Auskunftsbericht.
145. BStU-Potsdam, AIM 26/79, 58; Dec.12, 1978, Einschätzung.
146. BStU-Schwerin, AIM 766/55, 12–13; Nov. 30, 1954, Beurteilung, gez. Bachmann; Jan. 6, 1954, Vorschlag als Hauptinformator, gez. Bachmann.
147. BStU-Potsdam, AIM 26/79, 57; Apr. 30, 1974, Einschätzung.
148. BStU-Schwerin, AIM 766/55. See the set of reports following p. 77 in that file.
149. Grimmer et al., *Die Sicherheit*, 73.
150. Miller, *Narratives*, 55.

151. Jörg Doll, Marc Damitz, "Zur Bedeutung des wichtigsten inoffiziellen Mitarbeiters für die Bewältigung der Bespitzelung durch das MfS der DDR," in *Politisch motivierte Verfolgung*, eds. Ulrich Baumann and Helmut Kury (Freiburg: Edition iuscrim, 1998), 249.
152. Peter Holquist has remarked along similar lines for Bolshevik surveillance. See "'Information is the Alpha and Omega of our work': Bolshevik surveillance in its pan-European context," *Journal of Modern History* 69 (Sept. 1997): 449.
153. Interview with Florian Tenbrock, Aug. 8, 2003.
154. Miller, *Narratives*, 53.
155. BStU-Potsdam, AIM 2326/80, 100; Oct. 3, 1980, Abschlussbericht gez. Kessel.
156. Interview with Matthias Piekert, Wittenberge, May 23, 2006; interview with Bernd Lohre, Wittenberge, June 7, 2006.
157. BStU-Potsdam, 173/88, 147; diagram (date unclear).

## Chapter 4

1. Names were blacked out in the documents; therefore all names related to this operation who are *not* Stasi are pseudonyms.
2. BStU-Schwerin, AOP 774/82, 175; May 26, 1982, Schlussbericht.
3. BStU-Schwerin, AIM 473/94, vol. 1, 37; Feb. 5, 1981, Bericht, gez. Major Kunzmann, HA Kader und Schulung, bestätigt von Erich Mielke.
4. Ibid.
5. BStU-Schwerin, AIM 473/94, vol. 1, 94; Apr. 24, 1981, Vorschlag zur Verpflichtung.
6. BStU-Schwerin, AIM 473/94, vol. 1, 17; Aug. 4, 1981, Bericht, gez. Axel.
7. BStU-Schwerin, AIM 473/94, vol. 1, 20; Nov. 20, 1981, Bericht, gez. Axel.
8. BStU-Schwerin, AIM 473/94, vol. 1, 25; Dec. 9, 1981, Bericht, gez. Axel.
9. A very similar escape attempt to the one fictionalized by Klaus Kordon is detailed in Anke Jauch, *Die Stasi packt zu: Freiheitsberaubung 1980* (Frankfurt: August von Goethe Literaturverlag, 2007).
10. BStU-Schwerin, KD Perleberg 10627; Apr. 14, 1989, Einleitungsbericht zur OPK Vater, gez. Kramp, bestätigt von Ryll.
11. BStU-Schwerin, AIM 473/94, vol. 1, 6–8; Dec. 13, 1981, Einleitungsbericht zur OPK Ballon, gez. Ultn. Giese, bestätigt von Tilse.
12. BStU-Schwerin, AIM 473/94, vol. 1, 34–35; Dec. 29, 1981, Bericht, gez. Axel.
13. BStU-Schwerin, AIM 473/94, vol. 1, 55; Jan. 28, 1982, Operativplan zum OV Ballon, gez. Wolgast, bestätigt von Tilse.
14. BStU-Schwerin, AIM 473/94, vol. 1, 93; Mar. 18, 1982, Ermittlungen, gez. Giese.
15. Reinhard Grimmer et al., eds., *Die Sicherheit: zur Abwehrarbeit des MfS*, vol. 1 (Berlin: Edition Ost, 2002), 373.
16. Mike Dennis, *The Stasi: Myth and Reality* (London: Longman, 2003), 64–65.
17. Reinhadt Hahn, *Ausgedient: Ein Stasi-Major erzählt* (Halle: Mitteldeutscher Verlag, 1990), 44. Hahn calls the protection of the informant the "highest commandment."
18. Interview with Matthias Pickert, May 23, 2006.
19. This tactic was also used in OV *Idol* against a twenty-three-year-old student at the Martin Luther University in Wittenberg. Steffen Reichert, *Unter Kontrolle: Die Martin-Luther-Universität und das Ministerium für Staatssicherheit 1968–1989* (Halle: Mitteldeutscher Verlag, 2007), 386.
20. BStU-Schwerin, AIM 473/94, vol. 1, 115; Apr. 1, 1982, Vermerk.
21. BStU-Schwerin, AIM 473/94, vol. 1, 100; Mar. 26, 1982, Bericht, gez. Loth, Abt. VIII.
22. BStU-Schwerin, AIM 473/94, vol. 1, 145; May 20, 1982, Vermerk, gez. Wolgast.
23. Interview with Matthias Piekert, May 23, 2006.
24. Interview with Christian Klenk, May 23, 2006.
25. Grimmer et al., *Die Sicherheit*, 282–89.
26. Klaus Schroeder, *Die veränderte Republik: Deutschland nach der Wiedervereinigung* (Munich: Ernst Vögel, 2006), 358.
27. Interview with Bernd Lohre, June 7, 2006.
28. Dennis, *Stasi: Myth and Reality*, 65, 113–14.

29. BStU-Schwerin, BdL Nr. 002600, 4. Jan. 1971, Richtlinie 1/71 über die operative Personenkontrolle (OPK).

30. Ibid., 9.

31. Ibid., 10.

32. See for example Theo Mechtenberg, *30 Jahre Zielperson des MfS* (Halle: Landesbeauftragte für die Unterlagen des Staatssicherheitsdienstes der ehemaligen DDR in Sachsen-Anhalt, 2001).

33. Directive 1/81 is reprinted in David Gill and Ulrich Schröter, *Das Ministerium für Staatssicherheit: Anatomie des Mielke-Imperiums* (Berlin: Rowohlt, 1991), 323–24.

34. Directive 1/81 in Gill and Schröter, *Ministerium*, 331.

35. Ibid.

36. Gill and Schröter, *Ministerium*, 128.

37. Directive 1/76 is reprinted in Gill and Schröter, *Ministerium*, 354–55.

38. Gill and Schröter, *Ministerium*, 132.

39. Martin Debes, *Durchdringen und Zersetzen: Die Bekämpfung der Opposition in Ostthüringen durch das MfS im Jahre 1989* (Manebach: Goldhelm Verlag, 1999), 20.

40. Directive 1/76 in Gill and Schröter, *Ministerium*, 378.

41. See BStU-Schwerin, KD Perleberg, 10468.

42. See the many operations in signature BStU-Schwerin, KD Perleberg, 10445, vols. 1 and 2.

43. BStU-Schwerin, KD Perleberg, 10445, 8; Mar. 30, 1988, Bericht, gez. IME Ulrich.

44. Interview with Klaus-Peter Schmid, Neuruppin, May 6, 2006.

45. Jens Gieseke, *Mielke-Konzern: Die Geschichte der Stasi* (Stuttgart: DVA, 2001), 54.

46. Mary Fulbrook, in promoting a history of the GDR that does not focus solely on repression, has written: "If we turn our attention away from the repression apparatus, then not everything looks so evil." Mary Fulbrook, "Jenseits der Totalitarismustheorie?" in *German Monitor: The GDR and Its History: Rückblick und Revision*, ed. Peter Baker (Amsterdam: Rodopi, 2000), 42.

47. BStU-Potsdam, AOV 62/59, 25; Mar. 20, 1957, Vermerk, BDVP Potsdam an VPKA Gransee.

48. BStU-Potsdam, AOV 62/59, 33–36; Mar. 15, 1958, Sachstandsbericht über das operative Material über den Pferdezuchtverein in Falkenthal, gez. Meyer, bestätigt von Oltn. Meuschke, Dienststellenleiter.

49. BStU-Potsdam, AOV 62/59, 84; Apr. 14, 1958, Schlussbericht, gez. Meyer and Meuschke.

50. BStU-Potsdam, AOV 62/59, 104–7; Jan. 8, 1959, Operativplan zum ÜV 89–58 gez. Lippert.

51. BStU-Potsdam, AOV 62/59, 116; Mar. 26, 1959, Schlussbericht zum ÜV 89–58, gez. Lippert und Meuschke.

52. Gieseke, *Mielke-Konzern*, 50.

53. BStU-Potsdam, AOV 455/65, 31; Dec. 1, 1956, Ermittlungsauftrag.

54. BStU-Potsdam, AOV 455/65, 167; May 13, 1957, Sachstandsbericht zum Operativvorgang Wahrheit, gez. Ultn. Lüdecke.

55. BStU-Potsdam, AOV 455/65, 172; May 14, 1957, Operativvorgang für den Operativvorgang Wahrheit, gez. Lüdecke.

56. BStU-Potsdam, AOV 455/65, 260; Dec. 15, 1964, Schlussbericht zum OV Wahrheit.

57. BStU-Potsdam, AOV 8/59, 7; May 21, 1958, Bericht, gez. Singer, Hauptsachbearbeiter.

58. BStU-Potsdam, AOV 8/59, 89; Jan. 7, 1959, Schlussbericht zum ÜV 14–58, gez. Schölzel und Meuschke.

59. BStU-Potsdam, AOV 22/59, 6; Feb. 14, 1957, Beschluss für das Anlegen eines Überprüfungsvorganges.

60. BStU-Potsdam, AOV 22/59, 54; Feb. 5, 1959, Schlussbericht, gez. Wallert and Meuschke.

61. Gieseke, *Mielke-Konzern*, 122.

62. BStU-Schwerin, AOV 1068/68, 180; Aug. 24, 1968, Einschätzung zum OV Maler, gez. Pippig.

63. BStU-Schwerin, AOP 866/62, unpaginated; June 15, 1962, Beschluss über Einstellen eines OV, gez. Pippig.

64. BStU-Schwerin, see AOP 89/61.

65. BStU-Potsdam, AOV 898/79, 29–30; Oct. 28, 1977, Eröffnungsbericht zur Anlage des operativen Vorganges "Student" nach 213 StGB, gez. Gaeth.

66. BStU-Potsdam, AOV 898/79, 33; Aug. 20, 1976, Bericht über postalischen Kontakt zu einem inhaftierten BRD-Bürger, gez. Gaeth.

67. BStU-Potsdam, AOV 898/79, 56; Sept. 26, 1977, Zwischenstand der OPK Fischer, gez. Gaeth.

68. BStU-Potsdam, AOV 898/79, 58; Sept. 26, 1977, Zwischenstand der OPK Fischer, gez. Gaeth.

69. BStU-Potsdam, AOV 898/79, 219; Mar. 14, 1978, Bericht über durchgeführtes Vorbeugungsgespräch mit (blacked out), gez. Gaeth.

70. BStU-Potsdam, AOV 898/79, 93;Feb. 26, 1979, Vorschlag zum Abschluss des OV Student.

71. BStU-Potsdam, AOV 898/79, 83; May 13, 1978, Bericht über durchgeführtes Vorbeugungsgespräch mit (blacked out), gez. Gaeth.

72. Grimmer et al, *Die Sicherheit*, 359.

73. Bernd Eisenfeld, "Die Ausreisebewegung—eine Erscheingungsform widerständigen Verhaltens," in *Zwischen Selbtsbehauptung und Anpassung*, ed. Ulrike Poppe et al. (Berlin: Links, 1995), 202.

74. BStU-Schwerin, AOPK 243/89, 18; Feb. 9, 1984, Massnahmeplan zur OPK Zahn gez. Wolgast, bestätigt von Tilse.

75. BStU-Schwerin, AOPK 243/89, 72; Feb. 21, 1984, Bericht from IMS Pluto.

76. Ibid.

77. BStU-Schwerin, AOPK 243/89, 203; July 29, 1985, Bericht gez. GMS Andrea.

78. BStU-Schwerin, AOPK 243/89, 224; Jan. 31, 1986, Sachstandsbericht zur OPK Zahn, gez. Major Bless.

79. BStU-Schwerin, AOPK 243/89, 138; Sept. 19, 1984, Bericht from IMS Pluto.

80. BStU-Schwerin, AOPK 243/89, 252; Apr. 13, 1986, letter to Staatsratsvorsitzender der DDR. See also 302, 307 for letters of Aug. 25, 1987, and Dec. 1, 1987, to Honecker.

81. BStU-Schwerin, AOPK 243/89, 339; Mar. 1, 1988,Vernehmungsprotokoll.

82. BStU-Schwerin, AOPK 243/89, 379; Mar. 2, 1988, Schlussbericht, gez. Untersuchungsführer Klüssendorf.

83. BStU-Schwerin, AOPK 41/89; Apr. 11, 1988, Einleitungsbericht zur OPK Transport, gez. Major Rosenbaum.

84. BStU-Schwerin, AOPK 41/89; Dec. 12, 1988, Abschlussbericht zur OPK Transport, gez. Major Rosenbaum.

85. See for example BStU-Potsdam, AOPK 619/84, 205; Nov. 3, 1983, Durchführung eines erneuten Gespräches mit der Mutter über die Zielperson der OPK Sänger, gez. Käpernick.

86. BStU-Potsdam, AOV 420/83, 55; Aug. 24, 1981, Eröffnungsbericht über die Anlage eines OV zu dem Bürger (blacked out), gez. Kessel and Ribbecke.

87. See BStU-Potsdam, AOPK 783–86, vol. 1, 6–182.

88. BStU-Potsdam, AOPK 2283/89, 14; July 29, 1987, Einleitungsbericht zur OPK Observant, gez. Käpernick, Töpfer, and Zachow.

89. BStU-Potsdam, AOPK 2283/89, 15; July 29, 1987, Einleitungsbericht zur OPK Observant, gez. Käpernick, Töpfer, and Zachow.

90. BStU-Potsdam, AOPK 2283/89, 251; Apr. 21, 1989, Abschlussbericht zur OPK Observant, gez. Zachow, Mehlmann, and Töpfer.

91. BStU-Potsdam, AOPK 2283/89, 88–88a; undated telegram from the Kreis police office in Gransee.

92. BStU-Potsdam, AOPK 2283/89, 127; June 16, 1987, Information zum Stand der Untersuchung, gez. Major Kasche of Department IX/7.

93. BStU-Potsdam, AOPK 2283/89, 223; June 17, 1987, Massnahmeplan, gez. Generalmajor Schickart, Leiter BV Potsdam.

94. BStU-Potsdam, AOPK 2283/89, 116; June 15, 1987, Information zum Vorkommnis am Objekt der GSSD Drögen, gez. Töpfer.

95. BStU-Potsdam, AOPK 2153/89, 69; July 28, 1987, Schlussbericht.

96. Volker Koop was the first to discuss this case in *Deckname 'Vergeltung': Die Stasi und der Tod der Brüder Baer* (Bonn: Bouvier, 1997). The events are also mentioned in Ilko-Sascha Kowalczuk and Stefan Wolle, *Roter Stern über Deutschland: Sowjetische Truppen in der DDR* (Berlin: Links, 2001). An interview with the father appears in Annette Leo, "Schmerzhafte Erinnerungen," in *Fürstenberg-Drogen. Schichten eines verlassenen Ortes*, eds. Florian Buttlar et al. (Berlin: Hentrich, 1994)

97. BStU-Potsdam, AOPK 2283/89, 148-49; June 17, 1987, Treffbericht IMS Eigenheim, gez. Oltn Wünsch.

98. BStU-Potsdam, AOPK 2283/89, 176-77; undated Information über die Beisetzung der durch Anwendung der Schusswaffe, gez. Oberst Weissbach.

99. BStU-Potsdam, KD GS 112, 92; Oct. 29, 1986, Bericht, gez. Töpfer.

100. Annette Leo, *Das ist so*, 170.

101. BStU-Potsdam, AOPK 2283/89, 98; June 12, 1987, telegram, Töpfer an BV Potsdam.

102. BStU-Potsdam, AOPK 2283/89, 16-19; Massnahmeplan zur OPK Vergeltung, Aug. 14, 1987, gez. Leiter KD Gransee, Oberstleutnant Töpfer.

103. BStU-Potsdam, AOPK 1983/88, 5; Aug. 14, 1987, Übersichtsbogen zur OPK Vergeltung.

104. BStU-Potsdam, AOPK 2283/89, 78-81; Telegram, Aug. 5, 1987. Töpfer an BV Potsdam, Oberst Hauck.

105. BStU-Potsdam, AOPK 2283/89, 368-71; Aug. 8, 1988, Abschluss bericht zur OPK Vergeltung, gez. Töpfer.

106. Interview with Matthias Piekert, May 23, 2006; Interview with Klaus-Peter Schmid, May 6, 2005.

107. Interview with Klaus-Peter Schmid, May 6, 2005.

108. Gieseke, *Mielke-Konzern*, 87.

109. Helmut Müller-Enbergs, *Inoffizielle Mitarbeiter des Ministeriums für Staatssicherheit* (Berlin: Links, 2001), 86.

110. Grimmer et al, *Die Sicherheit*, 352.

111. Gieseke, *Mielke-Konzern*, 113.

112. BStU-Potsdam, AOPK 1618/88, 21-23; Dec. 11, 1981, Aktenvermerk zu einer Information, die der Gen. (blacked out), Direktor der POS (blacked out), am Dec. 11, 1981, in der DE über den Schüler (blacked out), Schüler der 9. Klasse der POS vorgetragen hat, gez. Oberleutnant Lindenberg.

113. BStU-Potsdam, AOPK 1618/88, 24-26; Jan. 12, 1982, Bericht, gez. Oschim.

114. BStU-Potsdam, AOPK 1618/88, 71; July 10, 1987, Bericht über Kontaktgespräch.

115. BStU-Potsdam, AOPK 1618/88, 197; Mar. 7, 1988, Vorschlag zur Umregistrierung IMS Frank, gez. Bracklow.

116. BStU-Potsdam, AOPK 1618/88, 234-36; May 12, 1988, Abschlussbericht IMB Frank.

117. BStU-Potsdam, AOPK 619/84, 205; Nov. 3, 1983, Durchführung eines erneuten Gespräches mit der Mutter über die Zielperson der OPK Sänger, gez. Käpernick.

118. BStU-Potsdam, AOPK 619/84, 211; Mar. 8, 1984, Abschlussbericht zur OPK Sänger, gez. Tamme und Käpernick.

119. BStU-Potsdam, AOPK 619/84, 109; Nov. 16, 1979, Aktenvermerk über das Gespräch mit Genn. Dr. (blacked out), Kaderleiter VEB Grüneberger.

120. BStU-Potsdam, AOV 420/83, 55; Aug. 24, 1981, Eröffnungsbericht über die Anlage eines OV zu dem Bürger (blacked out), gez. Kessel und Ribbecke.

121. BStU-Potsdam, AOV 420/83, 114; Aug. 28, 1981, Aktenvermerk zum Einsatz einer KP der KD Lübz zur Aufklärung der Absichten und Vorbereitungshandlungen zum UGÜ des (blacked out).

122. BStU-Potsdam, AOV 420/83, 167; June 8, 1982, Vernehmungsprotokoll des Beschuldigten.

123. BStU-Potsdam, AOV 420/83, 16; Dec. 14, 1982, Beschluss über die Archivierung des umseitig genannten Vorganges.

124. This is a suggestion in Andrew Port's fine study, *Conflict and Stability in the German Democratic Republic* (New York: Cambridge University Press, 2007), 107.

125. An outstanding work on this strategy which covers a range of *Zersetzen* examples is Sandra Pingel-Schliemann, *Zerseten: Strategie einer Diktatur* (Berlin: Robert-Havemann-Gesellschaft, 2002), 13.

126. Jürgen Gottschalk, *Druckstellen: Die Zerstörung einer Künstler-Biographie durch die Stasi* (Leipzig: Evangelische Verlagsanstalt, 2006), 9.

127. Jens Gieseke, *Die hauptamtlichen Mitarbeiter der Staatssicherheit* (Berlin: Links, 2000), 312.

128. Gieseke, *Mielke-Konzern*, 186.

129. Dennis, *Stasi: Myth and Reality*, 112.

130. In *Backing Hitler* (Oxford: Oxford University Press, 2001), Robert Gellately convincingly argues that Nazi concentration camps were well known to the German population, and in many cases supported.

131. Hubertus Knabe, "Strafen ohne Strafrecht, Zum Wandel repressiver Strategien in der Ära Honecker," in *Die DDR: Recht und Justiz als politisches Instrument*, ed. Heiner Timmermann (Berlin: Duncker and Humblot, 2000), 94.

132. Clemens Vollnhals, "Das Ministerium für Staatssicherheit. Ein Instrument totalitärer Herrschaftsausübung," in *Sozialgeschichte der DDR*, ed. Hartmut Kaelble et al. (Stuttgart: Oldenbourg, 1994), 514.

133. BStU-Schwerin, KD Perleberg, 10521, unpaginated; Sept. 20, 1976, telegram Tilse an Schwarz.

134. BStU-Schwerin, KD Perleberg, 10521, unpaginated; May 23, 1977, Bericht, gez. Robert.

135. Interview with Dr. Woronowicz, Spandau. May 29, 2006.

136. Gieseke, *Mielke-Konzern*, 185.

137. Gieseke, *Die hauptamtlichen Mitarbeiter*, 451

138. For more on the environmental movement, see Ehrhart Neubert, *Geschichte der Opposition in der DDR 1949–1989* (Bonn: Bundeszentrale für politische Bildung, 2000), 744–52.

139. BStU-Potsdam, KD Gransee 147, 20; Mar. 9, 1988, Stellungnahme zu der durch die KD Gransee vorgeschlagenen Anlage des OV Anarchist, gez. Oberstleutnant Kleine, Leiter Abteilung XX in Potsdam.

140. BStU-Potsdam, KD Gransee 147, 236; May 26, 1988, Zwischenbericht zum OV Anarchist, gez. Captain Bracklow.

141. BStU-Potsdam, KD Gransee 147, 272; Aug. 30, 1988, Einschätzung des Bearbeitungsstandes OV Anarchist, gez. Captain Bracklow.

142. Ibid.,275.

143. BStU-Potsdam, KD Gransee 147, 561; Oct. 8, 1989, Aktenvermerk zum OV Anarchist, gez. Captain Bracklow.

144. Ibid.

145. BStU-Schwerin, AOP 75/67.

146. BStU-Schwerin, AOP 013/88, unpaginated; Oct. 27, 1987, Abschlusseinschätzung, gez. Bloßfeld.

147. Interview with Bernd Lohre, June 7, 2006.

148. Ibid.

149. BStU-Schwerin, AOPK 243/89, 266; Abschlussbericht zum OPK Meister.

150. BStU-Schwerin, AOP 452/71, unpaginated; Aug. 12, 1970, Bericht, gez. Pippig.

151. BStU-Potsdam, 2140/83, 47–48; Sept. 21, 1981, Eröffnungsbericht über die Wiederaufnahme der Bearbeitung des archivierten OV Impressionist.

152. BStU-Potsdam, 2140/83, 48; Sept. 21, 1981, Eröffnungsbericht über die Wiederaufnahme der Bearbeitung des archivierten OV Impressionist.

153. BStU-Potsdam, 2140/83, vol. 2, 19–20; May 20, 1982, Bericht über die durchgeführte konspirative Durchsuchung der Wohnung des (blacked out), gez. Fischer und Keil.

154. BStU-Potsdam, 2140/83, 143; Dec. 17, 1981, Brief Unrath an KD Gransee.

155. BStU-Potsdam, 2140/83, vol. 2, 192–93; Aug. 2, 1982, Abschlussbericht, gez. Hauptmann Rügen.

156. BStU-Potsdam, 2140/83, vol. 2, 373–75; Oct. 20, 1983, Abschlussbericht, gez. Oschim und Oberstleutnant Tamme.

157. BStU-Schwerin, ZMA 739-1; Jan. 20, 1987, Eröffnungsbericht zum OV Schreiber, gez. Major Kleiss-Schmid, bestätigt von Ryll.

158. BStU-Schwerin, ZMA 739-1; July 30, 1987, Bericht der Abt. 32.

159. BStU-Potsdam, A/S 9.60, vol. 2, 10; July 26, 1958, Bericht der Arbeitsgruppe für Anleitung und Kontrolle über den Einsatz in der BV Potsdam in der Zeit vom June 23 bis zum July 23, 1958, gez. Major Kairies.

160. BStU-Schwerin, KD Perleberg 10586; July 8, 1987, Bestandsaufnahme, gez. Hauptmann Hummel, Referat A/I, bestätigt von Ryll.

161. BStU-Potsdam, AKG 1335, 255; Dienstversammlung—KD Gransee. Ansprache des Leiters BV Nov. 1, 1985.

162. Ibid., 256.

163. Robert Service, *Comrades: A World History of Communism* (London: MacMillan, 2007), 481.

164. BStU-Schwerin, KD Perleberg 10586; July 8, 1987, Bestandsaufnahme, gez. Hauptmann Hummel, Referat A/I, bestätigt von Ryll.

165. As quoted in Debes, *Durchdringen und Zersetzen*, 97.

166. See also Grimmer et al., *Die Sicherheit*, vol.1, 62.

167. Interview with Tenbrock, May 11, 2006.

168. As quoted in Grieder, "In Defence," 576.

## Chapter 5

1. Jens Gieseke, *Die hauptamtlichen Mitarbeiter der Staatssicherheit* (Berlin: Ch. Links, 2000), 442; Mike Dennis, *The Stasi: Myth and Reality* (London: Longman, 2003), 83–84.

2. BStU-Schwerin, Abt. Kader und Schulung, 105, Joachim Abraham.

3. Francesca Weil, *Zielgruppe Ärtzeschaft: Ärzte als inoffizielle Mitarbeiter des Ministeriums für Staatssicherheit* (Göttingen:Vandenhoeck & Ruprecht, 2008), 14.

4. Interview with Rolf Schwegel, May 31, 2006, in Wittenberge.

5. Weil, *Zielgruppe Ärtzeschaft*, 294.

6. Based on interview with physician, Wittenberge, June 30, 2006.

7. Jens Gieseke, "Staatssicherheit und Gesellschaft—Plädoyer für einen Brückenschlag," in *Staatssicherheit und Gesellschaft: Studien zum Herrschaftsalltag in der DDR*, ed. Jens Gieseke (Göttingen: Vandenhoeck & Ruprecht, 2007), 14.

8. Gary Bruce, "Access to Secret Police Files, Justice, and Vetting in East Germany since 1989," *German Politics and Society* 26, no.1 (Spring 2008): 95.

9. Babett Bauer, *Kontrolle und Repression: Individuelle Erfahrungen in der DDR (1971–1989)*. (Göttingen: Vandenhoeck & Ruprecht, 2006) 142.

10. Interview with Lutheran minister, Bad Wilsnack, May 2, 2006.

11. Interview with resident of Perleberg, May 23, 2006.

12. Interview with physician in Wittenberge, Wittenberge, June 30, 2006. Interview with Fürstenberg physician, May 9, 2006.

13. Interview with resident of Perleberg, Apr. 26, 2006.

14. Interview with physician, Fürstenberg, May 9, 2006.

15. Interview with grocery clerk, Fürstenberg, May 5, 2006.

16. Interview with inn owner, Zehdenick, May 19, 2006.

17. Interview with grocery clerk, Fürstenberg, May 5, 2006.

18. Interview with former Gransee resident, Kitchener, Ont., Aug. 9, 2006.

19. Interview with architect, Gransee, Apr. 25, 2006.

20. Interview with kindergarten teacher, Gransee, May 17, 2006.

21. Interview with teacher, Wittenberge, May 15, 2006.

22. Interview with physician, Fürstenberg, May 9, 2006.

23. Interview with inn keeper, Zehdenick, May 19, 2006.

24. Merrilyn Thomas, "The Evangelical Church in the GDR," in *The Workers' and Peasants' State: Communism and Society under Ulbricht, 1945–1971*, ed. Patrick Major and Jonathan Osmond (Manchester: Manchester University Press, 2002), 212.

25. Thomas, "Evangelical Church," 211, 224.

26. Klaus Behnke, "Zersetzungsmassnahmen," in *Politisch motivierte Verfolgung: Opfer von SED-Unrecht*, ed. Ulrich Baumann and Helmut Kury (Freiburg: Edition iuscrim, 1990), 389.

27. Interview with Dr. Woronowicz, Spandau, May 29, 2006.

28. Interview with Herr Heiser, Bad Wilsnack, May 2, 2006.

29. Timothy Garten Ash, *The File: A Personal History* (New York: Random House, 1997).

30. Barbara Miller, *Narratives of Guilt and Compliance in Unified Germany: Stasi Informers and their Impact on Society* (London: Routledge, 1999), 59.

31. Interview with Herr Jung, Bad Wilsnack, May 12, 2006.

32. Siegfried Grundmann, "Der DDR-Alltag im Jahre 1987," in *Die DDR: Analyse eines aufgegebenen Staates*, ed. Heiner Timmermann (Berlin: Duncker & Humblot, 2001), 144.

33. Bernd Eisenfeld, "Flucht und Ausreise, Macht und Ohnmacht," in *Die SED-Herrschaft und ihr Zussamenbruch*, ed. Eberhard Kuhrt (Opladen: Leske & Budrich, 1996), 383–96. Mary Fulbrook correctly points out that an important aspect of the Helsinki Final Act was that the East German government had *publicly* committed itself to human rights. See Fulbrook, "Popular Discontent and Political Activism in the GDR," *Contemporary European History* 2, no. 3 (Nov. 1993): 277.

34. Bernd Eisenfeld, "Die Ausreisebewegung–eine Erscheinungsform widerständigen Verhaltens," in *Zwischen Selbtsbehauptung und Anpassung*, ed. Ulrike Poppe et al. (Berlin: Ch. Links, 1995), 202.

35. Eisenfeld, "Die Ausreisebewegung," 203.

36. Interview with teacher, Wittenberge, May 31, 2006.

37. Interview with kindergarten teacher, Gransee, May 17, 2006.

38. Interview with grocery clerk, Fürstenberg, May 5, 2006.

39. Siegfried Kuntsche, "Das Bauerndorf in der Nachkriegszeit. Lebenslagen und Alltag," in *Befremdlich anders: Leben in der DDR*, ed. Evemarie Badstübner (Berlin: Dietz, 2000), 90.

40. Interview with Gustrow resident, Gustrow, May 1, 2006.

41. Günter Fromm, "Eisenhüttenstadt, sein Störsender und die verbotenen Antennen," in Badstübner, *Befremdlich*, 219.

42. Fromm, "Eisenhüttenstadt," 227.

43. Interview with Perleberg resident, May 23, 2006.

44. Interview with teacher, Wittenberge, May 31, 2006.

45. Interview with local historian, Gransee, May 8, 2006.

46. Fromm, "Eisenhüttenstadt," 226.

47. As quoted in Sandra Pingel-Schliemann, *Zersetzen: Strategie einer Diktatur* (Berlin: Robert-Havemann-Gesellschaft, 2002), 50.

48. Interview with Perleberg resident, Apr. 26, 2006.

49. Interview with owner of wood-product factory, Wittenberge, May 22, 2006; interview with teacher, Wittenberge, May 31, 2006.

50. Czeslaw Milosz, *The Captive Mind*, trans. Jane Zielonko (New York: Vintage, 1981), 54.

51. Johannes Huinink et al., eds., *Kollektiv und Eigensinn: Lebensverläufe in der DDR und danach* (Berlin: Akademie Verlag, 1995), 373.

52. Stefan Wolle, "Sehnsucht nach der Diktatur? Die heile Welt des Sozialismus als Erinnerung und Wirklichkeit," in *Der Schein der Normalität: Alltag und Herrschaft in der SED-Diktatur*, ed. Clemens Vollnhals and Jürgen Weber (Munich: Olzog, 2002), 17–21.

53. Joachim Gauck's address in *Opfer und Täter der SED-Herrschaft: Lebenswege in einer Diktatur. XVI. Bautzen-Forum der Friedrich-Ebert-Stiftung* (Leipzig: Friedrich-Ebert-Stiftung, 2005), 37. See also Ehrhart Neubert, "Opfer in strafrechtlichen nicht faßbaren Bereich," in *Politisch motivierte Verfolgung: Opfer von SED-Unrecht*, ed. Ulrich Baumann and Helmut Kury (Freiburg: Edition iuscrim, 1998), 295.

54. Interview with physician, Fürstenberg, May 9, 2006.

55. Interview with former Gransee resident, Kitchener, Ont., Aug. 9, 2006.

56. On the nature of fear see B. Bauer, *Kontrolle und Repression*, 362.

57. Johannes Raschke, *Zwischen Überwachung und Repression: Politische Verfolgung in der DDR 1971 bis 1989* (Opladen: Leske + Budrich, 2001), 30.

58. Renate Hürtgen, "Stasi in die Produktion," in Gieseke, *Staatssicherheit und Gesellschaft*, 316.

59. Hannelore Kleinschmid, "Der Mut zum Nein," *Deutschland Archiv* 8 (1995): 348.

60. B. Bauer, *Kontrolle und Repression*, 445.

61. B. Bauer, *Kontrolle und Repression*, 13.

62. Ulrike Helwerth, "kann man in hoyerswerda küssen?" in *Das kollektiv bin ich: Utopie und Alltag in der DDR*, ed. Franziska Becker et al., (Weimar: Böhlau, 2000), 33–34.

63. See in particular Stefan Bollinger and Fritz Vilmer, eds., *Die DDR war anders: Kritische Würdigung ihrer wichtigen sozialkulturellen Einrichtungen* (Berlin: Edition Ost, 2002), 8.

64. Bollinger and Vilmer, *Die DDR war anders*, 19.

65. Robert Proctor, *The Nazi War on Cancer* (Princeton: Princeton University Press, 1999).

66. Linde Wagner, "Polikliniken—ein gesundheitspoltisches Modell," in Bollinger and Vilmer, *Die DDR war anders*, 229-230.

67. Interview with physician, Wittenberge, June 30, 2006.

68. Ulrich Mielke, *Das Bezirkskrankenhaus Magdeburg-Altstadt* (Magdeburg: Bürgerkomitee Sachsen-Anhalt, 2007), 9.

69. Weil, *Zielgruppe Ärtzeschaft*, 281.

70. Weil, *Zielgruppe Ärtzeschaft*, 283.

71. Weil, *Zielgruppe Ärtzeschaft*, 291.

72. Orlando Figes, *The Whisperers: Private Life in Stalin's Russia* (New York: Metropolitan, 2007), 180.

73. Figes, *Whisperers*, 122-26.

## Chapter 6

1. Between August 1989 and April 1990, demonstrations took place in 522 locations in East Germany, but very few of these have been the subject of scholarly investigation. See Uwe Schwabe, "Der Herbst '89 in Zahlen," in *Die SED-Herrschaft und ihr Zusammenbruch*, ed. Eberhard Kuhrt (Opladen: Leske & Budrich, 1996), 719-35.

2. These elections dealt with local governing bodies like district councils and mayorships. These were not elections to the national parliament. See Karl Wilhelm Fricke, "Die DDR-Kommunalwahlen '88 als Zäsur für das Umschlagen von Opposition in Revolution," in Kuhrt, *Die SED-Herrschaft*, 467.

3. BStU-Schwerin, BV Schwerin, KD Perleberg 10556 (unpaginated), "Symbol 89" Lagefilm.

4. BStU-Schwerin, BV Schwerin AKG, KD Perleberg 10410 (unpaginated), "Zum Ergebnis der Kommunalwahlen am 7 Mai 1989," Ryll an BV Schwerin, May 16, 1989.

5. Ibid.

6. Ibid.

7. "Hinweise über ausgewählte bedeutsame Probleme in Zusammenhang mit den Ergebnissen der Kommunalwahlen am 7. Mai 1989." Document from BStU Central Archive, ZAIG 5352 as printed in Armin Mitter and Stefan Wolle, *Ich liebe euch doch Alle!: Befehle und Lageberichte des MfS Januar-November 1989* (Berlin: Basisdruck, 1990). See also the discussion of opposition to the election results in Ehrhart Neubert, *Geschichte der Opposition in der DDR 1949-1989* (Bonn: Bundeszentrale für politische Bildung, 2000), 813.

8. BStU-Schwerin, BV Schwerin AKG 06b, 6, Feb. 3, 1989, "Zu beachtenden Probleme in Vorbereitung der Kommunalwahlen 1989."

9. BStU-Schwerin, BV Schwerin, KD Perleberg 10471 (unpaginated). Mar. 16, 1989. "Zu beachtenden Probleme in Vorbereitung der Kommunalwahlen 1989."

10. BStU-Schwerin, BV Schwerin, AKG 01b, 158, Mar. 21, 1989, "Information über sicherheitspolitische Aspekte sowie weitere Reaktionen der Bevölkerung im Zusammenhang mit der Vorbereitung und Durchführung der Kommunalwahlen am 7 Mai 1989."

11. BStU-Schwerin, BV Schwerin AKG 46b, 74, Aug. 18, 1989, "Information über einige bedeutsame Aspekte der Versorgung der Bevölkerung mit Konsumgütern und Dienstleistungen im Kreis Perleberg."

12. Ibid., 76.

13. Ibid., 77.

14. BStU-Schwerin, BV Schwerin AKG 46b, 73, Aug. 3, 1989, "Information über weitere Reaktionen der Bevölkerung des Bezirkes Schwerin," BV Schwerin an ZAIG. See also BStU-Schwerin, BV Schwerin AKG 46b, 74, Aug. 18, 1989, "Information über einige bedeutsame Aspekte der Versorgung der Bevölkerung mit Konsumgütern und Dienstleistungen im Kreis Perleberg."

15. Walter Süß, "Die Durchdringung der Gesellschaft mittels des MfS—Fallbeispiel Jena im Jahre 1989," in Kuhrt, *Die SED-Herrschaft*, 241-46.

16. BLHA Rep. 531, Gransee 1489, Oct. 19, 1989, Vorlage für das Sekretariat der KL der SED Gransee,

17. BLHA Rep. 531, Gransee 1498, May 30, 1989, Information über die Realisierung eingegangener Verpflichtungen zur gezielten Überbeitung des Planes.

18. BStU-Potsdam, AKG 1054, 362; Referat Leiter BV zur DV in der KD Gse am Aug. 30, 1989.

19. BStU-Schwerin, BV Schwerin, KD Perleberg 10471 (unpaginated), July 31, 1989, "Information über die Nichtrückkehr eines NSW-Reisekaders aus Österreich," KD Perleberg an BV Schwerin.

20. Although Hungary cut away, to great fanfare, the barbed wire on its border with Austria, other border defenses remained intact. More than four thousand people were arrested at this border between May and the full opening of the border in August. Karsten Timmer, *Vom Aufbruch zum Umbruch: Die Bürgerbewegung in der DDR 1989* (Göttingen: Vandenhoeck & Ruprecht, 2000), 99.

21. Ilse Spittmann and Gisela Helwig, *Chronik der Ereignisse in der DDR* (Cologne: Verlag Wissenschaft und Politik, 1989), 2–3; Timmer, *Vom Aufbruch zum Umbruch*, 101.

22. BStU-Schwerin, BV Schwerin, Leiter, 16, 198–99. Memorandum of Aug. 25, 1989, from Korth to all KD leaders.

23. BStU-Schwerin, BV Schwerin AKG46b, 116, Sept. 5, 1989, "Information über weitere Reaktionen der Bevölkerung auf erpresserische Botschaftsbesetzungen sowie das ungesetzliche Verlassen der DDR über die Ungarische Volksrepublik."

24. Bernd Eisenfeld, "Flucht und Ausreise, Macht und Ohnmacht," in Kuhrt, *Die SED-Herrschaft*, 360.

25. A continuation of former policy does not always translate into "paralysis," a label some have applied to the East German government in face of the exodus. See Damon Terrill, "Tolerance Lost: Disaffection, Dissent and Revolution in the German Democratic Republic," *East European Quarterly* 28, no. 3 (Sept. 1994): 366. Similarly, Jonathan Grix argues that the GDR leadership "did not respond" to this crisis. Jonathan Grix, *The Role of the Masses in the Collapse of the GDR* (New York: St. Martin's, 2000), 97.

26. BStU-Schwerin, BV Schwerin, KD Perleberg 10471 (unpaginated), Aug. 16, 1989, "Aktuelle Lageschwerpunkte in Vorbereitung der 750-Jahr Feier der Stadt Perleberg."

27. Mitter and Wolle, *Ich liebe euch doch Alle*, 151.

28. BStU-Schwerin, BV Schwerin AKG 06b, 58, June 2, 1989, "Information über die Lage auf dem Gebiet der Antragstellung auf ständige Ausreise nach nichtsozialistischen Staaten und Westberlin sowie bei Privat-und Touristenreisen und damit im Zusammenhang stehende feindlich-negative Handlungen im Kreis Perleberg." (This date is likely wrong since "June 20" is referred to in the document).

29. BStU-Schwerin, BV Schwerin AKG 03a, 138, June 15, 1989, "Information über die Lage auf dem Gebiet der Antragstellung auf ständige Ausreise nach nichtsozialistischen Staaten und Westberlin sowie damit im Zusammenhang stehende feindlich-negative Handlungen im Bezirk Schwerin."

30. Ibid., 143.

31. BStU-Schwerin, BV Schwerin, KD Perleberg, 10556 (unpaginated), "Zur op. Kontrolle vom OV und OPK Personen am 7 Mai 1989." See also chap. 3 and chap. 4 respectively for a fuller explanation of OV and OPK.

32. BStU-Schwerin, BV Schwerin KD Perleberg 10376, 10377, series of reports on OPKs 1985–1989. "Darstellung der politisch-operativen Lage der KD Perleberg," by Hauptman Giese. he percentage of OPKs dealing with applicants to emigrate was also similar to years past. In 1987, nineteen of forty-six OPKs dealt with applicants to emigrate. See BStU-Schwerin, BV Schwerin, KD Perleberg 10586, unpaginated, July 8, 1987, "OPK Bestandsaufnahme."

33. BStU-Schwerin, BV Schwerin KD Perleberg 10586 (unpaginated), July 8, 1987, "OPK Bestandsaufnahme."

34. BLHA Rep. 531, Gransee 1493, Apr. 20, 1989, Monatsinformation (monthly report).

35. BLHA, Rep. 531, Gransee 1498, Apr. 3, 1989, Bericht über die inhaltliche und organisatorische Vorbereitung der Kommunalwahlen.

36. BLHA, Rep. 531, Gransee 1493, Sept. 20, 1989, Monatsinformation.

37. BLHA, Rep. 531, Gransee 1493, Aug. 20, 1989, Monatsinformation.

38. BStU-Potsdam, BVfS Potsdam, AKG 1054, 374–75. Referat Leiter BV zur Dienstversammlung in der KD Gransee am Aug. 30, 1989.

39. BStU-Schwerin, BV Schwerin 573/94 (unpaginated), July 11, 1984. "Vorschlag zur Verpflichtung des Kandidaten," gez. Leutnant Besenbiel.

40. BStU-Schwerin, BV Schwerin 573/94 (unpaginated), Jan. 13, 1986, "Leistungseinschätzung des IMB Robert," gez. Besenbiel.

41. BStU-Schwerin, BV Schwerin, 573/94 (unpaginated), Feb. 14, 1989, "Einsatz und Entwicklungskonzeption für den IMB Robert," gez. Besenbiel.

42. BStU-Schwerin, BV Schwerin, AOPK 414/90, (unpaginated), Apr. 23, 1987, "Eröffnungsbericht zum OV Tendenz," gez. Besenbiel und Ryll.

43. BStU-Schwerin, BV Schwerin, AKG o6b, 36–37, Apr. 10, 1989, "Zum Stand der Beziehungen Staat-Kirche im Kreis Perleberg," gez. Ryll.

44. BStU-Schwerin, BV Schwerin, AOPK 414/90 (unpaginated), Mar. 20, 1989, "Sachbestandsbericht zum OV Tendenz," gez. Besenbiel und Ryll.

45. BStU-Schwerin, BV Schwerin, AOPK 414/90, Apr. 5, 1989, "Aktennotiz," gez. Major Fenster.

46. BStU-Schwerin, BV Schwerin, AKG o3a, 182, 180, June 15, 1989, "Information über einige Aspekte des aktuellen Wirksamwerdens innerer feindlicher, oppositioneller und anderer negativer Kräfte in personellen Zusammenschlüsse im Bezirk Schwerin."

47. BStU-Schwerin, BV Schwerin, Oct. 24, 1989. Report by Robert.

48. BStU-Potsdam, KD Gransee 147, 219. Apr. 7, 1988, Befragungsprotokoll.

49. BStU-Potsdam, AKG 1612, 37. Dec. 23, 1988, Jahresplan 1989.

50. BStU-Potsdam, AKG 1054, 362–63. Referat Leiter BV zur DV in der KD GSE am Aug. 30, 1989.

51. BStU-Potsdam, KD GS 112, IM Vorgang IV 1117/86, 175.,Nov. 5, 1986, Verpflichtung,.

52. See the records contained in KD GS 112, IM Vorgang IV 1117/86.

53. BStU-Schwerin, KD Perleberg, 10441, 240, "Entschluss des Leiters der VPKA Perleberg," by Laskeweitz, July 3, 1989.

54. BStU-Schwerin, BV Schwerin, AKG 27b, 5–13, "Abschlussbericht zur Aktion "Stadtjubiläum 89," by Lieutenant Colonel Ryll, Aug. 28, 1989.

55. BStU-Schwerin, KD Perleberg 10441, 17, "Massnahmeplan zur politisch-operativen Sicherung der Vorbereitung und Durchführung der Veranstaltungen anlässlich der 750-Jahrfeier der Stadt Perleberg," by Fluch, July 7, 1989.

56. Ibid. 6–9.

57. BStU-Schwerin, KD Perleberg 10441, 83 "IM-Einsatz Stadtjubliäum 89," Aug. 4, 1989.

58. BStU Schwerin, KD Perleberg 10441, 85 "Einsatz der IM zum Stadtjubliäum 89," Aug. 10, 1989.

59. BStU-Schwerin, BV Schwerin, AKG 27b, 8, "Abschlussbericht zur Aktion "Stadtjubiläum 89," by Lieutenant Colonel Ryll, Aug. 28, 1989.

60. BStU-Schwerin, BV Schwerin, AKG 27b, 82, Memorandum of Aug. 31, 1989, from Ryll.

61. BStU-Schwerin, KD Perleberg 10441, 8, "Abschlussbericht zur Aktion "Stadtjubiläum 89," by Lieutenant Colonel Ryll.

62. Neubert, Geschichte der Opposition, 830, 851.

63. BStU-Schwerin, BV Schwerin, KD Perleberg 10471, 134, "Die am 20 Oktober 1989 stattgefundene Veranstaltung in der evangelischen Kirche in Wittenberge," Oct. 22, 1989. None of the other fledgling organizations like Demokratie Jetzt or Demokratischer Aufbruch had a presence in Perleberg. For more on these groups, see Neubert, Geschichte der Opposition, 856–63.

64. BStU-Schwerin, BV Schwerin, KD Perleberg 10471, 136, "Aktivitäten oppositioneller Kräfte im Kreis Perleberg," Oct. 25, 1989.

65. Grix, Role of the Masses, 113.

66. Stefan Wolle, Die heile Welt der Diktatur: Alltag und Herrschaft in der DDR 1971–1989 (Berlin: Links, 1998), 324.

67. BStU-Schwerin, BV Schwerin KD Perleberg 10471, 136, "Aktivitäten oppositioneller Kräfte im Kreis Perleberg," Oct. 25, 1989. See also BStU-Schwerin, BV Schwerin, KD Perleberg, 10471, 145–48, "Aktivitäten antisozialistischer Kräfte im Kreis Perleberg," Oct. 30, 1989.

68. BStU-Schwerin, BV Schwerin, Leiter 2a, 33, "Information über das Wirken des Neuen Forums, weiterer Sammlungsbewegungen und damit im Zusammenhang stehende beachtenswerte Probleme," Nov. 7, 1989.

69. BLHA, Rep. 531, Gransee 1493, Monatsinformation zum Oct. 20, 1989.

70. BStU-Potsdam, KD Gransee, Sach 254, Oct. 18, 1989, Schreiben BV Leiter an KD Leiter.

71. BStU-Potsdam, KD Gransee, Sach 254; Oct. 31, 1989, Bericht zur Veranstaltung im Jugendklubhaus Zehdenick am Oct. 30, 1989.

72. Interview with Zehdenick innkeeper, May 19, 2006.

73. Ibid.; and interview with Perleberg resident, May 23, 2006.

74. An excellent discussion of the role of Intershops in creating disenchantment is found in Jonathan Zatlin, *The Currency of Socialism: Money and Political Culture in East Germany* (Cambridge: Cambridge University Press, 2007).

75. BLHA, Rep. 531, Gransee 1490, Protokoll der Sitzung des Sekretariats der Kreisleitung am Nov. 8, 1989.

76. BStU-Potsdam, KD Gransee, Sach 254, Oct. 30, 1989, Schreiben BV Leiter an KD Leiter.

77. Andreas Niemann and Walter Süß, *Gegen das Volk kann nichts mehr entschieden werden*, 37.(Berlin: BStU, 1996).

78. BStU-Schwerin, KD Perleberg, 10610, Nov. 28, 1989, telegram.

79. Interview with Perleberg physician, Perleberg, May 27, 2006.

80. Gareth Dale, *The East German Revolution* (Manchester: Manchester University Press, 2006), 154.

81. See Edward Peterson's conclusion in *The Secret Police and the Revolution* (Westport: Praeger, 2002). Ross's discussion of the standard of living is somewhat cursory, considering the depth of the rest of his work. Corey Ross, *The East German Dictatorship: Problems and Perspectives in the Interpretation of the GDR* (London: Arnold, 2002), 136.

82. Gale Stokes, *The Walls Came Tumbling Down: The Collapse of Communism in Eastern Europe* (New York: Oxford University Press, 1993), 138.

83. Konrad Jarausch, *The Rush to German Unity* (New York: Oxford University Press, 1994), 24.

84. Daniel Chirot, "What happened in Eastern Europe in 1989?" in *The Revolutions of 1989*, ed. Vladimir Tismaneanu (London: Routledge, 1999), 38.

85. See Charles Maier, *Dissolution: The Crisis of Communism and the End of East Germany* (Princeton: Princeton University Press, 1997), 124; and Dietrich Staritz, "Ursachen und Konsequenzen einer deutschen Revolution," in *Der Fischer Weltalmanach* (Frankfurt: Fischer Taschenbuch-Verlag, 1990), 15.

86. Rainer Eckert, "Die Aktivitäten kleiner oppositioneller Gruppen" in Kuhrt, *Die SED-Herrschaft*, 696.

87. See for example BStU-Schwerin, BV Schwerin AKG 46b, 57–73, "Information über erste Reaktionen der Bevölkerung des Bezirkes Schwerin zur 8.Tagung des ZK der SED," AKG Schwerin to ZAIG Berlin, June 29, 1989; "Information über die Reaktion der Bevölkerung des Bezirkes Schwerin im Zusammenhang mit den Entwicklungstendenzen in den sozialistischen Staaten sowie weitere aktuell-politische Ereignisse," AKG Schwerin to ZAIG Berlin, July 20, 1989; "Information über weitere Reaktionen der Bevölkerung des Bezirkes Schwerin auf gegenwärtige Entwicklungstendenzen in den sozialistischen Staaten sowie damit im Zusammenhang stehende Probleme der weiteren Ausgestaltung der entwickelten sozialistischen Gesellschaft," AKG Schwerin to ZAIG Berlin, Aug. 3, 1989.

88. BStU-Schwerin, BV Schwerin, AKG46b, 113, "Information über weitere Reaktionen der Bevölkerung auf erpresserische Botschaftsbesetzungen sowie das ungesetzliche Verlassen der DDR über die Ungarische Volksrepublik," May 5, 1989.

89. BStU-Schwerin, BV Schwerin, AKG 46b, 111, "Information über weitere Reaktionen der Bevölkerung auf erpresserische Botschaftsbesetzungen sowie das ungesetzliche Verlassen der DDR über die Ungarische Volksrepublik," BV Schwerin to ZAIG, Sept. 5, 1989.

90. BStU-Schwerin, BV Schwerin, AKG 46b, 120, "Information über die Reaktion der Bürger des Bezirkes Schwerin auf die illegale Nacht-und-Nebel-Aktion zur Abwerbung in Ungarn befindlicher DDR-Bürger," AKG BV Schwerin to ZAIG, Sept. 12, 1989.

91. BStU-Schwerin, BV Schwerin, AKG 46b, 124, "Information über die Reaktion der Bürger des Bezirkes Schwerin auf die zeitweilige Aussetzung des pass-und visafreien Reiseverkehrs zwischen der DDR und der CSSR," AKG BV Schwerin to ZAIG, Oct. 5, 1989.

92. BStU-Schwerin, BV Schwerin, AKG 46b, 151, "Information über weitere Reaktion der Bevölkerung auf die Erklärung des Politbüros des ZK der SED vom 11 Oktober 1989," AKG BV Schwerin to ZAIG, Oct. 13, 1989.

93. Ross accurately points out that the balance of these elements (rather than the denial of the importance of one or the other) is what separates historians. Ross's account suggests priority for the changing international situation in providing the framework for demise. Ross, *East German Dictatorship*, 135.

94. Grix, *Role of the Masses*, 138.

95. Interview with Wittenberge factory owner, May 22, 2006.

96. Timmer, *Vom Aufbruch zum Umbruch*, 189.

97. BStU-Schwerin, BV Schwerin, KD Perleberg, 10590, 26–42, "Zuarbeit für den Plan 1990," signed by Ryll, Sept. 20, 1989. Karsten Timmer argues that illegal exodus was the "critical event" in the fall of the regime, although the evidence presented here suggests that the exodus did not affect the GDR uniformly and, accordingly, different districts had different priorities. Timmer, *Vom Aufbruch zum Umbruch*, 103.

98. Madarasz believes that the Stasi was a key institution for keeping the Party informed of popular developments, although she downplays the accuracy of the information given its ideological blinders. See Jeannette Madarasz, *Conflict and Compromise in East Germany 1971–1989: A Precarious Stability* (New York: Palgrave, 2003).

99. BStU-Schwerin, BV Schwerin, AKG 46 b (unpaginated), "Information über einige bedeutsame Aspekte der Versorgung der Bevölkerung," Aug. 18, 1989.

100. Madarasz, *Conflict and Compromise*, 157.

101. Peterson, *Secret Police*, 268. Several historians have gone so far as to call Stasi officers conspirators. The discovery immediately following the revolution of key oppositional figures having links to the Stasi—Minister President Lothar de Maziere, the lawyer Wolfgang Schnur, and the speaker for the newly formed Social Democratic Party, Ibrahim Böhme—led in part to this conspiracy theory, formulated initially by the journalist Henryk Broder. See Armin Mitter and Stefan Wolle, *Untergang auf Raten* (Munich: Bertelsmann, 1993), 530–33; and reiterated in Wolle, *Die heile Welt*, 338. Mitter and Wolle point, however, to a lack of evidence to support the theory of a Stasi conspiracy to overthrow the East German regime. The conspiracy theory has also been dismantled in Walter Süß, "Selbstblockierung der Macht," in *Weg in den Untergang: Der Innere Zerfall der DDR*, ed. Konrad Jarausch and Martin Sabrow (Göttingen: Vandenhoeck & Ruprecht, 1999). Mike Dennis's *The Stasi: Myth and Reality* (London: Longman, 2003), 231, calls the conspiracy theory "unsatisfactory." Jens Gieseke is adamant that Stasi officers were not in any way democratic reformers: Jens Gieseke, *Die Hauptamtlichen Mitarbeiter der Staatssicherheit* (Berlin: Links, 2000), 471.

102. BStU-Potsdam, KD Gransee, Sach 254, 358, Referat Leiter BV zur DV in der KD GSE am Aug. 30, 1989.

103. Hans-Hermann Hertle, *Der Fall der Mauer: Die Unbeabsichtigte Selbstauflösung des SED-Staates* (Opladen: Westdeutscher Verlag, 1996), 115. Karsten Timmer also argues this point of view. Timmer, *Vom Aufbruch zum Umbruch*, 185.

104. BStU-Potsdam, BV Potsdam, KD Gransee, SACH 264, 40–42, "Gewährleistung der Sicherheit der Dienstobjekte," from head of BV,Schickart, to KD leaders, Oct. 30, 1989.

105. Landeshauptarchiv Schwerin, 10-20-10-22 F10, Bericht des Sekretariats an die KL am May 17, 1989.

106. BLHA, Rep. 531, Gransee 1498, Aug. 23, 1989, Bericht über die politische Lage, die Stimmung und Meinungen der Werktätigen zu aktuellen innen- und aussenpolitischen Fragen.

107. Ibid.

108. BLHA, Rep. 531, Gransee 1493, Monatsinformation zum Aug. 20, 1989.

109. BLHA, Rep.531, Nr. 1498, Sept. 21, 1989, Bericht über die politische Lage, die Stimmung und Meinungen der Werktätigen zu aktuellen innen- und aussenpolitischen Fragen.

110. The minutes of these meetings are found in BLHA, Rep. 531, Gransee, Nr. 1481, 1487, 1488, 1489, 1490.

111. BLHA, Rep. 531, Gransee 1488, Protokoll der Sitzung des Sekretariats der Kreisleitung am Oct. 11, 1989.

112. BLHA, Rep. 531, Gransee 1493, Monatsinformation zum Oct. 20, 1989.

113. Landeshauptarchiv Schwerin, 10–20–10–22 FII, Nov. 11, 1989, KL Sitzung.

114. Udo Grashoff, *"In einem Anfall von Depression ..."*: *Selbsttötungen in der DDR* (Berlin: Links, 2006), 243.

115. Richard Popplewell has argued a similar conclusion for the Stasi at the leadership level, based on documents in Mitter and Wolle *Ich liebe euch doch Alle!*. See Richard Popplewell, "The Stasi and the East German Revolution of 1989," *Contemporary European History* 1, no. 1 (1992): 56.

116. Popplewell, "The Stasi," 56.

117. BStU-Schwerin, BV Schwerin, KD Perleberg, 10471 (unpaginated), "Die Lage im Kreis Perleberg und damit im Zusammenhang stehende feindlich-negative Handlung," Oct. 12, 1989.

118. Interview with Zehdenick innkeeper, May 19, 2006.

## Conclusion

1. Hubert Spiegel, "Das wahre Gesicht des Joseph Klempner," *Frankfurter Allgemeine Zeitung* 17 May 2006, 33.

2. Thomas Reichel, "Die 'durchherrschte' Arbeitergesellschaft," in *Der Schein der Stabilität: DDR-Betriebsalltag in der Ära Honecker*, eds. Renate Hürtgen and Thomas Reichel (Berlin: Metropol, 2001), 109–10.

3. Jonathan Zatlin, *The Currency of Socialism* (Cambridge: Cambridge University Press, 2007), 318.

4. See Gauck's address in Friedrich-Ebert-Stiftung, *Opfer und Täter der SED-Herrschaft: Lebenswege in einer Diktatur*, vol. 16, *Bautzen-Forum der Friedrich-Ebert-Stiftung* (Leipzig: Friedrich-Ebert-Stiftung, 2005), 37.

5. In particular Götz Aly, *Hitler's Beneficiaries* (New York: Metropolitan, 2005) and Peter Fritzsche, *Life and Death in the Third Reich* (Cambridge, MA: Harvard University Press, 1998).

6. Landeshauptarchiv Schwerin, IV/4/08/95x96, 27.10.1953, Bericht "Entfaltung einer offensiven Agitationsarbeit unter den Massen."

7. Landeshauptarchiv Schwerin, IV/4/09/93X94, 12.6.1953, Direktive des Sekretariats der Bezirksleitung vom 12.6.1953.

8. Landeshauptarchiv Schwerin, IV/4/08/99, Protokoll der Sekretariatssitzungen nr. 2 der SED-KL Perleberg am 3.3.1954.

9. Landeshauptarchiv Schwerin, IV/4/09/93X94, 25.6.1953, Beschlussvorlage der SED KL Perleberg Agitationskommisison; Protokoll der Sekretariatssitzungen am 2.7.1953.

10. Landeshauptarchiv Schwerin, IV/4/08/110XIII, 21.9.1955, Erfahrungen der Kreisparteiorganisation Perleberg bei der Durchführung von Landsonntagen.

11. Reinhard Grimmer et al., *Die Sicherheit: zur Abwehrarbeit des MfS*, 2 vols. (Berlin: Edition Ost, 2002). vol. 1, 63.

12. Peter Schaar, *Das Ende der Privatsphäre* (Munich: Bertelsmann, 2007), 61–63, 140–44.

# Bibliography

*Primary Sources*

*Federal Commissioner for the Files of the State Security Service of the former GDR–Potsdam branch.*
*(Bundesbeauftragte für die Unterlagen des Staatssicherheitsdienstes der ehemaligen DDR–*
*Aussenstelle Potsdam)*

*Record Groups*

Allgemeine Sachablage
Abteilung VII
Abteilung XX
KD Gransee
Kaderakten
IM-Vorgänge
OPK (Personal Surveillance Operation)-Vorgänge
OV-Vorgänge

*Federal Commissioner for the Files of the State Security Service of the former GDR–Schwerin branch*
*(Bundesbeauftragte für die Unterlagen des Staatssicherheitsdienstes der ehemaligen DDR–*
*Aussenstelle Schwerin)*

*Record Groups*

AKG
ZMA
KD Perleberg
Kaderakten
Bezirksleitung
IM-Vorgänge
OPK-Vorgänge
OV-Vorgänge

*Landeshauptarchiv Schwerin*

*Record Groups*

Sekretariatsitzungen
Bürositzungen der KL Perleberg
BPO der Sicherheitsorgane
Feindliche Gruppierungen
Protokolle der Sitzungen der KL der SED

*Brandenburgisches Landeshauptarchiv–Potsdam*

*Record Groups*

Rep. 531 Gransee
Sekretariatssitzungen der KL Gransee
Informationsberichte

## Interviews with Residents of Districts Gransee and Perleberg

Kindergarten Teacher, Gransee, May 17, 2006
Teacher, Wittenberge, May 19, 2006
Factory director, Wittenberge, May 22, 2006
Perleberg resident, Perleberg, May 23, 2006
Senior physician, Wittenberge, June 30, 2006
Dr. Woronowicz, Spandau, May 29, 2006
Teacher, Wittenberge, May 31, 2006
Physician, Perleberg, June 1, 2006
Architect, Gransee, April 25, 2006
Director, Retail Co-operative, Perleberg, April 26, 2006
Frau Vogt, Gustrow, May 1, 2006
Lutheran minister, Bad Wilsnack, May 2, 2006
Grocery store clerk, Fürstenberg, May 5, 2006
Local historian, Gransee, May 8, 2006
Physician, Fürstenberg, May 9, 2006
Teacher, Wittenberge, May 10, 2006
Herr Jung, Bad Wilsnack, May 12, 2006
Teacher, Wittenberge, May 15, 2006
Support staff, Zehdenick Brick factory, Kitchener, Ont., August 9, 2006
Dr. Jürgen Schmidt-Pohl, Warnemünde, September 25, 2006

## Interviews with Stasi personnel

Rolf Schwegel, Wittenberge, May 31, 2006
Reinhard Kuhlow, Wittenberge, May 22, 2006
Anne Klenk, Wittenberge, May 23, 2006
Antje Müller, Quitzow, May 24, 2006
Matthias Piekert, Wittenberge, May 23, 2006
Herr and Frau Paupst, Wittenberge, May 31. 2006
Bernd Lohre, Wittenberge, June 7, 2006
Horst Sauer, Perleberg, June 8, 2006
Florian Tenbrock, Häsen, August 8, 2003 and May 11, 2006
Klaus-Peter Schmid, Neuruppin, May 6, 2006
Rudolf Schulze, Wittenberge, April 28, 2006
Markus Schram, Zehdenick, May 4, 2006
Werner Beuster, Löwenberger Land, May 8, 2006

## Secondary Sources

Abke, Stephanie. *Sichtbare Zeichen unsichtbarer Kräfte: Denunziationsmuter und Denunziationsverhalten 1933–1945*. Tübingen: Diskord, 2003.

Allen, William Sheridan. *The Nazi Seizure of Power*. New York: Watts, 1984.

Ammer, Thomas, and Hans-Joachim Memmler. *Staatssicherheit in Rostock: Zielgruppen, Methoden, Auflösung*. Köln: Verlag Wissenschaft und Politik, 1991.

Arnswald, Ulrich, et al., eds. *DDR-Geschichte im Unterricht: Schulbuchanalyse-Schülerbefragung-Modellcurriculum*. Berlin: Metropol, 2006.

Ash, Timothy Garten. *The File: A Personal History*. New York: Random House, 1997.

Baldwin, Peter. *Reworking the Past: Hitler, the Holocaust, and the Historians' Debate*. Boston: Beacon, 1990.

Bauer, Babett. *Kontrolle und Repression: Individuelle Erfahrungen in der DDR (1971–1989)*. Göttingen: Vandenhoeck & Ruprecht, 2006.

Bauer, Yehuda. *A History of the Holocaust*. New York: Watts, 1982.

——— . "Overall Explanations: German Society and the Jews: or Some Thoughts about Context." In *Probing the Depths of German Antisemitism: German Society and the Persecution of the Jews, 1933–1941*, ed. David Bankier, 3–16. New York: Berghahn, 2000.

Behnke, Klaus. "Zersetzungsmassnahmen." In *Politisch motivierte Verfolgung: Opfer von SED-Unrecht,* ed. Ulrich Baumann and Helmut Kury. Freiburg: Edition iuscrim, 1990.

Bessel, Richard, and Ralph Jessen, eds. *Die Grenzen der Diktatur: Staat und Gesellschaft in der DDR.* Göttingen: Vandenhoeck & Rupprecht, 1996.

Bollinger, Stefan, and Fritz Vilmer, eds. *Die DDR war anders: Kritische Würdigung ihrer wichtigen sozialkulturellen Einrichtungen.* Berlin: Edition Ost, 2002.

Bracher, Karl Dietrich. *Die totalitäre Erfahrung.* München: Piper, 1987.

Bräutigam, ed. *Fremdarbeiter in Brandenburg in der NS-Zeit.* Potsdam, 1996.

Browning, Christopher. *Ordinary Men: Reserve Police Battalion 101 and the Final Solution in Poland.* New York: Harper, 1992.

Bruce, Gary. "Access to Secret Police Files, Justice and Vetting in East Germany since 1989." *German Politics and Society* 26, no. 1 (Spring 2008): 82–111.

———. " 'In our District, the State is Secure': The East German Secret Police Response to the Events of 1989 in Perleberg District." *Contemporary European History* 14, no. 2 (2005): 219–44.

———. "The Prelude to Nationwide Surveillance in East Germany: Stasi Operations and Threat Perceptions, 1945–1953." *Journal of Cold War Studies* 5, no. 2 (2003): 3–31.

———. *Resistance with the People: Repression and Resistance in Eastern Germany, 1945–1955.* Lanham, Md.: Rowman & Littlefield, 2003.

———. "Wir haben den Kontakt zu den Massen nie verloren." In *Staatssicherheit und Gesellschaft: Studien zum Herrschaftsalltag in der DDR,* ed. Jens Gieseke, 365–79. Göttingen: Vandenhoeck & Ruprecht, 2007.

Childers, Thomas. *The Nazi Voter: The Social Foundations of Fascism in Germany, 1919–1933.* Chapel Hill: University of North Carolina Press, 1983.

Childs, David, and Richard Popplewell. *The Stasi: The East German Intelligence and Security Service.* New York: New York University Press, 1996.

Chirot, Daniel. "What happened in Eastern Europe in 1989?" In *The Revolutions of 1989,* ed. Vladimir Tismaneanu, 19–50. London: Routledge, 1999.

Connelly, John. *Captive University: The Sovietization of East German, Czech, and Polish Higher Education, 1945–1956.* Chapel Hill: University of North Carolina Press, 2000.

Dahrendorf, Ralf. *Der Moderne Soziale Konflikt.* München: DTV Verlag, 1994.

Debes, Martin. *Durchdringen und Zersetzen:Die Bekämpfung der Opposition in Ostthüringen durch das MfS im Jahre 1989.* Manebach: Goldhelm Verlag, 1999.

Deletant, Dennis. "Romania." In *A Handbook of the Communist Security Apparatus in East Central Europe 1944–1989,* ed. Krzysztok Persak, Lukasz Kaminsi, and David L Burnett. Warsaw: Institute of National Remembrance, 2005.

Demps, Laurenz. "Die Provinz Brandenburg in der NS-Zeit." In *Brandenburgische Geschichte,* ed. Ingo Materna and Wolfgang Ribbe. Berlin: Akademie Verlag, 1995.

Dennis, Mike. *The Stasi: Myth and Reality.* London: Longman, 2003.

Diekmann. "Boykott–Entrechtung–Pogrom–Deportation." In *Verfolgung, Alltag, Widerstand,* ed. Dietrich Eichhotlz. Berlin: Volk & Welt, 1993.

Döbert, Frank. *Mit dem Ernstfall konfrontiert: Die Stasi und der VEB Carl Zeiss.* Geschichtswerkstatt Jena 3/96, 1996.

Doll, Jörg, and Marc Damitz. "Zur Bedeutung des wichtigsten inoffiziellen Mitarbeiters für die Bewältigung der Bespitzelung durch das MfS der DDR." In *Politisch motivierte Verfolgung: Opfer von SED-Unrecht,* ed. Ulrich Baumann and Helmut Kury. Freiburg: Edition iuscrim, 1998.

Donnersmarck, Florian Henckel von. *Das Leben der anderen: Filmbuch.* Frankfurt: Suhrkamp, 2006.

Dördelmann, Katrin. "Aus einer gewissen Empörung hierüber habe ich Anzeige erstattet: Verhalten und Motive von Denunziantinnen." In *Zwischen Karriere und Verfolgung: Handlungsräume von Grauen im nationalsozialistischen Deutschland,* ed. Kristen Heinsohn, Birgit Vogel and Ulrike Weckel, 189–205. Frankfurt: Campus Verlag, 1997.

Eckert, Rainer. "Schuld und Zeitgeschichte: Zwölf Thesen zur Auseinandersetzung mit der deutschen Diktatur." *Deutschland Archiv* 41, no. 1 (2008): 117.

Editorial, *Deutschland Archiv* 40, no. 6 (2007): 960.

Eicholtz, Dietrich. "Soziale Umbrüche in Brandenburg 1943–1945." In *Terror, Herrschaft und Alltag im Nationalsozialismus: eine Sozialgeschichte des deutschen Faschismus*, ed. Brigitte Berlekamp and Werner Röhr. Münster: Verlag Westfälisches Dampfboot, 1995.

———, ed. *Verfolgung, Alltag, Widerstand*. Berlin: Volk & Welt, 1993.

Eisenfeld, Bernd. "Die Ausreisebewegung—eine Erscheingungsform widerständigen Verhaltens." In *Zwischen Selbtsbehauptung und Anpassung*, ed. Ulrike Poppe et al. Berlin: Ch. Links, 1995.

———. "Flucht und Ausreise, Macht und Ohnmacht." In *Die SED-Herrschaft und ihr Zussamenbruch*, ed. Eberhard Kuhrt, 383–96. Opladen: Leske & Budrich, 1996.

Eisenfeld, Bernd, Ilko-Sascha Kowalczuk, and Erhart Neubert, eds. *Die verdrängte Revolution: der Platz des 17. Juni 1953 in der deutschen Geschichte*. Bremen: Edition Temmen, 2004.

Ellmenreich, Renate. *Frauen bei der Stasi: Am Beispiel der MfS-Bezirksverwaltung Gera*. Erfurt: Landesbeauftragte des Freistaates Thüringens, 1999.

Engelmann, Roger. "Eine Regionalstudie zu Herrschaft und Alltag im Staatssozialismus." In *Staatssicherheit und Gesellschaff: Studien zum Herrschaftsalltag in der DDR*, ed. Jens Gieseke, 167–86. Göttingen: Vandenhoeck & Ruprecht, 2007.

Ensikat, David. *Kleines Land, große Mauer: Die DDR für alle, die (nicht) dabei waren*. München: Piper, 2007.

Evans, Richard. *The Coming of the Third Reich*. New York: Penguin, 2004.

Faulenbach, Bernd. http://www.bundestag.de/Ausschuese/a22/Anhoerungen/ Gedenkstaettenkonzept/Stellungnahmen/Faulenbach.pdf.

Feldmann. "Das Städtische Lyzeum zu Wittenberge–Geschichte einer Schule." *Mitteilungen des Vereins für Geschichte der Prignitz* 5 (Perleberg 2005).

Figes, Orlando. *The Whisperers: Private Life in Stalin's Russia*. New York: Metropolitan, 2007.

Fitzpatrick, Sheila. *Everyday Stalinism: Ordinary Life in Extraordinary Times: Soviet Russia in the 1930s*. New York: Oxford University Press, 1999.

Fitzpatrick, Sheila, and Robert Gellately. "Introduction to the Practices of Denunciation in Modern European History." In *Accusatory Practices: Denunciation in Modern European History, 1789–1989*, ed. Sheila Fitzpatrick and Robert Gellately, 1–29. Chicago: University of Chicago Press, 1997.

Fricke, Karl Wilhelm. "Die DDR-Kommunalwahlen '88 als Zäsur für das Umschlagen von Opposition in Revolution." In *Die SED-Herrschaft und ihr Zussamenbruch*, ed. Eberhard Kuhrt. Opladen: Leske & Budrich, 1996.

Fricke, Karl Wilhelm, and Roger Engelmann. *Konzentrierte Schläge: Staatssicherheitsaktionen und politische Prozesse in der DDR 1953–1956*, Berlin: Ch. Links, 1998.

Friedrich-Ebert-Stiftung. *Im Visier der Geheimpolizei: Der kommunistische Überwachungs-und Repressionsapparat 1945–1989*. Leipzig: Friedrich-Ebert-Stiftung, 2007.

———. *Opfer und Täter der SED-Herrschaft: Lebenswege in einer Diktatur: XVI. Bautzen-Forum der Friedrich-Ebert-Stiftung*. Leipzig: Friedrich-Ebert-Stiftung, 2005.

Fritzsche, Peter. *Life and Death in the Third Reich*. Cambridge, Mass.: Harvard University Press, 2008.

Fromm, Günter. "Eisenhüttenstadt, sein Störsender und die verbotenen Antennen." In *Befremdlich anders: Leben in der DDR*, ed. Evemarie Badstübner. Berlin: Dietz, 2000.

Fulbrook, Mary. "Jenseits der Totalitarismustheorie?" In *German Monitor: The GDR and Its History: Rückblick und Revision*, ed. Peter Baker, 36–42. Amsterdam: Rodopi, 2000).

———. *The People's State: East German Society from Hitler to Honecker*. New Haven, Conn.: Yale University Press, 2005.

———. "Popular Discontent and Political Activism in the GDR." *Contemporary European History* 2, no. 3 (Nov. 1993): 265–82.

———. "Putting the People Back in: The Contentious State of GDR History." *German History* 24, no. 4 (Oct. 2006): 608–20.

Funder, Anna. *Stasiland*. London: Granta Books, 2003.

Gellately, Robert. *Backing Hitler: Consent and Coersion in Nazi Germany*. Oxford: Oxford University Press, 2001.

———. "Denunciations in Twentieth Century Germany: Aspects of Self-Policing in the Third Reich and the German Democratic Republic." *Journal of Modern History* 68, no. 4 (Dec. 1996): 931–67.

———. *The Gestapo and German Society: Enforcing Racial Policy 1933–1945.* Oxford: Clarendon Press, 1990.

Gieseke, Jens. "Die Einheit von Wirtschafts-, Sozial- und Sicherheitspolitik: Militarisierung und Überwachung als Probleme einer DDR-Sozialgeschichte der Ära Honecker." *Zeitschrift für Geschichtswissenschaft* 51, no. 11 (2003).

———. *Die hauptamtlichen Mitarbeiter der Staatssicherheit.* Berlin: Ch. Links, 2000.

———. *Mielke-Konzern: Die Geschichte der Stasi.* Stuttgart: DVA, 2001.

———. "Referat." In *Im Visier der Geheimpolizei: Der kommunistische Überwachungs- und Repressionsapparat 1945–1989.* Leipzig: Friedrich-Ebert-Stiftung, 2007.

———. "Staatssicherheit und Gesellschaft —Plädoyer für einen Brückenschlag." In *Staatssicherheit und Gesellschaft: Studien zum Herrschaftsalltag in der DDR,* ed. Jens Gieseke. Göttingen: Vandenhoeck & Ruprecht, 2007.

———, ed. *Staatssicherheit und Gesellschaft: Studien zum Herrschaftsalltag in der DDR.* Göttingen: Vandenhoeck & Ruprecht, 2007.

Gill, David, and Ulrich Schröter. *Das Ministerium für Staatssicherheit: Anatomie des Mielke-Imperiums.* Berlin: Rowohlt, 1991.

Glöwen, Thomas. "Zwangsarbeit im Beutelager: das KZ-Aussenlager Glöwen." In *Havelberg: Kleine Stadt mit grosser Vergangenheit.* Havelberg: Mitteldeutscher Verlag, 1998.

Gottschalk, Jürgen. *Druckstellen: Die Zerstörung einer Künstler-Biographie durch die Stasi.* Leipzig: Evangelische Verlagsanstalt, 2006.

Grashoff, Udo. "*In einem Anfall von Depression...*": Selbsttötungen in der DDR.* Berlin: Ch. Links, 2006.

Grieder, Peter. "In Defence of Totalitarianism Theory as a Tool of Historical Scholarship." *Totalitarian Movements and Political Religions* 8, no. 3–4 (Sept. 2007): 563–89.

Grimmer, Reinhard, Werner Irmler, Willi Opitz, and Wolfgang Schwanitz, eds. *Die Sicherheit: zur Abwehrarbeit des MfS,* 2 vols. Berlin: Edition Ost, 2002.

Grix, Jonathan. *The Role of the Masses in the Collapse of the GDR.* New York: St. Martin's, 2000.

Grundmann, Siegfried. "Der DDR-Alltag im Jahre 1987." In *Die DDR: Analysen eines aufgegebenen Staates,* ed. Heiner Timmermann. Berlin: Duncker & Humblot, 2001.

Hahn, Reinhardt. *Ausgedient: Ein Stasi-Major erzählt.* Leipzig: Mitteldeutscher Verlag, 1990.

Harsch, Donna. "Society, the State, and Abortion in East Germany, 1950–1972." *American Historical Review* 102, no. 1 (Feb. 1997): 53–84.

———. "Squaring the Circle: The Dilemmas and Evolution of Women's Policy." In *The Workers' and Peasants' State: Communism and Society in East Germany under Ulbricht 1945–71,* ed. Patrick Major and Jonathan Osmond, 151–70. Manchester: Manchester University Press, 2002.

Helwerth, Ulrike. "Kann man in Hoyerswerda küssen?" In *Das kollektiv bin ich: Utopie und Alltag in der DDR,* ed. Franziska Becker et al. Weimar: Böhlau, 2000.

Henckel von Donnersmarck, Florian. *Das Leben der anderen: Filmbuch.* Frankfurt: Suhrkamp, 2006.

Henke, Klaus-Dietmar. "Aufarbeitung verstärken, Gedenken vertiefen: Grundsätzliche Bemerkungen zum Gedenken an deutsche Diktaturen." *Deutchland Archiv* 40, no. 6 (2007): 1052–55.

———. "Zu Nutzung und Auswertung der Unterlagen des Staatssicherheitsdienstes." *Vierteljahrshefte für Zeitgeschichte* 41, no. 4 (1993): 575–87.

Henke, Klaus-Dietmar, and Roger Engelmann, eds. *Aktenlage: die Bedeutung der Unterlagen des Staatssicherheitsdienstes für die Zeitgeschichtsforschung.* Berlin: Ch. Links, 1995.

Henke, Klaus-Dietmar, Siegfried Suckut, Clemens Vollnhalls, Walter Süß, and Roger Engelmann. *Anatomie der Staatssicherheit: Geschichte, Struktur und Methoden.* Berlin: BStU, 1996.

Hertle, Hans-Hermann. *Der Fall der Mauer: Die Unbeabsichtigte Selbstauflösung des SED-Staates.* Opladen: Westdeutscher Verlag, 1996.

Hertle, Hans-Hermann, and Franz-Otto Gilles. "Stasi in der Produktion." In *Aktenlage: Die Bedeutung der Unterlagen des Staatsicherheitsdienstes für die Zeitsgeschichtsforschung*, ed. Klaus-Dietmar Henke and Roger Engelmann. Berlin: Ch. Links, 1995.

Hertle, Hans-Hermann, and Stefan Wolle. *Damals in der DDR: der Alltag im Arbeiter- und Bauernstaat*. München: Bertelsmann, 2004.

Hilberg, Raul. *The Destruction of the European Jews*. Chicago: Quadrangle Books, 1967.

Holquist, Peter. "'Information is the Alpha and Omega of our work:' Bolshevik surveillance in its pan-European context." *Journal of Modern History* 69, no. 3 (Sept. 1997): 415–50.

Huinink, Johannes, et al., eds. *Kollektiv und Eigensinn: Lebensverläufe in der DDR und danach*. Berlin: Akademie Verlag, 1995.

Hürtgen, Renate. "Stasi in die Produktion." In *Staatssicherheit und Gesellschaft: Studien zum Herrschaftsalltag in der DDR*, ed. Jens Gieseke. Göttingen: Vandenhoeck & Ruprecht, 2007.

Jacobeit, Sigrid, and Lieselotte Thoms-Heinrich. *Kreuzweg Ravensbrück: Lebensbilder antifaschistischer Widerstandskämpferinnen*. Köln: Röderberg, 1987.

Jarausch, Konrad. "Care and Coercion: the GDR as Welfare Dictatorship." In *Dictatorship as Experience: Towards a Socio-Cultural History of the GDR*, ed. Konrad Jarausch, 47–69. New York: Berghahn Books, 2000.

———. *The Rush to German Unity*. New York: Oxford University Press, 1994.

Jauch, Anke. *Die Stasi packt zu: Freiheitsberaubung 1980*. Frankfurt: August von Goethe Literaturverlag, 2007.

Jessen, Ralph. "Die Gesellschaft im Staatssozialismus." *Geschichte und Gesellschaft* 21, no. 1 (1995): 96–110.

Johnson, Eric. *Nazi Terror: The Gestapo, Jews, and Ordinary Germans*. New York: Basic Books, 1999.

Joshi, Vandana. *Gender and Power in the Third Reich: Female Denouncers and the Gestapo 1933–1945*. New York: Palgrave MacMillan, 2003.

Jung, Christian. *Geschichte der Verlierer: Historische Selbstreflexion von hochrangigen Mitgliedern der SED nach 1989*. Heidelberg: Universitätsverlag, 2007.

Kaienburg, Hermann. "Zwangsarbeit für das 'deutsche Rohstoffwunder.'" *1999 Zeitschrift für Sozialgeschichte des 20. und 21. Jahrhunderts* (Köln 1994).

Kaiser, Roswitha. "'Stille Helden:' Eine empirische Untersuchung über Verweigerungen und Ablehnungsgründe zur inoffiziellen Zusammenarbeit mit dem MfS am Beispiel der Bezirksverwaltung Potsdam." Diplomarbeit, Fachhochschule Potsdam, 1997.

Kaminski, Lukasz, et al., eds. *Handbuch der kommunistischen Geheimdienste in Osteuropa 1944–1991*. Göttingen: Vandenhoeck & Ruprecht, 2008.

Karau, Gisela. *Stasiprotokolle: Gespräche mit ehemaligen Mitarbeitern des Ministeriums für Staatssicherheit*. Frankfurt: Dipa, 1992.

Karpenko, Fjodorovitch. "Letter." In *Verschleppt nach Deutschland! Jugendliche Häftlinge des KZ Neuengamme aus der Sowjetunion erinnern sich*, ed. Herbert Dierks. Bremen: Edition Temmen, 2000.

Kielmansegg, Peter Graf. "Krise der Totalitarismustheorie?" In *Totalitarismus im 20. Jahrhundert*, ed. Eckhard Jesse, 286–304. Baden-Baden: Nomos, 1996.

Kleinschmid, Hannelore. "Der Mut zum Nein: Ein Bericht über Menschen, die sich der Stasi verweigerten." *Deutschland Archiv* 28 (1995): 348–59.

Kluge, Gerhard, and Reinhard Meinel. *MfS und FSU: Das Wirken des Ministeriums für Staatssicherheit an der Friedrich-Schiller-Universität Jena*. Erfurt: Landesbeauftragter des Freistaats Thüringen für die Unterlagen des Staatssicherheitsdienstes der DDR, 1997.

Knabe, Hubertus. "Strafen ohne Strafrecht, Zum Wandel repressiver Strategien in der Ära Honecker." In *Die DDR-Recht und Justiz als politisches Instrument*, ed. Heiner Timmermann. Berlin: Duncker and Humblot, 2000.

———. *Die Täter sind unter uns*. Berlin: Propyläen Verlag, 2007.

———. "Weiche Formen der Verfolgung in der DDR. Zum Wandel der repressiven Strategien in der Ära Honecker." *Deutschland Archiv* 5 (1997): 709–19.

Koehler, John. *The Stasi: The Untold Story of the East German Secret Police*. Boulder, Colo.: Westview Press, 1999.

Kohl, Ulrike. "Quellen zur Geschichte der NSDAP und ihrer Gliederungen in Berlin-Brandenburg." In *Jahrbuch für brandenburgische Landesgeschichte*, ed. Henning, Neugebauer, 177–215. Berlin, 1999.

Koop, Volker. *Deckname "Vergeltung": Die Stasi und der Tod der Brüder Baer*. Bonn: Bouvier, 1997.

Kopstein, Jeffrey. *The Politics of Economic Decline in East Germany*. Chapel Hill: University of North Carolina Press, 1997.

Kott, Sandrine. "Stasi als Teil der Gesellschaft," In *Staatssicherheit und Gesellschaft: Studien zum Herrschaftsalltag in der DDR*, ed. Jens Gieseke. Göttingen: Vandenhoeck & Ruprecht, 2007.

Kowalczuk, Ilko-Sascha, and Stefan Wolle. *Roter Stern über Deutschland: Sowjetische Truppen in der DDR*. Berlin: Ch. Links, 2001.

Krause, Werner. "Zum 60. Jahrestag der Reichspogromnacht vom 9. November 1938." *Gransee Zeitung 7/8* (November 1998).

Kuntsche, Siegfried. "Das Bauerndorf in der Nachkriegszeit. Lebenslagen und Alltag." In *Befremdlich anders: Leben in der DDR*, ed. Evemarie Badstübner, 64–116. Berlin: Dietz, 2000.

Leide, Henry. *NS-Verbrecher und Staatssicherheit: die Geheime Vergangenheitspolitik der DDR*. Göttingen: Vandenhoeck & Ruprecht, 2005.

Leo, Annette. *"Das ist so'n zweischneidiges Schwert hier unser KZ ..." Der Fürstenberg Alltag und das Frauenkonzentrationslager Ravensbrück*. Berlin: Metropol Friedrich Veitl-Verlag, 2007.

———. "Schmerzhafte Erinnerungen." In *Fürstenberg-Drogen: Schichten eines verlassenene Ortes*, ed. Florian Buttlar, Stefanie Endlich, and Annette Leo. Berlin: Hentrich, 1994.

Lindenberger, Thomas. "Everyday History: New Approaches to the History of the Post-War Germanies." In *The Divided Past: Rewriting Post-War German History*, ed. Christoph Klessmann, 43–67. New York: Berg, 2001.

———. *Herrschaft und Eigen-Sinn in der Diktatur: Studien zur Gesellschaftsgeschichte der DDR*. Köln: Böhlau Verlag, 1999.

———. "SED-Herrschaft als soziale Praxis, Herrschaft und 'Eigen-Sinn': Problemstellung und Begriffe." In *Staatssicherheit und Gesellschaff: Studien zum Herrschaftsalltag in der DDR*, ed. Jens Gieseke, 23–48. Göttingen: Vandenhoeck & Ruprecht, 2007.

———. *Volkspolizei: Herrschaftspraxis und öffentliche Ordnung im SED-Staat 1952–1968*. Köln: Böhlau Verlag, 2003.

Löser, Grit. "Die Stellung der Kreisdienststellen im Gefüge des MfS, dargestellt am Beispiel der Kreisdienststelle Freiberg und deren Bearbeitung als Bestand." PhD diss., Fachhochschule Potsdam, 1995.

Lüdtke, Alf. "Helden der Arbeit-Mühen beim Arbeitem." In *Sozialgeschichte der DDR*, ed. Hartmut Kaelblre et al. Stuttgart: Klett-Cotta, 1994.

Madarasz, Jeannette. *Conflict and Compromise in East Germany 1971–1989: A Precarious Stability*. New York: Palgrave, 2003.

Maier, Charles. *Dissolution: The Crisis of Communism and the End of East Germany*. Princeton, N.J.: Princeton University Press, 1997.

Malia, Martin. "To the Stalin Mausoleum." *Daedalus* 119 (Winter 1990): 295–344.

Mann, Reinhard. *Protest und Kontrolle im Dritten Reich*. Frankfurt: Campus Verlag, 1987.

Mechtenberg, Theo. *30 Jahre Zielperson des MfS*. Halle: Landesbeauftragte für die Unterlagen des Staatssicherheitsdienstes der ehemaligen DDR in Sachsen-Anhalt, 2001.

Merkel, Ina. "Leitbilder und Lebensweisen von Frauen in der DDR." In *Sozialgeschichte der DDR*, ed. Hartmut Kaelblre et al. Stuttgart: Klett-Cotta, 1994.

Merz, Kai-Uwe. *Kalter Krieg als antikommunistischer Widerstand: Die Kampfgruppe gegen Unmenschlichkeit, 1948–1959*. München: Oldenbourg, 1987.

Mielke, Ulrich. *Das Bezirkskrankenhaus Magdeburg-Altstadt*. Magdeburg: 2007.

Miller, Barbara. *Narratives of Guilt and Compliance in Unified Germany: Stasi Informers and their Impact on Society*. London: Routledge, 1999.

Milosz, Czeslaw. *The Captive Mind*. Translated by Jane Zielonko. New York: Vintage, 1981.

Mitter, Armin, and Stefan Wolle. *Ich liebe euch doch Alle!: Befehle und Lageberichte des MfS Januar-November 1989*. Berlin: Basisdruck, 1990.

———. *Untergang auf Raten*. München: Bertelsmann, 1993.

Muchow, Heinz, and Hans Joachim Eichel, Günter Rodegast, eds. *Chronik der Stadt Wittenberge 1933 bis 1944*. Wittenberge: Eigenverlag der Stadtverwaltung Wittenberge, 1997.
————. *Wittenberge im Jahre 1945: Eine Chronologie*. Wittenberge: Eigenverlag der Stadtverwaltung Wittenberge. 1998.
Müller-Enbergs, Helmut. *Inoffizielle Mitarbeiter des Ministeriums für Staatssicherheit*. Berlin: Ch. Links, 2001.
Murphy, David, Sergei Kondrashev, and George Bailey. *Battleground Berlin: CIA vs. KGB in the Cold War*. New Haven, Conn.: Yale University Press, 1997.
Naimark, Norman. *The Russians in Germany*. Cambridge, Mass.: Harvard University Press, 1995.
————. "Die Sowjetische Militäradministration in Deutschland und die Frage des Stalinismus." *Zeitschrift für Geschichtswissenschaft* 43 (1995): 293-307.
Neubert, Ehrhart. *Geschichte der Opposition in der DDR 1949–1989*. Bonn: Bundeszentrale für politische Bildung, 2000.
————. "Opfer in strafrechtlichen nicht faßbaren Bereich." In *Politisch motivierte Verfolgung: Opfer von SED-Unrecht*, ed. Ulrich Baumann and Helmut Kury. Freuburg: Edition iuscrim, 1998.
Niemann, Mario. *Die Sekretäre der SED-Bezirksleitungen 1952–1989*. Paderborn: Schöningh, 2007.
Otto, Wilfriede. "Die politischen Systeme." In *Deutsche Zeitgeschichte von 1945 bis 2000: Ein Handbuch*, ed. Clemens Burrichter et al., 292–93. Berlin: Karl-Dietz-Verlag, 2006.
Palmowski, Jan. "Staatssicherheit und soziale Praxis." In *Staatssicherheit und Gesellschaft*, ed. Jens Gieseke, 253–72. Göttingen: Vandenhoeck & Ruprecht, 2007.
Paul, Gerhard. *Staatlicher Terror und Gesellschaftliche Verrohung: Die Gestapo in Schleswig-Holstein*. Hamburg: Ergebnisse Verlag, 1996.
Peterson, Edward. *The Limits of Secret Police Power: The Magdeburger Stasi 1953–1989*. New York: P. Lang, 2004.
————. *The Secret Police and the Revolution: The Fall of the German Democratic Republic*. Westport, Conn.: Praeger, 2002.
Pfaff, Steven. "*The Lives of Others:* East Germany Revisited?" *GHI Bulletin* No. 41 (Fall 2007): 110–15.
Pingel-Schliemann, Sandra. *Zersetzen: Strategie einer Diktatur*. Berlin: Robert-Havemann-Gesellschaft, 2002.
Popplewell, Richard. "The Stasi and the East German Revolution of 1989." *Contemporary European History* 1, no. 1 (1992): 37–63.
Port, Andrew. *Conflict and Stability in the German Democratic Republic*. New York: Cambridge University Press, 2007.
Proctor, Robert. *The Nazi War on Cancer*. Princeton, N.J.: Princeton University Press, 1999.
Püschel, Almuth. *...der Angeklagte ist Jude*. Potsdam: Brandenburgische Landeszentrale für politische Bildung, 1996.
Raschke, Johannes. *Zwischen Überwachung und Repression—Politische Verfolgung in der DDR 1971 bis 1989*. Opladen: Leske + Budrich, 2001.
Reichel, Thomas. "Die 'durchherrschte' Arbeitergesellschaft." In *Der Schein der Stabilität: DDR-Betriebsalltag in der Ära Honecker*, ed. Renate Hürtgen and Thomas Reichel. Berlin: Metropol, 2001.
Reichert, Steffen. *Unter Kontrolle: Die Martin-Luther-Universität und das Ministerium für Staatssicherheit 1968–1989*. Halle: Mitteldeutscher Verlag, 2007.
Reuband, Karl-Heinz. "Denunziation im Dritten Reich: Die Bedeutung von Systemunterstützung und Gelegenheitsstrukturen." *Historical Social Research* 26, no. 2/3 (2001): 219–34.
Riecker, Ariane, Annett Schwarz, and Dirk Schneider. *Stasi intim: Gespräche mit ehemaligen MfS-Angehörigen*. Leipzig: Forum Verlag, 1990.
Ritter, Gerhard. "Der 17. Juni 1953: Eine historische Ortsbestimmung" In *Volkserhebung gegen den SED-Staat: eine Bestandsaufnahme zum 17. Juni 1953*, ed. Ilko-Sascha Kowalczuk and Roger Engelmann, 16–44. Göttingen: Vandenhoeck & Ruprecht, 2005.

Ross, Corey. *Constructing Socialism at the Grass-roots: The Transformation of East Germany, 1945-65.* Houndmills, Basingstoke: Palgrave, 2000.

——. *The East German Dictatorship: Problems and Perspectives in the Interpretation of the GDR.* London: Arnold, 2002.

RTL. "Die DDR Show – Von Ampelmännchen bis Zentralkomitee." August 28, 2003. http://www.stern.de/unterhaltung/film/512202.html?eid=512223.

Sabrow, Martin, et al., eds., *Wohin treibt die DDR-Erinnerung?* Göttingen: Vandenhoeck & Ruprecht, 2007.

Sagolla, Bernhard. *Die rote Gestapo.* Berlin: Hansa Druck, 1952.

Saldern, Adelheid von. "Öffentlichkeiten in Diktaturen: Zu den Herrschaftspraktiken im Deutschland des 20. Jahrhunderts." In *Diktaturen in Deutschland- Vergleichsaspekte,* ed. Günther Heydemann and Heinrich Oberreuter, 442–75. Bonn: Bundeszentrale für politische Bildung, 2003.

Schaar, Peter. *Das Ende der Privatsphäre.* Munich: Bertelsmann, 2007.

Scherzer, Landolf. *Der Erste.* Berlin, 2002.

Schilling, Walter. "Die Bearbeitung der Landeskirche Thüringen durch das MfS." In *Staatspartei und Staatssicherheit: Zum Verhältnis von SED und MfS,* ed. Siegfried Suckut and Walter Süß, 211–66. Berlin: Ch. Links, 1997.

Schmeidel, John. *Stasi: Shield and Sword of the Party.* New York: Routledge, 2008.

Schmeitzner, Mike. "Der Totalitarismusbegriff Kurt Schumachers." In *Totalitarismuskritik von links,* ed. Mike Schmeitzner, 249–82. Göttingen: Vandenhoeck & Ruprecht, 2007.

Schneider, Michael. "Nationalsozialismus und Region." *Archiv für Sozialgeschichte* 40 (2000): 423–39.

Schroeder, Klaus. *Der SED-Staat: Partei, Staat und Gesellschaft 1949–1990.* München: Hanser, 1998.

——. *Die veränderte Republik:Deutschland nach der Wiedervereinigung.* München: Ernst Vögel, 2006.

Schwabe, Uwe. "Der Herbst '89 in Zahlen." In *Die SED-Herrschaft und ihr Zusammenbruch,* ed. Eberhard Kuhrt, 719–35. Opladen: Leske & Budrich, 1996.

Semystiaha, Volodymyr. "The Role and Place of Secret Collaborators in the Informational Activity of the GPU-NKVD in the 1920s and 1930s." *Cahiers du monde russe* 42, nos. 2, 3, 4 (2001): 231–44.

Service, Robert. *Comrades: A World History of Communism.* London: Macmillan, 2007.

Siegel, Günther. "Die Kreisdienststelle Mühlhausen des Ministeriums für Staatssicherheit der DDR im Herbst 1989." In *Mühlhausen 1989/1990: Die Wende in einer thüringischen Kreisstadt,* ed. Josef Aldenhövel et al., 197–228. Münster: 1993.

Spittmann, Ilse, and Gisela Helwig. *Chronik der Ereignisse in der DDR.* Köln: Verlag Wissenschaft und Politik, 1989.

Staadt, Jochen. "Werkeln am Paradigmenwechsel: Die DDR als 'Konsensdiktatur'?" *Horch und Guck* 58, no. 2 (2007).

Stan, Lavinia. "Spies, Files and Lies: Explaining the failure of access to Securitate Files." *Communist and Post-Communist Studies* 37, no. 3 (2004): 341–59.

——, ed. *Transitional Justice in Eastern Europe and the former Soviet Union: Reckoning with the Communist Past.* New York: Routledge, 2008.

Staritz, Dietrich. "Ursachen und Konsequenzen einer deutschen Revolution." In *Der Fischer Weltalmanach. Sonderband DDR.* Frankfurt: Fischer Taschenbuch-Verlag, 1990.

Stokes, Gale. *The Walls Came Tumbling Down: The Collapse of Communism in Eastern Europe.* New York: Oxford University Press, 1993.

Süß, Walter. "Die Durchdringung der Gesellschaft mittels des MfS—Fallbeispiel Jena im Jahre 1989." In *Die SED-Herrschaft und ihr Zusammenbruch,* ed. Eberhard Kuhrt, 115–37. Opladen: Leske & Budrich, 1996.

——. "Selbstblockierung der Macht." In *Weg in den Untergang: Der Innere Zerfall der DDR,* ed. Konrad Jarausch and Martin Sabrow. Göttingen: Vandenhoeck & Ruprecht, 1999.

Tantzscher, Monika. " 'In der Ostzone wird ein neuer Apparat aufgebaut': Die Gründung des DDR-Staatssicherheitsdienstes." *Deutschland Archiv* 31 (1998): 48–56.

———. "Die Vorläufer des Staatssicherheitsdienstes in der Polizei der Sowjetischen Besatzungszone." *Jahrbuch für Historische Kommunismusforschung* 7 (1998): 125–56.

Terrill, Damon. "Tolerance Lost: Disaffection, Dissent and Revolution in the German Democratic Republic." *East European Quarterly* 28, no. 3 (Sept. 1994): 356–65.

Thiede, Carsten Peter. "Granseer Chronik 1918 bis 1945." Unpublished manuscript.

Thomas, Merrilyn. "The Evangelical Church in the German Democratic Republic." In *The Workers' and Peasants' State: Communism and Society under Ulbricht, 1945–1971*, ed. Patrick Major and Jonathan Osmond, 210–26. Manchester: Manchester University Press, 2002.

Timmer, Karsten. *Vom Aufbruch zum Umbruch: Die Bürgerbewegung in der DDR 1989*. Göttingen: Vandenhoeck & Ruprecht, 2000.

Vollnhals, Clemens. "Das Ministerium für Staatssicherheit: Ein Instrument totalitärer Herrschaftsausübung." In *Sozialgeschichte der DDR*, ed. Hartmut Kaelble et al., 491–518. Stuttgart: Oldenbourg, 1994.

Vollnhals, Clemens, and Jürgen Weber, eds. *Der Schein der Normalität: Alltag und Herrschaft in der SED-Diktatur*. München: Olzog, 2002.

Wagner, Linde. "Polikliniken—ein gesundheitspoltisches Modell." In *Die DDR war anders: Kritische Würdigung ihrer wichtigen sozialkulturellen Einrichtungen*, ed. Stefan Bollinger and Fritz Vilmer. Berlin: Edition Ost, 2002.

Weil, Francesca. *Zielgruppe Ärtzeschaft: Ärtze als inoffizielle Mitarbeiter des Ministeriums für Staatssicherheit*. Göttingen: Vandenhoeck & Ruprecht, 2008.

Welsch, Wolgang. *Widerstand und MfS im SED-Staat*. Schwerin: Schmidt-Pohl, 1999.

Wilkening, Christina. *Staat im Staate: Auskünfte ehemaliger Stasi-Mitarbeiter*. Berlin: Aufbau-Verlag, 1990.

*Wittenberge—eine Chronik mit Bildern*. Nordhorn: BVB-Verlag, 2000.

Wolle, Stefan. *Die heile Welt der Diktatur: Alltag und Herrschaft in der DDR 1971–1989*. Berlin: Ch. Links, 1998.

———. "Sehnsucht nach der Diktatur? Die heile Welt des Sozialismus als Erinnerung und Wirklichkeit." In *Der Schein der Normalität: Alltag und Herrschaft in der SED-Diktatur*, ed. Clemens Vollnhals and Jürgen Weber. München: Olzog, 2002.

Zatlin, Jonathan. *The Currency of Socialism: Money and Political Culture in East Germany*. Cambridge: Cambridge University Press, 2007.

# Index

# THE OXFORD ORAL HISTORY SERIES

J. TODD MOYE (University of North Texas), KATHRYN NASSTROM (University of San Francisco), and ROBERT PERKS (The British Library Sound Archive), *Series Editors*
DONALD A. RITCHIE, *Senior Advisor*